THE SOCIAL PROJECT

THE SOCIAL PROJECT

HOUSING POSTWAR FRANCE

KENNY CUPERS

University of Minnesota Press
MINNEAPOLIS • LONDON

The University of Minnesota Press gratefully acknowledges financial assistance provided for the publication of this book from the Van Eesteren-Fluck & Van Lohuizen Foundation and the Campus Research Board of the University of Illinois at Urbana–Champaign.

For additional resources and projects related to this book, including photography of contemporary suburban Paris, see the book's website at www.upress.umn.edu.

Published by the University of Minnesota Press
111 Third Avenue South, Suite 290
Minneapolis, MN 55401-2520
http://www.upress.umn.edu

Library of Congress Cataloging-in-Publication Data
Cupers, Kenny.
    The social project : housing postwar France / Kenny Cupers.
        Includes bibliographical references and index.
    ISBN 978-0-8166-8964-4 (hc) — ISBN 978-0-8166-8965-1 (pb)
    1. City planning—France—History—20th century. 2. Housing—France—History—20th century. 3. Architecture and state—France—History—20th century. 4. Architecture and society—France—History—20th century. I. Title.
    HT169.F7C87 2014
    363.5′8094409045—dc23
                                                                        2014001572

Printed in the United States of America on acid-free paper

The University of Minnesota is an equal-opportunity educator and employer.

20 19 18 17 16 15 14   10 9 8 7 6 5 4 3 2 1

CONTENTS

ABBREVIATIONS

AUA   Atelier d'urbanisme et d'architecture (Studio of Urbanism and Architecture)

CDC   Caisse des dépôts et consignations (Deposits and Consignments Fund)

CEDER   Centre d'études des équipements résidentiels (Study Center for Residential Facilities)

CERFI   Centre d'études, de recherches et de formation institutionnelles (Center for Institutional Studies, Research, and Training)

CES   Centre d'études sociologiques (Center for Sociological Studies)

CGP   Commissariat général du Plan (Plan Commission)

CIAM   Congrès internationaux d'architecture moderne (International Congresses of Modern Architecture)

CNL   Confédération nationale du logement (National Confederation for Housing)

CNRS   Centre national de recherche scientifique (National Center for Scientific Research)

CSTB   Centre scientifique et technique du bâtiment (Scientific and Technical Center for Construction)

DATAR   Délégation à l'aménagement du territoire et à l'action régionale (Delegation for Territorial Planning and Regional Action)

DGRST Délégation générale de la recherche scientifique et technique (General Delegation for Scientific and Technical Research)

ENSBA École nationale supérieure des Beaux-Arts (National School of Fine Arts)

HLM   Habitations à loyer modéré (Dwellings at Moderated Rents)

IAURP Institut d'urbanisme et de l'aménagement de la Région parisienne (Institute for Urbanism and Planning of the Paris Region)

INED   Institut national d'études démographiques (National Institute of Demographic Studies)

INSEE Institut national des statistiques et des études économiques (National Institute for Statistical and Economic Studies)

IUP   Institut d'urbanisme de l'Université de Paris (Urbanism Institute of the University of Paris)

SCC   Société des centres commerciaux (Commercial Centers Company)

SCIC   Société centrale immobilière de la Caisse des dépôts (Central Real Estate Company of the Deposits and Consignments Fund)

UIOF   Union internationale des organismes familiaux (International Union of Family Organizations)

ZUP   Zone à urbaniser par priorité (Priority Urbanization Zone)

ACKNOWLEDGMENTS

In the time of researching and writing this book, I have incurred many debts that I am delighted to acknowledge. Everyone at the University of Minnesota Press, and Pieter Martin especially, has been tremendously helpful and accommodating. At Harvard University, where this project first took shape, my mentors Antoine Picon, Eve Blau, and Margaret Crawford nourished my thinking in innumerable ways. Jean-Louis Cohen, Liz Cohen, Mary Lewis, Ted Bestor, Michael Hays, Hilde Heynen, Rosemary Wakeman, Susan Fainstein, Annie Fourcaut, Marie-Hélène Bacqué, and Dominique Rouillard strengthened this project with feedback at various stages of my research. During my years in Paris, Christian Topalov and Susanne Magri provided me not only with institutional support at the École des hautes études en sciences sociales and the Centre de sociologie urbaine but also with guidance and insight.

This book would not have been written without the generous feedback and unrelenting encouragement of many other colleagues and friends. In Cambridge, Mariana Mogilevich, Bill Rankin, Max Hirsh, Jennifer Mack, Matt Lasner, Jennifer Hock, Robin Schuldenfrei, Timothy Hyde, and others created a unique intellectual environment that enriched this project in the most fundamental ways. I thank the Society of Architectural Historians, the Society for American City and Regional Planning History, the Urban History Association, the Society for French Historical Studies, and the European Association for Urban History for allowing me to present research in progress at their meetings. I am grateful for the intellectual exchange resulting from invited talks at the University of Michigan, Taubman College; the Faculty of Architecture, Landscape, and Design at the University of Toronto; the International New Town Institute in the Netherlands; and the Eidgenössische Technische Hochschule

Zurich. Many other voices contributed to this book as a result of such scholarly exchange, including Bob Bruegmann, Dell Upton, Vanessa Schwartz, Brian Newsome, William Piggot, Michael Mulvey, Nichole Rudolph, Max Page, Eric Avila, Omar Khan, Zeynep Çelik Alexander, Gwenaëlle Legoulon, and Brad Hunt. For carefully reading and commenting on sections of the manuscript, I thank Catherine Roth, Tom Avermaete, Claire Zimmerman, James McHugh, and Heather H. Minor. Mariana Mogilevich, Curt Gambetta, and Venus Bivar have been extraordinarily generous with feedback during my final stages of writing.

The support of many institutions has made this book possible. I am grateful to have received the Chateaubriand Fellowship from the French Embassy to the United States, as well as grants from Harvard University, including the Frederick Sheldon Fellowship and the Center for European Studies Dissertation Research Grant. The support of a Fulbright Fellowship during my first three years of graduate school was also crucial to this project. I benefited from logistical support, intellectual stimulation, and the generosity of time during my tenure as the Reyner Banham Fellow at the University at Buffalo. Gratitude goes to Mary Woods for pointing me toward the Clarence Stein Award at Cornell University, which also provided support for my research. Financial support for the publication of this book has come from the Van Eesteren-Fluck & Van Lohuizen Foundation in the Netherlands, as well as from the University of Illinois at Urbana–Champaign.

Like every historian, I owe a great debt to archivists and librarians. The staff at the Centre des archives contemporaines in Fontainebleau, the Centre de documentation de l'urbanisme, the Forney library in the Marais, and the many other libraries and archives where I worked in and around France gave me indispensable assistance and created a welcoming environment. I owe special thanks to Josette Vivanz at the municipal archives of Sarcelles for our unplanned archival hunts in the basement of the town hall and for her infinite patience with my many requests. I admire the unrivaled professionalism of Alexandre Ragois at the Centre d'archives d'architecture du XXe siècle. I also thank many people who offered their time for in-depth interviews, including Gérard Guenon, Alain de Vulpian, Jacques Windenberger, Paul Chemetov, Marie-Geneviève Dezès, Anne Querrien, and Bernard Weil. Thanks to David Liaudet for lending me some evocative postcards from his extensive collection for inclusion in this book.

The moral support of many close friends during the long journey that this book has been for me has undoubtedly been most critical. My friends in Paris made my time there unforgettable. Isabelle Doucet was a very special companion who provided relentless encouragement and stimulating conversations during the many hours we spent together writing side by side. Curt Gambetta, Hadas Steiner, Jordan Geiger, Miriam Paeslack, and Mariana Mogilevich gave similarly all-round support, and very special thanks goes to Theodore Gilliam and Filip Cleynen. Last but not least, I thank my family for their absolute and unconditional support throughout.

INTRODUCTION

BUILDING THE *BANLIEUE*

EVEN ITS PUBLIC TRANSPORT has a different name. To visit the other Paris, you take not the metro but a different network of regional express trains. You cross underneath the *péripherique*, the circular highway that has replaced Paris's nineteenth-century city wall but has the same effect of demarcating the center from the rest. After this threshold, still the official city limit of Paris, the familiar city quickly peters out through the window. Then suddenly, the other Paris—perhaps the truly modern one—appears. Housing slabs and tower blocks in bright white, daring pink, and drab gray. Palaces for the people, giant but mostly less than glamorous. Ten-story pyramids imitating Mediterranean hilltop villages. Expansive multilevel plazas and exuberantly designed playgrounds. Graffitied concrete and postmodernist cladding. Well-intentioned community centers and monstrous shopping-mall megastructures. Highways, parking lots, and patches of green space, large and small, among it all. In the popular imagination this landscape, the unplanned result of planned developments, is the opposite of all that "Paris" stands for today. It is the city tourists rarely get to see but where most Parisians actually live. The situation is not all that different in Bordeaux, Marseille, Lille, or Grenoble. Their suburban landscapes, which make up so much of contemporary France, in some ways still seem to be the product of another society, altogether different from the one that produced the grand boulevards and monumental architecture of so many French cities. From an inner-city Paris that seems ever more set in its ways, the suburban excursion is uncanny. Although a new world has materialized where sixty years ago there was little more than fields of cabbage and a few cottages, the lingering sensation is that of visiting the puzzling remains of a long-lost civilization whose aesthetics no longer has a voice.

This new world has its equivalent in paper. The vast proliferation of paperwork that made possible France's frenzied urbanization has been poured into a subterranean city of dusty boxes in a far-flung suburb beyond the end of the commuter rail line.[1] This is France's National Archive for the postwar period, housing a greater volume of documents than was produced in all other periods of French history combined. With a uniquely French fervor for bureaucracy, the archive's paperwork breathes the now outmoded ambitions that shaped much of the urban landscape that flashes by the train window. Housing for all. A rational organization of the national territory. Universal access to public services of all sorts. A modern nation of socially mixed neighborhoods. Even if such rhetoric was accompanied by far less lofty motives, it was unparalleled in its consequences. The French postwar suburbs constitute one of the twentieth century's largest, and perhaps least understood, social and architectural experiments.

This book is about the making of that world. In less than three decades after World War II, France transformed from a largely rural country with an insufficient and outdated housing stock into a highly modernized urban nation. This transformation was in large part the result of the massive production of publicly funded housing projects and state-planned New Town developments on the outskirts of existing cities. The sheer speed and unprecedented scale of these developments—tens of thousands of housing units rising simultaneously—makes the interwar modernist housing of the New Frankfurt look almost as quaint as the prewar garden cities on which it was modeled. The upshift in housing production during the postwar decades was therefore not just a quantitative shift but a qualitative one. It changed the role of modern architecture at large. During these few decades of the twentieth century, architecture undertook a social project both unprecedented at the time and unparalleled since. Modern architecture did not belong to an avant-garde of architects alone; it was shared and shaped by government officials, construction companies, residents' associations, developers, and social scientists alike. And yet, despite such broad ground, its logic and language were remarkably consistent. Never before were modernization and modernism so pervasive and so closely allied, nor would they ever be again. Never before was modern architecture built on such a massive scale and at such a frantic pace, shaping the urban landscape at large. And never before was an entire generation so aware of how much better off they were than their parents—measured first of all in the social and material realm of everyday life. As the older agendas of social reform gave way to rationalization under the aegis of the state, architecture participated in the spatial organization of welfare and progress. The central argument of this book is that modern architecture and postwar urbanization in France developed in tandem, through a process of continual experimentation centered on everyday life as a target of modernization and an emerging domain of expertise.

It is hard not to read the resulting built environments through the lens of current events. In recent decades, a significant part of the housing stock from this period has undergone physical degradation and has gradually been left to those with no choice to live elsewhere. As predominantly white middle-class families left collective housing in favor of suburban single-family homes, poor families, particularly those of African origin, moved in. Many of the larger collective housing areas today—especially those built in the 1950s and 1960s—suffer from high youth unemployment and crime rates. More than seven hundred of them have been officially marked as "urban problem areas" by the French government, stigmatizing more than five million inhabitants, predominantly from ethnic minorities. The continuing unrest in a relatively small number of these deprived neighborhoods—the riots of November 2005 and 2007 being the most notorious—has become symbolic for the country's (sub)urban crisis. Critical observers in France and abroad have decried this condition as a blatant sign of social and racial apartheid. Two images, whose opposition reinforces their symbolic weight, continue to dominate our understanding of urban France: on the one hand, the monumental splendor and richness of Paris's historic city center, and, on the other, the poverty and hopelessness of its suburban landscapes of tower blocks and slabs. By the early 1980s, less than 16 percent lived in the city itself.[2] The majority inhabits the sprawling suburbs known as the *banlieue*. Other French cities mirror this pattern.

Despite its national particularities, suburban France is inscribed in a wider global narrative about modern architecture and state planning. During the postwar decades of unprecedented economic expansion—roughly between 1945 and 1975—large-scale urban renewal, mass housing estates, and ambitious New Town projects proliferated not only in France but also in places as diverse as Britain, Scandinavia, the Middle East, the Soviet Union, and the United States. Despite, or perhaps because of, the global front lines of the Cold War, these regions shared remarkably similar ideas about the virtues of planning and mass housing. With important exceptions, such as Singapore and Hong Kong, the overwhelming majority of the environments that resulted from these assumptions now appear as relics of long-lost convictions: the belief in modern architecture as a vehicle of social progress, and the confidence in the government to provide directly for individuals and families. A few decades after their construction, mass housing developments such as Pruitt-Igoe, Sarcelles, Bijlmermeer, and Aylesbury, came to represent a social crisis that cut deep into the public consciousness of their respective societies.

The dominant perception, among scholars and the public alike, is that postwar housing is therefore a monstrous human catastrophe. Many have laid the blame with the architects and planners who drafted the schemes. How could they conceive of siting near-identical towers and slabs, some of them hundreds of meters long and fifteen stories high, in vast areas of ill-defined open space generally disconnected from their surroundings? With Le Corbusier usually taking the blame, three decades of building production have become synonymous with modernism's failure: its rationalistic hubris, its inflexible and inhumane treatment of urban space, and its outright denial of people's needs and aspirations. Architects and planners themselves actually participated in such portrayals: their often-virulent critiques of monotonous housing schemes were not without self-interest. Physical determinism became convenient once again. If the origin of social malaise lay in design, so would its solution. Newer architects and planners could thus write themselves a future by demonizing what their older colleagues had produced. The problem with handing out this kind of blame is not that it would incriminate the wrong culprits. Rather, it reduces the history of a significant part of the urbanized world to a singular error. Meanwhile, shortsightedness has helped to legitimize the current policy of massive demolition. The famous image of an imploding Pruitt-Igoe—the housing development near Saint Louis, Missouri, that led the architect and critic Charles Jencks to proclaim the death of modern architecture—stands as a symbol here for what has become the clearest way out of mass housing.[3] Since the first demolitions in the 1970s, the decision to destroy these places, rather than to improve them, has gained purchase. This ignores the fact that only in few cases does such action accomplish anything more than simply displacing the social problem of poverty. Meanwhile, the products of the welfare state's golden age are disappearing even before their making has been properly understood.

Architectural history has done little so far to challenge this state of affairs. Reducing the history of mass housing to that of architectural discourse, English-language scholarship has continued to neglect the complex genesis of what are often dismissed as mediocre projects. At best, they are watered-down versions of a once-genius idea, at worst, equally thoughtless iterations of a revolting idea. But how can the forms and concepts in Le Corbusier's sketches of the 1920s, or the discourse of a self-appointed elite of architects such as the Congrès internationaux d'architecture moderne (CIAM) possibly suffice to explain a process of urbanization that has literally changed the face of the earth? Mass housing remains an excluded topic in architectural history because it falls through the gaps of the discipline.[4] It is neither a vernacular expression of local culture nor easily taken up in the canon of "high" architecture. Mass housing developments are often pervasively global and yet nationally specific, never quite unique nor completely alike. It is no wonder they challenge the norms of the discipline—despite being modern architecture's most widespread manifestation to date.

In many respects, the French suburbs epitomize these contradictions. In no other country were modern architecture and state planning so strongly united that they shaped both the image of contemporary urbanity and our understanding of the social ambitions of architecture at large. This convergence cannot be explained by the predominance of a single political ideology. France was midway between the Soviet bloc, where housing was a direct expression of Communist ideology, and the United States, where it never became the dominant model of urban development. Postwar housing in France was shaped both by the workings of a centralized state and by the social dynamics of liberal capitalism. During the *trente glorieuses,* the three decades of unprecedented economic growth and prosperity after World War II, mass housing was France's preeminent tool of national modernization.[5] Its cornerstone was the modern standard four-room apartment, resulting from mass production and typified in France as the "F4"—just as the nuclear family was to be the backbone of the nation. Despite the increasing engagement of private capital and the gradual liberalization of planning procedures, the centralized state remained the country's main urbanist, de jure and de facto, until well into the 1970s.[6] This period is consequently known as "the era of the technocrats," a time in which the country was steered by a class of leaders with a penchant for authoritarianism and technocracy inherited from wartime and colonialism.[7] The pervasive towers and slabs on the horizon of metropolitan France today stand as symbols of a regime bedeviled by a history of violence breeding violence.

This book sidesteps the morass of myth, symbol, and representation in which this history has been buried. Without dismissing the social and political debates that some of these places continue to generate—and should generate—it examines the complex construction of the *banlieue* on its own terms.[8] If accepted wisdom about this topic relies on overarching judgment—public housing is a necessary good; public housing always fails—this study historicizes such normative approaches.[9] Against the prevailing impulse to blame architectural modernism, its principles, typologies, and materials for the so-called failure of public housing, the study situates such physical determinism as itself part of the historical development of mass housing and New Towns. Causalities between built form and social life were discursively constructed and contested, not only by architects and experts but also by inhabitants and various other publics. The aesthetic monotony of facades, construction methods resistant to interior alterations, technically deficient building materials, and insufficient sound insulation are just a few of these materials that became active when harnessed by specific actors to specific ends—tenants and owners, sociologists or policy makers. In short, to understand the making of the French suburbs we need to favor situated agency over abstract forces and contingency over determinism.

Contrary to accepted wisdom, this perspective reveals that the postwar city in France is more than the product of a single utopian blueprint gone awry. But the idea that French urbanism amounts to a poor imitation of Le Corbusier's Unité d'habitation in Marseille continues to be a persistent fiction in both popular and scholarly accounts. Even if formally there are some striking resemblances between France's mass housing and certain CIAM projects, they cannot be reduced to it under the blanket category of "influence." Even if discussions between Corbusian modernists and urbanists such as Gaston Bardet reveal the ideological struggle over the proper shape of French reconstruction, they do little to explain the circumstances that informed mass housing "on the ground." What were the conditions that supported architects' and planners' participation in these projects across France? What shared ways of

thinking and doing made this massive architectural production possible over decades of
social, economic, and political change? If French postwar urbanization was driven by economic growth and guided by state bureaucracy, the actual shapes it took were not predeter-
mined. Why and how were things built the way they were? How did planners know and
decide what to build, and for whom? What factors outside of the domain of architecture
made architects' ideas convincing to those in charge? How did the public receive them, and
how did people occupy these environments, once built? To answer these questions one must
understand how architectural ideas hybridized as they trickled down and building transformed as it proliferated. This is a study therefore of how architecture *moves*—not just in
architectural discourse but through government and civil society institutions, social science,
and popular media.

The French suburbs were not built in a day or according to a singular principle. With their
designs and experiments being carried out at often unprecedented scales, architects and planners were engaged more than ever in the large-scale reorganization and modernization of
everyday life. But this hardly implied a unified agenda or one-off implementation. Motives
competed and projects conflicted. Problems with everyday life in France's mass housing and
New Town areas did not just appear in the last decades. Female depression and youth delinquency were only the most sensational of issues reported by journalists and social scientists at
the height of construction during the 1960s. Such concerns accompanied rather than succeeded the rapid urbanization of France after World War II. During this period, architecture
was not only planned and built, but also inhabited, criticized, studied, modified, and revised.
Mass housing was not just produced but also consumed. And these processes of production
and consumption became intimately intertwined. Instead of the prevailing assumption of tri-
umphant rise and spectacular fall, this period was one of accumulative experimentation and
continual revision. Without an embedded account of such processes, the course of architectural modernism cannot be understood.

The kind of history that can take account of such complexity and interaction is necessarily
a hybrid one. This study in fact contributes to a broader shift in architectural history, moved by
a rejection of the limited focus on discourse, representation, and authored work. It advances
instead an explicitly relational history of architecture that includes multiple disciplines, mainstream practice, and the built environment at large. Although architecture and urban planning
are now almost entirely different disciplines, with the latter squarely located in social science,
that was not the case in the postwar decades. Especially in mid-twentieth-century France,
architecture and urban planning were often indistinguishable under the rubric of *urbanisme*.
This period's architectural history therefore cannot be written without taking account of
urban planning, and most important, the dynamics of the postwar city more generally. As
such, this study stands on the shoulders of three distinct bodies of scholarship: histories of

postwar architectural modernism, an impressive body of mostly French-language scholarship in urban history, and an emerging history of the social sciences.[10]

This study has no pretensions to be a social history "from below." By focusing on the role of institutions, buildings, concepts, and organizations as much as the agency of individuals, it trains a hybrid lens that follows the composite production of the built environment itself. In the case of postwar France, that environment was both cause and result of interaction between the realms of design, construction, inhabitation, and scientific study. Such interactions, for which the state supplied a central platform, shaped the encounter between modern architecture and social science.[11] The social project that linked them was neither static nor univocal. It evolved from standard housing provision to lively neighborhoods, participatory planning, social integration, urban diversity, and the right to the city. And it changed under the influence of rising middle-class prosperity, the increasingly contested role of government in housing production, and inhabitants' growing expectations of agency in the shaping of their everyday lives.

The social agenda of interwar modernism—architecture as the vehicle for a new, egalitarian society—was reversed in the postwar decades. Architecture was now to facilitate societal changes already under way. This was in many ways a far more complex task, involving an increasingly complex set of actors and institutions. As modernism turned mainstream, the production of the built environment in postwar France went hand in hand with an unprecedented expansion of expertise. The production of specialized knowledge accompanying material production marked a revolution in both quantitative and qualitative terms. Architecture has rarely been considered as an integral part of this development. Its role has too often been reduced to the artistic, utopian, and paper projects of the 1950s and 1960s.[12] Yet, postwar architectural modernism was about more than radicalism and technophilia; architectural experimentation was a determining factor in, and the result of, an unprecedented regime of knowledge production.

Concerning areas as diverse as social life, building technology, and economic policy, a growing body of empirical knowledge provided architecture's intellectual context between the 1950s and 1970s. It brought architects, policy makers, developers, social scientists, and resident associations together as they experimented with urban planning principles, prefabricated construction, modern housing typologies, collective amenities, and commercial centers, from the first mass housing projects until the fundamental reorientation of the mid-1970s. Contrary to our contemporary intuition, the prevalence of technocratic expertise and functionalist doctrine at this time did not exclude "humanist" concerns with the social and the desire to accommodate inhabitants' diversity of needs. Such concerns were in fact shared by leftist, populist, and antimodernist critics and the makers of the mass housing projects they so vehemently critiqued. What did change over time was the way planners and critics came to actually understand inhabitants, their everyday lives, and their needs.

To chart this evolution, this study takes account of three perspectives. First of all, the book situates architecture in a regime of production and consumption resulting from both state-led modernization and liberal capitalism. This fundamentally shaped the way experts—including architects—approached inhabitants, who became "users" at the crossroads of technocracy and consumerism. The second and concomitant line of inquiry in this study is how the course of postwar architecture and urbanism was shaped by specialized knowledge. If housing and urbanization evolved as an experimental process in which the realms of construction and habitation were in continual interaction, the domain of the social sciences came to supply the essential knowledge assuring these exchanges. Third, this study offers an alternative framework for analyzing the politics and agency of architecture, beyond both the representational narrative of art and architectural history and the master narratives of draconian modernization and heroic contestation found in much urban history.

The User: Technocracy Meets Consumerism

French housing, both before and after 1968, was in many ways less about its inhabitants than about those who spoke and built in their name. It involved political elites and government administrators, large semipublic and private developers and construction companies, modern yet mainly Beaux-Arts–trained architects, scientific experts, and engineers in large consultancy firms—and increasingly, local and national associations of inhabitants, tenants, and consumers, assembled under the rubric of *usagers* or "users." This term not only emerged "in action," through the reactions of individuals and groups to large-scale urban development, but was also constructed as a register of understanding. The white nuclear family with a male bread-winning father, stay-at-home mother, and two or three children remained the central reference point for many architects and policy makers—almost all male—until well into the 1960s. At the same time, people also pushed back against such racial and gendered definitions—sometimes reinforcing them, as when housewives collaborated with policy makers on kitchen designs, sometimes subverting them, as when an Algerian construction worker moved into an "F4." Whether as an abstract universal, a statistical entity identified with the nuclear family, a normative figure subject to modernization, an active participant of neighborhood life, a free consumer, or a protesting militant, the user was a category of policy and design as much as an agent of the built environment. This category was fundamental both in the course of mass housing estates or *grands ensembles* and in the *villes nouvelles*, France's official program of New Towns officially launched in 1965.

Situated ambivalently between the mass subject and the individual—and between the realms of citizenship and private consumption—this particular type was in fact emblematic of architecture and urbanization in postwar Europe more generally.[13] As a term, *usager* first appeared in the *Petit Robert* dictionary during the 1930s, referring to "a person who uses (a public service, the public domain)."[14] This definition implied the responsibility of the state to furnish goods and services in expanding domains of social and personal life, at a moment in history when social welfare and modern state planning were in a crucial stage of formation.[15] This approach then became dominant during the "golden age" of the welfare state in postwar Europe, when governments became involved with their citizens' well-being in novel ways. From natalism to mental health and cultural policy, administration seemed to bear no longer just on subjects but on their very subjectivity. This was exactly the kind of shift that guided Michel Foucault's search for a definition of power beyond discipline, as the organization of social and personal life in general.[16] But, contrary to the conspiratorial tone of many subsequent interpretations, the new type of government was hardly experienced as a dark machination. In the eyes of policy makers and citizens alike, the function of the state was no longer just to rule but to serve.[17] Most accurately, perhaps, the state would rule by serving.

The figure of the user typified this new role of government. Neither simply a consumer (an independent actor in the private realm of the market) nor simply a citizen (subject to the state and thus in direct political relation to it through rights and obligations), the user was relatively autonomous from the state, yet at the same time linked to it as beneficiary of "public service." This kind of state provision was based on rights and thus on the basis of estimated need rather than individual want. Calculations were devoid of individuality, and in particular of race and ethnicity—absent categories in an otherwise meticulous bureaucratic system of social classification.[18] At the same time, as this study demonstrates, state provision was increasingly understood as a consumer relationship, whether defined individually or as "collective consumption."

The figures of citizen and consumer were indeed often conflated in a country marked by the welding of state-led modernization with a mass consumer culture grafted upon the American model.[19] If the United States was a Consumers' Republic, a term coined by Lizabeth Cohen for a regime in which "the consumer satisfying personal material wants actually served the national interest,"[20] France was a "Users' Republic" in which mass consumption was guided by an elaborate system of state planning and welfare provision. French consumer culture was shaped by conflict between the European emphasis on "collective consumption" as a social right and the American notion of the sovereign consumer whose satisfaction was guaranteed by the free market. The authority of the French state in consumption led observers such as Henri Lefebvre to speak of a "bureaucratic society of controlled consumption."[21] National economic planning, with its roots in the 1930s, its experimental phase during World War II, and its maturation under Jean Monnet and the Marshall Plan made France a "planning state" in which the government had a pervasive presence in everyday life. The ambiguity of the user— partly citizen, partly consumer—was constituent of this intertwining of state, market, and society that marks the postwar decades in France.

The built environment was not only shaped by this condition; it also helped shape it. In the first postwar years, the government prioritized infrastructure and heavy industries, but when rapid urban and demographic growth exacerbated the housing shortage, it assumed unprecedented responsibilities in housing production. Far exceeding its prior involvement in social housing and national reconstruction, by the mid-1950s the state began to promote the mass production of standardized dwelling units in large collective housing estates. With this development, architecture was granted a prominent role in the modernization of postwar society. At the same time, social engineering was restricted by the confines of a liberal capitalist democracy, the impact of private development, and the dynamics of mass consumerism. This tension brought the unknowable universe of the inhabitant to the heart of French urban and architectural expertise. It triggered new questions not only for planners and policy makers, but also for architects, who were now faced with a new, anonymous client in their design briefs. This user was to postwar architecture what the "modern subject" was to interwar modernism.

Housing was more than a straightforward service such as postal delivery or electricity. It was claimed as a basic citizens' right, increasingly built as a modern consumer product, and meanwhile remained a complex feature of personal identity, collective belonging, and social life. The state did not refrain from intervening in these various aspects. The democratization of rights, goods, and services that was one of the primary goals of French welfare generated a continuum between the public realm and the private domains of market and household. Urbanism was a key factor in this thoroughgoing reorganization of public and private. When inhabitants—organized in local associations and national civil society organizations—formulated demands for participation, they did so in the name of an all-encompassing user, more than as only tenants, citizens, or consumers alone. Mass housing and New Town development thus changed what it meant to be a Frenchman and an inhabitant. The urbanism of "collective facilities"—urban amenities from shops to churches that were to be included in mass housing developments—became a key element of the state-led project to improve life in what was built. In a system in which production and consumption were separate yet interdependent realms, the question of how one could inform the other thus became crucial.

Concrete and Knowledge

During the postwar decades, new types of experts circulated in the hallways of government—not just in France—and the social sciences in particular grew exponentially, both within the state apparatus and in the academy.[22] While that development was certainly reinforced by Cold War politics and came to define the global influence of American social science, French social scientists were in the first place shaped by their own intellectual traditions. Even in postwar France, however, the figure of the autonomous intellectual was increasingly replaced by that of the expert, a shift captured by Michel Foucault's notion of the "specific intellectual." No longer the intellectual of universal claims, the "master of truth and justice," this was the new knowledge producer who combined theory and practice by working in specific contexts.[23] Against the background of a decolonizing and rapidly urbanizing France, housing and urban development were particularly crucial fields for the development of this culture of expertise. French urbanists and social scientists had first encountered each other in the colonies, which since the late nineteenth century served as *champs d'expérience*, laboratories for controlled tests that could eventually be applied to France itself.[24] With the return of colonial administrators and their redeployment in French bureaucracy during the 1950s and 1960s, this experimental approach was now definitively folded back onto the metropole.

But in postwar France the intersection of architecture and social science was not just a matter of pragmatic state planning, of overcoming problems with the construction of housing estates or new neighborhoods. The relationship between built space and society was in fact one of the most fruitful themes in postwar French intellectual culture. In all its dimensions, whether in inner-city Paris or the country's mushrooming suburbs, urban space informed the work of thinkers and artists from a wide variety of disciplines and perspectives—from Situationist critiques of urban boredom to Jacques Tati's sterile world of glass and steel in *Playtime*. While such cultural production might seem far removed from the workings of government or the actual economic and political forces shaping the built environment, many intellectuals—Henri Lefebvre most famously—moved quite fluidly between avant-garde circles and the French state administration. Their work was often both critical of and instrumental to government planning and its consequences on the ground. Of these burgeoning intellectual cultures, sociology became increasingly central over the course of the postwar decades, as it promised access to the elusive realm of how built environments were actually "consumed."

Initially, however, that realm was practically irrelevant to state planners faced with the daunting task of rebuilding France during and after World War II. Their primary focus was on the scientific management of production. High-level civil servants, graduated from France's elite *grandes écoles* and hardened by wartime experience, made up a class of planning experts who cultivated technology as a means to achieve national modernization and reinstate French grandeur.[25] In the country's politically unstable climate of the immediate postwar decade, this elite of nonelected administrators was convinced that technology and applied science would transcend the deadlock of politics. This conviction—as old as Saint-Simonianism—set off an intellectual debate about technocracy, a term used pejoratively by opponents who considered it disregarding of human values.[26]

Such opposition, however, only disguised the formation of a shared culture of expertise. As the mind-set of national planning infiltrated large parts of the bureaucratic apparatus, the

French state became a knowledge-producing institution as much as an interventionist one. By the end of the 1950s, state planning included a range of social and cultural domains, and high-level administrators acknowledged the social sciences as key auxiliaries to political action and decision making. Such expertise included first of all economic science and demography, but increasingly also "softer" sciences such as geography and sociology. National economic planning gradually engaged these "human sciences," especially in growing policy areas such as education, public health, and housing. It was not that policy makers espoused science and technology to dissolve politics altogether, but rather that they aspired to a kind of objectivity that was modeled on the hard sciences. While some scientists overtly espoused political ideologies, the view that social science constituted a neutral form of expertise that could advance political decision making, if not overcome politics, was more common. The boundaries between technocracy and humanism were thus blurred at best.[27] This conflation was perhaps most pronounced in the realm of housing and urban policy, for which state administrators increasingly endorsed the use of social-scientific methods.[28] Initially, they prioritized economic and demographic methods, but what rose to become the legitimate domain of expertise about housing and urban planning was sociology. The construction of some of the first *grands ensembles* in the mid-1950s was in fact already accompanied by sociological inquiry, both independent and commissioned by the government. Although the sociologist Chombart de Lauwe was an absolute pioneer of this new field and Henri Lefebvre his most famous critic and successor, the role of social science in postwar urbanization—as that of architecture—cannot be understood through the work of a few "great men." France's centralized state apparatus channeled a massive, largely empirical and quasi-anonymous production of social science into its urban policies over the postwar decades.

Sociology is to be understood here not only as a purely academic discipline, but as a heterogeneous domain of expertise that far exceeded the initially weak and relatively uninstitutionalized discourse of theorists or academics at this time. What in postwar France was labeled sociology constituted a dispersed realm of knowledge production that included not only academic research, but also social work, popular studies, journalistic reportage, and, most important, a huge mass of government-commissioned studies. The latter were conducted by a burgeoning sector of semipublic and private *bureaux d'études*, research institutes and consultancy firms that had emerged in response to growing government demand for research, especially after 1958. Many housing projects functioned as life-sized laboratories under the scrutiny of social-scientific experts. They were experimental, not necessarily in the sense that they were innovative or radical, but in that their built form embodied hypotheses about everyday life and gave rise to a process of testing, evaluating, and adapting. Apartment layouts, housing blocks, public spaces, and collective amenities were revised and improved in subsequent projects, often on the basis of sociological models and observations of built projects.

Sociological expertise thus assumed a crucial role of mediation between what policy makers, developers, and architects produced in their offices and everyday life "on the ground."

French sociology grew up in the housing estates and New Towns of the postwar period. As these projects subjected everyday life to rationalization and modernization at an unprecedented scale, they became sociologists' quintessential barometer of French society. Their far-reaching effects on everyday life were accompanied by a conceptual revolution of what this realm was and could be. Henri Lefebvre's work—beginning with his 1947 *Critique de la vie quotidienne*—was at the forefront of a new generation who would turn everyday life into a fertile domain of sociological investigation.[29] The stakes were deemed high. While everyday life was seen as a victim of the alienating forces of capitalism and bureaucracy, and—following the fervent critiques of Guy Debord—of a consumer society that colonized it, it also harbored the seeds of change because critique could open it up to the authentic and the meaningful.

Meanwhile, architects did not remain at the sidelines. For an international avant-garde of architects and artists, the everyday had become a crucial vehicle to revise modernism for the postwar world. It allowed them to expand the principles of functionalism and to incorporate social life more directly into architectural design. The 1953 CIAM meeting in Aix-en-Provence, which signified the birth of Team X, was a landmark in this project, in which sociology was assigned a crucial role. In France, however, it was not Team X but the centralized state that figured as the primary meeting ground for sociology, architecture, and urbanism. From the mid-1960s on, work in multidisciplinary planning teams—most importantly for the *villes nouvelles*—allowed French architects and state planners to channel social and sociological critiques into new urban models, alternative to the *grands ensembles*. After the events of 1968, which "reintellectualized" French architectural culture and inspired a newly critical generation of architects, sociological ideas such as Lefebvre's notions of everyday life, appropriation, and the right to the city became staple references. Taken up by young collaborative architecture offices such as the Atelier de Montrouge and Atelier d'urbanisme et d'architecture, as well as younger state administrators, sociology was thus at once the main source for social critiques of urbanism and the instrument for generating new urban models. Although it proved impossible to effectively instrumentalize sociology for design, it provided architects and planners with a unique entryway into the practices of dwelling and with concrete design techniques such as "programming." Under the aegis of an increasingly self-critical state apparatus, the shift to new housing typologies and urban centers was only possible because of the insertion of sociological expertise in design. That would help architects and planners not only to instill citizen participation but also to entice consumers in novel ways. This development thus traverses what are conventionally understood as fundamentally opposing approaches to the city—modernist architecture and participatory planning.

Politics beyond Ideology

Sidestepping the dominant three-step narrative—with a first moment of architectural invention, a second one of massive construction, and a final one of contestation and crisis—the
study examines processes of co-construction and the importance of *gradual* sociocultural
change in the built environment. This reveals an alternative to the narrative of top-down
power versus bottom-up revolt that has characterized many studies of postwar urbanization,
especially in France.[30] As such, this study follows in the footsteps of Paul Rabinow's history
of welfare as an essential component of French modernity.[31] Yet, contrary to the tendency in
much Foucault-inspired scholarship to take this approach in a determinist direction, the study
brings the notion of power closer to the ground by demonstrating the historical importance
of a much larger set of actors and materials in shaping the built environment. That in turn
allows for a contingent account of how historical change unfolds.

The fact that both the embrace of state-funded housing and calls for citizen participation
cross the political spectrum in France reduces the explanatory force of political ideology. Left
and Right were, of course, rarely in full agreement, but modern state-led urbanism was supported by both sides, be it in different ways and for different reasons. What for the Right
could be a matter of economic rationality and national pride could be an issue of affordable
housing and social solidarity to the Left. If politicians generally agreed about the virtues of
mass collective housing in the 1950s and found themselves in agreement again when pro-
hibiting such housing in the 1970s, how can this history be cast as primarily a matter of party
politics or political ideology? This study traces the making and unmaking of such remarkable
consensus by focusing on the built environment itself. Although in architectural discourse
the lens of political ideology would suggest categorical oppositions—the Situationists' radical
leftist critiques, for instance, as diametrically opposed to the bureaucratic architectural production of a right-wing state during the de Gaulle years—a closer look at the complex agency
of architecture in the postwar city suspends such conventional registers.

Modern urbanism in France was politically eclectic, to say the least. At the level of the
national government, big decisions were made by centrist and right-wing politicians, in particular after 1958 with the arrival of de Gaulle, for whom participation was primarily a matter
of patriotism. At the same time, the urban policies of this government were developed by an
elite of nonelected officials with left-leaning but hardly radical political agendas—not rarely
social Catholics. On the local government level, the *grands ensembles* were enthusiastically
received by Communist mayors, while conservative municipalities tended to resist them. The
concentration of modern housing projects in the "red suburbs" of Paris is not an accident.[32]
Yet many large-scale housing and urban projects across the nation were planned from offices
in Paris. The *villes nouvelles* program was one such unmistakably Gaullist invention, drawn up

by nonelected technocrats against the demands of local government. Nevertheless, it was exactly in these New Town projects that sociology—surely more on the political Left than on the Right—inspired various New Town planners, whose political leanings were not often socialist. The architects they commissioned included an older, conservative generation of Beaux-Arts–trained architects as well as newly established offices of young radicals, many of whom had explicitly Communist affiliations. Moreover, the many programs and plans springing from specific political agendas at the national level were often transformed through local negotiation.

The emergence of participation in France is not a matter of one political ideology supplanting another but is part of a larger shift that confounds clear distinction between (right-wing) authoritarian planning and (left-wing) citizen empowerment. During the presidency of Giscard d'Estaing (1974–81), participation and quality of life became central preoccupations in architectural culture and urban policy. Yet these themes had been developing for more than two decades in what continues to be seen as the heyday of technocratic France.[33] Concerns with the recipients of mass housing did not first emerge from "the beach underneath the paving stones" after 1968, but as a part of these welfare state interventions themselves.[34] Similarly, the aesthetics of participation changed gradually from the modern to the postmodern: rather than being naturally opposite to the spatial homogeneity and visual repetition of midcentury modernism, participatory urbanism shifted over time to find its most "logical" expression in postmodern form, often recalling a preindustrial urban past. Most important, any a priori registers for understanding the politics or aesthetics of postwar architecture and urbanism were thrown off by the dynamics of a consumer society in which power also meant *purchasing power*. The latter constituted emerging forms of agency rarely acknowledged, yet increasingly of greater importance than those given by decree or demanded in protest. The proliferation of big-box shopping malls and predominance of the single-family home from the late 1960s onward, when a newly prosperous middle class could increasingly afford them, were clear signs of this emerging power threatening France's state-led urbanism. It is not surprising, then, that participation and lifestyle—or shared decision making and consumerism—were often conflated in urban and architectural debate during the 1960s and 1970s, at the height of the *villes nouvelles* project.

Fueled by growing prosperity, expanding social welfare, and mass consumerism during the postwar decades, the understanding of what it meant to be an inhabitant gradually evolved from a uniform, passive beneficiary of public services to a diverse set of active participants and consumers of lifestyle. This shift in mind-set took place during the "long sixties," the period between the late 1950s and early 1970s that is usually described as one of prosperity and relative stability, at least within the borders of the French metropole. This account thus contributes to recent scholarship, which has revised the dominant idea that the years between

Liberation and the economic downturn of the mid-1970s constituted a coherent period distinguished from the turbulence of World War II and the economic and social uncertainties after 1975. While some scholars, Philip Nord most recently, have traced the French postwar welfare state back to the 1930s and thus refute the idea that World War II introduced an absolute break, others, such as Rosemary Wakeman, have distinguished the 1940s and early 1950s as a quiet period distinct from the rapid urban modernization after the mid-1950s.[35]

Rather than challenging the bookends of the period, this study demonstrates crucial *qualitative* changes at the heart of the *trente glorieuses*. These changes do not correspond to political events, such as the founding of the Fifth Republic in 1958, but rather to the insidious transformations of everyday life in a country faced with unprecedented economic growth. Mass production based on the uniform consumption of material goods was increasingly subjected to diversification geared toward the consumption of lifestyle. The evolution from the mass urbanism of the first *grands ensembles* in the late 1950s to the branding of the *villes nouvelles* as showcases for new urban lifestyles little more than a decade later was an important factor of this dynamic. In France and many other countries, that shift took place under the aegis of a centralized state, which liberalized but by no means retreated. Liberalization in many ways meant privatization, which affected not only state-owned industries and the financial sector but also housing development. And with the privatization of housing, from real-estate development to individual home ownership, came marketing. In an increasingly prosperous France, individual families amassed savings that allowed them to act as middle-class consumers on the housing market. Developers both anticipated and tapped into this evolution by creating new housing products and shopping experiences, in which lifestyle became dominant.

This evolution of French dwelling culture was not just a factor of the market; it was also facilitated by a dynamic interplay between social contestation and state action. Critiques of state-led urbanism ran parallel to its historic development. While the *grands ensembles* helped to overcome the housing shortage and were celebrated by many as the advent of modern living and social progress, they were also criticized from day one. Some journalists reported nothing less than a moral panic, local associations and civil society organizations broadcast inhabitants' discontents, and sociologists formulated problems and solutions based on their extensive surveys. Especially after 1958, with Pierre Sudreau's tenure as minister of construction, the government took an active interest in these critiques. State administrators commissioned studies in order to understand and overcome what they saw as potential resistance to unquestionably benevolent modernization. They often took such critiques to heart in order to improve people's experience of the modernization process, making the centralized state not only a self-justifying but also a self-criticizing institution. That process led to a continual tweaking of design doctrines during the 1960s, but it was only after the social contestation of May 1968 that profound changes were proffered. That period's critiques of state capitalism—focused on the alienation of everyday life, the lack of participation, freedom, and creativity—were subsequently harnessed in new design and development strategies.[36] But not just private enterprise capitalized on critique. The well-known denunciations of government capitalism voiced by the Situationists in the late 1950s were rapidly recuperated by that same government after 1968 and informed new "user-oriented" approaches to state-led urban development during the 1970s.

Only in the mid-1970s did the French government finally shift away from large-scale housing production and a new regime of fully privatized housing development begin. The reasons were not altogether internal. The French economy was already showing signs of change and trouble by the late 1960s, but the oil crisis of 1973 sealed the end of the country's postwar golden age.[37] The Guichard directive, the official death knell for the *grands ensembles*, was signed earlier that year. It signified the official abandonment of the kind of urbanism that had guided a rapidly urbanizing and modernizing France. Meanwhile, participation and lifestyle—first tested in that same kind of urbanism during the 1960s—came to reign supreme in the private urban developments of the decades to come. Seemingly emerged from the ashes of a withering welfare state, this mind-set came in fact directly from the culture of the French welfare state itself, at the height of its success. By promoting active participation, free agency, and the consumption of lifestyle, government-led late-modern urbanism in France thus helped shape the social imaginary of the era that would follow. Despite the potentials of state-sponsored critique, these new approaches failed to arrest the logic of uneven development that ultimately shaped France's suburban crisis up until today. While the effort to attract middle-class families with images of new urban lifestyles intensified in the *villes nouvelles*, such families moved out of collective housing projects in increasing numbers, leaving large swaths of older, less desirable housing gradually to the immigrant poor.[38] The building boom stopped, and when it picked up again after the crises of the mid-1970s it was no longer in the form of "projects" but rather single-family homes. Expertise nevertheless continued to proliferate, but it would now be put to use not to build a social vision but to fix the "problem of the *banlieue*."[39]

Structure of the Book

The book's narrative unfolds in three parts. The first part, "1950s: Projects in the Making," examines how an unprecedented regime of mass housing production took shape in response to acute housing needs after World War II and throughout the 1950s. Chapter 1 describes why housing policies privileging industrialized production methods, large sites, and modern architectural forms came to prevail and how such policies entered into the purview of national modernization. The result was a new mode of development epitomized by the *grands ensembles*—mass housing estates on large, consolidated areas often at the peripheries of exist-ing cities. Chapter 2 examines how a bureaucratic epistemology emerged in correspondence with the mushrooming of new housing developments. Domestic and community life became a central focus in the attempts of architects, planners, policy makers, and especially social sci-entists to satisfy housing needs for French working- and middle-class nuclear families. Social science—shifting from the quantitative approach of economists and demographers to the qualitative research of urban sociologists—developed in relation to in the housing projects it both analyzed and helped create. It became central to a new machinery of knowledge produc-tion for which the centralized state served as primary platform.

The second part, "1960s: Architecture Meets Social Science," analyzes how mass housing production—a regime that produced knowledge as much as buildings—shaped architectural and social experimentation in the French suburbs during the "long sixties." Fueled by rising prosperity, mass consumerism, and the expansion of social welfare, the idea of overcoming the perceived shortcomings of mass housing increasingly dominated political and architec-tural discourse. Inhabitants expected to be addressed increasingly as active individuals rather than passive or uniform beneficiaries. This informed the continual revision of mass hous-ing and the French New Town projects. Architecture and social science met at a time when intellectuals from many stripes read urban space as the barometer of contemporary culture and society. They engaged in particularly productive exchange around the notion of *animation*, the discourse of participation, and the approach to programming. Chapter 3 demonstrates how the social and political ambition to "animate" the *grands ensembles* shaped their plan-ning and design. Experts and policy makers understood *animation* as a social and technical approach to create liveliness and foster community life in newly built and often large-scale housing areas. While that was initially seen as a matter of providing the right kind and num-ber of collective facilities following the *grille Dupont*, architecture and urban design played an increasingly important role as modernist principles were gradually reoriented toward commu-nity and street life. Chapter 4 examines the development of citizen participation in French planning and architecture. Focusing on Sarcelles, a notorious housing project that served as a major laboratory for this development, it demonstrates how calls for inhabitant participa-tion coincided with a surge in sociological and architectural expertise. Such expertise was subsequently harnessed in housing projects such as Villeneuve in Grenoble, whose brutal-ist aesthetics correlated with participatory aspirations. Chapter 5 investigates the method of *programmation* in the planning and design of the *villes nouvelles* or French New Towns. In the context of the city, *programmation* or "programming" referred to ways of spatially organizing and relating a mix of urban functions and activities. The social critiques of the late 1960s infused the work of multidisciplinary teams with a sociological sensibility in which city build-ing was increasingly thought of as a science of programming.

The third part, "1970s: Consuming Contradictions," describes the turning point away from public housing and toward private development during the 1970s. The cusp and decline of France's regime of housing production and experimentation were epitomized by extravagant large-scale urban projects and alternative housing types. Chapter 6 focuses on the making of new urban centers—a crucial component of *villes nouvelles* planning—in the sprawling suburbs of the Paris region. Designed with modern consumers in mind, these giant megastructures-in-denial integrated a vast number of commercial and residential functions in an attempt to re-create urban density and centrality in the metropolitan sprawl. Their designers were inspired by the popular success of privately developed shopping malls, which proliferated rapidly in the 1960s. Yet that very success became a major cause in the decline of what were ultimately inflexible and often very costly urban projects. Chapter 7 focuses on the development of alternative housing models such as flexible dwelling (*habitat évolutif*) and intermediary housing (*habitat intermédiaire*), which were meant to combine qualities of single-family home living with the economies of scale in mass production. These ultimate projects of French welfare's golden age were cut short by financial trouble at mid-decade. Yet, increasing discontents with mass housing, privatization, and the gradual rise of middle-class prosperity and residential mobility had already undermined their success. More flexible private developments—both housing and commercial—picked up in response to the volatile agency of individuals as private consumers. They had a fundamentally different suburban logic. Both government and the field of architecture lost their role as a primary force in urban development and the expertise of dwelling. The single-family home became the dominant model, and the user lived on as the contemporary consumer.

The conclusion explores how this history shapes our understanding of architecture's social ambitions today. It contextualizes the predominant understanding of the social in negative terms, as a result of changing housing policies and the shift toward private housing development. Finally, it discusses the book's main findings in light of the concealment of architecture's social project in postmodernism from the 1970s onward and the reemergence of social engagement in architecture and urbanism today.

1950s

PROJECTS IN THE MAKING

1

STREAMLINING PRODUCTION

The preference of the French for individual homes, rather than apartments in collective housing, is obvious. In fact, nine out of ten in small towns, more than three-quarters in towns of more than 30,000 inhabitants, and—what might be surprising by the way—more than half in Paris, prefer this kind of dwelling.[1]

THIS WAS THE STARTLING CONCLUSION of a 1947 survey published by the recently established Institut national d'études démographiques (INED, or National Institute of Demographic Studies). Using polling techniques imported from the United States, the public opinion survey was pioneering in its kind for a country still paralyzed by the trauma of war. Its organizers had sent extensive questionnaires to more than two thousand families in an attempt to reveal the general preferences of French men and women with regard to housing. The results might not be surprising today, but they bewildered observers of the construction boom that would come to define the following decades. The authors emphasized that surveys of this type were lacking in France but had already taken place in other European countries, where experts were well aware of their usefulness for shaping future housing policy and urban design. They hoped that the survey would be a beacon for those in charge of rebuilding France.

That task was colossal. Three million French people had come out of the war without a home. No fewer than one in five buildings had been damaged. And France's existing housing stock was severely outdated to begin with—most homes had been built before 1914 and had been insufficiently maintained. In 1946, 48 percent of French homes lacked running water,

80 percent did not have an indoor toilet, and no less than 95 percent were short of a shower or bathtub within the unit.[2] To many of those in charge, the gravity of the situation legitimized extreme measures and offered unprecedented opportunity. A decade later, collective housing blocks had sprung up like mushrooms all over the country. Their apartments featured modern kitchens with running water and new appliances, fully equipped bathrooms, and spacious rooms with large windows. In 1959, of the 320,000 homes built that year, more than 90 percent were at least partly state-financed and the vast majority were in the form of collective housing.[3] The new housing blocks and slabs were built by large companies often using industrialized techniques such as wall-sized prefabricated panel construction. They were grouped in *grands ensembles*, consolidated areas of modern housing most often at the periphery of existing cities.

Although this development itself was unprecedented, some of its underlying ideas were not entirely novel. During the 1920s, an international avant-garde of modernist architects had begun to experiment with new types of collective housing. Their work was inscribed in municipal housing programs with strong Social-Democratic support. Thousands of housing units were built to create the New Frankfurt and Red Vienna, but nothing of this scale took place in France. Of the few modern housing projects erected during these years, the best known is probably the Cité de la Muette in Drancy. Its notoriety, however, is as much owing to its architectural features as to its use as a Jewish internment camp during the war (Figure 1.1). Although the term *grand ensemble* appeared in the interwar period to describe such new types of housing, it only proliferated during the 1950s when large-scale collective housing became the norm for new development all over the country.[4]

In contrast to the United States, Britain, or Belgium, few single-family homes were built in France at this time. The ideal of the single-family home seemed eclipsed, for the time being at least, by the spectacular construction of *grands ensembles* and their much-celebrated modern comforts. Those inhabiting the new dwellings often came from slums and considered themselves lucky to be part of this new France, despite long commutes to work and the frequent lack of amenities in their often-remote estates. But why did high-rise collective housing in large estates predominate? How did this become the answer to France's challenges—in the aftermath of World War II—to regain national confidence, overcome the housing shortage, and boost the national economy? What was its intellectual foundation, and how did it differ from the interwar period?

The Planning State

France came out of World War II with a housing shortage that was both acute and long-standing. Contrary to popular perception, it was caused not only by wartime destruction but also by severe lack of development during the first half of the century.[5] Private housing

408 DRANCY. — Les Premiers Gratte-Ciel de la Région Parisienne

Figure 1.1. Cité de la Muette in Drancy, designed by Marcel Lods, Eugène Beaudouin, and Jean Prouvé for the Office public HBM de la Seine, 1931–34. Postcard by Godneff.

development had been sluggish for decades and had now practically come to a halt. Stringent rent-control laws had obstructed a revival, particularly in the lower segments of the housing market where need was most dire. Scarcity was further exacerbated by population growth in the immediate postwar years. Surprisingly, and despite the destitution, France initially lacked Britain's or Germany's commitment to boosting housing production or to building New Towns. Emergency measures such as the confiscation of unoccupied homes, loans and training programs for the construction industry, and forced rent increases to encourage private development had relatively little direct impact on the situation: by 1950, only seventy thousand new homes had been built, a small number considering the pressing need at the time and the yearly production of over five hundred thousand units a decade later.[6] There was no real public debate about housing in the immediate postwar years. In contrast to the emphasis on mass housing in architecture culture internationally, French architects and planners were surprisingly mute on the issue. The focus was on the cleanup of war-damaged areas, the reconstruction of historic town centers, the remaking of national infrastructure, and the decentralization of industry.[7]

The primary means through which France addressed postwar reconstruction and economic development was centralized national planning. Of course, the country was hardly alone in this orientation. What held Europe together in the immediate postwar decades was an incontrovertible faith in planning. The "political religion of postwar Europe," as the historian Tony Judt has called it, planning was derived less from the Soviet Union than from earlier ideas of liberal reformism, organized capitalism, and Keynesianism, and was strengthened by the experiences of fascist and wartime planning.[8] While this mentality dominated policy making in many European nations at this time, France's planning ideology proved particularly strong. As Britain developed an international reputation in welfare reform, France became a world expert in supply-side economic planning aimed at stable, long-term growth.[9]

Planning in France was guided by a long-standing tradition of political thought advocating resolute leadership in the form of neutral expertise. This technocratic view, which had roots in Saint-Simonianism, was further cultivated by political elites during the 1930s and formed the ideological basis of the postwar welfare state in France.[10] In the aftermath of the 1929 economic crash, various technocratic movements had sprung up to advocate for *planisme* or expert planning. Cast in direct opposition to the dominant ideology of economic liberalism and nourished by the crisis of parliamentary politics during the 1930s, these views found enthusiastic supporters—including modern architects such as Le Corbusier—but could not be put into practice until wartime when the Vichy government took them on.[11] Strengthened in its views by the emergencies of war, Vichy's political elite promoted authoritarian decision making guided by science and technology. Public engineers, who had played an important role in the French state administration over centuries, became even more central to decision making during this period.[12] As an influential group of what were called *techniciens* or technocrats, they supported the idea that rational, centralized planning by state experts was the only vehicle to attaining national progress. Because such an approach to expertise was cast as politically neutral—"ni gauche, ni droite"—it would be able to transcend the deadlock of national and local politics. A paragon of this conviction was Raoul Dautry, who had been widely praised for modernizing the French railways in the interwar period and became the first minister of reconstruction and urbanism upon the ministry's establishment in 1944.[13] In his eyes, state intervention was the only way France could be properly rebuilt and overcome its housing crisis. The ministry, a principal inheritor of Vichy authoritarianism, was run accordingly and would become the main organ of French reconstruction in the decade after the war.[14]

While they distanced themselves from Vichy, the postwar governments of the Fourth and Fifth Republics continued to promote expert planning, which was fundamentally shaped by a faith in the centralized state and in its superiority in directing economic and social affairs. The remarkably unscathed confidence in science and technology after the Second World War allowed a range of experts—often the same public engineers that had risen to power during the 1930s and early 1940s—to legitimate themselves at the level of national policy making. Although the country was not simply ruled by technocracy, as some critics claimed, technical expertise nevertheless had a particularly strong appeal within French political circles, transcending the different political camps.[15] In the highly unstable political climate of the first postwar decade—no less than eight successive governments were formed in the first five years of the newly established Fourth Republic—a powerful class of civil servants assured continuity in policy.[16] Often from Parisian bourgeois backgrounds, these men (rarely women) attended elite schools such as the École polytechnique and the École nationale des ponts et chaussées. These two institutions produced the country's strong network of government engineers, who were systematically distributed over the nation and operated in a strictly hierarchical and highly centralized way. (The state was able to employ the country's brightest as social status for government jobs was higher than for jobs in the private sector.) This organizational structure was the basis for how the centralized state governed the national territory until the decentralization of the 1980s.

France's elite of highly educated civil servants functioned quasi-invisibly yet very effectively inside the state apparatus and provided the expertise on which different ministers came to rely.[17] Because of their status as neutral experts, they were able to shape long-term policies that were relatively independent from the uncertain dynamics of party politics. In the immediate postwar years, many administrators had stayed on from the Vichy government and had received quick pardons for wartime collaboration. What drove many of them in the 1940s was national pride. The Second World War—and particularly the defeat of 1940—had left many French with the desire to assert a strong national identity. In a postwar climate of international competition and development, this desire was expressed in the urge to "catch up." The display of technological and economic progress was one particularly appealing way of doing so. The country's move from an unstable political economy and a cautious pattern of industrial development to an efficiently managed and dynamic order in the decade after World War II was in part the result of this perceived need to overtake other advanced industrial nations.[18]

The French postwar state thus became an *état planificateur* or "planning state" in which national pride and economic modernization went hand in hand. Although this development had its roots in the 1930s, it was the Monnet Plan (1946–50) that set its basic parameters for the decades to come. Under the direction of Jean Monnet, the economist and diplomat who would later become one of the main architects of the European Union, the Monnet Plan was a product of enlightened bureaucracy, crafted behind the scenes of public politics. In 1946, the Commissariat général du Plan (CGP, or Plan Commission), a governmental think tank established by Monnet, was charged with the creation of a detailed five-year plan for industrial modernization. Although it officially depended on the finance ministry, the commission had a long-term leadership structure transcending the short-lived positions of the finance ministers: between 1945 and 1963, there were twenty-two ministers but only three directors of the commission.[19] French planning thus developed in part as the result of American aid. The Monnet Plan was only viable thanks to the counterpart funds mechanism of the Marshall Plan, warmly welcomed a year after its establishment. Ironically, the strings attached to the American money included the construction of public housing. What in domestic politics would certainly have led to hysterical accusations of Communism was understood by American policy makers to be an appropriate solution for France: a necessary bulwark against French Communism. Perhaps even more ironic, considering the building boom that would follow, was that French planners resisted such demands.[20] They focused on what they saw as the sole guarantee for future growth: the development of basic industries, energy and agriculture, the production of primary materials, and the (re)construction of basic infrastructure. This meant neglecting social provisions such as housing. Between 1948 and 1951 only 13 percent of the counterpart funds was spent on housing, severely inadequate considering the enormity of the housing shortage.[21]

Planners' focus was instead on what they considered to be the underlying fundamentals—not the superstructure but the infrastructure. During World War I already, it had become clear to military strategists that war was won in the air through aerial bombardment of national infrastructure. The targets of military action—transportation and infrastructure nodes, vital basic industries, and cities themselves—thus turned into the basic targets of postwar reconstruction. The kind of strategic thinking employed in warfare could also serve national development in times of peace, something that became even more clear during World War II. The military view from the air thus changed the purview of postwar planning, which was no longer simply a matter of disparate entities—homes, cities, or industrial plants—but the organization of the national territory at large.[22] Yet, seeing territory as a matter of volition rather than fact was not just a consequence of war, the deployment of new technologies, or aerial perspective. It was also in part the product of a rather ill-defined but influential intellectual tradition of *géographie volontaire* or "volitional geography." This notion was firmly rooted in nineteenth-century Saint-Simonianism, according to which politically neutral experts would organize territorial space at a vast scale through large infrastructural projects.[23] But the origins of the term itself lay in the authoritarian regime of the Vichy government. In 1942, a team of engineers, geographers, and historians was commissioned by that government to study industrial relocation and the modernization of rural areas. Eventually published as *Matériaux pour une géographie volontaire de l'industrie française* in 1949, this study expounded a comprehensive theory for the geographic localization of French industry.[24] On the road to victory, centralized planning was of paramount importance, and the geography of France became a crucial arena of thought and action.

For many, that conviction did not change fundamentally after Liberation. In fact, the notion of *géographie volontaire* continued to shape official state policy when Eugène Claudius-Petit, minister of reconstruction and urbanism from 1948 until 1953, presented his case for a "National Plan for Territorial Planning" (Plan national d'aménagement du territoire) in 1950. His agenda, which was neglected by subsequent leaders but continued to implicitly influence French planning over the following decades, was rooted in the ideal of a "harmonious distribution" of people and activities over the national territory. This meant first of all that the chaotic urban growth of Paris needed to be limited and the rapid emptying out of rural and small-town France reversed. Ideas about the capital's "disproportionate development" and the need to develop the countryside were in part inspired by the projects of the Tennessee Valley Authority, which Claudius-Petit visited together with Le Corbusier in 1945, and in part by the work of Jean-François Gravier.[25] In his influential book *Paris et le désert français* (*Paris and the French Desert*) of 1947, he posited that the overwhelming concentration of people, industry, infrastructure, and culture in the capital—only intensified by the recent immigration from the countryside—constituted a territorial imbalance that was not just economically inefficient but also generative of all sorts of social ills.[26] Similar arguments had supported the 1943 Abercrombie Plan for London, whose ideas of green belts and satellite towns directly informed the planning of the British New Towns over the following decades. Gravier's denunciatory analysis of the country's hypercentralization in Paris also included concrete remedies, and these would similarly come to define the mind-set of a generation of French planners. His solution was a radical decentralization of industry away from the Paris region altogether, to be accompanied by a large-scale redistribution of the population to the provinces. This was more than simply a reactive measure in the eyes of Gravier, Claudius-Petit, and their followers: national economic development could only be pushed by resolute geographic strategizing. Such an approach encompassed not just housing or new neighborhoods, but everything from the relocation of large-scale industries and the modernization of transport to the regional development of hydroelectric energy.[27] The establishment in 1963 of France's state institution for regional planning, the Délégation à l'aménagement du territoire et à l'action régionale (or Delegation for Territorial Planning and Regional Action), and the official *villes nouvelles* or New Towns project launched in 1965 would be belated realizations of this intellectual ambition.[28]

Housing mattered to many of these administrators insofar as it was part of a more comprehensive approach to territorial development. And yet, while the French government failed to adequately address the acute housing shortage in the immediate postwar years, it set many of the basic parameters for the proliferation of the *grands ensembles* over the following decades. As administrators such as Claudius-Petit turned the territory of the French hexagon into the principal lens for his policies, they rendered the city a mere second-order phenomenon.

The complexity of social and spatial relationships of cities could subsequently be abstracted and emphasis placed instead on national development through mass housing in self-contained neighborhood units whose relationship to the larger context was of lesser importance. But perhaps most important, it was the growing dominance of planning as expertise that allowed administrators to place the relationship between people and place outside the realm of politics.

Roads to (Re)construction

Despite the overarching ambitions of state planning, day-to-day policy making in France remained preoccupied with the rebuilding of town centers and did not lead to a comprehensive approach to new construction and urbanization until well into the 1950s. The reconstruction of war-damaged areas and structures—begun not after Liberation but after the first destructions of 1940—was the most visible sign of change in the built environment at this time. Reconstruction projects varied enormously not only in size and spatial organization, but also in construction method, urban morphology, and formal language. For the small historic town of Gien on the Loire, disfigured by three waves of destruction during the war, the rebuilding was almost identical to what was lost. The reconstruction of Saint-Malo, a walled city on the Brittany coast, was inspired by a similar desire to return to the past but ultimately led to rationalized perimeter blocks with rustic facades carefully inserted into the existing urban fabric (Figure 1.2). The town of Saint-Dié, associated with Le Corbusier, whose project the inhabitants turned down in favor of a more historicist reconstruction, was indicative of modernists' limited role at this time. For the rebuilding of the heavily destroyed port city of Le Havre, tabula rasa helped legitimize Auguste Perret's comprehensive urban design project, whose "structural classicism"—a stark monumentality of reinforced concrete—was meant to instill national pride (Figure 1.3). And in Marseille, Fernand Pouillon and others provided a series of monumental "imperial facades" for the city's Old Port area.[29] Perhaps most exceptional, in fact, were wholeheartedly modernist designs, such as the arrangement of collective housing blocks in a sea of green at Sotteville-lès-Rouen (Figure 1.4).[30]

In their formal and typological diversity, these reconstruction projects provided little indication of what would follow. One type, however, was quickly excluded from the mix: the suburban single-family home. The dismissal of the single-family home as a valid option for new housing—despite the unambiguous results of the 1947 survey discussed at the beginning of this chapter—was motivated by a mind-set that seemed to categorize it as a thing of the past and not of the future. Shared almost universally across the French political spectrum, this view transcended the bounds of rational planning. One of the few experiments with mass-produced single-family homes took place in the late 1940s at Noisy-le-Sec in suburban Paris.[31] More than sixty model homes—a mix of bungalows and two-story houses—were

Figure 1.2. The reconstruction of Saint-Malo by architects Auffret & Hardion, with Louis Arretche and Marc Brillaud de Laujardière, 1952. From *Architecture française* 125–26 (1952): 21 and Fonds Arretche. Académie d'architecture/Cité de l'architecture et du patrimoine/Archives d'architecture du XXᵉ siècle/2014.

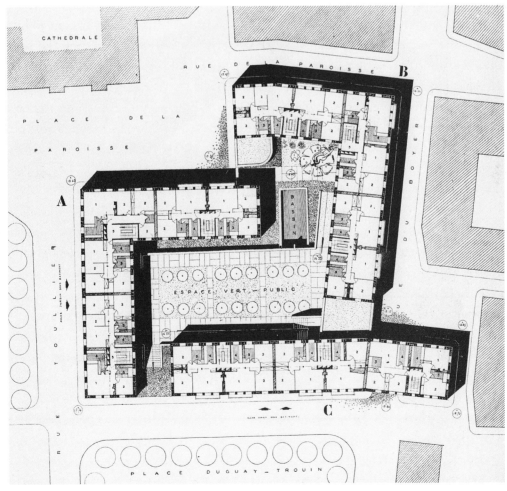

Figure 1.3. The reconstruction of Le Havre, begun in 1945, by the architect Auguste Perret. Fonds Perret. CNAM/Service interministériel des Archives de France/UFSE/CAPA/Archives d'architecture du XXᵉ siècle.

erected there by architects and construction companies employing a variety of experimental construction methods and materials, including precast concrete, steel, and aluminum (Figure 1.5). They were part of an experimental competition organized by the Ministry of Reconstruction and Urbanism to encourage mass housing construction. More such competitions and programs followed, but all focused on collective housing. Single-family homes were built in France at this time but remained in the realm of artisanal self-building by working- and lower-middle-class families, just as it had been during the interwar period. The production of mass collective housing eclipsed that of single-family homes in the mid-1950s and continued to have the upper hand until the mid-1970s.[32]

Rather than the result of socialist consensus or an authoritarian government careless about its citizens, the condemnation of the French *pavillon* or suburban single-family home—strongest in bourgeois intellectual circles but accepted in a much wider social arena—was shaped by convictions about the aesthetic face of national modernization. Despite the fact that

Figure 1.4. The housing estate of Sotteville-lès-Rouen, by the architect Marcel Lods, 1944–52. Fonds Lods. Académie d'architecture/Cité de l'architecture et du patrimoine/Archives d'architecture du XXᵉ siècle.

a

b

Figure 1.5. Prefabricated single-family model homes at Noisy-le-Sec, result of the 1946 experimental competition. (a) American wood-frame model "City-Lumber"; (b) French model "SO-TE-BA" (architect: Besse), made of a reinforced concrete frame and cement panels; (c) French model "C.I.M.A.P." (architect: L. Bailly), a reinforced concrete frame with cement coat and wood-frame roof with zinc cladding. From *Petites maisons construites depuis la guerre: La cité expérimentale de Noisy-le-Sec* (Paris: Ch. Massin & Cie/Librairie Centrale des Beaux-Arts, 1951).

C

in some neighboring countries, Belgium most remarkably, the massive construction of modern single-family houses rendered collective housing estates both unnecessary and unwanted, many French observers and policy makers saw this type as synonymous with the allotments of often shabby and self-built cottages on the urban periphery.[33] The interwar experiments with garden cities were seemed forgotten and the seductive models imported by American home builders such as Levitt would only reach France in the mid-1960s. The lack of positive imagery about middle-class suburban dwelling in postwar France helped cast the *pavillon* as the opposite of modernity.[34] As Kristin Ross has shown, "modern" in postwar French culture meant orderly, white, and clean; on the urban level this basically meant everything that the existing suburbs were not.[35] Urban planners and architects deplored the "chaos" of the working-class allotments built during the interwar period and referred to them as *lotissements défectueux*, substandard allotments (Figure 1.6). State administrators shared similar convictions: they were equally adamant on breaking with the past, in this case the disorderly suburbanization of France.[36] And many social scientists would soon join in by dismissing the suburban single-family home as a harbinger of extreme individualism and questionable petit-bourgeois values.[37] When modern architecture became widely embraced during the 1950s, it

Figure 1.6. The fabric of the Parisian suburbs, photographed in 1933. From Jean Bastié, *La croissance de la banlieue parisienne* (Paris: Presses Universitaires de France, 1964), 241.

certainly did not include the single-family home. But even as the language of the unmodern was clear, that of the *modern* was still an open question—at least for the time being.

The political support for architectural modernism in France was surprisingly weak during the era of Reconstruction. Despite the work of important champions like minister Claudius-Petit—a well-known friend of Le Corbusier who as major of Firminy in the mid-1950s commissioned the architect for the town's urban extension—modernism was still far from mainstream. The Congrès internationaux d'architecture moderne (CIAM) contained several important French architects, but they had limited influence within France itself. State-sponsored architectural culture was determined by the Beaux-Arts system of education and awards. The architects winning government competitions, those employed by the ministry, and those directly commissioned by the state for its public buildings and reconstruction projects came predominantly from the École nationale supérieure des Beaux-Arts (ENSBA), the national Beaux-Arts school in Paris. Despite the fact that this institution—the government's primary instrument for shaping its corps of architects—would become known as an untiring bastion of academism, it did not simply ignore international modernism. An influential interpretation of the 1933 CIAM Athens Charter found its way into the school through the teachings of André Gutton and, later on, Robert Auzelle.[38] Nevertheless, the government often favored prestigious Prix de Rome winners over hardline modernists. Wholesale change was further impeded by the hierarchical structure of decision making by state-employed architects and urbanists.[39] Despite his international renown, Le Corbusier's influence remained limited in France, and his failure to realize his plans for the reconstruction of Saint-Dié only further confirmed his relatively marginal position—at least politically.[40]

Behind the scenes, however, crucial steps were being taken toward the development of mass housing following decidedly modernist principles. Most important was the radical overhaul of the French construction industry during the 1940s and early 1950s. Its transformation was based on the promises of industrialization to mass-produce housing units of approved, standard quality in inexpensive and expeditious ways. The idea itself was hardly new. Industrialization had been one of the staples of architectural modernism since the early twentieth century. With his Maison Domino project of 1914–15, Le Corbusier was only one of many designers borrowing enthusiastically from Taylorism at this time. Industrialization and standardization had also been part of French reconstruction debates since 1940—albeit it in a less radical cloak and with a less explicitly social agenda. Not only modernist architects but also progressive politicians were keen to make the virtues of industrialization known to the mainstream of French industry and political culture.

During the 1940s, French home building was still a largely traditional and small-scale affair. Family-owned businesses based in traditional skills and craftsmanship dominated the housing construction sector as they had done for decades. Some very large construction companies had emerged in the interwar period, but they focused primarily on public works. Housing construction was an unimportant sector for such companies as it was dominated by piecemeal developments and informal self-building. When during the 1940s the government sought to accomplish large-scale infrastructure and public-works projects, only large companies with the necessary expertise and capital benefited from its commissions. This only exacerbated the opposition between small-scale artisans and large construction companies. In order to boost housing production to a level that would help overcome the enormous shortage, state administrators were increasingly convinced about the potential of these large firms. Encouraging them to expand into the domain of housing construction thus became a crucial strategy.

Many of the industrial techniques for housing construction were not entirely novel in and of themselves. In interwar Europe, not just architects but also industrialists had begun to emphasize the rationalization of construction through the mass production of prefabricated building components. Precast concrete window frames and wall-cladding elements were mass-produced in France at this time by companies such as Coignet. Vichy's Comité d'organisation du bâtiment et travaux publics (Committee for the Organization of Construction and Public Works) and the Association française pour la normalisation (French Association for Standardization) further promoted such techniques in the belief that a focus on individual components was the best way to modernize construction. The techniques were premised on the rationalization of traditional construction rather than a radical overhaul in method, form, or typology. Others, however—especially modernist architects—considered the complete industrialization of building as the best way forward for mass housing. German architects had first begun to experiment with this more radical approach almost two decades earlier, and one of the first large-scale employments of prefab floor-to-ceiling panels was Ernst May's municipal social housing project of Westhausen, part of the New Frankfurt program. Such prefabrication techniques would proliferate quickly in a postwar France increasingly convinced by the possibilities of concrete.

The state policies, competitions, and experimental programs of the late 1940s and early 1950s were crucial to this development. Part of the Monnet Plan was a Committee for the Modernization of Construction and Public Works, which proposed the development of prototype projects featuring industrialized construction processes. Out of the same ambition, the government also established the Centre scientifique et technique du bâtiment (Scientific and Technical Center for Construction), which encouraged a close collaboration between the state and the private construction sector and provided a test bench for experimental projects. But the most important initiatives were undoubtedly launched by the Ministry of Reconstruction and Urbanism itself. In many ways, this ministry functioned as France's central laboratory for the development of mass housing techniques and typologies. Focused first of all on the reconstruction of existing cities, the ministry did not directly or solely develop the *grands ensembles*. But its experimental programs and competitions encouraged architects, engineers, and construction companies to rethink housing production and thus established the basis for the streamlined production regime of the following decades.

Two competitions in particular—one for two hundred dwelling units in Villeneuve-Saint-Georges and another for eight hundred in Strasbourg, resulting in the famous Cité de Rotterdam—were crucial to this development.[41] Their explicit goal was to promote efficient, industrialized construction based on the complete standardization of the building process. Despite the large number of competitors, most entries proposed variations on the modernist theme of slabs and blocks. This was not surprising considering the provenance of participating architects and the competition's stringent requirements in terms of density and repetition. The winning schemes were those promising a reduction of cost by minimizing the number of different building components and maximizing the degree of repetition (Figure 1.7).

The competitions successfully demonstrated the advantages of heavy prefabrication, and spin-off projects by the competition's prize winners were built across the nation. As such, the initiative succeeded in drawing large contractor firms into the house-building industry and intensified technical research in the realm of housing construction. Engineers, organized in often semipublic *bureaux d'études techniques* or technical research firms, were thus able to

Figure 1.7. A housing project at Pont de Sèvres near Paris by Zehrfuss and Sebag, 1949–52. This project was based on their design for the experimental competitions of 1949 at Villeneuve-Saint-Georges organized by the Ministry of Reconstruction and Urbanism. From *L'Architecture d'aujourd'hui* 45 (1952): 1–2.

assert their expertise not only in the state administration but also in large construction companies. Their success only exacerbated the long-standing competition between architects and engineers in France, two professions that would undergo profound mutation in the task of building postwar France.[42] The government's requirements in terms of quantity, economy, and speed spoke directly to the expertise of engineers, rather than that of architects. As technical knowledge increasingly functioned as the glue between government and private industry and engineers came to occupy an increasingly important role not only in the construction but also in the conception of housing projects, the role of the architect changed. Rather than an artistic, solitary authority, the architect operated increasingly as mediator between engineers, developers, and construction companies. The role of the architect in the development of the *grands ensembles* would thus be far more limited than what the popular image of the master builder would suggest.

That said, neither technical expertise nor industrialization in and of themselves automatically implied uniformity or even collective housing types—as the experiments with prefabricated single-family homes at Noisy-le-Sec had demonstrated. Yet, many engineers considered the most efficient and rational method to be that of the *chemin de grue*. This was a construction system that generated linear blocks of collective housing using a construction crane that ran along a continuous rail track (Figure 1.8). In his 1943 *Bauordnungslehre*, Ernst Neufert had already suggested something similar with his *Hausbaumaschine* or "house-building machine," an idea for a mobile factory that could excrete infinite ribbons of multistory housing.[43] The reconversion of large-scale construction from military to civilian purposes after World War II brought such ideas within the realm of possibility and led to prioritizing some methods of prefabrication over others. Exceptional proposals, such as Jean Prouvé's *maison des jours meilleurs*, a prototype of which was exhibited on the Parisian banks of the Seine, would never make it to mass production (Figure 1.9). While its prefab kitchen and bathroom module and steel

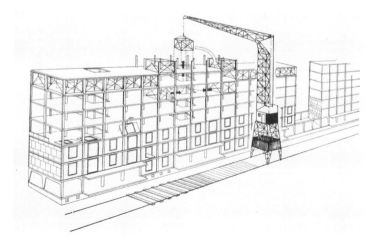

Figure 1.8. The *chemin de grue* method, illustrated for the project at Villeneuve-Saint-Georges by the architects Zehrfuss and Sebag with construction company Balancy & Schuhl. From *L'Architecture d'aujourd'hui* 30 (1950): xv.

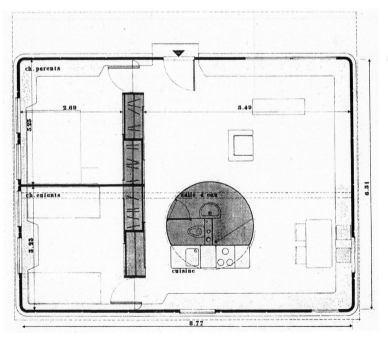

Figure 1.9. Jean Prouvé's *maison des jours meilleurs,* exhibited on the banks of the Seine River in Paris, 1956.
Copyright 2012 Artists Rights Society, New York/Société des auteurs dans les arts graphiques et plastiques, Paris.

construction allowed it to fall within the cost limits of government housing programs, it was refused on the grounds of its unorthodox interior organization. The most typical response to the impetus of mass housing production was the linear multistory housing block made of factory-produced, on-site-assembled elements. These were often floor-to-ceiling concrete panels, which included window details and finishings. Concrete thus won out over steel in French prefabrication, and its patented methods were championed by large construction companies such as Camus, Coignet, and Boussiron. The Coignet company had been founded in the nineteenth century by François Coignet, one of the very inventors of reinforced concrete. Raymond Camus only established his company in 1949, but three years later, a government commission of four thousand housing units to be built in two years allowed the firm to establish its first factory for large-panel prefabrication with a capacity of two thousand housing units a year (Figure 1.10). By 1966, the company owned six large factories in France and no less than twenty-three abroad. Coignet was its main competitor on the booming global market of mass housing construction.[44]

Following the success of these experimental competitions and the logic of economies of scale, minister Claudius-Petit launched a more ambitious program with the name *secteur industrialisé* or industrialized sector in 1951. The goal was to build ten thousand housing units over the next five years. Hoping to avoid some of the technical mistakes and problems of previous experiments, administrators shifted gears from concentrated experimentation to mass production on a national scale. The ambitions were both technical and social: industrializing construction and lower construction costs, solving the housing crisis, and planning for a "balanced" development of the French territory. The first phase of the program led to the construction of six housing estates of between 600 and 2,600 units in Angers, Bron-Parilly, Boulogne, Le Havre, Pantin, and Saint-Étienne. These projects were in effect the first *grands ensembles* of postwar France, and the fact that only one of them was in the Paris region was not coincidental. It followed Claudius-Petit's agenda for national decentralization. Other programs, ever more ambitious in size, rapidly followed.

Administrators' much-employed slogan "massivement, rapidement, économiquement" offers an accurate summary for the evolution of state policies in the 1950s. Most measures tended toward prioritizing big companies, big projects, and big buildings. The result was a dramatic shift in housing production. With the surge in scale of housing development—from a single unit or building to hundreds and then thousands of units at once—small-scale business quickly lost ground. Large-scale corporate construction companies took over, much as state administrators had intended with their policies. Once their machinery was in place, these firms had the expertise and technologies to exert continuing influence on the built form and typologies of mass housing production, despite growing criticism. The ties between the centralized state and corporate construction industry would remain close over the next decades,

Groupe de Farebersviller (Camus-Dietsch)

procédés industriels de construction

RAYMOND CAMUS

Cité de Méricourt (Camus-Génie Civil de Lens)

H.L.M. de Nanterre (S.E.R.P.E.C.)

SHAPE, Saint-Germain (S.E.R.P.E.C.)

Plus de
18.000 logements
construits
depuis 1950

Abaissement du prix de revient

Gain de temps

Souplesse de l'expression architecturale:
le procédé se prête aux constructions
les plus diverses : pavillons individuels,
ensembles de grand standing, groupes d'H.L.M.

RAYMOND CAMUS & Cᴵᴱ

40, rue du Colisée, PARIS (8ᵉ)

CAMUS-DIETSCH
usine à Marienau-lès-Forbach (Moselle)

C. G. C. L.
usines à COURCHELETTES (Nord)
et à Fort de Scarpe DOUAI (Nord)

S. E. R. P. E. C.
usine à MONTESSON (S.-&-O.)

R. L. Dupuy

Figure 1.10. Advertisement for the Camus heavy prefabrication system, 1959. "More than 18,000 dwelling units built since 1950. Lowering of construction costs. Gain in time. Flexibility in the architectural expression. The technique lends itself to the most diverse constructions: individual homes, luxury housing developments, and social housing areas." From *Urbanisme* 62–63 (1959): xxxvii.

until the mid-1970s when housing development decreased again in scale and new kinds of piecemeal suburban home building emerged.[45] Despite the all-pervasive calls for complete industrialization, however, it was rarely achieved, and traditional methods of construction continued to persist, even if the results looked similar. The first phases of Sarcelles and other large-scale housing projects in the mid-1950s were built using traditional techniques such as load-bearing stone masonry.[46] Although industrialization failed to guarantee the exponential gains in efficiency and productivity it delivered in other economic sectors, it did lead to a significant increase in speed and a reduction in both cost and working hours—in many cases by more than half.[47]

Apart from supplying the material technologies of mass housing production, the importance of government competitions, programs, and policies at this time was certainly also nonmaterial. By expanding the culture of technical expertise into the social domain of housing, they positioned the organization of the everyday realm of dwelling both outside of the realm of politics and outside of the private sphere. Because the architects, policy makers, and especially engineers in charge saw themselves as neutral experts developing a universally valid product, they expected that future inhabitants could at best optimize the dwellings provided for them, and not criticize them fundamentally. Consequently, the reception and inhabitation of mass-produced housing could later be treated as a matter of efficient management, not politics or individual choice.

A Decisive Turn

Only by the mid-1950s, then, did French housing take a resolute turn toward mass production, and modern collective housing in large estates—*grands ensembles*—become the logical expression of economic and social modernization. By this time, strong migration and the French baby boom had led the situation in metropolitan areas to become so acute that public discontents over the housing shortage now directly shaped national politics. Outcry about miserable housing conditions had been an important part of public debates throughout the 1940s, but government had steered a laissez-faire course in housing policy during this time. During the early 1950s, however, housing conditions reached an unprecedented level of emergency in the eyes of public observers and government elites alike. The seriousness of the problem was manifested in the growth of *bidonvilles* or shantytowns on the urban periphery, most notoriously those of Nanterre in the suburbs of Paris.[48] Faced with such an eyesore, which seemed to fundamentally contradict the national ambition to build a victorious modern France after the war, the government was compelled to address the housing shortage head-on. Fuel was added to the fire during the particularly cold winter of 1953–54, when the Catholic cleric and social activist Henri de Groués, known as Abbé Pierre since his Resistance days, gained national attention with his public protests against the miserable conditions of the homeless in the notorious zone around Paris. With his enormously successful campaigns, from open letters to the minister to the setting up of homeless tent camps along the Parisian banks of the Seine, he brought the grievances of the housing shortage to the center of national attention and, consequently, of national policy.[49]

Nonetheless, it was not only social activism but also a series of laws passed in the previous summer that provided the vehicle of change, away from the disparate experiments of Reconstruction and toward the streamlined housing production of the *grands ensembles*. Known as the Plan Courant because it was fabricated under the brief tenure of Pierre Courant as minister of construction, the legislation aimed to encourage the rapid and massive construction of low-cost standardized housing. The plan was unprecedented in that it tied together land-use legislation, a way to finance housing, and a program of normalized dwelling units known as *Logécos* (*logements économiques et familiaux* or low-cost family dwellings).[50] The reform of land-use legislation was crucial because it facilitated expropriation and thus allowed for the acquisition of substantially larger swaths of land for housing developments. The economies of scale insinuated by the state competitions were thus taken to their logical end point. Financing, another key constraint, was addressed by expanding state subsidies and by obliging employers to contribute 1 percent of salaries toward housing for employees.[51] Courant's goal was the production of 240,000 housing units per year, a target easily surpassed before the end of the decade (Figure 1.11).[52]

The combination of the plan's measures—supplying land and money while standardizing the program and process of building—is what ultimately allowed for the rapid proliferation of the *grands ensembles* in the second half of the 1950s. Initially, however, the program seemed to result in a very different kind of housing. Spurred by public outrage about the inhumane consequences of the housing shortage, the government first used the Plan Courant legislation to build low-cost emergency housing. During the harsh winter of 1954, officials organized a competition for the construction of *cités d'urgence*, emergency housing areas consisting of low-rise strips of very simple, expediently built units. These turned out to be very similar to the much-despised barracks built by the wartime government and were soon denounced for being nothing more than "new slums."[53] This result lent force to the concerns of social housing organizations, who lamented the *Logécos* for their degradation in size and quality of housing. The public scandal did not weaken the *Logéco* program, however; on the contrary, it informed an even more comprehensive approach to mass housing in which doing well and doing big became the one and the same thing.

The *Logécos* marked the golden age of a new category of state-subsidized housing called the *secteur aidé*. This new sector would be responsible for the largest part of housing production during the postwar decades, more than the private sector and the social housing sector in

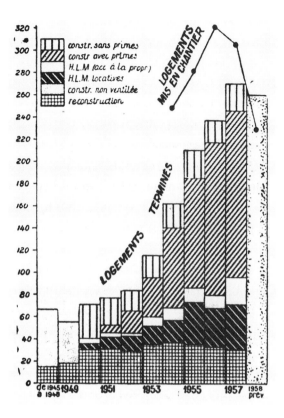

Figure 1.11. The evolution of housing construction in France between 1945 and 1958, showing a spectacular rise in the number of state-aided housing units (white and black diagonal hatches plus white in-between). From Gilbert Mathieu, "Logement, notre honte," *Le Monde* (April 11–18, 1958).

the strict sense.[54] The initial goal of the *Logécos* was not collective rental housing; they were meant to stimulate individual home ownership for the French lower-middle classes. The situation turned out differently. *Logéco* housing could be purchased by intermediaries, and many middle-class families thus preferred to rent out their dwellings in a market where offer was far below demand.[55] When the initiative was relaunched in 1958 under the influence of Pierre Sudreau's *grands ensembles* policies, the *Logécos* then became officially rental units.[56] Many administrators also believed that rental housing, which effectively prevailed until the 1970s, would stimulate the geographic mobility of the country's workforce as new large-scale industries developed across the national territory.

In contrast to the Reconstruction period, when the Ministry of Reconstruction and Urbanism often acted firsthand as the project developer, the state was no longer directly in charge of building mass housing. Instead, social housing organizations and semipublic and large private developers were. In order to further stimulate mass production, the government also created its own housing developer, the Société centrale immobilière de la Caisse des dépôts (SCIC, or Central Real-Estate Company of the Deposits and Consignments Fund), with funds from the national finance institution Caisse des dépôts et consignations.[57] Despite the more distributed nature of commissioning housing projects, decision making about qualitative issues with regard to housing was still largely concentrated in the centralized state apparatus. It controlled large parts of the banking and construction sectors, either directly or indirectly. The purely private sector amounted to less than 10 percent of the total housing production in the 1950s.[58] The housing market was thus overwhelmingly defined by the state, first of all through the technical norms it imposed on the housing construction it would help finance, and second as a result of the hierarchical structure of national and local planning procedures. While housing production remained distributed over different state bodies, social housing organizations, semipublic institutions, and private companies, it was no longer the weak and fragmented domain it was during the 1940s.[59] Despite the complex and dynamic relationships between these various entities, and the proliferation of different norms and categories, housing production became a unified domain held together by the indirect yet central role of the "planning state."

This development blurred some of the crucial distinctions between state and market housing. In fact, it transformed the very nature of housing. Contemporaneous developments in the United States, of which Levittown would become the staple reference, offer an instructive comparison here. Despite their fundamental dependence on the financial regulation of the federal government, they were privately developed and sold as consumer goods in the private market. In 1950s France, the equivalent in housing production was at once carrier of modern consumer comfort and product of the centralized state. Epitomized by places such as Sarcelles (Plate 1), many of these projects were perceived by local inhabitants as "landing from Paris," and thus as interventions of the centralized state. Consequently, because of their relationship with the state—in this case SCIC as developer, financier, and landlord—the new inhabitants of these housing areas were less private consumers than denizens of a "welfare state city."

The brief history of the Castor movement offers a clear indication of how the multitude of initiatives of the immediate postwar years were gradually channeled into a generally state-aided mass housing paradigm. The Castors or "Beavers" groups grew out of militant youth, worker, and consumer organizations in the late 1940s.[60] They became popular self-building organizations in which individual members contributed their own labor to housing construction projects, mainly single-family home allotments. The movement had a vision of cooperative living and direct participation, which, according to Michel Anselme, member of Monnet's CGP and spokesperson of the newly established Union nationale des Castors, was derived from nineteenth-century utopianism.[61] After having united nationally, the Castors lost momentum but then joined the larger "cooperative movement." This movement, of which Bâticoop was the most prominent, only selectively adopted the Castors' ideology of self-building. Created in 1952 by Michel Anselme himself, Bâticoop was less interested in utopian lifestyles or the idea of building one's own home than in providing members with affordable homes as rapidly and efficiently as possible. The movement's projects shifted toward collective housing, and cooperation was often limited to everyday management such as the cleaning of communal spaces.[62] In short, it ultimately did not offer a veritable alternative to state-led housing production. The Castors' self-help ideology ended up merely underlining the shortcomings of the national government in housing construction, rather than contesting its very responsibility or authority in this realm. While some of the initial movements' militants tended to be mistrusting of state initiative, the cooperative societies replacing them tapped into state resources just as regular social housing organizations did. Ultimately, they actively contributed to rather than questioned state-led urbanism and housing production. In 1953, Bâti-coop submitted plans for *Logéco* approval, which were subsequently used by other cooperative societies to build standardized housing projects financed by the state.[63] The company would build several *grands ensembles*, one of which was La Dame Blanche in the Parisian suburb of Garges (Figure 1.12). The project was a *grand ensemble* similar to that of Sarcelles, located just on the other side of the nearby railway tracks. Their morphological similarities expressed how

Figure 1.12. Aerial photograph of La Dame Blanche in Garges, near Paris, by Noël Lemaresquier, early 1960s. Neighboring Sarcelles is visible at upper left. Archives départementales du Val d'Oise, Fonds Henrard 29Fi 202.

political alternatives, like that of self-building, had converged into the dominant paradigm of state-led urbanism.

The dominance of state-aided mass housing production went hand in hand with a broader cultural shift in the realm of dwelling. Part of the reason why the state could assume unprecedented responsibilities in the realm of housing was that during the 1950s the meaning of publicly funded housing moved away from the realm of social reform. During the interwar period, when centralized state intervention was limited and social housing was first of all a municipal affair, the work of reformers was concentrated on improving the lives of the working classes. Philanthropic projects such as those of the Fondation Rothschild on Paris's former fortifications embodied the social-reform ideology that circulated among independent reformers, intellectuals, and administrators at the Musée social.[64] This private institution became an important center of expertise for social reform and set a basis for the architectural standardization of publicly funded housing in France. But it was only after the Second World War that such expertise was fully incorporated in the new rationalist paradigm of state-sanctioned housing production. Despite the continuity of certain reform practices targeting the "socially unadapted," the state's growing stake in housing was no longer legitimized by the idea of social reform or even social justice, but by a more abstract idea of rationalization—economic, technical, and functional—in the name of national modernization.

The mass housing regime of the *grands ensembles* enabled a radical extension of the social groups for whom housing should be provided. The government's new role in housing could no longer be considered as a domain pertaining only to a single segment of society—the war-stricken homeless or the working poor. Calls for a universal "right to housing" and the view, increasingly common, that providing housing was a government responsibility further encouraged the centralized state to take a more overarching position in the realm of housing. The official name change in 1950 from Habitations à bon marché or "cheap dwellings" to Habitations à loyer modéré (HLM) or "dwellings at moderated rent" was part of this move to distance the category of social housing from a particular social class.[65] The change in state competency over housing from the Ministry of Health to the Ministry of Reconstruction and Urbanism in 1947 was indicative of the same shift. State housing was no longer stigmatized as pertaining primarily to a single social class. The widespread perception in postwar France that traditional class lines were becoming blurred, or that they would become irrelevant in a rapidly democratizing society, only strengthened such views.

In short, the transition from Reconstruction to the *grands ensembles* that ultimately shaped French postwar urbanization was possible because of a streamlining of housing production in which the state took on a more indirect and at once more overarching role. Housing, as a generalized good assured by a centralized state, at least in principle, entailed a novel relationship between the state and those for whom it was built. No longer framed as part of "les classes dangereuses" or "les bons Français," the beneficiaries of housing were the French citizenry as a whole. The way people were addressed, however, was individual rather than collective: not as "la population" or "le peuple"—ways of address perhaps more common to the regimes on the other side of the Iron Curtain—but instead as *usagers* (users). When they lamented any short-comings of their new mass housing environments, inhabitants often did so in the name of this new social category. The user became the central figure accompanying the development of mass production in the 1950s and would remain the common register for both understanding and producing the built environment over the following decades.

This term conveys the complexity of forces in which housing production was situated in a country shaped by both liberal capitalism and a centralized state apparatus. While it never completely replaced other terms such as citizen (*citoyen*), consumer (*consommateur*), client (*client*), or *utilisateur*—another word for user in the context of a device or machine—the term *usager* predominated in the realm of housing and urban planning. In this spatial context, users were ambiguously positioned in between the realms of citizenship and private consumption. The term *user* was thus a spatialized notion, but differed from *inhabitant* or *urbanite* in that it referred to spatial yet placeless relationships with both state and market.

Instead of the efforts to base housing design on what in France was called a "minimum vital" for the working classes, housing production was increasingly geared toward a social average rather than a biological minimum. Alfred Sauvy—the demographer, anthropologist, and director of France's national statistics institute—had pointed out that the targets for housing needed to be socially determined and dynamic rather than fixed if they were to reflect the country's rising prosperity and social progress.[66] Modern architects were equally aware that the *Existenzminimum* ideal of the interwar avant-garde needed to be adjusted to the postwar world. Compared to the modernist subject, the figure of the user was no longer the radical projection of a cultural elite or the imagined destiny of the working class, but represented the actually existing social body of postwar society. It was, at least initially, an anonymous average to which class, race, and gender were no more than statistical variations. At the same time, it personified the unknown and complex world of architecture's everyday use and experience. The idea of a new dwelling that would give rise to a modern subject stripped of the cultural particularities of class was imagined long before the advent of the *grands ensembles.* But the notion of an actually existing, anonymous average replaced that of a revolutionary subject-in-becoming in the machinery of mass housing as it was put in motion during the 1950s—not only in France but internationally.[67]

When, after the completion of the Plan Monnet, national planning began to focus on mass housing and urbanism, it was with this category in mind. The centralized state, as the carrier of a rationality superior to that of the market, was to guide the housing sector indirectly but comprehensively, and this conviction informed subsequent four-year plans. The Second Plan

(1954–57) prepared under Étienne Hirsh, outlined a policy shift away from heavy industry and toward "social provisions" such as housing and education. The plan was different not only in its content but also in method: it was more comprehensive in its attention to other economic sectors and moved away from direct interventionism and the nationalization of industry. In the realm of housing, national planning initially meant nothing more than the establishment of quantitative targets for yearly production. Such targets implied a simple quantification of need: the number of people who needed to be housed and the number of dwelling units to be provided. For calculations to be accurate, however, a range of factors had to be taken into account, including demographic growth, internal migration, the effects of slum clearance, new housing projects, and the gradual phasing out of overpopulation in the existing housing stock.[68] Such methods of calculation had been pioneered by Louis Henry in 1950 and were subsequently refined during the 1950s as planners were challenged to take an ever more complex set of factors into account.[69] They were also increasingly aware that their work was not just based on facts, but also on norms. And to determine what constituted terms such as "overpopulation," planners needed a series of norms for which an—albeit rough—social-scientific survey was needed. Norms thus entered into the discourse of planning as both a solution and a problem that required further elaboration. While planning methods initially reduced inhabitants to generic, interchangeable entities in objective, quantified need, planners continually refined their evaluations of housing need and began to include more sophisticated, qualitative aspects.[70] After the questions about numbers, the logical next question was: what kind of dwellings to build? To this end, the CGP commissioned France's national statistics institute, the Institut national des statistiques et des études économiques (INSEE) in 1955 to pursue a large-scale social-scientific survey, questioning inhabitants about their households, rents, opinions, and intentions.[71] This and other studies served as the basis for determining objectives for future housing construction. Yet, however more detailed such objectives, they could never fully determine the architectural form of mass housing.

Modernization Meets Modernism

As housing construction became increasingly streamlined and yearly production more than quadrupled over the span of a decade, its quality changed fundamentally. Compared to the architectural variety during Reconstruction, the outcome was undeniably more homogeneous: by the end of the decade, concrete slabs and blocks of *modern* collective housing separated by green lawns prevailed. Out were the single-family homes. Out were masonry and steel construction. Out were traditional urban forms. Some smaller-scale projects, such as modernist infill blocks in city centers, persisted under the radar, but the large-scale, the modern, and the monumental set the tone. Why was it that the *grand ensemble* became practically the sole model of mass housing in the mid-1950s? And what kind of modern was this, three decades after modernist architects' first experiments with collective housing estates in Europe?

A key factor in the architectural homogenization of housing production in France was the *Logéco* program of the 1953 Plan Courant. Not just any way to increase housing production, it was a concerted effort by government officials, architects, engineers, and leaders of civil society organizations to create a specific standardized architecture of mass housing. By imposing norms for the housing financed through this program, the state had an unprecedented role in shaping the architecture of housing production nationally. It was hardly the first time the state enforced housing norms; technical norms for social housing had long been in existence. But the application of such a comprehensive set of technical *and* architectural norms on different categories of housing—far beyond social housing proper—was unprecedented.

The program began in early 1953 when the Ministry of Reconstruction and Urbanism created regional committees led by state-appointed engineers to study housing projects from all over France. Based on projects submitted by architects, sent in by professional journals, and dug up from the archives of the ministry, these committees created a series of *plans-type* or prototype plans to be promoted nationwide for large-scale reproduction. The projects were selected by a government-appointed jury of experts, which included representatives of social housing organizations and prominent architects. Among the architects were well-known modernists such as Le Corbusier and Prouvé but also Prix de Rome architects, some of whom, such as Alexander Persitz, Jacques-Henri Labourdette, and Bernard Zehrfuss, had already participated in the government's experimental housing competitions. The jury selected around fifty projects. Remarkably, only twelve of them were for collective housing blocks; the others were for either terraced housing or semidetached single-family homes. State-employed architects then transformed the selected projects into *plans-types* through uniform presentation and by eliminating construction details, materials, and facades. These stripped-down plans were subsequently assembled in a two-volume catalog, published as the *Catalogue des plans types: Logements économiques et familiaux* in June 1953.[72] The publication only contained basic floor plans divided into those suitable for collective housing and those for individual home construction. The deal was simple: if they chose from this catalog of typical plans, interested developers would receive a state subsidy and be able to borrow 80 percent of the funds from the Crédit foncier for their housing project, for which the legal procedures, controls, and building permits would subsequently be simplified.[73]

The impetus of architectural standardization was written in the plans themselves. The catalog contained no sections and no facades. Hardly any distinctions were made in the norms and descriptions between individual and collective housing units. And yet, despite minister Courant's claim that they would leave plenty of individual freedom to designers and builders, these typical plans were, if not entirely restrictive, highly prescriptive in their application. The

Plan Courant specified maximum floor areas below that of even the most stringent HLM norms of the time, a maximum construction price, and minimum standards of comfort. In the eyes of policy makers, the sense of urgency and the goal of affordability justified a normative reduction in the size of dwelling units compared to the social housing of both the interwar period and the 1940s. The stringency of these stipulations forced developers into either standardized production or shoddy construction, or both. Despite the absence of any indication of how these units would fit into their surroundings or how they would facilitate social life outside the dwelling unit, the catalog implicitly promoted an architectural context in which the units would fit: for the collective housing types, almost all plans assumed a thin eight-meter slab in which the units would be placed parallel, each staircase giving access to two apartments per floor. Only two of the fifty-some plans contained an exterior corridor, and another two suggested isolated blocks around a single core staircase. These would not be commonly used. The floor plans of the first generations of *grands ensembles*, from Sarcelles to places such as Chevilly-Larue, were almost exact copies of the most common catalog plans (Figure 1.13).

Soon after the publication of the catalog, the ministry extended the *Logéco* procedure to include not just typical plans but entire housing projects, to be proposed by architects and construction companies and then converted into types. The goal was a further streamlining of the process of government-regulated mass construction. Invited submissions varied and consisted of both single-family home projects and collective housing, submitted by developers such as the single-family home builder Maisons Phénix, social housing organizations such as Bâticoop, and young architects such as Claude Parent and Ionel Schein (Figure 1.14).[74] The ministry's selection drastically reduced this diversity. In its attempt to smooth the process of evaluation, administrators explicated their selection criteria in an internal note, which conveyed the government's agenda of architectural standardization cum social modernization in surprisingly clear terms.[75] First of all, state administrators assumed a strict functional specialization per room. This practically reduced the purview of architectural design to a puzzling together of a given set of boxes. Design thus amounted to the organization of efficient connections between already defined spaces. The ministry assumed as much when it prescribed that "the relative position of the rooms needs to satisfy a double condition: 1) to reduce to a minimum the routes most frequently taken by the dwelling's occupants, 2) to guarantee family life the options of socializing during certain hours (meals, collective recreation) and of isolation at other times (at night, for toilette, or focused work)." This kind of floor plan rationalization was not new. It went back to the domestic reforms of home economists and the experiments of interwar modernist housing, most famously those of the New Frankfurt.[76] But the fact that the centralized state issued such principles for general housing production all over the nation dramatically changed their societal stakes. It meant that a rationalized conception of modern dwelling now entered the mainstream of French society.

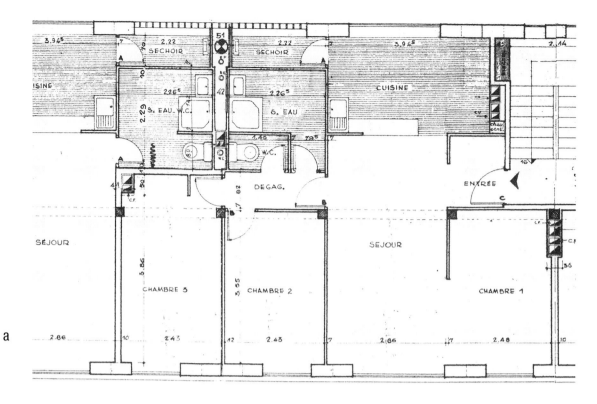

a

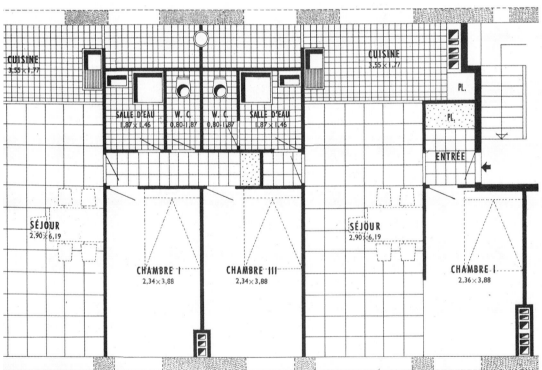

b

Figure 1.13. A comparison between (a) Boileau and Labourdette's first phase of housing slabs at Sarcelles in 1957, and (b) one of the *Logéco* typical plans as published in the 1953 catalog. Archives municipales de Sarcelles and Archives nationales, France, CAC 19771096/001.

PROJET TYPE HOMOLOGUÉ DE LOGEMENT ÉCONOMIQUE ET FAMILIAL

TYPE	REGION	Nº DU DEPARTEMENT	Nº D'ENREGISTREMENT
COLLECTIF **F2 - F3 - F4 - F5 - F6**	**ILE-DE-FRANCE**	**75**	**135**

NOM ET ADRESSE DU BENEFICIAIRE DE L'HOMOLOGATION
ASSOCIATION BATICOOP, 6, rue Halévy, PARIS.

a

Figure 1.14. *Logéco* projects, 1953: (a) proposal by Bâticoop; (b) proposal by Maisons Phénix; (c) proposal by Lionel Schein and Claude Parent. Archives nationales, France, CAC 19771096/002.

PROJET TYPE HOMOLOGUÉ DE LOGEMENT ÉCONOMIQUE ET FAMILIAL

TYPE	REGION	Nº DU DEPARTEMENT	Nº D'ENREGISTREMENT
COLLECTIF F2 - F3 - F4	ILE-DE-FRANCE	75	143

NOM ET ADRESSE DU BENEFICIAIRE DE L'HOMOLOGATION
SOCIETE DES MAISONS PHENIX, 19, rue François-1er, PARIS (8e)

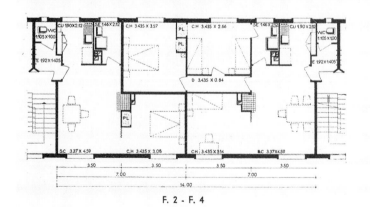

F. 2 - F. 4

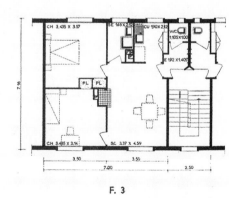

F. 3

b

PROJET TYPE HOMOLOGUÉ DE LOGEMENT ÉCONOMIQUE ET FAMILIAL

TYPE	REGION	Nº DU DEPARTEMENT	Nº D'ENREGISTREMENT
F 4	ILE-DE-FRANCE	75	54

NOMS ET ADRESSE DES BENEFICIAIRES DE L'HOMOLOGATION
C. PARENT et I. SCHEIN, 22, avenue de Versailles, PARIS

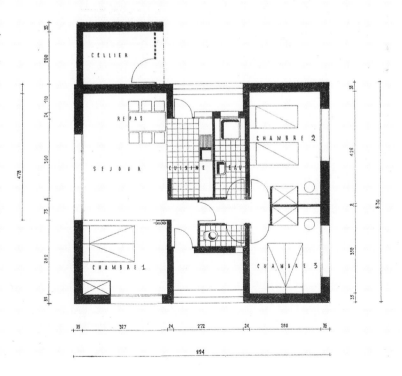

C

While many modernist architects had long been eager to be able to exert such influence in society, the assumption that modern housing could help realize the national project of modernization only became shared among state administrators in the 1950s. Like modernists, they thus tended to implicitly promote an approach to the inhabitant that, at least initially, conceived of her or his actions as a direct and logical consequence of good planning and design. Some architects continued in the postwar period to understand their social role as part of an older conviction, a "civilizing mission" of guiding inhabitants by means of the architecture provided for them. Marcel Lods, for instance, still proclaimed in an interview in the late 1950s that "the role of the architect is to teach them how to live. They do not know and there is no literature on the question."[77] Yet many other architects, including Émile Aillaud, did not deem such guidance appropriate, and if they did think in terms of educating inhabitants, it was less driven by social reform than inspired by the way product designers conceived of user manuals.

The design of the kitchen was undoubtedly the most important terrain where these approaches were played out. Some of the *Logéco* plans proposed to integrate the kitchen with the living room, while others proposed a small, separate "laboratory kitchen," which only allowed for meal preparation (Figure 1.15). None of them suggested a proper eat-in kitchen, which was well known to be in popular demand at least since the 1947 INED survey, in particular with the working classes (Figure 1.16). The architects and state administrators behind the plans seemed to have been in general agreement that the function of the eat-in kitchen, a space of familial sociability around the activity of cooking, derived from traditional, nonurban habits that did not belong in the modern middle-class family home. In the new modern culture of dwelling, the living room and not the kitchen was to be the central space for socializing. As such, the *Logécos* not only supplied basic principles of architectural standardization, but also continued to carry some highly normative conceptions of everyday life and domestic culture.[78]

To many postwar architects however, the social agenda of interwar modernists—architecture as the vehicle for the making of a new, egalitarian society—seemed to have simply been reversed: architects' mission now was to accommodate the changes already under way in a new, rapidly transforming postwar society. The rise of a new middle class, which overturned traditional class hierarchies, seemed to affirm the inevitability of France's ongoing democratization. That conviction helped architects across the political and aesthetic spectrum to embrace a simple, modern architectural language for housing.[79] The more traditional architectural forms and decorations of the interwar social housing projects built by municipal organizations—and whose apartment types were clearly organized in terms of social class—had become anathema.[80] The architecture of mass housing was to be built around a universal *cellule* (cell) or basic dwelling unit, whose rational design and modern comfort promised to satisfy both workers and a novel middle class less committed to status and expensive appearance.

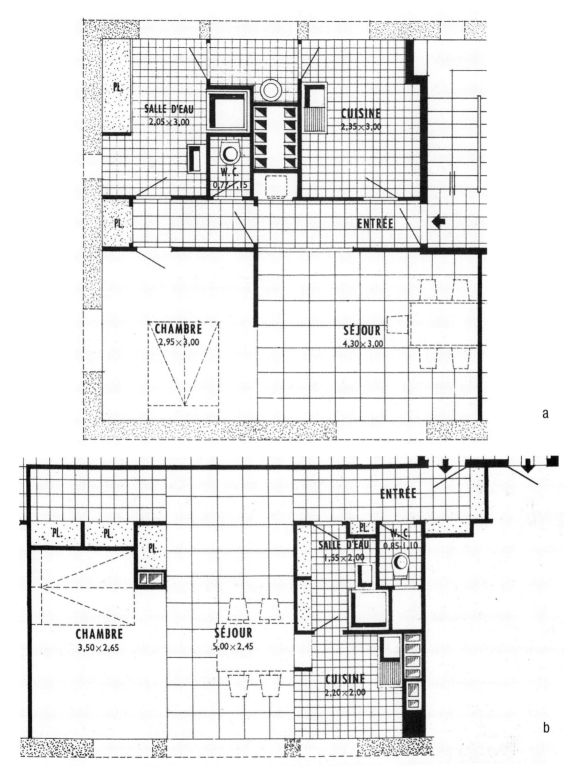

Figure 1.15. Two *Logéco* plans from the 1953 catalog, with (a) a laboratory kitchen separated from the living and dining area, and (b) a kitchen integrated into the living and dining room. Archives nationales, France, CAC 19771096/001.

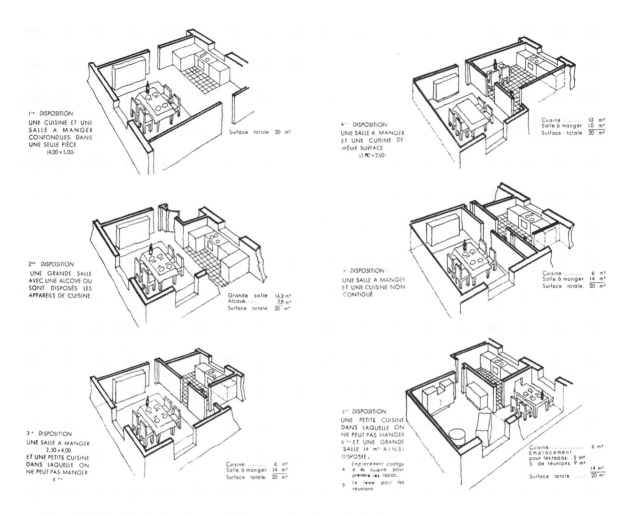

Figure 1.16. Six options for the kitchen and dining space layout, presented to the interviewees of the 1947 INED survey on housing. The first option (upper left) featured kitchen and dining room in a single space; 6 percent of interviewees preferred this option. The second option (middle left), preferred by 4 percent, was similar but with the kitchen in an alcove. The third option (lower left), preferred by 19 percent, featured a small kitchen and a separate dining room. The fourth option (upper right), generally the most popular with workers, civil servants, and salaried employees, and preferred by 28 percent of the interviewees, had a large eat-in kitchen and a separate formal dining room. The fifth option (middle right), preferred by 18 percent, separated the kitchen and dining room with a hallway. The final option (lower right), popular with 24 percent, featured a small kitchen, linked to a dining area integrated into the living room. From Alain Girard, *Une enquête par sondages: Désirs des Français en matière d'habitation urbaine* (Paris: Presses Universitaires de France/Institut national d'études démographiques, 1947), 48–49.

Functionalism was no longer the radical ideology of an avant-garde; it was the logical way to design a one-size-fits-all apartment for a minimum budget.

Equivalent to the universality of the *cellule* was the universality of its occupants, who now entered the machinery of housing production as statistical variations of an unquestioned average. The modern architects working within the dominion of the centralized state were faced with a new category of anonymous users. No longer working for an individual patron, with whom they were in direct contact, architects now needed to design for this unknown mass, behind which a multitude of different inhabitants and dwelling cultures remained hidden. The development of a single, standardized architecture of mass housing further entrenched the assumption of an average to which class, gender, and age were no more than statistical details.

Ultimately, the Plan Courant and *Logécos* resolved the question of the *cellule* for architects to the extent that the government could subsequently employ it as a basis for further regulation.[81] Through a Règlement national de la construction established between 1955 and 1960, the construction of any type of new housing unit—publicly or privately built—became directly regulated by the state.[82] Per dwelling unit and per functionally specialized room, the legislation specified minima for inhabitable volume, floor area, natural lighting, and ventilation. It also stipulated minimum norms with regard to comfort, utilities, and appliances. Collective spaces were subjected to similar rules for hygiene and security. Despite the fact that these norms did not stipulate spatial relations between the rooms in the dwelling unit, nor a particular housing typology or architectural form, their rigor and detail were more than just symbolic of the new mass housing regime that was emerging at this time. Norms did not in and of themselves determine the architecture of mass collective housing during the subsequent decades. But when accompanied by the will to modernize the nation's domestic sphere and by a powerful set of principles and precedents derived from interwar modernism, norms became an easy vehicle for streamlining production. As they aligned modernization and modernism in an unprecedented way, the *Logécos* constituted a watershed in French housing, on which the urbanism of the *grands ensembles* would be based. By developing a systematic solution to the individual dwelling unit, the program delivered the unquestioned building block for the *grands ensembles*, the design of which could subsequently be limited to issues of land purchase and spatial composition.

Statistical Beaux-Arts

In popular accounts, mass collective housing estates are often brought back to Le Corbusier. The role played by this "high priest of modernism" in the development of French mass housing and postwar urbanism more generally is nevertheless much less important than is usually assumed. Despite his outspoken critique of the *grands ensembles,* the conviction that he was responsible for the errors of modern urbanism in France seems indelible. In an accusatory book titled *The Mistakes of Le Corbusier and Their Consequences,* Jacques Riboud proclaimed in 1968 that "the concentration, density, and implantation 'in dominos' of the *grands ensembles* derive from his precepts."[83] The positive reception in the press of his "Unité d'habitation" project for Marseille, its general praise by architects, and minister Claudius-Petit's outspoken enthusiasm for it were all instrumental in creating this impression. In a 1948 article published in the French demography journal *Population,* Le Corbusier had proposed the Unité as a national prototype whose mass production could solve the housing crisis.[84] His article offered a rational defense of collective living fueled by outright condemnation of the single-family home and its suburban fabric (Figure 1.17). This vision corresponded to that of many state planners, for whom collective housing was the only efficient solution to the acute housing shortage at the time.

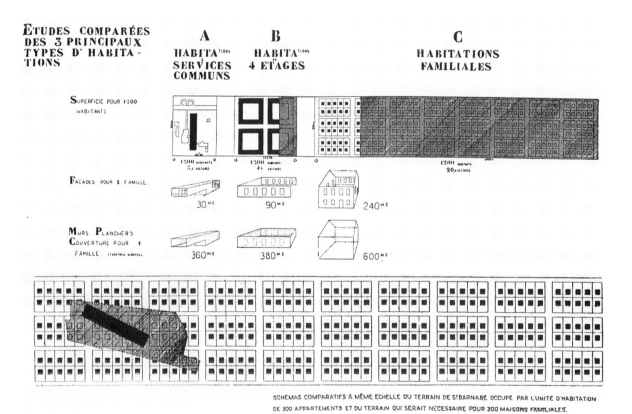

Figure 1.17. A diagram by Le Corbusier explaining the land-use rationality of his Unité d'habitation, which would contain the same number of housing units (300) in its compact slab as the sprawling repetitive subdivision shown for comparison. From Le Corbusier, "L'habitation moderne," *Population* 3, no. 3 (1948): 424. Copyright 2012 Artists Rights Society, New York/Société des auteurs dans les arts graphiques et plastiques, Paris/Fondation Le Corbusier.

In formal terms, however, the *grands ensembles* of the 1950s did not have much to do with the Unité d'habitation as it was built in Marseille. The concept of a free-floating and self-contained "city in a building" was miles away from the compositional massing of the first generation of *grands ensembles*. The Unité remained very much a unique and isolated sculpture, repeated only four times in entirely different places—Nantes, Briey, Firminy, and Berlin—despite the design's promise to solve housing shortage through the simple proliferation of such self-contained units in large park landscapes. The inclusion of a diverse set of collective amenities on different floors inside the housing block at Marseille, crucial to its conception and expressed in the facade, was an idea never taken up in the design of the *grands ensembles*. Collective amenities were a matter of second-order importance, if only for the fact that in many projects they simply were not part of the initial project funding. More important than the morphology or typology of the housing block itself—as innovation in this realm was impeded by strict government norms—was their spatial composition within the estate.

By the 1950s, the composition of freestanding housing blocks in a park landscape was a familiar theme in international modernism. French architects could build on a wide-ranging collection of precedents from earlier decades. The *Siedlungen* or modern housing areas of Frankfurt and Berlin built in the 1920s had taken the prewar garden-city model as a basis but established new formal principles for urban extension and housing typology. The *Zeilenbau* layout would become the most well known of these, despite the fact that many projects did not in fact follow this logic in all of its rigor and often featured carefully sculpted housing blocks to emphasize natural topography or landscape features, such as the pond in the middle of the *Hufeisensiedlung* by Bruno Taut and Martin Wagner. The increase in density of subsequent projects—at the *Großsiedlung* of Siemensstadt by Hans Scharour and others, for instance—amounted to a shift away from the suburban garden ideal. In the United States, housing models diverged more markedly—ranging from Clarence Stein and Henry Wright's suburban greenbelt community of Radburn to William Lescaze's dense urban housing project in Brooklyn. What came to represent a similar divergence in France was the Cité de la Muette in Drancy by Marcel Lods, Eugène Beaudouin, and Jean Prouvé, built between 1931 and 1934 (see Figure 1.1). Not only was it much larger than the bulk of new housing projects in France at this time, it was also the first to establish a clear shift away from the garden-city tradition and toward what would become the *grand ensemble* model—no longer suburban neighborhoods of individual homes with gardens, but decidedly *urban* landscapes featuring monumental sculptures of collective dwelling.

Two decades later, however, the architects commissioned for the *grands ensembles* of the mid-1950s faced a new reality: dense collective housing in large estates was no longer an ideological choice for them to project the creation of a new society. It was simply the brief to which they had to respond. As government institutions, corporate construction firms, engineers, and developers—only partially under the influence of architects—had set the basic parameters of urban development by the mid-1950s, the role of the commissioned architects was limited by many constraints, including the size of the development, the required density and thus choice of collective housing, basic layouts for the dwelling units, and so on. The question for postwar architects was therefore not whether or not to continue the modernist model of the collective housing estate, but what the specific forms and urban compositions were that it could allow for. To answer this question, the language of architectural modernism was not the only reference for French architects in charge of mass housing design. The basic concepts of the *grands ensembles* proliferating during the second half of the 1950s were certainly derived from interwar modernist dogma as it had been espoused in the 1933 CIAM Athens Charter—the separation of functions, the hostility to the traditional street and the perimeter block, and the imperative of air, light, and space. Yet, their compositional qualities were in fact equally close to the traditions of the Beaux-Arts. The overwhelming majority of *grands ensembles* architects were trained in the formal and compositional principles of the Beaux-Arts rather than in the kind of modernism that had flourished at the Bauhaus. The principles of composition that provided the urban vocabulary for the *grands ensembles* thus originated in architectural theories about monumentality and composition as they were taught at the ENSBA during the 1930s and 1940s. Georges Gromort set out such theories during his tenure at the school, arguing for the universal applicability of compositional order to any kind of program on any kind of site.[85] Nevertheless, Beaux-Arts theory was not something that could be applied mechanically to mass housing, because it constituted an unprecedented challenge and thus spawned new ideas as well.

The phenomenal increase in the size of housing projects and the technical demands for repetition of construction elements and techniques required new formal strategies. The architectural conception of the *grands ensembles* thus moved in between two at times contradicting principles. On the one hand, attention needed to be given to the sculptural quality of the individual housing block, slab, or tower. On the other hand, there was the need for formal consistency of the ensemble and thus the question of how to express the whole through its parts. Many architects resolved this dilemma through an aesthetic celebration of quantity, size, and repetition. Giving pathos to the impetus of "housing for the greatest number" often meant expressing the beauty of massification. The architectural historian Bruno Vayssière, one of the first to give serious attention to the mass housing of this period, has described its architecture as "le hard French" because of what he called its statistical beauty. After the defeat of 1940, architects' work was necessarily inscribed in the heroic modernization of the country, and the monumentalizing of sheer quantity was thus for many architects not just a matter of international modernism but also of national pride and identity. Grand compositions of housing blocks were explicitly meant to elicit awe and thus to express the dignity of the new France under construction. This confirmed one of the basic premises of national modernization in France: the desire to break with the past while remaining undeniably French.

Architects reinterpreted familiar principles of classical monumentality as a way of expressing the dignity of mass housing. Zehrfuss's housing project at Haut-du-Lièvre in Nancy, for example, featured two colossal slabs of housing, a 400-meter-long fifteen-story one and a 300-meter-long seventeen-story one (Figure 1.18).[86] At Lyon La Duchère, a similarly grand effect was achieved by locating the slabs on top of a steep hill, which magnified the impression of overwhelming scale upon the approach (Figure 1.19). With such strategies, the architects seemed to want to recall the monumentality of classical French monuments. Yet the approach to conceive collective housing projects as the new Versailles for the average man dovetailed as much with Beaux-Arts tradition as it did with the ideas of the French Communist Party, for

Figure 1.18. Bernard Zehrfuss's housing project of 3,400 dwelling units at Le Haut-du-Lièvre, financed in large part by the Office public HLM de Nancy, 1956–62. Fonds Zehrfuss. Académie d'architecture/Cité de l'architecture et du patrimoine/ Archives d'architecture du XXᵉ siècle.

Figure 1.19. The housing project of Lyon La Duchère by the architects Coulon, François Régis Cottin, and Franck Grimal, 1957–66. The project was developed by the Société d'équipement de la région de Lyon, a subsidiary of SCIC, and contained around 5,300 dwelling units. Archives nationales, France, CAC 19771142/019.

whom the future was Soviet and the goal to build palaces for the people. Axiality was another favored compositional technique that served similar purposes. For the Surville neighborhood, located on the hill above the town of Montereau, Xavier and Luc Arsène-Henry placed the housing blocks along a single boulevard crossing the terrain, articulated by a large square in the center (Figure 1.20). Such projects translated the monumentality of Hausmannian Paris into a new postwar suburban condition.

Serial and sequential composition also became common to emphasize monumentality and celebrate quantity. The *grand ensemble* of Bron-Parilly, by Pierre Bourdeix, René Gagès, and Franck Grimal, also near Lyon, featured four near-identical T-shaped housing slabs along a new monumental boulevard (Figure 1.21). The design did more than just serve the logic of economies of scale. The rhythmic experience of repetitive volumes alongside a main route would inculcate the feeling of a large new spatial order. Yet, more often than not, such intentions suffered from a lack of imagination about the concrete experience of architectural concepts. Regardless of the specific composition, it was often the bird's-eye view that supplied the architects with the essential lens for judging their design. The experience of the pedestrian, the driver, and even that of the inhabitants from the windows of their apartment, was often the ill-considered result, rather than the starting point, of this top-down compositional order.

But this was not always the case. At Marly-les-Grandes-Terres, a housing project by Marcel Lods, Jean-Jacques Honneger, and the Arsène-Henry brothers, couples of parallel housing slabs sharing collective park space were carefully yet systematically distributed across the terrain. This arrangement gave pedestrians and drivers on the encircling road a perspective of dynamic repetition (Figure 1.22).[87] But the design did more than that. It actually engaged the landscape at three different but interrelated scales. By placing housing slabs right across

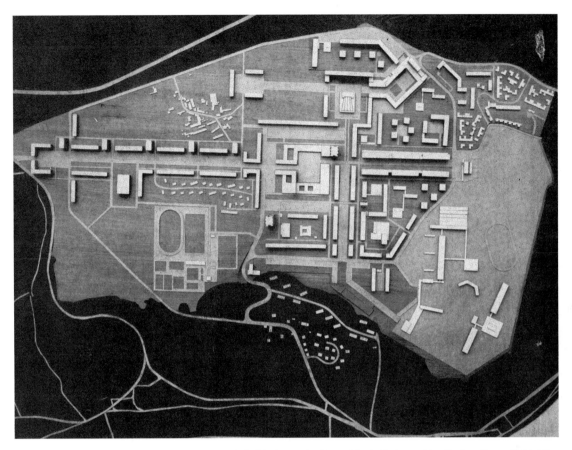

Figure 1.20. Model of the *grand ensemble* of Surville in Montereau by the architects Xavier and Luc Arsène-Henry, 1961–74. From *Urbanisme* 75–76 (1962): 147.

from each other, the architects created the feeling of a half-open courtyard, an enclosed urban landscape framed by the apartments looking out onto it. This provided an intimate collective garden for the inhabitants of the two adjoining blocks. At the same time, the placement of these slabs also framed a larger open green space in the middle of the new development. This space was conceived as the grand central park that tied the entire neighborhood together. The third kind of landscape was purely visual: the neighborhood was located on top of a hill overlooking the western suburbs of Paris, and each individual dwelling unit was afforded a view onto this expansive metropolitan landscape.[88]

With their compositions, many architects were in search of a balance between open and closed forms, between small-scale intimate collective spaces and the experience of the new collectivity at large. Orthogonality in composition helped to marry these seemingly contradictory aspirations. At Sarcelles, Mont-Mesly, and Massy-Antony, for example, the composition of the *grand ensemble* was based on an orthogonal grid of towers and blocks that were grouped

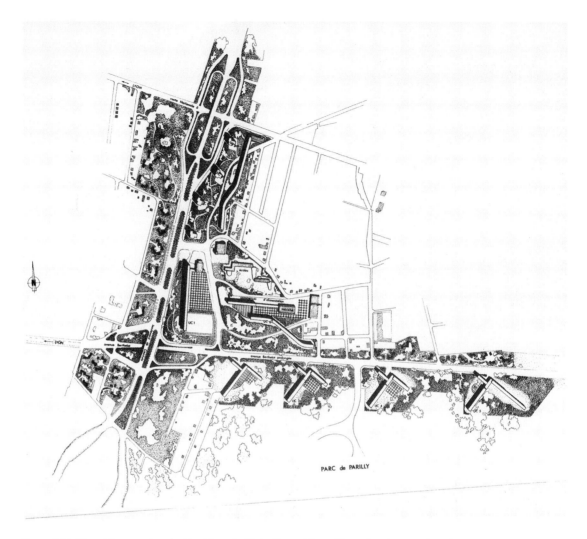

Figure 1.21. Plan of the *grand ensemble* of Bron-Parilly by the architects Pierre Bourdeix, René Gagès, and Franck Grimal, 1954–60. The project was for 2,600 dwelling units by the Office départementale HLM du Rhône. From René Gagès, *Les chemins de la modernité* (Brussels: Pierre Mardaga, 1988), 24–25. Courtesy of Mardaga.

so as to create relatively open centrifugal figures (see Figure 3.4). The collective and intimate nature of the resulting open spaces could then be reinforced by the placement of small-scale collective amenities and shops meant to serve only the surrounding housing blocks.

Despite the diversity in compositional strategies, the pages of leading magazines such as *L'Architecture d'aujourd'hui* and *Urbanisme* during this time revealed the limits of variety. The standardization of dwelling units was mirrored in the similarity between *grands ensembles* nationally: just as the F4, France's standard four-room apartment, appeared thousands of times with minimal layout variations across the country, so did the *grands ensembles* they made

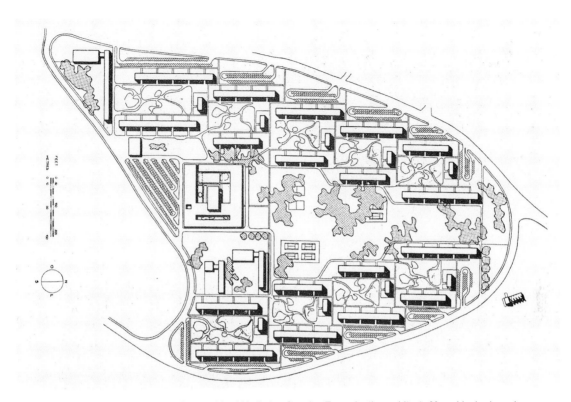

Figure 1.22. Master plan for the *grand ensemble* of Marly-les-Grandes-Terres by the architects Marcel Lods, Jean-Jacques Honneger, and Xavier and Luc Arsène-Henry, 1955–58. From *L'Architecture française* 205–6 (1957): 54.

up appear as ever so many variations on a theme—whether they were built in the suburbs of Lille or the outskirts of Marseille. Even when architects such as Émile Aillaud attempted to create an entirely different architecture for mass housing, as at Les Courtillières, the project's odd-shaped windows and curved facades hardly distracted the inhabitants from the fact that they were living in the exact same standardized units (Figure 1.23).[89]

Housing for All, All the Same?

In *Les petits enfants du siècle*, Christian Rochefort's classic novel about the life of a young girl in Paris's new suburban housing, the protagonist expressed her ambivalent reaction to this new environment when she observed its nocturnal state:

In the evening, the windows were illuminated and behind them were nothing but happy families, happy families, happy families, and happy families. In passing you could see, under the lightbulbs, all the happiness in a row, all equal like twins, or like a nightmare. The happiness of

Figure 1.23. Les Courtillières in Pantin, a nearby suburb of Paris, by the architect Émile Aillaud, 1954–57. Fonds Aillaud. Service interministériel des Archives de France/Cité de l'architecture et du patrimoine/Archives d'architecture du XXᵉ siècle.

the west facade could see from their homes the happiness of the east facade as if they were watching each other in the mirror. Eating noodles from the co-op. The happiness was piling up, I could have calculated its volume in cubic meters and in tons, me who loved creating problems.[90]

Such feelings were not unlike American suburban blues, articulated by Malvina Reynolds in her 1962 song "Little Boxes" in which she decried the culture of conformism in American suburbs with homes "made out of ticky-tacky" and "that all look just the same." The monotony of modern lifestyle when it reached every single household similarly across the country—at least so it seemed—was also that of the *grands ensembles* in postwar France.

The 1950s marked a paradoxical turn in the production of the built environment in France, as the variety of architectural experiments during Reconstruction gave way to the imperative of mass housing. The *grands ensembles* that ultimately embodied the country's postwar prosperity were only possible thanks to a streamlining of production in which the state took on a more indirect, yet at once more central, role. Housing moved away from the realm of social reform to become a generalized good assured—at least in principle—by the welfare state. As in other Western European nations, mass housing was part of a larger agenda of national modernization in the context of postwar economic growth. That agenda rendered politics in the language of technology, rationality, and progress. In France, more than elsewhere, the direction toward mass housing was strengthened by the radical dismissal of both traditional dwelling cultures and the popular desire for the single-family home. Neither state-led normalization nor industrialization really completely determined the architectural form or urban typology of housing. At the root of the standardized architecture and urbanism of mass housing was a more implicit set of shared cultural norms solidified by the exchanges between government officials, architects, engineers, and a growing range of experts. Modern, collective, efficient, rational, and planned: those were the shared cultural norms guiding the decision toward a homogeneous production of mass housing.

Already in 1953, however, Auzelle's *Technique de l'urbanisme* published in the popular French book series "Que sais-je?" implicitly revealed the questionable conformity to which such a proclaimed universalism could give rise. The popular edition of Auzelle's book suggested that modern urbanism in France could be considered a well-oiled technique and unquestionable virtue. In the book's section on housing, the fundamental starting point was an evaluation of basic "needs and aspirations of inhabitants." These were summarized in a chart listing basic needs according to four categories: men, women, children, and the elderly. For women, for instance, these included a variety of demands from shops to "the proximity of a small park or a boulevard to walk the stroller."[91] Yet, when it came to the design and layout of such housing areas, his "theoretical implantation diagrams" did not seem to be able to translate this variety in spatial terms. In contrast to the spatial diversity he had advocated for in his housing project for Petit-Clamart in the late 1940s, he only provided a rigorously systematic approach that prefigured the spatial monotony so widely perceived by visitors of the *grands ensembles* later in the decade (Figure 1.24). How easily could such a radically standardized approach to dwelling be carried by the lofty humanism of satisfying inhabitants' every need and aspiration?

Throughout the 1950s, the government, professions, and civil society organizations all contributed to the idea of universalizing access to housing: anybody in need of housing should be afforded it. Of course, the beneficiaries of social housing did not include the wealthy bourgeoisie and the French government did not suddenly abolish existing hierarchies and classifications of social class, race, or gender. State housing production continued to discriminate, and not everybody was effectively provided with equivalent housing options. The poor would in fact largely be neglected in social housing policy until the late 1960s. Those performing the precarious labor of actually building the new mass housing complexes on the urban periphery—

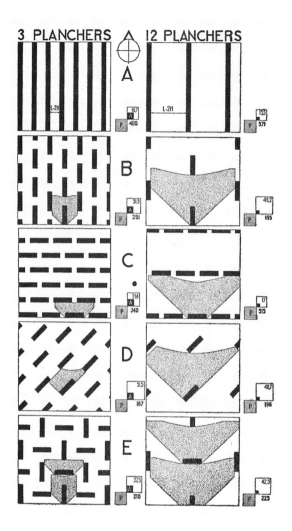

Figure 1.24. A theoretical diagram showing infinitely repeatable patterns for the layout of 10 m-wide housing slabs of either 3 (left) or 12 (right) stories, based on the shadows they throw over a flat, empty site. From Robert Auzelle, *Technique de l'urbanisme* (Paris: Presses Universitaires de France, 1953), 48–49.

many of whom were immigrants from Portugal, Italy, Spain, or North Africa—were often forced to live in shantytowns situated in the margins of the suburban landscape or in shacks near the construction sites themselves.[92] Only a minority of immigrant families found their way into new social housing, while others, considered "isolated" and in need of both assistance and control, were housed in "homes" following an authoritarian paternalism inherited from colonial rule.[93]

To answer who exactly were the initial inhabitants of the *grands ensembles*, social housing statistics are of only limited use. Not only does the profusion of categories of publicly and privately financed housing units in such housing estates distort these statistics, it also fails to account for the rapid social mobility of many inhabitants at this time. Mass housing in part *made* its beneficiaries middle-class. Despite these caveats, it is safe to say that the initial inhabitants were predominantly French white-collar and middle-class nuclear families, often coming from substandard housing in Paris or the provinces. What the French called middle-class at this time were families with (almost always male) breadwinners in liberal professions or mid-level administrative positions in state institutions or large private companies. The 1955 INSEE survey showed that newly built housing often did not benefit those in dire need of shelter, but rather those whose incomes were already significantly on the rise. Sometimes even upper-middle-class people such as business owners and upper-level managers found their way into social housing at this time—something that frustrated many social housing advocates and informed subsequent policy. Blue-collar working-class households, which made up almost a third of France's total population, were thus not the primary beneficiaries of the first *grands ensembles*, at least not in the 1950s. Even if rising wages and employment stability fostered the working-class nuclear family, many workers at this time were still living in furnished rooms, provisional buildings, and lodging houses—a way of life that was often adapted to their geographic mobility. Only during the 1960s, when mass housing production was at its height and half a million new units were finished every year, did blue-collar working-class families become the dominant beneficiaries of social housing and inhabitants of the *grands ensembles*.

This situation led the sociologist Alain Touraine to go so far as to label the first *grands ensembles* quintessentially petit-bourgeois.[94] Despite such specificity, existing identifiers of social class were in part being reshaped by the rapidly changing stock of mass housing. Many observers characterized the *grands ensembles* as harbingers of a new *mass* culture. Paul-Henry Chombart de Lauwe and Henri Lefebvre both reported on the dissolving of traditional class boundaries, the "dilution of the proletariat," in the new housing areas they studied.[95] Also, in terms of age, the population of the *grands ensembles* was both unique and rapidly changing. They predominantly housed nuclear families with young children with a large family size relative to the national average. There were almost no poor, adolescents, or elderly and few non-French people among them, and many came from the same factories and companies. Some housing estates, especially those facilitating large-scale industries such as in the Lorraine and the north, housed larger percentages of foreign workers—Italians, French Antilleans, Algerians, Moroccans, Germans, Belgians, and so on.[96]

Race and ethnicity were officially invisible and thus practically absent in the bureaucratic paper mill. At times they could be read between the lines in the official norms and social-scientific parameters—for instance, in what were called the "socioprofessional categories," such as "immigrant workers" (*travailleurs immigrés*) and "managers" (*les cadres*). Despite its promises of a universal average, the advent of mass housing was accompanied by an increasingly sophisticated social categorization: the nuclear family became the basic norm, while youth, women, the elderly, and so on became subject to a specialized taxonomy of expected behavior, and thus, again, specific yet standardized needs. The user that was implicitly constructed in the architecture of mass housing was thus a highly ambiguous one. As soon as this figure was constructed, concrete identity became a question: if experts agreed on the need for norms and standards, they increasingly disagreed on what these should be.

The state was not the only institution establishing norms for mass housing during the 1950s: national civil society organizations such as the Union internationale des organismes familiaux (UIOF, or International Union of Family Organizations) were also engaged with norm making and as such had their own role in housing design. Established in 1947 to act as a common platform for family organizations, UIOF quickly became a crucial organization in France, operating on both national and international levels.[97] Its subcommittee on housing focused on ways to "better adapt housing to the needs and desires of the family." In 1957, at its yearly conference in Cologne, the organization established a new set of norms based on surface minima for national housing production (Figure 1.25). Aiming to address a more

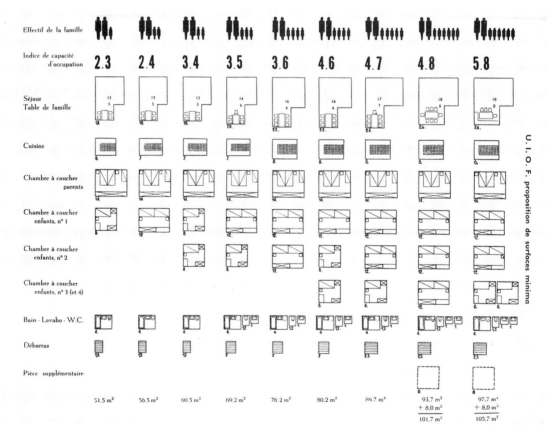

Figure 1.25. Diagram by the Union internationale des organismes familiaux illustrating the calculation of minimum surface norms for apartments, 1959. From *Techniques et architecture* 19, no. 2 (1959): 121.

encompassing definition of need, including "both physical and spirituals needs," these norms included ideal floor plans that were subsequently employed in France.[98] The plans were based on activities rather than floor areas only, and instead of the official types promulgated by the state, they proposed a larger set of different types. Yet, as much as the organization criticized existing norms, its work further confirmed rather than questioned the need for universal norms to be applied to all forms of housing. The norms, known as the "Cologne norms," were disseminated internationally.[99] Naturally, they assumed the nuclear family as the central and only category for designing and evaluating housing. Caught in a larger complex of social and cultural norms promoting the modern middle-class family, the process of architectural standardization and technical normalization was thus an ongoing and a contested one, centering on, yet expressly exceeding, the domain of the centralized state.

This process engendered a situation in which the notion of use soon appeared as a *question* for discussion rather than a given. As one of the presenters at the Cologne conference observed: "In contrast to the method of making plans for individuals of which the social milieu and needs are known—as it happens most often in the case of the single-family home—the making of plans for an 'anonymous' user demands a greater degree of reflection and imagination in the calculation of needs in order to attain satisfying results."[100] On the one hand, mass housing production implied a standardized, modern way of living. On the other hand, it prompted the question—more and more pressing—of how to adapt housing to increasingly complex and unknown needs. That question spawned a fast-growing domain of expertise. The appearance of housing blocks on the horizon of metropolitan France therefore cannot be understood without this expertise and the new bureaucratic epistemology it gave rise to.

2

A BUREAUCRATIC EPISTEMOLOGY

BOLD ASSERTIONS OF A NEW BEGINNING at times help ensure ambiguous continuities. In January 1959, Charles de Gaulle became president of the newly established Fifth Republic of which he had helped draft the constitution the year before. France had entered into seemingly irreversible political crisis over decolonization in general and Algeria in particular. For many, the return to power of this charismatic leader of the French Resistance would restore the country's power and grandeur, deemed lost ever since the invasion of 1940. Pierre Sudreau, appointed by de Gaulle to head the renamed Ministry of Construction (no longer Reconstruction), commissioned an ambitious housing survey. Its explicit goal was to improve state-aided housing production across the nation. With the new republic came renewed ambition for national modernization, and architecture and urbanism would play their part.

The survey was unprecedented. Or at least it was presented as such. Little mention was made of—let alone conclusions drawn from—by the Institut national d'études démographique (INED)1947 national housing survey, the landmark study that had indicated the desire of the French for the single-family home. Sudreau's was a similarly extensive survey of French households and their housing needs and desires. But rather than just working with the national demographics institute, he called in the help of "the French themselves." To this end, he hired Jeanne Picard, a prominent women's leader with a long-standing career in representing working-class families. She organized the public consultation of national women's associations in order to reveal not only inhabitants' dissatisfactions about their new homes but also their specific suggestions for improvement. On the basis of this information, the organizers came up with the design of a new ideal dwelling unit called the "referendum apartment."[1] Drawn up by the ministry's in-house architect Marcel Roux, the new apartment was considered both the summation of popular wants and a prototype for future housing production. It was exhibited as a life-sized model home at the popular household fair Salon des arts ménagers in 1959 and elicited an overwhelming amount of attention from the French public. The model apartment was a proud statement about the comforts of modern French family life and the national standard of living—not surprising in light of the famous "kitchen debate" between Richard Nixon and Nikita Khrushchev that same year. But, as it brought together commercial builders, provincial housewives, and Prix de Rome architects, the French initiative was to be first and foremost a tool to "adjust housing to people's needs and aspirations" (Figure 2.1).[2]

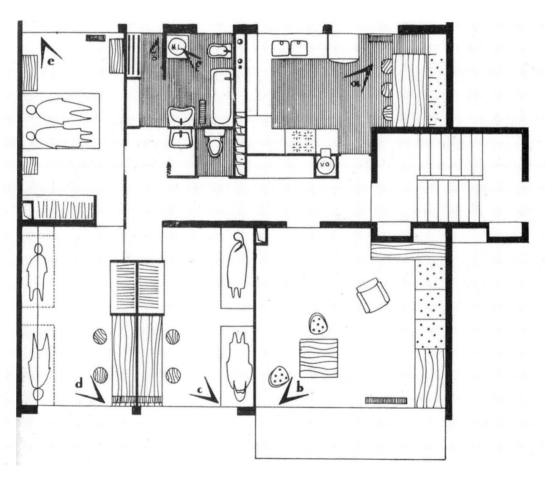

Figure 2.1. The referendum apartment of 1959 designed by Marcel Roux on the basis of surveys organized by Jeanne Picard for the Ministry of Construction. The apartment's size exceeded social housing norms at the time. One of its key features was the eat-in kitchen, a popular preference in France but discouraged by some housing experts. From *Techniques et architecture* 19, no. 2 (1959): 117.

Despite its aspirations for social inclusion and public participation, the "referendum apartment" actually further endorsed the standardization set in motion by mass production. Proposing a single apartment type that could appeal to all French nuclear households dovetailed conveniently with the impetus of building massively, cheaply, and quickly. At the same time, it exemplified a shift toward the need to know—whether through sociological research, opinion poll, or marketing study—inhabitants' needs and desires in the realm of housing. At the end of the war a little over a decade earlier, neither architecture culture and planning theory nor the state apparatus in France was particularly interested in such knowledge. The "referendum apartment" thus signaled an evolution. The evaluation of what was being built could no longer be only in the hands of professionals; its success or failure was now also defined by inhabitants, albeit indirectly, through expert studies of their opinions and of the way they inhabited the homes provided for them. Whether the initiative was a propaganda stunt or the sign of a real transfer of power from producer to inhabitant, it made one thing self-evident: questions about use and inhabitation had seeped into the core of planning and design. It was no longer enough to abstractly project social ambitions onto architectural and urban plans, as French intellectuals had been doing since the nineteenth century. Design now stood directly in the service of social and domestic life, which could be modernized only after being concretely apprised and understood. In the long tradition of turning society into an object of knowledge to facilitate intervention, something seemed to have changed. The technocratic modernism that over the preceding century had incessantly stripped away social and cultural particularities to create an abstract and standardized population was enriched by an increasingly complex encounter with those very particularities.[3] It was as if Adolphe Quetelet's *homme moyen*—the famous nineteenth-century statistician's "average man" so dear to social reformers in France and beyond—had splintered into a multitude of voices, eerily reverberating in the hallways of French bureaucracy.

Learning from the Everyday

The conviction that housing needed to be adjusted to inhabitants' "actual" needs, as they subjectively expressed them and could be empirically studied—rather than designed according to how they were objectively known—emerged in the margins of postwar reconstruction. In France and elsewhere, the general sense of emergency, aggravated by the destitution of war and the acute housing shortage during the immediate postwar years, prompted two very different kinds of responses. One came from the top, the other from the bottom. Rural French and foreign migrants in search of work in metropolitan and industrial areas settled wherever they could and built their own homes either in shantytowns or in suburban allotments. The Castor movement was only the most organized form of this boom in self-building.

The majority of this activity was perceptible to, but not at all under the control of, those in charge. In their eyes, what was needed was not self-help but sweeping intervention comprehensively organized from above. It was not so much that decision makers thought there was not the time for consultation or participation. Expertise in housing or urban planning simply did not require it. People's needs were not a question, but an objective, urgent given.

This way of thinking prevailed not just among policy makers but also among architects. Even in Le Corbusier's *constructions "murondins"* of 1942, a unique proposal for national reconstruction that relied on inhabitants as self-builders, the tone was fundamentally no different. Prefaced as a "small gift to my friends, the youth of France," the architect had designed a type of youth center that could be erected by anyone anywhere across the country in the name of national reconstruction.[4] Youth for him was the spiritual avant-garde for rebuilding the nation and thus needed to become "their own architects, urbanists, and builders." In striking contrast to his 1914–15 Maison Domino proposal of a reinforced concrete prototype for mass housing construction after World War I, this idea was remarkably low-tech. A simple combination of walls (*murs*) and logs (*rondins*) would allow people to build with materials they could find at a time of extreme scarcity. Aligning national reconstruction with autoconstruction, the self-assigned task of the architect was to offer the basic designs "to be built by their users."[5] The result was a set of simple rectangular volumes organized by L-shaped walls on an orthogonal grid (Figure 2.2). While the plans allowed—in theory, at least—for infinite variation based on site and program, people's needs were simply given to the architect, and their participation was essentially limited to execution.

After Liberation, at a relative distance from dominant architectural thinking and state policy making, certain architects nevertheless developed ways to engage inhabitants more directly in the process of design. One exceptional yet isolated project that attempted to do so was André Lurçat's reconstruction for the town center of Maubeuge.[6] Lurçat, a modernist architect with Communist allegiances, insisted that inhabitants' input during the making of the master plan was not only important for its success but also constituted a more efficient form of planning. In an article published in *Urbanisme* after the completion of the project, he summarized his new approach and declared that "only by collaborating directly with the population can the urbanist respond with maximum efficiency and speed to the problems at hand. Surveying in order to fix the exact facts of the whole problem, informing the population, educating and then convincing it in order to assure its help and well-considered approval, these are the essential and determining elements of success."[7] He illustrated his approach with a diagram of the planning process (Figure 2.3).

The diagram suggested a role for architects and planners that fundamentally differed from the one they were generally assigned. Rather than as designers and plan makers who were removed from the concrete experiences of the site and their inhabitants, the diagram

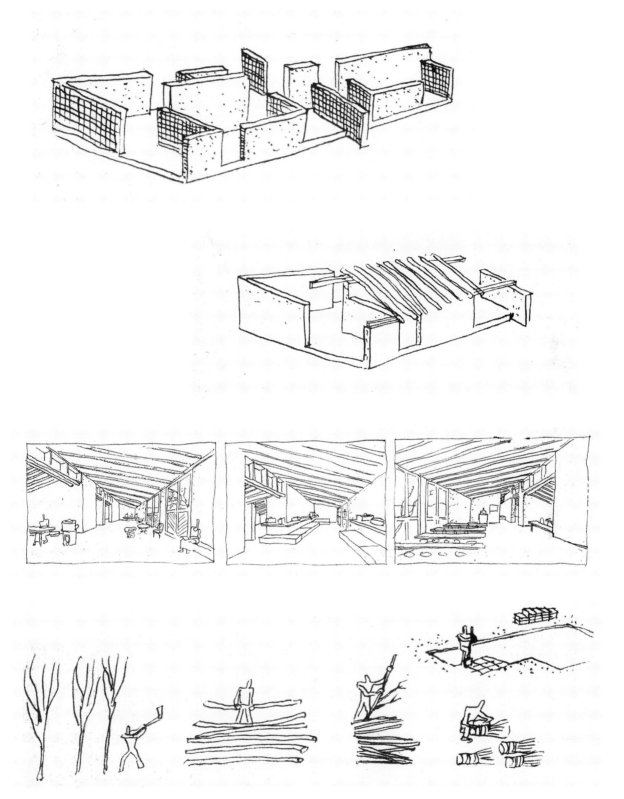

Figure 2.2. Sketches from Le Corbusier's *Les constructions "murondins"* (Paris: Étienne Chiron, 1942). Copyright 2012 Artists Rights Society, New York/Société des auteurs dans les arts graphiques et plastiques, Paris/Fondation Le Corbusier.

ETABLISSEMENT DU PLAN D'AMENAGEMENT ET DE RECONSTRUCTION

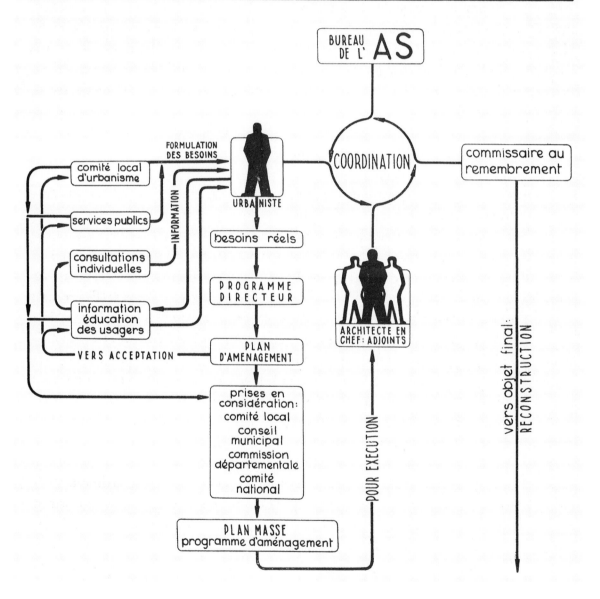

Figure 2.3. Diagram of the planning process for Maubeuge by André Lurçat, 1954. From *Urbanisme* 37–38 (1954): 100. Copyright 2012 Artists Rights Society, New York/Société des auteurs dans les arts graphiques et plastiques, Paris.

conceived of them first and foremost as mediators, working directly with the inhabitants to formulate solutions to their needs. These needs were not known in advance, based on the principles of the Athens Charter or any other doctrine; they needed to be formulated on the basis of a social process of exchange between professionals and the local population. Concretely, the project engaged inhabitants through a Comité local d'urbanisme, Lurçat's own interviews with local inhabitants, weekly information sessions, and a large public assembly. This approach thus implied a two-way flow of knowledge. Inhabitants needed to be educated about the possibilities and changes they faced, but they also needed to communicate their reactions and preferences. This knowledge, gained through mediation, would then serve as the basis for planning and design. Nevertheless, the architect and urbanist—often one and the same person in France at this time—remained the central conduit for this new approach: other forms of expertise, such as sociology, were absent in the process.

The final plan bore clear signs of this alternative approach, especially when compared to Le Corbusier's proposal for Saint-Dié, which was drawn up around the same time and had become heavily contested by the town's inhabitants. By explicit request of the inhabitants, Lurçat's final project preserved the old fortifications, emphasized existing and new commerce in the city center, and proposed a variety of housing types, including grouped single-family homes. The modernist rearticulation of the historic, war-torn urban fabric suggested an approach to modernizing urban life while refusing a radical break with the past (Figure 2.4). Despite the local success of the plan, however, its lessons remained unheard, and Lurçat himself was not able to further develop his method in subsequent housing projects. The architect's failure to directly influence the mainstream of French architecture and urbanism at the time was perhaps in part a consequence of his own ambivalent positioning—at times subverting and then again confirming the dominant ways of state-led reconstruction and housing development. Instead of the architect as mediator, empirical observation would turn out to become the accepted method to incorporate people's needs into design. Long before *Learning from Las Vegas*, learning *from* would win over directly listening *to*.[8]

One figure was crucial to this development in France and it was not an architect. Paul-Henry Chombart de Lauwe, now recognized as one of the preeminent urban sociologists of postwar France, provided the most compelling solution to the "problem" of people in large-scale, state-led urban development.[9] More than architectural modernism, it was the emerging field of urban sociology that would ultimately supply the tools for mediating between planners and people and be able to marry large-scale, top-down urban development with the ideals of social emancipation and democratic decision making. During the 1950s, Chombart became one of the most influential advocates for the inclusion of sociological expertise in the workings of the centralized state—in particular as it related to mass housing and urban development. Almost a decade before Sudreau's "apartment referendum" program, this young,

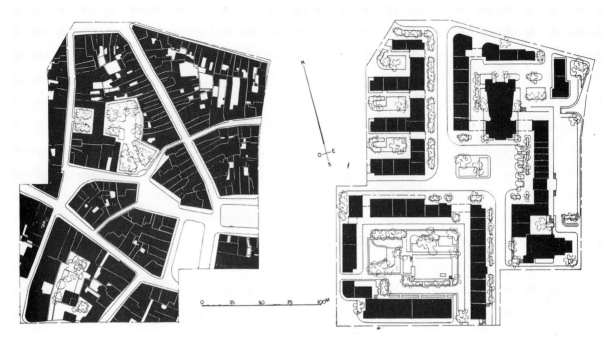

Figure 2.4. Comparison of the existing building block pattern of Maubeuge's historic city center and Lurçat's reconstruction project, 1954. From *Urbanisme* 37–38 (1954): 105. Copyright 2012 Artists Rights Society, New York/Société des auteurs dans les arts graphiques et plastiques, Paris.

ardent member of the French Resistance had begun to promote, in both academic and government circles, what he called "applied" urban sociology as the basis for planning and design.

His background and wartime experience had made Chombart a remarkably hands-on intellectual. At a young age, he attended the École nationale supérieure des Beaux-Arts (ENSBA) with the idea of becoming a sculptor but quickly opted for the social sciences instead. He studied anthropology under Marcel Mauss and by the mid-1930s, at the age of twenty-two, undertook his first ethnographic study on African Dogon communities under direction of the anthropologist Marcel Griaule. The war brought him in contact with prominent intellectual figures at the École des cadres d'Uriage, a unique wartime think tank established to create a strong political elite after the French defeat in 1940. The school was a crucial meeting ground for advocates of technocratic leadership and produced numerous engineers who would populate the ranks of the French state bureaucracy after the war. It fostered a culture of "men of action," fighting for national pride and grandeur. Chombart took this call very seriously and joined the Resistance movement in 1942 together with many of his colleagues. He escaped occupied France via Spain and joined the French liberation army that had been assembled in North Africa. Serving as a pilot, he took a fervent interest in aerial photography, which profoundly influenced his later research.[10] Coming out of the war, he began to use this technique in his social-scientific studies of urbanization commissioned by the Centre national de recherche scientifique (CNRS, National Center for Scientific Research).

At the heart of Chombart's concerns was the French working class. Like so many intellectuals gathering in the "heroic" capital after Liberation, Chombart believed in the universal ideal of human brotherhood, which he channeled into an almost sentimental sympathy for *le peuple*.[11] The experiences of Resistance and Liberation in France had engendered a deep feeling of human solidarity, which was shared across France's ideological and political spectrum. Whether of Marxist, Catholic, or technocratic stripe, intellectuals could identify almost naturally with the poor and the working classes. The intellectual culture of Paris and much of the nation during the 1940s and 1950s was permeated by a deep-seated humanism that was often both populist and poetic. The homes, streets, and hearts of "the people" were where not only the past but also the future of France was to be found. With a penchant for mystery and authenticity, the exploration of working-class Paris, with its nooks and crannies, its cafés, and its alleyways, thus became a staple of cultural production, from the historical scholarship of Louis Chevalier to the crime novels of Léo Malet.[12] This intellectual interest in urban space also pervaded the work of Chombart, who was an impassioned adherent of social Catholicism. This long-standing and influential movement of left-leaning Catholics in France promoted the application of their religious principles to the social problems of modern industrialized societies.[13] Ever since the French Revolution they had stood to fight the evils of urban poverty and to improve the lives of the working poor, but unlike that of the socialists, their message was one of reconciliation rather than class conflict. This ideological conviction directly informed Chombart's extensive sociological surveys of working-class living conditions, which he undertook from the late 1940s onward. By this time, Chombart had settled in what would become a crucial subject in his research, the Parisian working-class suburbs. With his wife Marie-José, also a member of the Resistance and a researcher in psychology at the CNRS after the war, he lived in Ivry-sur-Seine in the southern "first-ring" suburbs of the capital.

The first results of this research were published in 1952 as *Paris et l'agglomération parisienne*.[14] The study presented a new way to analyze both the social and spatial dimensions of the Paris region and combined aerial perspectives and descriptions of the physical fabric with detailed accounts of people's ways of life "on the ground." For Chombart, the view from above and the view from below were in fact constitutive of each other, as the innovative use of urban cartography by Louis Couvreur demonstrated (Figures 2.5 and 2.6).[15] The study had an important and lasting influence on a younger generation of French architects and planners and galvanized the validity of Chombart's sociological approach for architecture and urban planning in France and beyond. Most famous perhaps has been its appropriation by the Lettrists and the Situationists, more radical groups of intellectuals and artists that included Guy Debord and Henri Lefebvre. Ignoring Chombart's conciliatory Catholicism and his hardly

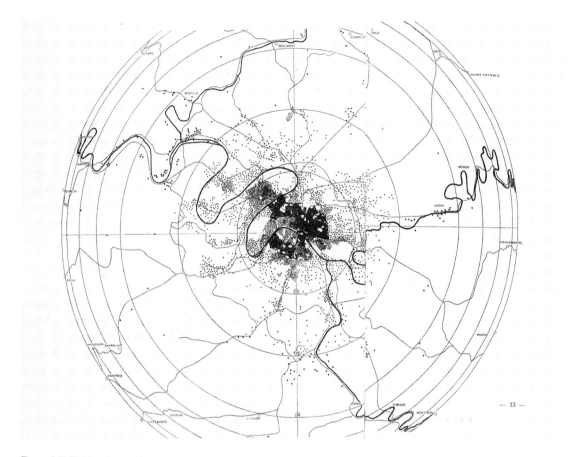

Figure 2.5. Plotting the residences of the staff of two Parisian department stores, this diagram demonstrated workers' long commutes within the growing metropolitan region. From Paul-Henry Chombart de Lauwe, *Paris et l'agglomération parisienne* (Paris: Presses Universitaires de France, 1952), 13.

revolutionary mission to have his research contribute to state-led urban planning, they re-tooled his work to construct a cartographic imaginary for their theories of the *dérive* or urban drift.[16] Despite Lefebvre's increasingly negative critique of Chombart, these avant-garde groups shared the same love for the authentic working-class neighborhood. At the basis of their otherwise divergent ideologies was a fundamental respect for the ephemeral uses and dynamic atmospheres of the contemporary city. The Situationists celebrated marginality and subversion where Chombart emphasized community and solidarity; but, like many other French intellectuals at the time, they all located the kernel of the future in the spatiality of everyday life.

Chombart's approach of capturing the authenticity of everyday life was not only in tune with the Parisian intellectual avant-garde; its importance was also clear to those at the forefront of modernist architectural culture. The postwar CIAM (Congrès internationaux d'architecture moderne) provided the key platform for an international renewal of modern architecture, and

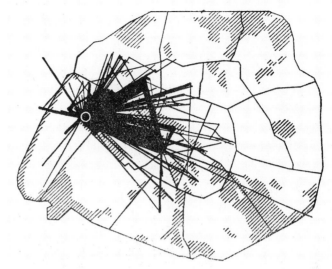

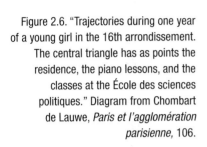

Figure 2.6. "Trajectories during one year of a young girl in the 16th arrondissement. The central triangle has as points the residence, the piano lessons, and the classes at the École des sciences politiques." Diagram from Chombart de Lauwe, *Paris et l'agglomération parisienne*, 106.

that renewal was based increasingly on interests in urban space and everyday life. Members of the group showed growing discontents with their governments' official reconstruction and modernization plans, and many discussions centered on the problematic public reception of modern architecture. Especially for the younger generation of architects not directly involved in the group's famous Athens Charter of 1933, the main challenge was how modern architecture could better respond to the "man in the street." That ambition prompted an increasing focus on the realm of everyday life and its importance for architectural design. Central to this shift was the notion of habitat. At the 1949 meeting in Bergamo, Le Corbusier had officially declared that the main goal of CIAM should be the creation of a "Charter of Habitat." He had remained silent, however, about what that would entail and how exactly it could replace the claims to universality of the Athens Charter. Since the mid-nineteenth century, the meaning of habitat in both French and English had shifted to refer not only to the living environment of a biological entity, plant, or animal, but, more specifically, to the human realm of dwelling in all its complexity.[17] Its transference from biology to modern architecture and planning, however, begged new epistemological questions. Was habitat an objective matter—of needs defined scientifically by quantities of air, light, and space as had been asserted during the 1929 CIAM on the *Existenzminimum?* Or was it a way of learning from the subjective, unquantifiable experiences of dwelling?

Despite the fact that the next meeting would largely ignore Le Corbusier's call, the notion of habitat became an implicit preoccupation in the debates.[18] For the French Beaux-Arts–trained architect André Wogenscky, who became a close collaborator of Le Corbusier, habitat included not only "the needs, activities, and aspirations of man within the family dwelling" but "all such things in the immediate environment as are necessary for a complete life."[19] How such a rich universe would be accessible to architects, let alone operative in design, was the big question. Although the concept of habitat never became all-encompassing, and concepts such as home, house, dwelling, *habitation, logement, foyer,* and *maison* continued be used, it was the term most consistently employed in the context of mass housing. The conceptualization of habitat as "dwelling plus its immediate surroundings" seemed founded on architects' attempts to improve such conditions for populations and social groups, rather than strictly individually. To many, the notion thus addressed the everyday as part of an architecture of mass production—not surprising, perhaps, considering the global proliferation of new construction techniques such as heavy prefabrication during the 1940s.

The discussions concerning habitat culminated in the 1953 CIAM at Aix-en-Provence, where, in the words of architectural historian Tom Avermaete, the "epistemological turn toward the everyday" became clear.[20] The most famous of the forty-some presentations was undoubtedly the Urban Reidentification Grid by Alison and Peter Smithson, which radically abolished the four functions of the Athens Charter—dwelling, work, transportation, and recreation—and brought the urban photography and ethnography of working-class London streets to the heart of architectural culture.[21] But this was only the tip of the iceberg. Another important contribution to the meeting was by the Groupe d'architectes modernes marocains, an interdisciplinary CIAM group from Morocco that included Michel Écochard, Vladimir Bodiansky, Georges Candilis, Shadrach Woods, and others. Their work was directly influenced by the extensive research on indigenous dwelling by Écochard's Service de l'urbanisme in Casablanca. The investigations of traditional casbahs and medinas included physical building surveys as well as ethnographic studies and were directly instrumental to experimentation with new housing typologies. The most famous of these, Sémiramis and Nid d'abeille by Atelier des bâtisseure-Afrique, would eventually be used by Candilis as the basis for mass housing design in the French suburbs.[22] A similar approach was developed by the CIAM-Algiers group, whose "Bidonville Mahieddine" presentation showed perhaps most clearly how architectural lessons could be drawn from ethnographic analyses of Algerian shantytowns and traditional dwellings.[23] Such presentations did not just bring "colonial laboratories" to the attention of modern architects; they proposed nothing less than a new knowledge base for design. Against what they perceived as the imposition of abstract principles, they attempted to derive design solutions directly from the analysis of existing social and spatial realities.

What brought this approach to the heart of the French metropole was perhaps more than anything the work of Chombart. In fact, one project at the 1953 CIAM meeting directly involved the sociological research he had just published in *Paris et l'agglomération parisienne.* The project, an "analytical study of habitat" of the Parisian suburb of Boulogne–Billancourt, was the work of a group called CIAM-Paris. The group included the architects Édith and Roger Aujame, Pierre Riboulet, Gérard Thurnauer, and Jean-Louis Véret, most of whom knew

Chombart well.[24] From the basic postulate that habitat was "the meeting point between sociology and architecture," their presentation offered a detailed analysis of Boulogne–Billancourt "from the perspective of everyday life" rather than as "abstract entity."[25] It included not only a quantitative survey of the population but also photographic documentation, cartographic analysis, and firsthand sociological observations—similar to Chombart's own study (Plate 2).[26] Although their approach had certainly been inspired by the colonial administrative lens of Êcochard, with whom Thurnauer had gained some working experience, it was unthinkable without the sociological work of Chombart.[27]

Just like that of the Smithsons and the North African groups, the project emphasized knowledge centered on "everyday life" as the new basis of modern architecture. Rather than giving up the dominant rational ambitions of architectural modernism, this amounted to an expansion of that rationality by moving from abstract principles to the study of concrete, everyday realities. These included both the objective world of facts and the subjective world of experience. Architecture could thus be built on social science—some architects mentioned psychology, others anthropology or ethnography, but most agreed on sociology. The Doorn Statement on Habitat, established the following year by a group of mainly Dutch and British architects, promoted this view by emphasizing the necessity of collaboration between architects and sociologists.[28] The concrete terms of such a collaboration, however, were never frontally addressed within CIAM or its successor, Team X. In many cases, they remained in the realm of rhetoric or theory. Yet, the practicalities of collaboration between architects, planners, and sociologists were directly explored by Chombart and others in France, in the context of urban projects that most members of CIAM and Team X would readily dismiss as having little architectural quality.

Defining Needs and the Need for Sociology

What made French policy makers, planners, and architects during the 1950s consider knowledge of "user needs and aspirations" was the work of sociologists such as Chombart more than that of architectural groups such as Team X. If, as the demographer Sauvy had pointed out, housing was less a matter of minimum norms than of *socially* defined needs that depended on rising prosperity and technological progress, these needs had to be studied not just quantitatively but also qualitatively if they were to determine future policy directions. Demography, a social science that had long been in the service of the modern state, would not suffice. Although experts and decision makers of many stripes increasingly agreed on this by the 1950s, it was unclear what particular kinds of study would be most useful. Chombart's pioneering research played a crucial role in steering the direction such studies would take over the following decade.

What allowed Chombart to do so were his direct contacts with some of the architects of the new housing projects that were being erected in the Parisian suburbs at this time. One encounter was particularly productive, that with the architect and state administrator Robert Auzelle. Around the time they met, Auzelle was working on the Cité de la Plaine, a housing project in the southern suburb of Clamart, an area that Chombart was studying. Their collaboration gave Chombart a close view of the housing problems and solutions that were in a crucial phase of development in France at the time—after the immediate reconstructions and before the massive proliferation of *grands ensembles* of the later part of the 1950s. The mayor of Clamart had initiated a large housing program right after the war, leading to the creation in 1947 of a departmental social housing organization and the plans for what would eventually be more than two thousand dwelling units.

When Auzelle was asked to design the master plan for this housing project, he was adamant on using Chombart's sociological study of the surrounding area. His research on this rather cutoff part of Clamart, called Petit-Clamart, revealed the intricate social and physical fabric of what Chombart referred to as a "fake village of the suburbs." Using aerial photographs and drawing maps, Chombart traced the fragmented little neighborhoods of suburban allotments the area was made up of. He mapped the clusters of small shops and amenities that their community life revolved around. He analyzed the area's social meeting places, recreational spaces, and existing public services. The result was a rich picture of the area's social life as shaped both by its geographic isolation from Paris and by its economic and social dependence on the capital (Figure 2.7).

But Chombart went further than mere description or analysis; his report also stipulated a number of specific recommendations for the future housing project that was planned for the area. First of all, he called for further sociological study of a larger surrounding region, including nearby suburbs and towns. He then recommended that new housing be accessible to workers of the same salary level as the existing population, "if not, there will be opposition between two neighborhood groups owing to the social classes present in them."[29] With the same concern in mind, he suggested that some of the existing inhabitants be allowed to move to the new housing area. He also advocated for better public transport connections to Paris and the surrounding suburbs, as well as more local cultural amenities and institutions. Another suggestion was to refurbish the infrastructure and roads of existing allotments so as to diminish the opposition between the old and the new. His ambition was to assure the social and spatial integration of the new development with the existing neighborhoods, a concern that was triggered by what he saw as the related dangers of segregation and social conflict.[30]

In his subsequent design of the housing area, Auzelle attempted to take on these recommendations insofar as they were within the realm of possibility. Moving in between Beaux-Arts academism and the architectural modernism of CIAM, he claimed to take "the social

a

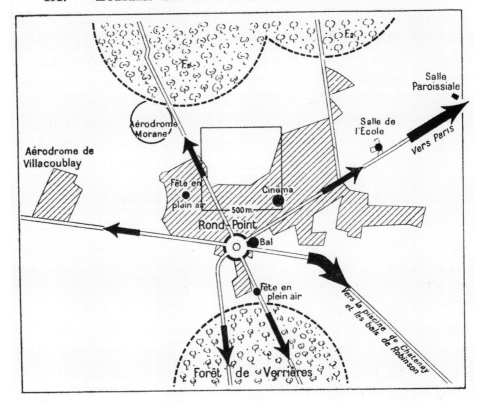

b

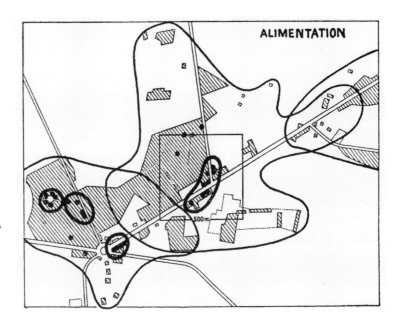

Figure 2.7. Aerial photographs and diagrams of Petit-Clamart, including (a) inhabitants' options for recreation (the airfield, the cinema, the open-air festival grounds, the dance hall, the forest, and the parish meeting hall), and (b) clusters of food stores. From Chombart de Lauwe, *Paris et l'agglomération parisienne,* 230, 235, 236.

organization of space" as the basis for planning. Auzelle was a moderate advocate of the Athens Charter but did not seem familiar with the ongoing discussions in the postwar CIAM. He was, in fact, more fundamentally influenced by the humanist urbanism of Gaston Bardet and the work of the urban historian Marcel Poëte. Following the philosopher Henri Bergson's concept of *élan vital* or the "vital impetus" in his 1907 book *Creative Evolution*, Poëte had conceived of the city as a complex "living organism" in continuous evolution.[31] Bardet had taken this historically informed, organicist concept of the city as the basis of his own design method, which he developed during the 1930s and 1940s. His research on Paris during this time led to a hierarchical concept of urban organization, ranging from the metropolis at large down to the micro-neighborhood. Like the proponents of social Catholicism, Bardet was convinced that the small, intimate neighborhood scale offered the ideal framework for individual self-development and community life and would protect the human spirit against the alienation of metropolitan life. Bardet's close association with Vichy tainted his reputation after the war. He left France in the late 1940s and turned away from urbanism to spiritualism in the 1950s. Yet he continued to exert significant influence on French urbanism with his magnum opus *Le nouvel urbanisme* of 1948, and in particular via students and followers such as Auzelle.[32]

For his project at Clamart, Auzelle used Bardet's urban design method of "polyphonic organization."[33] Concretely, this meant that Auzelle invited different architects to collaborate on the master plan and the architectural design. He invited Raymond Gervaise (architect in charge of Reconstruction), Édouard Déchaudat (the city architect of Clamart), André Mahé and Armand Taponier, and Émile Monvoisin, who was in fact an engineer. None of these were particularly well known. He first asked each of them to produce their own master plan individually and then synthesized them using the research findings and recommendations developed by Chombart. In collaboration with the sociologist, Auzelle chose a neighborhood unit size of thirty to sixty units grouped around a small public space. Apart from a section of individual houses built at the start of the project, the ensemble consisted of collective housing in blocks of four to five stories.[34] The resulting plan was then divided into five sectors that were allotted to the individual architects. This approach was meant to allow modern planning to emulate the diversity of an "organically grown" city (Figure 2.8).

During this time, Robert Auzelle was also the director in charge of the study center at the Ministry of Reconstruction and Urbanism. This allowed him to become Chombart's best advocate in the French government. Auzelle, in fact, helped him get some of his research projects funded: he convinced Eugène Claudius-Petit to sponsor Chombart de Lauwe's research for Paris and its eventual publication as *Paris et l'agglomération parisienne* in 1952. Yet, despite Chombart's considerable success, there was more than a single cause to the inclusion of sociological expertise in housing and urban policy. Another factor was the experience of slum clearance and, more particularly, the development of preliminary social surveys to guide this

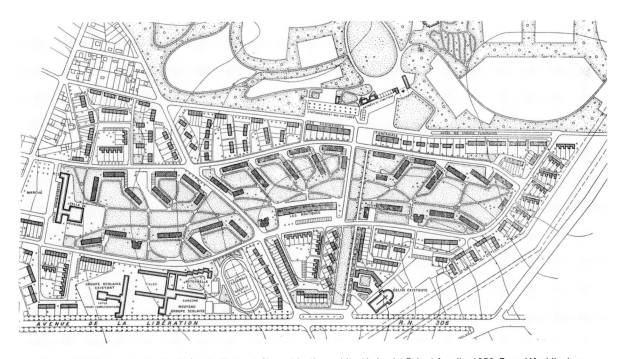

Figure 2.8. Master plan for the Cité de la Plaine at Clamart by the architect/urbanist Robert Auzelle, 1950. From *L'Architecture d'aujourd'hui* 32 (1950): 58.

process. Since 1947, Robert Auzelle had been in charge of this at the ministry, where he had developed a new method of surveying based on studies by the group Économie et humanisme and the Institut national d'hygiène. These two institutions focused on social problems in inner-city neighborhoods and positioned urban renewal squarely in the realm of reform and social justice. Founded in 1941 by Louis-Joseph Lebret, Économie et humanisme was a group of social Catholics who, like Chombart, with whom they were in contact, were looking for an ideological alternative to both liberal capitalism and communism.[35] In their urban surveys, they saw both an opportunity to help the poor and the outlines of a communitarian spirit. The basic method Auzelle derived from their studies was a system of two-sided index cards for each dwelling unit. One side contained information about the material condition of the dwelling or its *habitabilité*; the other side described its occupants and their social lives. This information was to guide the project of gradually moving inhabitants, using reusable temporary housing facilities, to appropriate new homes. He believed this method could ultimately guide a systematic renewal of the country's old city centers.[36] The experience of rehousing forced government planners for the first time to deal concretely with the problem of managing inhabitants and confronted them with the social repercussions of their plans. The approach to include a rudimentary sociological survey into the process of urban renewal thus established an important precedent for an approach to planning based in the social as much as in the physical.

The broad appeal of Chombart's approach, however, was that it offered a more general framework for understanding the relationship between the social and the physical aspects of France's rapid urbanization after the war. Under the influence of his anthropological work with Marcel Griaule, the urban morphological approach he had adopted from Maurice Halbwachs, and his own analytic approach to the city through aerial photography, Chombart used concepts such as "social space" to explore this relationship.[37] The notion corresponded closely with what some modernist architects within CIAM and especially Team X were after at this time when they used the term *habitat*. Although he did not seem to have had much direct contact with them, Chombart soon promoted the idea of *habitat* in similarly universal terms: "The house [*habitation*] cannot be separated from the material living environment of a society in space, in other words, from *habitat*. The topic we set out thus poses, in its essence, the general problem of relations between the material manifestations of a civilization, its social structures, and its modes of thinking. Studying *habitat* in this perspective is to observe the image of a society on the ground."[38]

In parallel with the dismissal of the Athens Charter's four functions by CIAM architects at this time, Chombart proposed a crucial redefinition of the notion of need as it was generally understood by French social scientists, planners, and architects during the late 1940s and early

1950s. Rather than a matter of function, biology, or even socioeconomics, as Sauvy had suggested, Chombart insisted that inhabitants' needs with regard to dwelling were physiological, psychological, and cultural in nature. Apart from minimum floor surface and standards of modern comfort, his research revealed a multitude of needs: "a need to organize and appropriate space, a need for independence of groups of inhabitants inside an apartment, a need for rest and relaxation, a need to separate functions, a need for well-being and freedom from material constraints, a need for familial intimacy, a need to be appreciated, a need for external social relations, and so on."[39]

While such a list threatened to test the elasticity of the notion of need, it was of crucial importance to Chombart in advancing his project for an engaged sociology. Whether under the rubric of need, social space, or *habitat*, Chombart's work was guided by an implicit message to those in charge of designing the built environments of a rapidly urbanizing France. As a sociologist, he saw two opposing ways of working, and he was clear about the policy implications of his own work and that of his discipline. Planning could either be shaped by economic and demographic calculations and the personal ideas of designers, thus imposing plans on the population, so he claimed, or it could take into account "a more profound knowledge of the real behavior and, most important, the motivations behind this behavior," which should allow architects and planners to "avoid the tensions and the revolts they threaten to encounter."[40]

Chombart was more than occasionally critical of state-led housing production and urban planning, but his repeated calls to take account of inhabitants' needs and desires did not imply a fundamental critique of state-led modernization in and of itself. On the contrary, he vindicated state-led modernization. Chombart vigorously criticized the "hard" way of bringing about modernization as it was supported by some policy makers during the 1950s, and he did so with the help of his sociological studies: "We have been able to observe at multiple occasions that some imposed behaviors, materialized by a certain disposition of the dwelling unit, are in flagrant opposition with the cultural models, desires, or aspirations of the households. In contrast, we have been able to notice changes in the traditional way of 'living' that fully satisfy the beneficiaries of these new dwellings. It is when the plan leaves a certain degree of freedom to the user in the choice of his lifestyle, without encouraging undesirable habits incurred in the old dwellings, not to say the 'slums,' that the progress is best experienced as a liberation and not like an obligation to give way to modernism." His own proposal was thus not to eliminate but to smooth the process of modernization, emphasizing that the "innovative quality" of the dwelling unit should not be experienced "as an inconvenience or hindrance to family life but as a liberation from old habits and outdated cultural models."[41] Ultimately, Chombart never questioned the basic premise of social modernization based on housing provision—a belief that kept him close to France's state officials and policy makers at the time.

An Experimental Science

The French turn to mass housing in large-scale urban developments—the outlines of which were becoming clear in the early 1950s—provided a unique opportunity in the eyes of forward-thinking social scientists. Could they, for the first time perhaps, do more than merely record and analyze social changes under way? Could they stop running behind the project of modernization and instead play an active role in better articulating it based on their knowledge of its social repercussions? As an intellectual who carried the *Légion d'honneur* and other military decorations for his heroic actions during the war, this question was certainly on Chombart's mind. During the postwar years, he consequently pursued a methodology for his urban sociology that rested on the mutual development of fundamental and applied research. He was convinced that these were not antithetical and would fertilize each other without compromising either one.

In 1950, during his research on Paris, Chombart established an institute for fundamental research, the Groupe d'ethnologie sociale. Three years later, a spin-off for applied research was created by him under the name Bureau d'études sociotechniques—soon renamed Centre d'étude des groupes sociaux (Center for the Study of Social Groups).[42] Whereas the first was more closely linked to the academic world, the latter was a private nonprofit organization. Researchers, projects, and money constantly flowed in between Chombart's institutions, much as he had envisaged. The Ministry of Reconstruction and Urbanism had already commissioned his fundamental research cell in 1951, but it was especially through his applied research cell that policy-oriented government-commissioned studies really took off. Chombart's work during the 1950s included research projects on cities such as Bordeaux, Maubeuge, Rouen, Saint-Étienne, and Paris, and he was commissioned by a variety of state institutions, including the Ministry of Reconstruction and Urbanism, the District of Paris, and the Centre scientifique et technique du bâtiment (CSTB, or the Scientific and Technical Center for Construction). Toward the end of the decade, the surge in demand for applied research would necessitate a new institutional structure emulating the private research and consulting firms that were rapidly growing at this time.[43] With this institutional structure for his research, Chombart envisaged urban sociology as an experimental endeavor that turned the built environment into a life-sized laboratory:

> Research needs to be oriented toward an experimental observation pursued in increasingly controlled conditions, methodically choosing the samples and terrains for comparison, and progressively developing hypotheses from the first observations onward, following the approach by Claude Bernard in the medical sciences. The second step is to move toward a veritable experimental intervention by preparing plans in which predefined elements following precise hypotheses are introduced in order to then observe the results. Research also needs to be

participatory, that is to say, obliging researchers to live close to local populations and engage them in researchers' work. Research needs to be active and dynamic to the extent to which it studies social phenomena in relation with transformations that are on their way. In such conditions, fundamental research, disinterested in the scientific sense of the term, will be most efficient and most useful for the applications themselves.[44]

Such conceptualizations of sociology as a rigorously experimental science dovetailed with what was referred to as the *attitude prospective* or prospectivist approach in France. While forward-looking and futurist perspectives were common at this time of widespread societal optimism—popular books abounded with visions of the near or distant future—prospectivist thinking was preoccupied more specifically with the relationship between technology and society. Guided by the belief that in postindustrial societies technological change would lead to social progress, prospectivists aimed to be rigorously scientific and wildly futuristic at the same time. One of their most fervent advocates was the industrialist, philosopher, and state administrator Gaston Berger, who in 1957 created the journal *Prospective* and a study center by the same name. Through such initiatives, a loose network of politicians, high-level civil servants, businessmen, and scientists came together in the 1950s.[45] During the following decade, prospectivism would become hugely popular in architectural culture—when imported by Michel Ragon and the Groupe international d'architecture prospective he founded in 1965 to promote utopian projects such as those of Yona Friedman.[46] But it was already during the 1950s that prospective thinking exerted its most profound influence by engendering powerful connections between the worlds of the artistic avant-garde, the academy, and national politics.

Social scientists, and not only those of the prospectivist stripe, were eager to portray themselves as contributors to the future of France, and often keen to prove the relevance of their discipline not only to day-to-day life but also to national decision making. Jean Fourastié, a well-known economist and government administrator who would later coin the term *les trente glorieuses* to describe France's three decades of economic prosperity after World War II, was undoubtedly moved by such ambitions.[47] As a professor at the Institut d'études politiques de Paris and director of research at the École des hautes études en sciences sociales (School for Advanced Studies in the Social Sciences), he was squarely rooted in the academy and had close connections to the Parisian artistic avant-garde.[48] At the same time, he occupied prominent positions in the state administration, first as commissioner in the Plan Monnet and later the Commissariat général du Plan, and even as an expert in international institutions such as the United Nations and the European Union. As such, Fourastié was the embodiment of the modern academic leaving the ivory tower to engage in the trenches of policy making. But even those who did not conceive of their discipline as explicitly interventionist seemed to perceive the social sciences as fundamentally shifting gears. At the Colloque national de démographie in 1960, the demographer and sociologist Alain Girard described this shift by claiming that "sociology has left the cabinet of the scholar and the thinker, in order to insert itself more and more into contemporary life, and apply itself to the observation of current problems."[49]

Lefebvre, a Marxist who tended to be as critical of the optimistic liberalism espoused by Fourastié as he was of the Catholic reformism of Chombart, described his research in terms not too dissimilar from Chombart's. Contrary to his contemporary Anglo-American reputation as a disengaged philosopher of social space, Lefebvre was intensely enmeshed with the bureaucracy of urban research and policy in France at this time.[50] Like Chombart, he consulted with multiple government institutions on ongoing debates in urban and housing policy. In his 1960 research of Mourenx, a new government-planned settlement in the French Pyrenees for workers of a nearby industrial complex, he considered "the new town as a social laboratory (not in the sense of Kurt Lewin, but nevertheless in a sufficiently specific sense: as a melting pot in which well-defined social forces take place and where tangible results of macro-decisions appear)."[51]

By the mid-1960s, the number of studies on housing estates and new large-scale urban developments had become so overwhelming in French sociology that Henri Coing, in the introduction to his well-known sociological study of Parisian urban renewal, felt the need to acknowledge that the fashionable domain of sociological inquiry was elsewhere: "Urban sociology in France has found in the housing groups that are localized at the periphery of our cities a vast field of research and experimentation: the spontaneous or directed suburban growth supplies a privileged terrain for the observation of ways of life and new behavior of urbanites. The 'grand ensemble' figures as an improvised laboratory."[52] Mass housing projects thus appeared as unprecedented sites of social and spatial experimentation under the observing gaze of sociologists, whether they partook or stood by. Some architects, state planners, and a variety of like-minded professionals crossing in and out of the state apparatus had already begun to gauge the repercussions of mass housing production and aimed to adjust it, as they could and saw fit, to their own criteria. When sociologists, including Chombart, advocated for their discipline to participate in this world of experimentation in the 1950s, they articulated a shift that was in fact much more encompassing.

If sociology was to be an experimental science, how would it concretely contribute to the construction of the new France? The answer, for Chombart, was multidisciplinary collaboration. Such an approach was already being employed in state institutions such as the Commissariat général du Plan, which consulted social scientists on a regular basis. In the eyes of Chombart, this way of working should now be expanded to encompass the overall process of urbanization, from policy, design, and planning to construction and inhabitation. Together with a small group of state administrators, civil society leaders, and architects from the mid-1950s onward, Chombart argued vigorously for multidisciplinary planning teams that would bring together policy makers, planners, architects, and sociologists.[53] After a sociological analysis of how modernist architects designed housing, he remained unconvinced that architects could really be left to their own devices. The simple reason was that they did not have the necessary expertise of inhabitants' complex needs in the realm of dwelling. Consequently, he contended, "the work of researchers in the human sciences needs to consist—in collaboration with architects, administrators, and social services—of analyzing these needs in all their complexity and variety so that housing can be adapted to families and allow them to flourish instead of imposing on them."[54]

Ultimately, his idea of such multidisciplinary collaboration was based on the conviction that "the basic approach shared by urban planners and sociologists consists of thinking people in space and research for them the means to appropriate space."[55] The notion of appropriation—which would become one of the main concepts in Lefebvre's thinking, partly inspired by Situationism—was in fact first formulated by Chombart. Appropriation for him did not entail a critical transformation that contested the original intentionality of architectural space as it would for Lefebvre and others from the late 1960s onward. Chombart spoke instead about appropriation in the way inhabitants' use of interior decoration in new apartments would help them to customize or personalize their everyday environments. In his eyes, the collaboration between architects conceiving of space and sociologists researching its usage was therefore as logical as it was unproblematic. Sociology would simply provide the "user data" for a better-adjusted architecture.

Despite Chombart's keen desire for a sociologically informed architecture of mass housing, his recommendations tended at times to fall into familiar formats. In 1959, at the end of a decade of intensive fundamental and applied research on modern housing, he stipulated maximum surface norms that varied according to geographic region, using the same universal method of calculation. Based on these surveys, he argued that tension would arise within the family when surfaces were too small, independent of the particular layout of the unit. He continued by stipulating that the ideal threshold for familial satisfaction was situated at about fourteen to sixteen square meters per person.[56] This figure came surprisingly close to Le Corbusier's spatial prescription almost three decades earlier, in his 1930 plan for the "biological unit" of man that required a cell of exactly fourteen square meters. What for Le Corbusier was a matter of biology and avant-gardism was a matter of sociology and meticulous statistics for Chombart, but their ultimate results were not dissimilar. Admittedly, the modernist architect had taken the singular subject of a "universal man" as the basis for his design, leading to a single room for a single occupant, whereas for the sociologist familial relationships and thus the space of the family unit were of key concern (see Figure 2.9).

Thus, despite the continuities of thought, Chombart did ultimately change the terms of the housing debates in 1950s France: instead of Euclidian space he proposed social space as

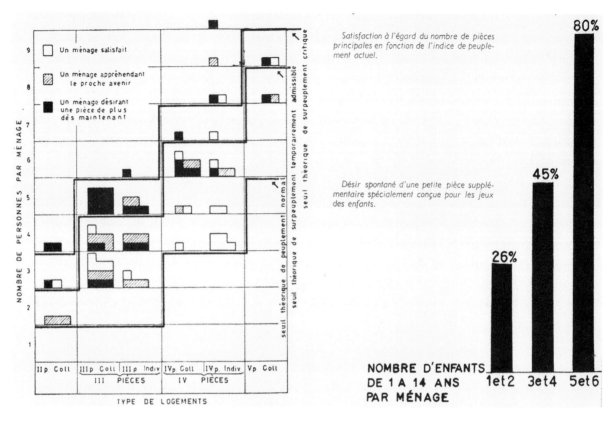

Figure 2.9. Results from a study by Chombart de Lauwe surveying eighty families in new housing in the region of Bordeaux, 1959. The left-hand graph displays families' satisfaction with the number of rooms in their apartment, varying with family size (vertical axis) and apartment type (horizontal axis). The right-hand graph demonstrates the more pronounced desire of larger nuclear families for a children's playroom. From Paul-Henry Chombart de Lauwe, "Sociologies de l'habitation," *Urbanisme* 65 (1959): 8–9.

the basis of design, instead of biological givens he analyzed sociopsychological needs, and instead of hard, technologically driven modernization he advocated a softer, socially oriented process. However, these shifts did not lead him to propose revolutionary changes. Many of the improvements he proposed were moderate, commonsensical, or well known, such as better sound insulation and more collective amenities in new housing estates. In many ways, Chombart's approach was still based on an objective science of human need. His belief that inhabitants' needs could be better known and subsequently better accommodated by experts was unwavering. In the same vein as Le Corbusier had done and as an army of state administrators continued to do, he espoused the dominant bias against the single-family home; he argued that opinion polls such as the 1947 INED survey could not reveal inhabitants' "real needs."[57] He ignored popular demand and preferred collective over individual housing because the latter was less efficient in his eyes and often resulted in "badly organized urbanization patterns."[58]

His applied research in Bordeaux revealed even more normative assumptions. The goal of this study, commissioned after the positive reception of his studies for Paris, was to help the developer, a regional social housing organization, in adapting its housing program to inhabitants' needs.[59] Based on sociological profiles of household types in three local housing estates, the study questioned the validity of generic norms that defined "this standard family or this average Frenchman, a rare sample that does not really exist if it were not for the arbitrary intervention of statistics or the lack of imagination of model makers."[60] Despite this critique, however, his study did not in fact question standardized mass production. On the contrary, a better understanding of how families used their domestic space further legitimized the mass production of identical housing units in the sociologist's eyes. If Le Corbusier during the 1920s had used technological arguments in his pleas for mass production based on a standard prototype, Chombart now advocated for a remarkably similar principle, but in explicitly sociological terms. To resolve what he saw as a contradiction between people's personal attachment to their homes and the need for flexibility as households move, grow, or change, he proposed the national distribution of mass-produced dwellings with identical layout and fittings:

> Analogous to other industrial sectors, one could talk of "brands" of dwellings, like makes of cars or brands of household appliances—independently of their characteristics of power or the capacity of the models. One could, moreover, reproduce these series in multiple geographic sections of a single urban agglomeration, in order to maximize exchanges of apartments from one estate to the other, and thus respond to the need for mobility prompted by change in workplace or school (to just cite these factors of mobility).[61]

Concepts of the home as a neutral, standardized cell were widely shared by modern architects during the 1950s. Perhaps surprisingly, they were not often accompanied by an agenda for direct social engineering. Asked if the architect "can or has to influence the lifestyle of his contemporaries," Émile Aillaud responded, in a 1958 meeting with Sudreau: "I do not think that we can or should weigh on the life of the tenant by way of the dwelling layout. To impose a mold adapted to intellectuals or the bourgeoisie would lead to inadequate results and a rapid degradation of the dwelling space. Therefore, I think the cell needs to be as anonymous and interchangeable as possible, so that 'anybody' could live in it."[62] The belief in a universal language of modern architecture as it went mainstream was thus shared by architects and sociologists alike. That does not mean Chombart always agreed with the architects. When in the late 1950s he interviewed prominent French architects, many of whom were in charge of mass housing projects, he was dismayed to see how resistant they still were to the idea of incorporating inhabitants' opinions and ways of life in their design process.[63] Where

Chombart differed was not in the ultimate goal but in the way to get there. And that path was not set in stone.

Expertise in Contest

Chombart was hardly the only advocate for the importance of expertise in housing and urban planning during the 1950s. The development of mass housing production and the processes of design and normalization that accompanied it created vast openings for the engagement of new domains of knowledge. Those opportunities were not unique to housing or urbanism. A wealth of new forms of expertise found its way into French policy making during this era of enthusiastic modernization. Apart from demographic studies, public opinion polls were becoming increasingly successful means of guiding policy. They had only recently been imported into France when Jean Stoetzel, professor of social psychology at the Sorbonne, founded the Institut français d'opinion publique as the French counterpart of the American polling firm Gallup in 1938. Soon after, the company was commissioned by the French government on a regular basis. Another emerging form of knowledge for policy was in the form of collaboration with civil society organizations aiming to bring the concerns of citizens and families closer to the state administration. One key such association was the Union nationale des associations familiales, established in 1945 to officially represent French families in the national government. The organization, structured as a union of local associations across France, had seats in the Conseil économique et sociale just as did the French labor unions. It would play an important part in the urban policies of the *grands ensembles* during the 1960s.[64]

While many of these new forms of knowledge were quantitative in nature, qualitative research also gained enormously in appeal, if only a little later. Chombart's calls to include qualitative sociology in national housing and urban policy were certainly pioneering when he first launched them, but by the mid-1950s public authorities were increasingly open to the claim that such research could in fact help them improve designs of new housing and plans for urban growth. The career of André Trintignac, a mid-level civil servant in the Ministry of Reconstruction and Urbanism, was representative of this changing mind-set within the state apparatus.[65] Trintignac began his career in the early 1950s in the ministry's section on regional planning and development, where he was responsible for establishing construction and financing programs based on the quantification of housing need. This led him to participate in international housing conferences such as those of the European Economic Community and the Union internationale des organismes familiaux (International Union of Family Organizations). At such conferences, which brought together specialists of diverse nations and disciplines, both governmental and private institutions, Trintignac advocated for more in-depth sociological research preliminary to programming housing. His calls were in fact remarkably similar to those of Chombart, who at the same kinds of conferences urged France to "catch up" with those countries where policy-oriented sociological study was more prominent, in his eyes. Guiding examples—not only for architects but also for the sociologist—were the well-known British and Scandinavian housing and New Town developments, as well as the efforts of various American and European architects to incorporate studies about inhabitant needs.[66]

Such international comparisons were equally important to civil servants including Trintignac and guided much of their intellectual convictions and subsequent policy making. At the momentous Congrès mondial de la famille in Paris in 1958, which Trintignac attended, conference-goers were in overall agreement that before the establishment of a construction program, a proper and careful sociological inquiry as well as a collaboration between sociologists, architects, urbanists, and social workers was indispensable.[67] Future inhabitants needed to be consulted and subsequently informed about the environments provided for them, and many countries were purportedly engaged in doing so. Other organizations such as the International Council for Building Research Studies and Documentation followed suit and confirmed this recent surge in the sociology of housing and urban planning.[68] In other words, by the end of the 1950s, the idea of sociology as an experimental science seemed to have become an international bureaucratic reality.

Trintignac was at the forefront of that reality in France. His involvement in the establishment of national housing norms during the earlier part of the decade had given him invaluable expertise that he could now harness for his career in the French government. As the director of the Bureau des études sociologiques de l'habitat (Office of Sociological Studies of Habitat), he became one of the main figures in the development of sociological studies within the ministry. He organized studies on inner-city neighborhoods, mass housing estates, and shantytowns, and led projects to specify the particular needs of what were called specialized groups of users, including the elderly, traveling bachelors, immigrants, and the "socially unadapted." This work continued to influence housing and urban policies throughout the 1960s and 1970s.

Yet, despite the mirroring of Chombart's calls for sociology within the state apparatus, there was more than one kind of expertise that vied for legitimacy in housing and urban policy. In fact, many policy makers, including Trintignac, deemed Chombart's research rather ill-suited for government policies. When Chombart applied for funding at the Commissariat général du Plan for a six-year urban research project in 1959, Trintignac sent in negative advice, fundamentally questioning the usefulness of his studies: "As you know, the Direction de l'aménagement du territoire has had numerous contacts with Mr. Chombart de Lauwe in the past: we have notably attempted to ensure a connection between the work of urbanists and that of sociologists; the agreement could not be realized with Mr. Chombart de Lauwe as he was oriented essentially toward a research with fundamental character. . . . We can question whether in these conditions the administration needs to subsidize studies that are not directly useful to it."[69] State administrators such as Trintignac preferred a type of expertise that was simpler, less time-consuming, and more efficient. They often deemed Chombart's work too academic—despite his own stated aims and his ambiguous position in between academic, professional, and government circles.[70] His research was at least partly meant to be inscribed in the growing academic field of sociology, and was generously supported by the prominent "prospectivist" and academic Berger. But his relation to the academy remained a tenuous one. Georges Gurvitch, a prominent sociologist at the Sorbonne, obstructed his entering the university, and the famous anthropologist Claude Lévi-Strauss seemed "embarrassed that he was doing ethnography in Paris and not in the tropics."[71] Despite its influence, Chombart's work thus threatened to fall in between two stools.

Other kinds of expertise, also focused on the social environment but in competition with the "properly sociological" kind—meaning academic and critical—emerged simultaneously with Chombart's. In the cracks between the epistemological machineries of the postwar state and the academy burgeoned another production of knowledge whose purpose was not wisdom or policy but rather business. Private consultancy and market research firms constituted a conspicuously new domain of knowledge production in a France only recently introduced to the purported virtues of American corporate practices.[72] A pioneer in this respect was the Office of Applied Sociology and Psychology (Bureau de sociologie et de psychologie appliquées), established in 1954 and shortly after renamed COFREMCA. Its founder, Alain de Vulpian, had attended the elite Paris school now known as Sciences-Po directly after the war and had subsequently worked for Stoetzel's Institut français d'opinion publique. This background had exposed him to both academic social sciences and the more pragmatic methods of opinion polling and interviewing. Wary of the dominant influences of Marxism and existentialism in French intellectual life at this time, he was instead heavily invested in American cultural anthropology and psychosociology.[73] For his new company, de Vulpian experimented with a variety of different approaches but remained ultimately pragmatic in scope. His company was a big success and allowed him to work with large corporate clients such as the cosmetics firm L'Oréal and Air France during the 1950s.[74] In opposition to the French proclivity for social structure and the continuing predominance of demography at this time, he endorsed what he would later call a "micro-systemic sociology." This approach aimed to give much more attention to individuals and their own understanding of the world. The firm mostly cultivated large corporate clients and never became a stable partner in state policy making. It was nevertheless commissioned regularly by local governments and centralized state institutions for a variety of studies, including in the realm of housing and urban policy. The company was first approached in 1957 by the CSTB to analyze the inhabitants' satisfaction in new housing projects.

The alternative kinds of expertise emerging at this time were often in direct competition. Perhaps not surprisingly, the centralized state offered the primary platform where many of these conflicts were played out. After the CSTB had received both Chombart and de Vulpian's commissioned study in 1957, it established a working group with them to compare the results and put them into practice. The goal was to improve the dwelling layouts of mass housing to better respond to inhabitants' needs and desires.[75] When, at one of the meetings, de Vulpian presented his methodology as a "new, efficient, and manageable" alternative to conventional sociological research, Chombart responded that this not only already existed, but that the results of "such market research" could not be compared with that of "properly sociological" studies "because the issue is not to study choices but [the underlying] situations and structures."[76] Chombart continued by proclaiming that statistical surveys of large samples were outmoded, and instead, in-depth surveys with a small number of participants were the way to go. The director of the group felt forced to remind both researchers of the ultimate goal, namely, "letting housing developers know what types of dwellings they should build." He went on to show the types of dwelling layouts created by the CSTB, and as a follow-up proposed a "botanical" classification of a large sample of existing units. Chombart nevertheless continued to insist on his own sociological method, while others—more in tune with de Vulpian—suggested radically pragmatic solutions. One of these was a "service 'après-vente,'" a post-purchase customer service for new government-aided housing units.[77] Such a concept, which conflated housing as private commodity with housing as state service, was a clear sign that the discussion removed housing from the realm of politics, despite the loud protests only a couple years earlier for a universal "right to housing."[78] Chombart's own research was ultimately perhaps not so different in that it equally depoliticized housing matters by framing them as expertise. What most members of the group agreed on was that ideal dwelling typologies based on sociological expertise were the only way to improve the quality of housing. In other words, the quibbles between Chombart and de Vulpian were the sign of mere differences in degree rather than fundamental questions over the status of knowledge.

A fundamentally different case was presented by experts such as Robert-Henri Hazemann. He advocated for an unrelated form of expertise that laid similar claim to the domain of housing and urbanism around this time. It was based on the medical sciences rather than the social. Hazemann was a medical doctor and inspector at the Ministry of Health who also taught at the Institut d'urbanisme de l'Université de Paris. During the late 1950s and early 1960s, he published prolifically about the *grands ensembles*. His attempts to medicalize the problems of everyday life in mass housing estates were based on an environmental determinism that was hardly new. Since mid-nineteenth century, medical scientists had produced a significant body of "slum knowledge" based on the assumed link between environment and behavior. Hazemann's work thus amounted not to a revolution but to a mere shift in focus, toward the psychosociological pathology not of slums but of newly built environments. He argued vehemently against what he saw as architects' and planners' *gigantisme*—the unjustifiable exaggeration in scale and monumentality of modern housing. He might have been right to point out the ultimate irrationality of seemingly rational projects, for instance, a four hundred-meter-long fifteen-story slab of housing at Haut-du-Lièvre in Nancy (see Figure 1.18). But rather than on the basis of aesthetics, he criticized such projects for their "devastating human consequences," which he understood to be first and foremost in psychosociological diseases. He thus argued: "When it is too tall and its units too low-ceilinged and cramped, the building does not allow low-income families to develop themselves freely both from a physical and a moral point of view. . . . The grouping of buildings poses psychosocial problems that are far from known. The neighborhood contacts, notably that of the children, certainly have very serious and permanent consequences in the formation of character."[79] Other medical specialists joined him in his alarming reportage of the presumed physical and mental consequences on the inhabitants of mass collective housing. Despite their immediate appeal in the popular press and success in mobilizing critiques of the *grands ensembles,* medical science never attained the legitimacy of sociology when it came to mass housing. It ultimately seemed proven wrong by contradiction: doctors' alarming calls of a dramatically sickened urban civilization probably wore off in the face of inhabitants' often-mundane experiences and problems of day-to-day life in France's sprawling new suburbs.

Knowledge and Building, a Mutual Production

The conviction that the production of mass housing needed to be better adjusted to inhabitants' "real" needs was increasingly shared by professionals and civil servants involved in housing and urban planning. Despite conflicting claims to expertise, the domain of inquiry that was ultimately believed to offer the legitimate tools for this task was sociology. Rather than an academically bounded discipline, sociology was a field that went beyond the initially weak and relatively uninstitutionalized discourse of academic sociologists. What could be labeled sociology constituted a dispersed realm of knowledge production including academic research such as that of Alain Touraine and his students, but also journalistic reportage, including Marc Bernard's *Sarcellopolis* and Jean Duquesne's *Vivre à Sarcelles,* works of social critique such as some of Lefebvre's, and, most important, a vast quantity of government-commissioned sociological reports.

The latter were executed by a burgeoning sector of semipublic research firms or *bureaux d'études.*[80] De Vulpian's private consultancy firm remained an exception, at least until the late 1960s. Most firms grew out of government initiatives and remained either public or semipublic. They were easily recognized by bureaucratic-sounding acronyms such as CRU, CEDER,

SOFRED, BERU, SEDES, or CERES. The last, which stood for the Centre de recherches économiques et sociales (Center for Economic and Social Research), was established in 1956 to collaborate with the Ministry of Construction in research on collective amenities for the *grands ensembles*. The center's research agenda was largely shaped by the ministry in concert with architects, social workers, and other experts.[81] Many other such research institutes were soon established with the same goal.[82] These emerging institutions often collaborated with each other and would supply much of the expert knowledge on which subsequent housing and urban planning policies were based. By 1965, the social research sector was already so wieldy and so intricately linked to policy making that it became a topic of research itself and needed to be mapped out by state planners (see Figure 2.10).[83] The sprawling suburbanization of France thus went hand in hand with a sprawl of networked knowledge.

This culture of networked knowledge production had as much to do with the celebration of science as a vehicle for social progress across the Cold War world as it did with the

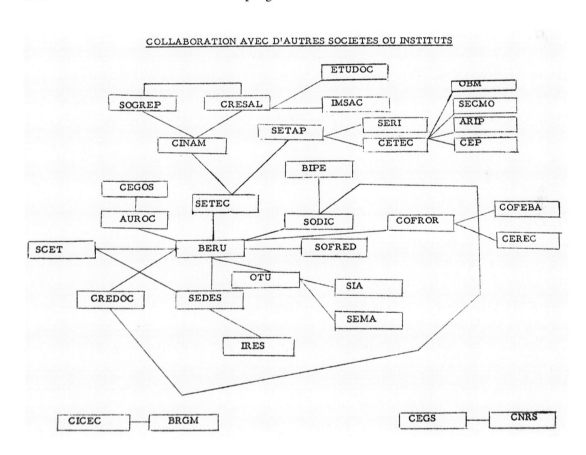

Figure 2.10. Diagram of urban research firms collaborating with the French government. From Commission de l'équipement urbain, groupe de travail no. 5, "Études urbaines," 1965. Archives nationales, France, CAC 19920405/009.

particularities of French modernization. Paul Rabinow has brilliantly explored the longer historical trajectory of French modernity by focusing on the development of techniques of social control and pacification based in the redefinition of the physical and social environment.[84] These techniques, which contributed to the foundations of welfare as a feature of enlightened government, were spurred by emerging domains of knowledge of the social world. They included first and foremost statistics, demography, geography, and sociology. Mass housing and urban planning, physical cornerstones of the postwar welfare state in France, are thus unthinkable without the role of social-scientific knowledge. Yet, after World War II, such knowledge was as much about social pacification as it was about national competitiveness. Social scientists during this time entered into a decidedly international arena defined by the new transatlantic bind between Europe and the United States and the geopolitical reordering of the Cold War more generally. Anxious to overcome the country's perceived "delay" on the international scene, French government officials were adamant on framing the task of science in terms of national progress. For social scientists, a crucial way of achieving such glory was to assert a model of objectivity inspired by the exact and natural sciences.[85]

In the United States such a positioning may have been a way to depoliticize the social sciences in an era of anti-Communist witch hunts, but French social scientists were often less concerned with ideological neutrality than they were enthralled by the empowering uses of technical and quantitative methods—many of which were of American vintage.[86] Embracing such "hard" models of knowledge production could increase legitimacy in the state apparatus and provide more leverage within the university. Perhaps not surprisingly, the inclusion of social-scientific expertise into state housing and urban policy had begun with more quantitative disciplines such as economics and demography, which prevailed in scientific credibility over the "softer" approaches of sociology and psychology. Yet, in the course of the 1950s, national planning increasingly expanded its view of the economy to include "humanistic" dimensions—triggered in part by increasing anxiety about the social and psychological repercussions of France's explosive postwar growth and rapid modernization of everyday life. This shift precipitated the inclusion of sociology, in particular the "prospectivist" kind that dovetailed with the mind-set of planning.

During the late 1950s, national economic planning, scientific expertise, and national pride thus became more closely intertwined than ever. Unlike its predecessors, which attracted little international attention and for which the government did little to bring them before the public eye, the Fourth Plan gained national and even international prominence.[87] The economic prosperity after the reforms of 1958–59 strengthened the belief in planned economic growth. But, more important, planning now found a strong spokesperson in the person of President de Gaulle, who turned the plan into France's big project—"la grande affaire de la France." In marked contrast with, for instance, West Germany, which had seen a quick return to a liberal market economy after the end of Marshall Plan aid, France strengthened its national planning. De Gaulle's Fourth Plan constituted a major change in emphasis and scope compared to previous plans, aiming not only to build a systematic picture of the national economy, but also to more comprehensively target social development and welfare. The widely distributed publication of the Fourth Plan in 1962 summed up this ambition by describing previous plans as "a less partial idea of the economy: more housing, a modernized agriculture, renewed industries, a growing purchasing power," and the new plan as "a less partial idea of Man: more hospitals, more schools, more youth and cultural centers, modernized cities and villages, less social injustice. A better way of life."[88]

The year 1958 was thus an important milestone, and not only in French politics. For the social sciences, it meant the affirmation of a course that had been more prudently embarked on earlier in the decade. Despite the consensus that modernization was led first of all by technological progress, state administrators were increasingly convinced that it now required a "humanistic approach." The way to assure this was by engaging the human sciences. Before 1958, institutional demand for social-scientific research was marginal and there was little political will to utilize it. Most of the knowledge production was fundamental, and the social sciences were institutionally poorly embedded. At the university, there were only a couple of chairs, and there was not even a full degree in sociology. Only the École des hautes études en sciences sociales had some faculty members specializing in sociology. During this time, the Centre d'études sociologiques (Center for Sociological Studies) was a principal place for sociological research in France, but its researchers, who mainly had backgrounds in philosophy and history, did not have much contact with the universities.[89] After 1958, however, the demand for social-scientific research grew spectacularly, in tune with rising interest from the government. National modernization came to be portrayed as a social project above anything else. The social sciences were to play an unprecedented role and were rapidly institutionalized during the following decade, first of all at the university, but gradually also inside the state apparatus. The number of researchers skyrocketed, and the overwhelming demand for social-scientific research now came from the state administration.[90]

The work of Chombart and many others was inscribed in this larger shift in the bureaucratic organization of knowledge production. Sudreau's famous "referendum apartment" and other efforts during his tenure as minister in 1958 were only the tip of the iceberg: they simply confirmed the success of a new set of ideas that had been in formation in the course of the decade. His Commission de la vie dans les grands ensembles (Commission for Life in the *grands ensembles*) was motivated by a growing concern with the social life of new housing areas and instigated an important moment of dialogue between high-level civil servants, politicians, architects, urbanists, social scientists, and representatives of national civil society organizations. But by 1958, this was hardly the first time they were at the same table.

The attempts to accurately determine housing needs and the growing concerns with the social repercussions of new housing projects, once built, had spurred the incorporation of such expertise in state-led housing and urban planning in the course of the late 1940s and 1950s. At the same time as it began to streamline housing production into mass collective housing estates, the government also developed ways to adjust it to perceived needs—within well-delineated but nevertheless changing boundaries. The conviction to improve housing on the basis of empirical research had first emerged at the margins of architecture and social science. As mass housing gradually dominated state intervention in the realm of the built environment, such convictions transformed and became part of the mind-set of state administrators. Thus emerged, during the 1950s, a generally shared understanding that the production of housing needed to be informed directly by investigations into its "consumption," or, in other words, how these environments, once built, would be used by their inhabitants.

While sociology was increasingly privileged as the appropriate domain of expertise with regard to these questions, the "feedback loops" between production and consumption were in fact generated by a diverse field of knowledge, for which the centralized state served as the primary platform. The proponents of this bureaucratic epistemology of mass housing were diverse, including state administrators such as Trintignac, representatives of civil society organizations such as the Union nationale des associations familiales, and social scientists external but linked to the state, for instance, Chombart. They were caught in the tension between the imperatives of standardization and the desire to know the specificity of people's needs.

The fervor of French humanism, which was in essence a Parisian culture of bohemian *intellos* during the 1940s, thus transformed during the 1950s and 1960s into a way of governing the nation. Just as the intellectual gaze expanded out from the Parisian "quartier populaire" onto the national territory at large, so was the culture of avant-garde urban exploration turned into a bureaucratic epistemology. In other words, by the time critical intellectuals such as the Situationists lambasted the "hygienic" state-led urbanism that was obliterating the organic and mysterious urbanity of the capital during the 1950s, some of their ways of thinking had already infiltrated that very bureaucracy.

This bureaucratic epistemology was shaped by the ambition to satisfy "users," the citizen-consumers of state services, while continuing to promote large-scale mass housing production as the only viable solution. As such, the shift from reconstruction projects to the mass production that would ultimately typify the *trente glorieuses* was one toward a new, paradoxical focus on the user. People were thus treated as abstracted factors in the calculations of state planning, generic citizen-consumers whom the state was to provide for, and, increasingly, who were the central focus for a more "humane" production and management of the built environment. The narrative of postwar French urbanism is not one from a ruthless, authoritarian

regime of mass production toward an emancipatory one focused on human needs and aspirations. The repercussions of mass housing production in 1950s France amount to the advent
of the user as a *category* of design, research, planning, and inhabitation. Rather than setting up
a "humanist" view of the user as an active participant of neighborhood life against a statistical
notion of the user based on functionalist or quantified need—an opposition that would eventually become dominant with the contestations of 1968—the former is in fact part and parcel
of the latter.

It is no longer surprising, then, that Sudreau continued to support the standardization of
mass production by increasing repetitiveness and efficiency while at the same time aiming
to satisfy people's desires and aspirations. In 1958, the same year of his Commission de la vie
dans les grands ensembles, his working group on industrialization and productivity (Étude de
l'industrialisation et l'accroissement de la productivité dans la construction) suggested that
developers always work with the same architects and the same construction companies,
"promoting the use of the same techniques, that is to say, the same materials with the same
operations and the use of the same elements."[91] The report further suggested that "this effort
to diminish the necessary variety in small as well as large projects" would be the task of the
state and would only be possible through rigorous regulation of the construction sector and
the promotion of prototype projects instead of merely prototype plans.[92] That such an
extreme standardization of housing was not seen as being in blatant conflict with the efforts
to satisfy the future inhabitants of these environments, once built, only illustrates how culturally ingrained the social project of architectural modernization had become in France.
This project, in short, entailed not just material or technological development but the rise of
a bureaucratic epistemology that would organize French urban culture and design over the
next decades.

1960s

ARCHITECTURE MEETS
SOCIAL SCIENCE

3

ANIMATION TO THE RESCUE

In France, numerous *grands Ensembles* have already been or will be inscribed into the land, from the mining and steel region of the Lorraine to the oil-rich Béarn, passing through the important industrial regions, old or new. But it is not enough to build dwellings adapted to needs, and to create the necessary facilities according to carefully established plans and norms, if those houses, social centers, schools, kindergartens, and parks do not bring happiness, and do not serve human and social progress. Even if the project is technically successful, inhabitants can be dissatisfied, the social atmosphere generate protest, families dissolve, and youth gangs emerge. It is not enough that the Urbanist and the Architect thought about the sociological problems and avoided errors in conception. What still needs to be done is to create a human Community in the sphere of individual freedom.[1]

APPEARING TO DISMISS AN URBANISM of numbers and norms, this statement served to introduce a highly consequential study that did in fact focus on detailed quantitative and technical guidelines. Its aim was to modulate the provision of what were called *équipements collectifs* in mass housing estates. A mix of basic public services, community and welfare institutions, and private amenities, these "collective facilities" were meant to transform housing estates into thriving new neighborhoods. A result of intensive research by a state-led commission of experts—including architects, sociologists, and leaders of civil society organizations—the study was published in the influential journal *Urbanisme* in 1959 and presented itself as a model for the *grands ensembles* (Figure 3.1). By this time, these large-scale modern collective housing estates had become the quintessential product of urban

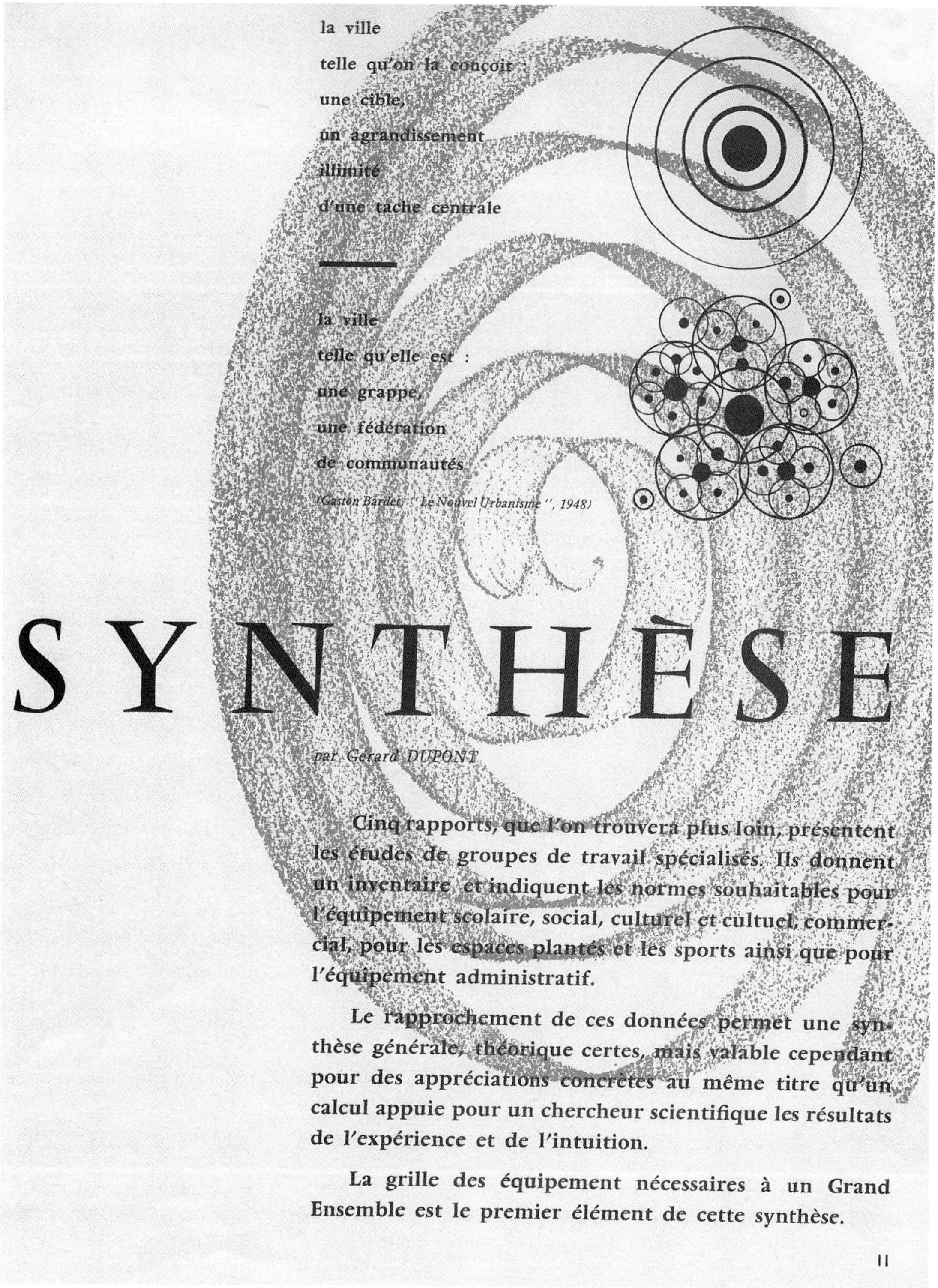

la ville

telle qu'on la conçoit :

une cible,

un agrandissement

illimité

d'une tache centrale

——

la ville

telle qu'elle est :

une grappe,

une fédération

de communautés

(Gaston Bardet, " Le Nouvel Urbanisme ", 1948)

SYNTHÈSE

par Gérard DUPONT

Cinq rapports, que l'on trouvera plus loin, présentent les études de groupes de travail spécialisés. Ils donnent un inventaire et indiquent les normes souhaitables pour l'équipement scolaire, social, culturel et cultuel, commercial, pour les espaces plantés et les sports ainsi que pour l'équipement administratif.

Le rapprochement de ces données permet une synthèse générale, théorique certes, mais valable cependant pour des appréciations concrètes au même titre qu'un calcul appuie pour un chercheur scientifique les résultats de l'expérience et de l'intuition.

La grille des équipement nécessaires à un Grand Ensemble est le premier élément de cette synthèse.

11

Figure 3.1. The *grille Dupont* as it was published in 1959. The dots adjacent to each collective facility correspond to the size of the urban unit at which it should be planned: residential groups of 200 to 500 dwellings, neighborhood units of 800 to 1,200 dwellings, *quartiers* of 1,500 to 2,500 dwellings, arrondissements of 3,000 to 6,000 dwellings, and the city or municipality of at least 8,000 dwellings. From *Urbanisme* 62–63 (1959): 11–14.

GRILLE D'ÉQUIPEMENT

D'UN GRAND ENSEMBLE D'HABITATION

La grille qui est ici présentée comprend 85 sortes d'équipements. Cette grille constitue pour l'urbaniste une nomenclature générale des équipements à prévoir.

Elle indique, en outre, pour chaque équipement le seuil à partir duquel son installation doit faire l'objet d'une étude.

Les échelons correspondant à ces seuils sont les suivants :

— Le groupe résidentiel (200 à 500 logements environ) représenté par ————————— ●
— L'unité de voisinage (800 à 1.200 logements environ) représenté par ————————— ● ●
— Le quartier (1.500 à 2.500 logements environ) représenté par ————————— ● ● ●
— L'arrondissement (3.000 à 6.000 logements environ) représenté par ————————— ● ● ● ●
— La ville ou la commune (ensemble d'au moins 8.000 logements ou ensemble ayant l'autonomie communale) représentée par ————————— ● ● ● ● ●

I. - Équipement Scolaire, Culturel et Cultuel.

11	**GROUPE SCOLAIRE DU PREMIER DEGRÉ** ————————— ● ●
	111 Classes maternelles. ————————— ●
	112 Classes primaires. ————————— ● ●
12	**ÉTABLISSEMENT DU SECOND DEGRÉ** ————————— ● ● ● ● ●
	121 Lycée.
	122 Enseignement technique.
	123 Collèges d'enseignement général (cours complémentaires).
13	**CENTRE CULTUREL** ————————— ● ● ● ● ●
	131 Salle de spectacle.
	132 Salle de conférences et concerts.
	133 Musée ou galerie d'exposition.
	134 Bibliothèques et salles de lecture pour adultes et enfants.
	135 Salles de réunions.
14	**MAISON DE JEUNES** ————————— ● ●
15	**LOGEMENTS ET FOYERS DE JEUNES** ————————— ● ● ●
	151 Logements de jeunes travailleurs.
	152 Logements d'étudiants.
	153 Foyers de jeunes.
16	**CITÉ PAROISSIALE** ————————— ● ● ●

II. - Équipement Commercial.

21	**CENTRES SECONDAIRES** ————————— ● ●
22	**CENTRE PRINCIPAL** ————————— ● ● ● ●
23	**HOTELLERIE** ————————— ● ● ● ● ●

III. - Équipement Social et Sanitaire.

31 ÉQUIPEMENT SOCIAL

311 Halte-garderie d'enfants.
312 Centre d'action sociale.
313 Pouponnière.
314 Crèche.
315 Jardin d'enfants.
316 Centre payeur de Sécurité Sociale.
317 Maison de retraite pour personnes âgées.
317bis Foyer pour personnes âgées.
318 Logements pour personnes âgées et pour infirmes.
319 Bureau d'aide sociale.

32 ÉQUIPEMENT SANTÉ

321 Centre Médical.
322 Dispensaire de soins.
323 Dispensaire de protection maternelle et infantile.
324 Dispensaire antituberculeux et d'hygiène mentale.
325 Hôpital public.
325bis Hôpital privé non commercial.
326 Hôpital psychiatrique.
327 Service d'ambulances.
328 Hôpital de malades de longue durée non commercial.
329 Maisons de santé privées et cliniques privées d'accouchement.

IV. - Espaces plantés, Parkings et Sports.

41 JARDINS D'IMMEUBLES

411 Zones de pré-habitation.
412 Aires de jeux libres.
413 Espaces clos pour enfants.
414 Cadre de verdure.

42 PARKINGS, VOIES ET PLACES PLANTÉES

421 Parkings.
422 Voies et places plantées.

43 PARCS ET JARDINS PUBLICS

431 Jardins publics.
432 Parcs urbains.
433 Grand parc boisé

44 JARDINS DE CULTURES INDIVIDUELLES

45 ÉQUIPEMENT SPORTIF NON SCOLAIRE

451 Terrains de volley-ball et basket-ball.
452 Courts de tennis.
453 Terrains d'entraînement pour le football, le rugby et le hand-ball.
454 Terrains ou stade de compétition omnisports.
455 Salle de sports.
456 Bassin de natation.
456bis Piscine couverte.

46 CIMETIÈRE

V. - Équipements généraux.

51 ADMINISTRATION MUNICIPALE OU D'INTÉRÊT LOCAL ——— ● ● ● ● ●

    511 Services administratifs municipaux.

    512 Services techniques municipaux (Direction et Bureau d'études).

    513 Bureaux de la Municipalité et locaux de cérémonie.

    514 Syndicat d'initiative.

    515 Bureaux des organismes constructeurs.

52 INSTALLATIONS ANNEXES DES SERVICES TECHNIQUES D'INTÉRÊT LOCAL ——— ● ● ● ● ●

    521 Abattoirs.

    522 Ateliers municipaux (garages, réserves, entretien).

    523 Eau et assainissement (usines et stations).

    524 Entretien de la voirie et des espaces plantés (parc à matériel, pépinières).

    525 Enlèvement des ordures ménagères (garages et usine de traitement).

    526 Pompes Funèbres (garages et magasins).

    527 Chauffage urbain.

53 POLICE INCENDIE

    531 Commissariats de Police. ——— ● ● ●

    532 Services de secours contre l'incendie. ——— ● ● ● ● ●

    533 Avertisseurs. ——— ● ●

54 ÉQUIPEMENT DE LA VOIE ET DES ESPACES PUBLICS ——— ●

    541 Éclairage public.

    542 Bancs, boîtes à papier, plans de la ville, plaques indicatrices, panneaux d'affichage, etc.

    543 Parkings publics.

55 SERVICES D'ÉTAT ——— ● ● ● ● ●

    551 Gendarmerie.

    552 Direction des Impôts.

    553 Recette-Perception.

56 P. T. T.

    561 Bureau de poste principal. ——— ● ● ● ● ●

    562 Recette succursale. ——— ● ● ● ● ●

    563 Central téléphonique. ——— ● ● ● ● ●

    564 Boîtes aux lettres. ——— ●

    565 Cabines de téléphone public. ——— ● ●

57 COMMUNICATIONS

    571 Stations autobus. ——— ● ●

    572 Gare routière. ——— ● ● ● ● ●

    573 Station S. N. C. F. ——— ● ● ● ●

58 MARCHÉS PUBLICS ——— ● ● ●

Les renseignements fournis et les réflexions suscitées par les différents rapports des groupes spécialisés permettent de dessiner une structure théorique des Grands Ensembles sous les aspects fondamentaux de la démographie, de l'économie et de l'espace.

development and would remain so for the decade to come. Yet, despite being cast as a "feature of social and human progress" in the rapidly expanding economy of postwar France, there was no blueprint for what a *grand ensemble* was or what kind of social life it should facilitate.

The premise of the study was to answer exactly those questions. With its "general nomenclature" of collective facilities—eighty-five types including schools, shops, cultural centers, hospitals, churches, retirement homes, playgrounds, dispensaries, social centers, youth centers, kindergartens, sports centers, police headquarters, fire departments, post offices, and many more—it seemed to be the planner's ultimate shopping list for city building.[2] Titled "Grille d'équipement d'un grand ensemble d'habitation" but soon known as the *grille Dupont* after the state administrator in charge, the publication set the parameters for intensive reflection on the design of mass housing estates and collective facilities during the following decades. The journal *Urbanisme* would become the key log of such reflection because it brought designers, state administrators, and social scientists into an intensive dialogue. The journal itself was as much a propaganda tool as the self-critical report of an ongoing exploration. Funded by the state-owned Caisse des dépôts (CDC, or Deposits and Consignments Fund) and cofounded by the Société française des urbanistes, France's professional association of urbanists, it embodied the close relationship between the profession and the state. Yet it was hardly the only journal that reported on the development of mass housing. Extensive reportage and special issues proliferated over the years to come. What these had in common was fundamental ambiguity when it came to a doctrine. Would the certainty of numbers and norms not assure the establishment of a clear recipe for mass housing, once and for all? Why, then, would the design and conception of the *grands ensembles* need to be continually revised? Even between the late 1950s and the late 1960s—a period when their basic policies, techniques, and formal examples were already in place and before they became fundamentally questioned—their conception was hardly set in stone. Evolving welfare policies, changing ideals and practices of social life, and continual reportage on the problems faced by inhabitants continued to unsettle established norms and principles. The result was a decade of intensive experimentation in design and social science revolving around the elusive idea of *animation*. The *grille Dupont* was only the beginning.

Stabilizing Critique

What set off the search for a doctrine for the *grands ensembles* was the pioneering research for Paris under direction of Pierre Sudreau.[3] As commissioner for construction and urbanism in the Paris region—before he became minister of construction—his main concern was how to manage the capital's rapid urban growth. In the fall of 1957, faced with the uncontrolled sprawl of new housing projects in the suburbs and concerned about their social repercussions,

Sudreau established a special committee, the Commission de la vie dans les grands ensembles (Committee for Life in the *grands ensembles*). This initiative brought together architects, urbanists, state administrators such as Gérard Dupont, social housing experts, social scientists, representatives of family and women's organizations, medical doctors, schoolteachers, and landscape architects to study the urbanism of the *grands ensembles*. The gathering also included Jacques-Henri Labourdette, the architect in charge of building Sarcelles at this time, as well as Hélène Gordon-Lazareff, founder and editor of the immensely popular women's weekly magazine *Elle*, and Jacques Goddet, editor of the nationwide sports daily *L'Équipe*.[4] The participation of such prominent public figures was certainly unusual, if not unprecedented. Because both publications interacted with a lot of average French people, their inclusion speaks to the organizers' ambition to reach a wide spectrum of the French population.

The meetings led to the creation of five different working groups focusing on social, cultural, and religious facilities, commercial facilities, studies of the urban environment, administrative and financial problems, and, finally, recreation and open-air sports. Following the basic assumption that collective facilities were crucial to life in mass housing areas, the principal goal was to "first of all define and subsequently finance and build these facilities."[5] In order to do so, social surveys, urban research, and public consultation were needed. The committee visited housing areas and individual apartments, interviewed inhabitants, and compiled lists of what they liked and disliked about their homes and neighborhoods.[6] The committee's reports exposed a variety of concerns, from kitchens that were too dark and too small and the ugliness ascribed to the new architecture to the unreasonably high prices of groceries in the new commercial centers and the need for more social centers. It consulted with social-scientific experts and public figures and gathered information through standard questionnaires sent to representatives of civil society organizations such as the Union féminine civique et sociale and the Scouts de France. On the basis of these, it compiled a detailed overview of "objective" criteria for different types of collective facilities—for instance, what a cultural center or a youth center should look like, what concrete activities it should facilitate.[7] Conspicuously absent from the list were cafés, bars, bistros, and restaurants. Although these could have been subsumed under the generic rubric of "commerce," it was clear that many committee members at the time considered such amenities inappropriate. That view would soon be criticized as "a sad mix of excessive puritanism and functionalism."[8]

When Sudreau became minister of construction in 1958, the work of the committee was not abandoned. On the contrary, it moved from the regional to the national level and resulted in the publication of the *grille Dupont* in 1959 (see Figure 3.1). The publication was presented as an important step in the making of an overarching doctrine, but not without a strategic ambiguity. Although in his introduction the minister was careful in calling the *grille* simply a "guide for practical use," the publication manifested the belief in a rigorous science for the design of mass housing estates, one that could enumerate "what needs to be done for a social and economic equilibrium, a happy individual and collective life."[9]

Around this time, a string of news articles and opinion pieces in national newspapers, popular magazines, and the specialized press brought the topic of the *grands ensembles* to public attention.[10] Journalists visited new housing projects in Sarcelles, Pantin, or La Courneuve and wrote hyperbolically about "cities without a past" and the "birth of a new civilization." Television reportage followed suit. The makers of "Sarcelles, 40 000 voisins," an episode from the popular series *Cinq colonnes à la une*, claimed to portray ordinary life in Sarcelles but ultimately mesmerized viewers by highlighting the alienating qualities of inhabitants' new environments. Journalists interviewed local inhabitants to reveal the challenges they faced, from muddy boots that were the result of living on a giant construction site to the absence of amenities and the long commutes to Paris. Sweeping helicopter views, emphasizing the inhuman scale of the new housing projects, dramatized their at times mundane plight (see Figure 3.2).

Figure 3.2. Stills from the television broadcast "Sarcelles, 40 000 voisins" in the series *Cinq colonnes à la une*, ORTF (Office de radiodiffusion-télévision française), December 2, 1960.

The lack of privacy was a key concern to many inhabitants. Despite the rhetoric of modern living, the reduction of norms for state-aided housing in the early 1950s had led to small rooms and minimum-sized apartments in the first generation of *grands ensembles*, as at Bron-Parilly and the first phases of Sarcelles (see Figure 1.20 and Plate 1). Many inhabitants deemed the number of units serviced per hallway or staircase too high; it produced a sense of overcrowding and lack of intimacy. Moreover, the pioneering use of novel prefabrication techniques on a large scale had in many cases led to technical deficiencies: unmanageable heating systems, windows that did not close properly, construction elements such as prefabricated staircases that suddenly collapsed, and, especially, bad sound insulation. Inhabitants seemed to constantly know what their neighbors were up to, even at the most inappropriate times. This ecology of sound had a direct impact on the perception of privacy: "From ten o'clock on, even in spring, the *grand ensemble* sleeps. Each and every sound is then unseemly, insolent; you have to apologize for being there, for having a friend over, for shaking the ashes from your pipe, for having the habit of brushing your teeth long before going to bed."[11]

Other complaints centered on the geographic location of many housing estates. Cut off from the rest of the city, they left residents socially isolated and with strenuously long commutes to work. Inhabitants of housing projects in the Parisian suburbs often took more than one hour to get into the city, which was the necessary transfer point for any other regional destination in the heavily centralized capital. In extreme cases, such as that of the Floréal housing area near Saint-Denis, two buses were needed just to go to the old center of Saint-Denis, and because the planned commercial center was not yet finished, the estate did not have a single shop: "Yes, really, we are here like on an island," the inhabitants concluded.[12] The lack of nearby amenities in such peripheral locations—schools and shops in the first place—only aggravated this sense of isolation.[13]

Public criticism was also focused on the architecture of the new developments. Their *gigantisme*, an explicit search for grandness and monumental scale, the uniformity of their buildings and dwelling types, and the absence of trees, streets, and other traditional socializing spaces were recurring themes of critique. Journalists were among the first to relate such characteristics to the spread of social and psychological disorders, depression and suicide among housewives being mentioned most often. According to the popular science magazine *Science et Vie*, this new suburban world was nothing less than "the evil of numbers, half-light, and noise; the evil of calculated space, of impossible solitude and overriding silence; the evil of the *grands ensembles*. . . . In one word, it is the world of isolation and promiscuity, of boredom and clamor: in the language of tenants as well as experts, it is hell."[14]

The government was attentive to these critiques, if only to subsequently rebut them. In a brief study commissioned in 1959 by the Ministry of Construction analyzed a variety of critiques from recently published news articles. Interested in who the public blamed for the perceived errors, it found that the centralized state administration was number one on the list, the architects second, and then the engineers and the construction and management companies. It tended to dismiss the bulk of critique on the basis of its "weak use of evidence": the statements made were "often personal" rather than accompanied by "real quantitative evidence."[15]

Negative reactions from inhabitants and the press only increased in subsequent years, but could not shake the conviction that the *grands ensembles* were the unavoidable face of contemporary urbanism and the logical expression of Western economic development. Pierre Randet, then in charge of the Direction d'aménagement du territoire but with a lifelong career in state-led urban planning, contended that, rather than the "diabolical invention of esthetes or technocrats," the formula of the *grands ensembles* was simply "imposed by the scale of the economic and social conditions of our era. Whether a factory for two thousand workers needs to be installed, or a city of eight or ten thousand inhabitants to be built, it is necessary to do in two or three years what used to take decades or centuries; we need to rationally find the secrets of a harmony that used to emerge by itself thanks to the unison of people with their territory. . . . We need to make an effort to insert more diversity in the recruitment of new inhabitants of the *grands ensembles,* as in the composition of volumes and forms."[16]

In the eyes of administrators, the *grands ensembles* were crucial to the national economy and the organization of labor. To facilitate the movement of workers to new industrial plants, often located in regions lacking the required labor, mass housing construction was indispensable. The New Town of Mourenx, built at the end of the 1950s to house the workers of the nearby industrial complex of Lacq in the Pyrenees, became a well-known example, just like the housing estates built around the industrial zones of Dunkerque. Marxist scholars during the 1970s would interpret such developments as vehicles of state-capitalist exploitation. At the time, however, even the studies of Henri Lefebvre—who would later earn the status of being one of their most outspoken critics—confirmed the dominant logic of the *grands ensembles.* In his 1960 sociological research on Mourenx and his critique of a Swiss New Town proposal in Furttal published the following year, he dismissed the rigid functionalism of these schemes but did not fundamentally question the basic premise of large-scale state-led development. In other words, his critique did not (yet) open up to a different kind of urbanism: the idea was to *improve* mass housing estates by combatting the everyday boredom they created.[17]

Voices outside of the realms of government and expertise further confirmed such convictions. Even from angles where alternatives to state-led collective mass housing could be most expected, such as the Castors communities of self-builders, the *grands ensembles* were regarded as practically inevitable.[18] Within the cultural worldview of France, there was no real alternative to them. The question was not *if* but *how* to build them. This state of affairs afforded policy makers and architects the space to proffer up critique without dismissing the *grands ensembles* altogether. Soon after the publication of the *grille*, *L'Architecture d'aujourd'hui*, another leading professional journal, joined in such critiques. In a 1960 overview of ongoing construction, it decried the "mediocrity and dispersion" of mass housing projects around Paris. The same issue, however, contained an alternative proposal for a *grand ensemble* that was based on very similar urban concepts (Plate 3).

Pierre Sudreau, throughout his tenure as minister of construction from 1958 until 1962, embodied this paradoxical situation, in which critique strengthened rather than debilitated the reigning paradigm. In 1960, he issued a long statement about his visions for architecture and urbanism, in which he condemned some errors of the *grands ensembles*: their disregard for the site in which they were implanted and the lack of architectural imagination.[19] Yet, despite his acknowledgment of "grave mistakes" already committed, he continued to proclaim that "the *grands ensembles* emerge from a logical prediction of needs; a healthy conception of Urbanism imposes them."[20] To avoid future mistakes, he issued guidelines focused on the importance of the natural landscape, the conservation of its beauty by a "harmony of forms," and the careful siting of construction projects. Nevertheless, his most important contribution to what would become the golden age of the *grands ensembles* would lie not in landscape preservation but rather in the development of facilities to animate the new estates.

Facilitations of Life

Earlier in the 1950s, civil society organizations, state administrators, and sociologists had already begun addressing problems with mass housing that had resulted from the lack of facilities or *équipement*. Denoting anything from post offices and grocery shops to community centers, this term was used to mean the collection of all amenities that support everyday life. In France, Paul-Henry Chombart de Lauwe had been one of the first to emphasize the relation between the life of a neighborhood and its *équipement*; he was convinced that better provision of collective facilities would help prevent social problems and encourage the development of more socially successful neighborhoods where people feel "at home."[21] He acknowledged the importance of quantitative studies to determine the appropriate program of facilities. Studying and equipping thus went hand in hand. By the end of the decade, the provision of collective facilities in new housing estates was advocated for by a variety of experts and users.[22] Although they did not necessarily link it explicitly to Chombart's ideal of community building, they did entrench the idea that the provision of facilities, in concert with sociological study of inhabitant needs, was the solution to social problems in mass housing.

Consequently, the Ministry of Construction made *équipement* central to its housing policy. The Centre d'études des équipements résidentiels (CEDER, or Study Center for Residential Facilities), a research cell established by Sudreau during the making of the *grille* in 1959, set the basic framework for studying and planning facilities. Its 1962 report relegated the study of inhabitants'"residential needs" to a detailed quantitative specification of collective facilities. These would minimize "tensions or deficiencies in social relations, maladjustment to collective life, the roving of children tending to certain forms of mental exasperation or pre-delinquency, and so on."[23] René Kaës's *Vivre dans les grands ensembles*, a 1963 sociological study based very much on Chombart's work, further galvanized these convictions.

Despite the fact that calls for collective facilities had initially emerged as criticism of large-scale mass housing, they actually helped to further the movement toward the large scale in housing policy. In order to do the *grands ensembles* better, they had to be done *bigger*. That would allow them to be more efficiently organized, more comprehensively planned, and better equipped. Faced with intensive speculation and the problem of finding available land, state planners became increasingly aware that the surge in mass housing production had not been accompanied with the necessary urban planning strategies. What demonstrated this was the unfortunate location of many recently built projects, far away from public transportation and existing town centers and sometimes even on land that was officially designated for agriculture and thus considered off-limits for housing construction, as at Sarcelles, Le Luth in Gennevilliers, and Les Courtillières in Pantin.[24] Such problems informed the 1957 law that allowed larger areas to be earmarked for urban development.[25] Subsequent legislation under Sudreau followed the same logic by instituting the ZUP (zones à urbaniser par priorité), a planning tool for large-scale urban development. While it reaffirmed the need for mass production through standardization and rationalization, this new legislation was also meant to regulate the integration of collective facilities in new housing projects.[26] The basic idea, shared by state administrators, urbanists, and many civil society leaders alike, was that the larger scale would be more efficient and not only encourage industrialized production techniques but also lead to a more fully equipped neighborhood environment. As such, *équipement*—the actual content of which continually evolved—became the common denominator of a range of corrective measures for that one decision that would remain untouched for the time being: the state-led production of mass collective housing in large estates.

While the *grille* linked the notion of *équipement* directly to mass housing estates, it was not entirely defined by them. The increasingly elaborate requirements for collective facilities in new housing estates were also part of a larger trajectory of state welfare. During the postwar boom, when economic growth expressed itself most visibly in a thriving consumer culture, the role of the French government came to be defined increasingly in terms of collective consumption. From child allowance to highway infrastructure, the state was understood as a provider of (politically neutral) public services and benefits. Some of these were taken over from civil society organizations and traditional institutions; others were meant to satisfy new needs. Furthermore, the massive state adoption of social welfare programs and organizations was accompanied by a redefinition of the meaning of *équipement*. During the late 1940s, the Plan Monnet still used the notion of *équipement* to refer to basic infrastructure such as ports, roads, and utilities. The term soon began to encompass an increasingly elaborate list of buildings and amenities, first including public administrative buildings such as fire stations and then modern collective facilities such as social and cultural centers. This shift surfaced in planning debates during the mid-1950s and became explicit in the preparations for the Fourth Plan, more particularly in its Commission de l'équipement urbain, which linked *équipement* directly to new housing developments. Part and parcel of this shift was the conviction that the provision of collective facilities was an apolitical matter. One of the planners, Jean Lemoine, best summarized this idea when he contended that "the morals and ideas have slowly evolved, charity imbued with paternalism was first replaced by the idea of social justice, and then simply by that of rational organization, whether it concerns the economy, social services, or culture."[27] That these collective facilities were focused first and foremost on the *grands ensembles* only underscores the importance of modern urbanism in the historical development of the French welfare state.

The *grille Dupont* was pioneering in that it brought a diversity of institutions within the purview of a single, systematic approach, one that aimed to translate all possible needs and types of facilities directly into an urban program. It reduced the variety of existing social institutions—from theaters to churches, each of which had its own distinct tradition and historical development—to differences in degree rather than kind. The fact that they could now all be understood as "facilitating entities" was a sign less of an all-encompassing modernist functionalism than of the prominence of the welfare state as a central form of oversight and source of provision in social life.

The term *grille* was a rather generic French management term, but its use in urban planning was not without ideology. As opposed to the still-dominant view of urbanism as "urban art," the *grille Dupont* rendered design into a scientific and efficient management process that could guarantee success. At this time, the *grille* had already been used as an urban planning tool by the Commissariat général du Plan (CGP). In response to the neglect by both private and public sectors of the development of commerce in the fast-growing suburbs, this planning think tank had proposed a *grille d'équipement commercial* that allowed planners to calculate the necessary commercial facilities of a given area.[28] Not unlike American approaches to shopping-mall development emerging at this time, this method implied both a market study of the purchasing power of the local and future population and a planning study to define the concrete commercial program. The *grille Dupont* closely followed this approach. In contrast to American practices, its use in France was fundamentally driven by what was perhaps the main conviction underlying French modernization, namely, the superiority of the state vis-à-vis the market in the rational management of economic affairs. Concomitant with this belief was the assumption that centralized planning would be more efficient than spontaneous development. The authors of the *grille* thus emphasized that "the solution to absolutely avoid is to realize the commercial facilities in the *grands ensembles* in the form of an assemblage of different shops, the nature and size of which would be defined only empirically or by the random application of merchants. This would lead to commercial amenities corresponding neither to inhabitants' needs nor to those of the merchants. Instead, commercial facilities need to be conceived in general, in their totality, and adopted in each *grand ensemble*."[29] The direct spatial translation of this idea was the planned commercial center, which remained unquestioned until the second half of the 1960s when economic failure and the criticism of bored consumers contested it. Until that time, the method of the *grille* was used widely inside the state apparatus.

A different sort of *grille* that might have inspired French planners at the time was used in the postwar Congrès internationaux d'architecture moderne (CIAM). In these famous meetings, the *grille* was first and foremost a system for graphically organizing information by means of coded panels that could be assembled into larger screens.[30] As such, it allowed systematic comparison of all projects presented at the meetings. Each project was initially broken down into objective characteristics: horizontally according to the four functions and vertically according to particular themes—environment, land use, constructed volume, and so on. The grid thus functioned not only as a tool for reading but also for conceiving of architectural and urban projects. Yet, its function was altered at the 1951 meeting, where the Modern Architectural Research Group had proposed a simplified grid. Under the influence of Jacqueline Tyrwhitt, whose ideas were partly inspired by Joseph Lluis Sert, the presentations now came to be organized according to the scale of settlements: the village or primary housing group, the neighborhood, the town or city sector, the city itself, and, finally, the metropolis or multiple city.[31]

Sudreau's committee developed a similar principle by organizing its list of collective facilities in five nested sociospatial scales: the residential group (200–500 dwelling units), the neighborhood unit (800–1,200 units or 3,000–4,500 inhabitants), the *quartier* (1,500–2,500 units), the arrondissement (3,000–6,000 units), and ultimately the city at large (see Figure 3.1).[32] The residential group would have a minimum number of facilities: parking spaces, green space, a children's playground, and street furniture. At the neighborhood unit level, a preschool and primary school should be provided, as well as social amenities such as a daycare center, a small medical center, a social center, a youth community center, and fifteen to twenty shops for everyday necessities. At the level of the *quartier*, composed of two neighborhood units, inhabitants would find a "religious center," a day nursery, additional social facilities for youth, other shops, a public market, and so on. Finally, a secondary school, more playgrounds, a dispensary, and a principal commercial center with larger and more specialized stores should be located at the level of the arrondissement. These hierarchical scales were based on the assumption that individual inhabitants' needs could be satisfied within strictly delineated spatial realms. The concept of the commercial and community center was part and parcel of this approach: local facilities would be concentrated in smaller, secondary centers for everyday necessities at the center of each unit, while the principal commercial center would serve a larger area's more specialized needs. This urbanism of "hermetic boxes" made it possible to specify for each type of facility an average square footage, and for each of the spatial units, an ideal proportion of surfaces allocated to housing, collective facilities, parking space and circulation, and finally, green space.

Of course, this ideal scenario was rarely built as such. In reality, many contingencies crossed planners' paths. A crucial limitation was the availability of land, which, together with fragmented ownership structures, land speculation, lengthy expropriation procedures, and physical restrictions—topography, infrastructure, or existing buildings—left architects and planners with less-than-ideal options for their schemes. Nevertheless, throughout the 1960s the *grands ensembles* continued to be thought of in terms of the neighborhood unit. Plans were based less on close-up sociological observation than on ideal spatial conceptions of everyday life. For François Parfait, director of the Société centrale pour l'équipement du territoire, a large state-owned developer, the ideal *grand ensemble* was "a coordinated planning operation of an entire Neighborhood Unit or a part of one or more units, conceived to satisfy the needs of the different categories of inhabitants that need to live together in it."[33]

The formal conception of many *grands ensembles* embodied such idealizations. In typical projects, including Sarcelles, Épinay-sur-Seine, or Massy-Antony, the housing blocks were arranged in a grid delineating the different neighborhood units, not unlike the pattern of an electronic chip. The dictum of light, air, and openness created a spatial framework in which collective facilities could be plugged in as independent entities, simple add-ons to the basic program of mass housing (Figure 3.3). This formal and functional independence coincided with the particular financing structure of the *grands ensembles*, for housing construction funding was readily available through state loans and subsidies, whereas that of collective facilities was problematic and initially dispersed over an unwieldy number of state institutions, including the Social and Economic Development Fund, the Ministry of National Education, the Ministry of Youth and Sports, the Ministry of Public Health, the Ministry of Culture, the Ministry of Construction, the Ministry of the Interior, local municipalities, public credit organizations, and social security organizations. This was an important reason why so many projects contained only housing, and lacked collective facilities, at least initially.[34]

Community, a Sociological Modernism

The notion of community that ran through French urban planning at this time was both an ideal and an understanding of the world as is. What linked the *grille Dupont* to earlier concepts

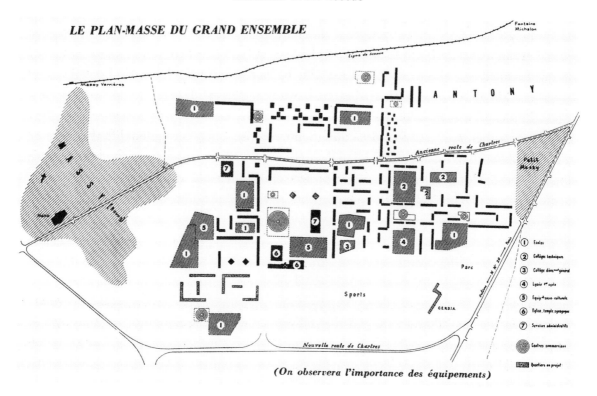

Figure 3.3. The *grand ensemble* of Massy-Antony by the architect Pierre-Édouard Lambert, 1954–61. Key: 1 = primary schools; 2 = technical schools; 3 = general high schools; 4 = lyceums; 5 = sociocultural facilities; 6 = church, temple, or synagogue; 7 = administrative services; round target = commercial centers. From *Hommes et Commerce—Revue de synthèses et de recherches économiques* 1, no. 72 (March–April 1963): 54.

of the neighborhood unit from Clarence Perry onward was the assumption that to a certain spatially delineated area corresponded a specific form of sociability. Despite its global applications from the American Greenbelt towns to the Soviet micro-rayons (micro-districts or residential complexes), the modernist concept of the neighborhood in postwar France was supported by a specific vision of community, often inspired by "slum sociology." The ideal of a closely knit community sharing local amenities bore remarkable resemblances to the sociological descriptions of poor inner-city neighborhoods that the *grands ensembles* were meant to replace. As Christian Topalov has shown in his comparative analysis of postwar urban sociology, working-class neighborhoods were "discovered" at the time they were about to vanish. Like William Foote Whyte and Herbert Gans in the United States or Michael Young and Peter Willmott in Britain, French sociologists such as Henri Coing no longer portrayed them as chaotic spaces of promiscuity and moral degeneracy but cast them as socially structured spaces in which the density of human interrelations produced an intimate sense of community.[35] Fundamental to such sociology in France was not only the work of Chombart, whose romantic solidarity with the French working classes paralleled Coing's, but also the surveys of working-class urban space by associations such as Économie et humanisme and the work of the urban historian Louis Chevalier.[36] They created a vivid image of Paris that was often as impassioned in its spirit as it was scientific in its ethnographic detail. Between the early 1940s and the mid-1950s, such studies made working-class neighborhoods visible in a new light. Emphasizing their informal, tightly knit communities, their density of encounters, their lively streets, their spontaneous sociability, their festivities, and their outdoor life, they became a model rather than a curse. As French planners and sociologists held up such ideals of community for the *grands ensembles*, they projected the lifeworld of the nineteenth-century *quartier populaire* onto suburban developments across the national territory of a modernizing France.

Despite international correspondences in postwar sociology and planning and the significant influence of the British New Towns in France at this time, the intellectual provenance of community as a concept in French urban design was distinct from that of the neighborhood unit in the Anglo-American planning tradition. Conceived as an intermediary sphere in between the centralized state and the individual citizen, the notion of community was inspired by social Catholicism and in particular by the work of urbanists such as Gaston Bardet and Robert Auzelle.[37] Their basic assumption was that communities were the building blocks of national solidarity and that their specific social morphology depended on a particular spatial organization, which could therefore be fostered by state intervention. Such isomorphism between the social and the spatial was well received in the French social sciences at the time, based on the pioneering work of Maurice Halbwachs and Marcel Mauss and subsequently developed by the ethnographer Marcel Griaule, who had used aerial photography to explain the community life of Dogon villages in West Africa.[38] Bardet, who was closely linked to the Économie et humanisme group and had positioned himself explicitly against what he saw as the excessively functionalist approach of CIAM and Le Corbusier, harnessed these basic propositions in his call for an urbanism of "community neighborhood units" ("unités communautaires de voisinage"). In other words, what in some contexts, such as Sweden, might have been considered a direct expression of functionalism came to be portrayed in France as a humanist remedy against its excesses.[39]

The publication of the *grille Dupont* featured one of Bardet's more famous citations from his book *Le nouvel urbanisme*: "The city as it is conceived: a spot, an endless expansion of a central point; the city as it is: a cluster, a federation of communities."[40] Concepts such as "cluster" were used both to describe the sociospatial structure of existing cities and to project a novel, "organic" structure for new urban development. By emphasizing the importance of local neighborhood life in housing estates and by organizing their own research in such spatial hierarchies, sociologists such as Chombart further strengthened the use of the neighborhood unit in urban planning.[41]

The *grille Dupont* thus entailed a "structuralization" and "sociologization" of architectural modernism. That direction was not altogether dissimilar from the intellectual currents within Team X at this time, with one crucial difference. Rather than casting their work as a radical break from an earlier modernism, the architects and planners of the *grands ensembles* under-stood their work as a continuation. Soon after the publication of the *grille Dupont*, Maurice-François Rouge thus contended that "the goals [of the Athens Charter] were too general and not accompanied by structural principles, which are needed to provide the vision for attaining them. . . . The Athens Charter does not give any indication in terms of structure; one could say it is a-structural. And yet, to propose structure is the raison d'être of any science."[42] He consequently conceived of the *grand ensemble* as the result of four structural layers—func-tional, physical, socioprofessional, and aesthetic. The physical structure was made up of basic elements: service facilities, production facilities, dwelling facilities, and so on (Figure 3.4). Such schemes contributed to the conviction that the urbanism of the *grands ensembles* could be a social-scientific "completion" of the Athens Charter.

Despite such bold assertions to comprehensiveness, some pretty straightforward aspects of urban life were conspicuously ignored. Employment was one of them. The *grille* offered some minor reflections on the relation between living and working, or what it called the "economic structure of the *grand ensemble*." Its authors calculated that the number of jobs generated inside a *grand ensemble* would be only 18 percent of the total jobs required for its population. While claiming to be against a strict separation of housing and employment zones, they nev-ertheless neglected to offer specific suggestions on how these zones could be integrated. Urban planners at the time could not really respond to the widespread public criticism that the *grands ensembles* were *banlieues dormitoires* just like the interwar allotments to which they were sup-posed to be the solution.

The idea that science, structuralism, and sociology would complement the doctrines of interwar modernism remained strong, but it did not lead to the establishment of an ultimate doctrine. On the contrary, it set in motion a gradual questioning of some of the Charter's basic stipulations—the separation of functions and the abolition of the street being the most obvi-ous ones. In the years following the publication of the *grille Dupont*, the CGP continued to revise it and the results were published in 1962, again under the direction of Dupont in the journal *Urbanisme*. In the introduction, Jacques Maziol, Sudreau's successor, reaffirmed the policy of the *grands ensembles*, as they "effectively assure the indispensable coordination of housing with collective facilities."[43] Repatriation to the metropole as a result of French de-colonization, large-scale migration from the French countryside, and the French baby boom all exacerbated the need for housing, which remained undiminished throughout the 1960s. Large-scale mass housing estates continued to be the only imaginable response.

LES STRUCTURES

plan de la structure fonctionnelle	plan de la structure socio-professionnelle	plan de la structure physique	plan de la structure esthétique
Données démographiques, économiques et administratives.	Données sociologiques.	Schéma des tracés.	Transcendance artistique.
Données quantitatives, fournies par la science et corrigées par l'éthique.	Données quantitatives, fournies par la science et corrigées par l'éthique.	Données formelles, élaborées par la science et l'éthique et fournies à l'art.	Élément qualitatif, qui relève de l'éthique et de l'art.
Relèvent de l'**économiste,** de l'aménageur et de l'urbaniste.	Relèvent du **sociologue** de l'aménageur et de l'urbaniste.	Relèvent de l'**urbaniste.**	Relève de l'**urbaniste** et de l'**architecte.**

plan de la structure physique

éléments de base : les " équipements "

Équipements de services	Équipements de production	Équipements d'habitat		Équipements de liaison
		Équipements de logements	Équipements d'espaces verts	

notion de base : la " polarisation "

POLE	**AIRE D'INFLUENCE**	**SCHÉMA DE POLARISATION**	
Pôle principal, noyaux et pôles subordonnés.	Rayon d'action, étendue, limite ou cadre.	Schéma de répartition des noyaux et pôles secondaires par rapport aux pôles auxquels ils sont subordonnés.	Tracé des réseaux de liaison, convergents et divergents.

Pôle de la zone urbanisée

Pôle	**Zone d'action**	**Schéma de polarisation**	
Équipements de services groupés au centre.	Tissu résidentiel entourant le pôle avec, à l'extérieur, les équipements de production.	Schéma de polarisation propre à la zone urbanisée : pôle principal et hiérarchie de noyaux secondaires.	Hiérarchie de réseaux, essentiellement piétonniers, autour du pôle principal et des noyaux secondaires.

Pôle constitué par l'ensemble de la zone urbanisée

Pôle	**Aire d'influence**	**Schéma de polarisation**	
L'ensemble précédent (pôle et sa zone d'action).	Territoire environnant (espaces cultivés ou non, avec leurs pôles subordonnés, villages et même villes d'un rang secondaire par rapport au pôle considéré).	Deux schémas de polarisation, concentriques mais distincts, ceux : — de la zone urbanisée, — de l'aire d'influence.	Réseaux routiers, polarisés sur les voies de pourtour de la zone urbanisée.

limites de validité de la polarisation

Limite inférieure (concentrations humaines de très faible importance : milieu rural)		**Limite supérieure** (concentrations humaines importantes : milieu urbain)	
C'est la limite inférieure de l'état infra-urbain (voir ci-dessous).		C'est la limite supérieure de l'état urbain, qui sépare celui-ci de l'état supra-urbain.	
Pôle	**Aire d'influence**	**Pôle**	**Zone d'action**
Doit avoir un minimum d'habitants à desservir.	Ce minimum dépend de l'étendue de l'aire d'influence, qu'il faut donc pouvoir « cadrer » en conséquence.	Les services n'ont de valeur, pour les tissus résidentiels, qu'en deçà d'un certain rayon qu'il ne faut pas dépasser.	Le tissu résidentiel ne doit pas s'étendre au-delà d'une certaine distance du pôle (limite maxima de l'ordre de 2.000 m.).

caractéristiques de polarisation des trois états des concentrations urbaines

NIVEAU « INFRA-URBAIN » (Villages et bourgs)	**NIVEAU « URBAIN »** (Villes, Cités, Unités urbaines)	**NIVEAU « SUPRA-URBAIN »** (Soit Agglomérations, soit Fédérations de Cités)
Un seul pôle principal, sans pôles subordonnés.	Un seul pôle principal, avec un nombre limité de pôles subordonnés.	Plusieurs pôles principaux, avec chacun leurs pôles subordonnés.

Figure 3.4. "D'une doctrine des structures à l'esquisse d'une charte" (From a doctrine of structures to the outline of a charter), by Maurice-François Rouge, 1960. The scientific method of dividing problems into smaller subsets reinforced the conviction of planners like Rouge that social life can be understood and comprehensively planned through the smallest details. From *Urbanisme* 66 (1960): 12.

Many of the 1962 *grille* revisions were of theoretical rather than practical importance. The hierarchical urban scales, for instance, were tweaked: compared to the five original ones, the arrondissement level disappeared, and the size of the *quartier* level was doubled. These entities, however, rarely corresponded to the actual makeup of *grands ensembles* once built. More significant was the introduction of a distinction between "small and medium-sized ensembles" and "large ensembles," the latter when the number of inhabitants was over 25 percent of the population of the surrounding urban agglomeration. The idea that the size of a *grand ensemble* was relative to its surroundings was a first, albeit modest, acknowledgment of the importance of context. In his article on the evolution of recent French urbanism, also published in 1962 in *Urbanisme*, Dupont alluded to a more fundamental change in mind-set when he emphasized "the respect for measure, the concern with the landscape, the importance of intimate spaces encouraging social contact, shopping boulevards, and lively centers" as crucial concerns for future urbanism. "Against strict zoning has now emerged the desire to situate places of activity in the middle of residential zones, in order to facilitate human contacts, to create liveliness, and to bring employment closer to the home."[44] These novel ideas would not have a concrete impact until the later part of the 1960s, after the publication of another adjustment to the *grille*.

This second official adjustment, again published in *Urbanisme*, was based on extensive research by several committees inside the Ministry of Construction between October 1963 and February 1965. Basically, four kinds of spatial levels were now envisaged, divided into two types: the *unité d'habitations* (itself divided into the *résidence* of 50–150 units and the *groupe* of 200–500 units) and the *unité d'organisation urbaine* (divided into the *voisinage* of 800–1,200 units and the *quartier* of 2,500–5,000 units). This reorganization gave more weight to cultural facilities and exterior spaces, which were to be more finely distributed over the projects. The level of the city at large was eliminated because it was now acknowledged as being "incontrollable."[45] However, the real shift was clarified in the qualitative study that accompanied the *grille*. Planners now set themselves the goal to rethink the *grand ensemble* in its totality, "from the individual home to the city." They would do so by addressing "the absence of certain sociocultural facilities directly linked to the housing" and by focusing on "the whole of the nonbuilt space available to inhabitants."[46] The study was shaped by the ambition to bring into the realm of design a number of previously ignored aspects of the built environment, most important being the sensuous perception of the natural site, its colors, light, and microclimate, and the urban context. The researchers involved attempted to infer sociopsychological data from the physical qualities of the built environment:

> These phenomena—because they are unconsciously experienced and thus simply undergone—leave individuals without defense and play a role depending on the temperaments, a role

that, in the sociological surveys, is revealed in banal sayings ("we don't like it," "we're bored") or
false reasons ("the elevator doesn't work properly," "the school is too far"), while the real grievances can be entirely different: the apartment building is too high, the road that leads to the
school is boring, complicated, and interrupted by roads.[47]

Statements such as these implied a more central role for social science in design, and for urban
sociology in particular. For the authors of the study, the emerging discipline of urban sociology promised to transcend the "functionalist division of human activity," to encourage local
community life, and to lead to better design. Urban space, they argued, should be designed
according to the complexity of inhabitants' needs. The design of playgrounds should consequently be based on a detailed analysis of sociologically defined age groups and by giving
attention to these groups' "sensorial and mental development" (Figure 3.5). Such an attention
to children's experience was particularly pertinent to the *grands ensembles*, whose inhabitants
were predominantly young families with children. Another priority for a sociologically enriched

Figure 3.5. A sociological analysis of play areas was central to the second revision of the *grille Dupont*. From *Urbanisme*
90–91 (1965): 30–31.

urbanism, which the policy makers responsible for revising the *grille Dupont* would take to heart over the next years, was to transpose the architectural and social qualities of the traditional urban street into new principles of urban design (Figure 3.6).

In his introduction to the second revision, Yves Aubert advocated for the employment of social-scientific expertise in the earliest stages of the design process.[48] During the first half of the 1960s, similar calls for the inclusion of sociology had begun to enter the mainstream of French urbanism. A few years earlier, Randet had already contended that "the introduction of economic and social sciences in the antechamber of urban plan making has transformed bit by bit the job of the urban planner *[aménageur]*. The urbanist can no longer make his plans by himself; he needs to participate in a team in which the part of the architect— who has been the pioneer in urbanism—remains nevertheless important because it is he who is ultimately responsible for the creation of form."[49] During a 1964 national conference on

Figure 3.6. A spread titled "What is the street?" was included in the second revision of the *grille Dupont*. From *Urbanisme* 90–91 (1965): 18.

urbanism, which was characterized by professional anxiety, commentators observed that "it is an idea now generally accepted that urbanism requires the work of a multidisciplinary team."[50]

As such, the 1965 *grille* did not propose a ready-made formula for the *grands ensembles*. While the quantitative grid itself was reduced to a practical tool for administrative and financial planning, the accompanying studies implied the need for in-depth sociological study and insisted on the development of local urban research. The conception of the *grands ensembles* thus moved away from the dogmas of the Athens Charter under the influence of sociological expertise focused on their inhabitation. Exemplary in this evolution was the work of the CEDER, established as part of the original *grille Dupont*. The primary goal of this research center was to deliver the necessary preliminary studies for the programming and management of collective facilities in *grands ensembles*. These entailed not only an economic, demographic, and sociological understanding of the local context but also a study of needs as expressed by local inhabitants. By the time the center was dismantled in 1970, its researchers had carried out more than two hundred studies for housing projects across the country.[51] This wealth of studies showed that the *grille Dupont* did not just constitute a static doctrine or unquestioned recipe for an automated production of *grands ensembles*. Rather, it was part and parcel of an experimental process pointing not only to a different knowledge base but also to new formal principles for urban design.

The Rise of the Sociocultural

While the *grille Dupont* listed anything from shops to police stations and sewer installations, its 1965 revision focused specifically on what were termed "sociocultural" facilities. This modifier was meant to target social, youth, community, and cultural centers. Guy Houist, a key representative of national family organizations and member of the Economic and Social Council (Conseil économique et social), explained in the publication that these facilities constituted the French counterpart to the British notion of community building.[52] The sociocultural sector thus entailed both the physical infrastructure of these centers and the organization of social and cultural activities in and around them. Other observers explained that the appearance of this sector in France was a direct consequence of the awareness that social work was necessarily cultural in its contents and that culture inevitably had a social basis.[53] What all proponents agreed on was its ultimate goal: the prevention of social problems by creating community life.

The ground for these centers had been laid by socialist and social reform movements at the turn of the century. Their efforts to create a space that was free from the oppression of the work floor and the control of the church led to a new type of institution, the *maison du peuple*, literally, "house of the people." Containing an auditorium, various meeting rooms, and often a restaurant and bar, such establishments facilitated working-class leisure, education, and political organizing. They were cast as the vehicle of a new working-class culture, and their architecture was to facilitate as well as symbolically represent this aspiration. For his *maison du peuple* in Brussels, Victor Horta embraced the vegetal motifs of the Art Nouveau and exploited the new possibilities of iron and glass to create a large top-lit auditorium. Several decades later, Jean Prouvé, Eugène Beaudouin, Marcel Lods, and Vladimir Bodiansky employed the same basic program for the *maison du peuple* in Clichy, but now used the modernist metaphor of the building as machine.[54]

Regardless of formal continuities during the postwar decades, momentous changes in welfare provision fundamentally affected this institution's very reason for existence. As the rationality of the bureaucratic state eventually replaced the social ambitions of reformers, the type of the *maison du peuple* splintered into a panoply of facilities—community, social, and cultural centers, depending on specific aims and audiences. The social center in particular was cast as the modern successor of the previous type. In a 1952 report, the United Nations defined it as "an organization that, with the collaboration of users, endeavors to resolve the problems of the population of a neighborhood or geographic sector, by putting at its disposal, in an appropriate space, a set of services and collective realizations of an educational, social, or sanitary character, animated by a social worker who is responsible for the general functioning of the Center, needs to assure a permanent presence, and, if possible, reside there."[55] Such definitions conveyed the new sociotechnical paradigm replacing the overtly ideological reform agendas of previous decades. In France, this shift was brought about by the centralized state, which in coordination with a range of institutions—familial associations, employers' organizations, social security organizations—now took the lead in planning and managing such facilities across the nation.[56]

Spurred by rapid urbanization, social centers proliferated over the national territory but were particularly pertinent to the *grands ensembles*.[57] The Commission de la vie dans les grands ensembles stipulated that they should be built in each and every new neighborhood unit and proposed that they be housed on the ground floor of new housing slabs.[58] The committee members followed the United Nations definition, but they also wanted more. In their view, the new social center could do more than just "facilitate users' initiatives, contribute to the coordination of diverse social services, and evaluate the needs of its beneficiaries." Social centers were deemed crucial because they could actually "create the social life that was initially absent in the *grands ensembles*."[59] Such ambitions were inscribed in a larger shift in French welfare, from a model based on paternalism and guardianship to one of mass consumption and personal and community development. It was a shift that affected not only the social center but a range of facilities for which the state took increasing responsibility.

One institution developed in particular proximity to it: the cultural center. Just as social centers were no longer to reform the socially "unadapted," so would these facilities no longer "uplift" the masses but instead provide the general public with access to culture. In France, the creation in 1959 of a new Ministry of Cultural Affairs led by the charismatic André Malraux marked not only the birth of a veritable cultural policy; it also formalized the new welfare project in cultural terms.[60] The ministry's official mission was "to make the most important works of humanities, and first of all of France, accessible to the largest possible number of Frenchmen."[61] In order to democratize culture, it had to be decentralized and disseminated over the national territory. With this in mind, Malraux made the construction of *maisons de la culture* and cultural centers the centerpiece of his political project. Shaped by earlier concerns with national heritage, as well as by the Gaullist project of national modernization, the initiative had affinity with popular education movements such as Peuple et culture, for whom the cultural center was first and foremost an instrument of social development. While Malraux's new institutions were architecturally innovative—taking formal cues from the popular *salle de spectacle*, for instance, in order to break with the bourgeois theater—their democratizing effects were nevertheless limited. Only six such cultural centers were finished by 1965. Experts in the social and cultural sector were quick to question their impact, not only because of the small number of new centers but also because their conservative definition of culture as artistic genius did not allow them to reach a broad enough audience.[62]

Another emerging type, initially confused with Malraux's initiatives, was the *maison des jeunes et de la culture*, or "youth and cultural center." Youth centers had been around since the interwar period but became more prominent in response to the rise of youth as a new social problem. Moral panic about youth violence erupted after a series of widely reported incidents with *blousons noirs*—groups of young delinquents held together by a new subculture of pop music, cars, and fashion—in the summer of 1959.[63] When the journalist Michel de Saint-Pierre responded to such incidents by claiming that "the *grands ensembles* are the factories of the *blousons noirs*," the problem of youth became associated specifically with mass housing projects.[64] This remained so throughout the 1960s and after. Because their first inhabitants were predominantly young families with children, adolescents constituted an increasingly important social group in such areas—if less because of sheer quantity than as a result of urban imagination. Movies such as Marcel Carné's *Terrain vague* of 1960 helped shape the popular image of bored youth gangs hanging out in the hallways, outdoor spaces, and construction sites of suburban housing estates (Figure 3.7). How to keep such adolescents busy thus became a key question. A growing number of sociologists—such as Jacques Jenny, a close collaborator of Chombart—concerned themselves with the "problem" of youth, and sociological analysis often suggested a clear solution: the creation of specialized facilities appropriate to the needs and aspirations of youth.[65]

In 1958, fewer than two hundred youth centers could be counted in France, and the majority of them were located in rural communities. By the end of the 1960s, there were more than

Figure 3.7. Film stills from the movie *Terrain vague* by Marcel Carné, 1960.

a thousand, primarily located in *grands ensembles*.[66] While older youth centers continued to operate, the new generation was fundamentally different in its focus on modern recreation. Facilitating activities from table tennis to theater performance, from judo to photography, and from poetry club to Esperanto course, the new centers often contained meeting rooms, conference rooms, offices, and, at times, an auditorium. When they were not incorporated in the housing slabs or the commercial centers, they were shaped as isolated pavilions in between the housing slabs. Some emulated the horizontality of the elongated housing slabs around them as if to express the same architectural language of openness and equality. Others performed their own sculptural identity to express a communal focal point. But they all avoided the hierarchy, monumentality, and sense of closure of traditional institutional architecture (Figure 3.8).

Despite the diverse origins and target audiences of social, cultural, youth, and other centers, planners increasingly emphasized their similarities. They saw parallels not only in terms of activities, funding, and management, but especially in terms of their social ambitions. Expert arguments for concerted planning at this time lent force to the idea of a systematic approach under the banner of the sociocultural sector. That ambition was fundamentally shaped by the notion of *animation*, by which planners meant the incitement of community life and activities. During the 1960s, neighborhood facilities were increasingly conceived of as *pôles d'animation* or "participatory centers."[67] The idea was specifically associated with mass housing estates and prompted by the government's attempts at improving life in them.[68] While the term *usager* or user remained predominant in describing the need for such facilities, it also became contested: people could no longer just be passive beneficiaries; they needed to assert themselves as active

Figure 3.8. The youth center of Sarcelles, early 1960s. Caisse des dépôts et consignations, CDC 2-C-006. Copyright Studio Martin.

participants.[69] Some proponents saw the sociocultural sector as being based on the principles of "self-help," referring explicitly to the English term.[70] Many state administrators agreed, contending that "the specific character of the sociocultural domain lies in the active participation of users. This is what distinguishes it from commercial leisure and certain forms of recreation in which the user remains simply a passive user."[71] Jean-Paul Imhof, a key proponent of the newly forged domain of intervention, defined it in similar terms as "comprising a variety of activities that take place principally during free time and that are consequently based on voluntary participation, the object of which is the development of the participant's physical, affective, and intellectual skills in a collective environment that stimulates the development of social relations, and, eventually, the assumption of responsibility."[72]

The social organizer Henri Théry went as far as to call *animation* a new paradigm for French society.[73] Until recently, he claimed, "emphasis was only on the creation and administration of things," but postwar consumerism, mass production, and state welfare had prompted "the imperative of *animation*. To animate is to give life, to create or activate a vital process through which individuals and groups affirm themselves and get going; it is to generate a dynamism that is at once biological and spiritual, individual and social." For Théry and others, this was a matter of distinguishing between active, participating citizens and passive consumers, and consequently between neighborhoods with and without a "soul."[74] *Animation*, state administrators and urban planners contended, used to be assured *spontaneously* by the local communities and municipalities. But because of large-scale migration to the city and the construction of entirely new urban areas, inhabitants were having problems settling into the housing projects built for them. To integrate them, planners argued, *organized* social and cultural activities and community events—in other words, *animation*—were needed. In the context of the *grands ensembles*, the meaning of the concept was thus fundamentally ambivalent: it referred both to the spontaneous liveliness of a neighborhood and to the artificial means of instilling community life in new housing areas through organized activities.

Since the early 1950s, an increasing number of experts became concerned with the question of how to transform mass housing into successful neighborhoods. As construction continued at an unprecedented pace during the 1960s, the impetus to "give life" to the *grands ensembles*, to "humanize the concrete," manifested itself only more acutely.[75] At least for some, the ultimate rationale was to quash potential social unrest: "Technically, *animation* appears as a specific response to new needs, born from the transformations of collective life, and consequently it has a function of adapting people to new forms of collective life. In particular, its goal is to make very complex social organisms work, like the new housing estates that are threatened by paralysis as a result of malfunctioning communications, dissenting attitudes, friction, and protest."[76] To others it was a means to address the growing dangers of human alienation, which had expanded from the realm of work to that of consumption and everyday life more broadly, and for which the *grands ensembles* had become the exemplar.

What experts and community leaders increasingly agreed on then was that the development of community life required *new* kinds of spaces that could facilitate activities in which inhabitants could freely participate. A first attempt to translate this idea into an urban planning strategy was the experiment with what were called *locaux collectifs résidentiels* or "residential meeting places" from 1960 onward. Planners thought of them as spaces in between the privacy of the home and the publicity of the park or the commercial center. Distributed inside the housing projects, primarily on the ground floor of the housing blocks, they would be used by local residents for a range of recreational activities—family parties, block meetings, creative workshops, youth meetings, children's games, and so on. This was an idea already tested in Soviet urbanism and in the architecture of municipal socialism during the interwar period.[77] It had also been conceptualized by architects including Le Corbusier, more particularly through his concept of the *prolongements du logis* or "extensions of the dwelling" that were essential to everyday life. And it had been proposed by sociologists like Chombart, who had argued on multiple occasions for the social importance of intimate spaces for inhabitants to socialize.[78]

The initiative was officially launched in 1960 when the Ministry of Construction recommended that developers provide 0.30 m² of collective meeting space per dwelling unit.[79] Not many were actually built: the lack of enforcement, absence of funding, unclear management, and difficulties of implementation disincentivized developers. Of the spaces that did get built, often on the ground floor of housing blocks, many were poorly managed and underused.[80] In subsequent years, planners and state administrators continued to emphasize the need for such spaces and obliged developers to provide them. A new law in 1965, pushed by Aubert at the ministry, raised the bar to one square meter per dwelling unit and suggested more concrete options for management.[81] Despite these efforts and the relative success of a few experiments, such collective spaces never became a standard feature of the *grands ensembles*. A 1969 law gave developers the choice, instead of obligation, to build them. This meant a de facto abandonment of the entire idea. If the discrete insertion of specialized facilities in otherwise unaltered mass housing schemes was not successful, what then would be? This question, increasingly shared by designers, planners, and policy makers, would lead to more fundamental revisions of the overall conception of mass housing during the 1960s. Designers became aware that bringing the built environment to life was not only a matter of sociology or social work; architecture and urbanism could play a part as well. It was the imperative of "animating" the *grands ensembles* that would thus have a direct impact on their urban design.

Animating Designs

The ideas around *animation* had in fact already begun to trigger architectural solutions, at least since the work of the Commission de la vie dans les grands ensembles in 1958. In one of the committee's working groups, on the "study of the urban environment," the notion of *animation* was considered as a way of synthesizing the concerns of all other working groups, and the reason was that it allowed members to think about environment in both social and architectural terms. Their concerns were both fundamental and mundane: "an important task of this [group] is to study the rules that can give life and animation to the street or to public spaces, by assuring their equipment (taxi phones, mailboxes, vending machines, public lighting . . .), by drawing conclusions from studies about the density of passersby each hour of the day, and by studying the rules of typical construction that can assure the harmony of architectural lines and avoid the monotony of facades."[82] Soon after, such an inclusive understanding of *anima-tion* inspired architects to rethink some of the urban design concepts for the *grands ensembles*.

The French architects of mass housing were, of course, hardly alone in this respect. Every-day sociability and urban liveliness had become major concerns for architects internationally during the 1950s, partly under the influence of Team X, and had informed new modernist designs, such as Alison and Peter Smithson's "streets-in-the-air." But this was just one version of how traditional urbanity could be reimagined. Many other Team X architects saw design potentials in the study of everyday life, which they appreciated in its "purest" form in Mediter-ranean hill towns and lively working-class streets. Aldo van Eyck's architectural language, at once poetic and anthropological, was perhaps most sophisticated and resulted from a struc-turalist rigor inspired by the work of the French anthropologist Claude Lévi-Strauss.[83] Such intellectual borrowing also informed new formal concepts of cluster, stem, and web, harnessed in designs of large-scale housing and urban projects across national borders. The work of Candilis-Josic-Woods, the only proponents of Team X in France, functioned as a conduit for translating some of these ideas into French mass housing design. By the late 1960s, the firm had designed about forty thousand dwelling units in France.[84]

Their most iconic large-scale housing project was that of Toulouse-le-Mirail. Begun in 1961, the project further developed the concepts of "stem" and "cluster," largely derived from the theories of the Smithsons (Figure 3.9).[85] The street, which the architects understood at once as a morphological urban structure and a crucial dimension of everyday life, functioned as the structuring device for the development, a massive New Town for a hundred thousand inhabitants. The project was a primary case study in the 1962 *grille* revision. Referring to Georges Candilis's 1962 article "À la recherche d'une structure urbaine,"[86] the research accom-panying its second revision acknowledged the pertinence of his ideas, often formulated as an implicit critique of the monotony of an older generation of *grands ensembles:* "it is necessary to reestablish the notion of the 'street,' which has disappeared in current projects. . . . The street becomes an active center through the diversity of its components; it reintegrates the spon-taneous character of everyday life, in opposition with the sphere of repetition, uniformity, and banality."[87]

Urban spontaneity, liveliness, and diversity were the conceptual ingredients of this new vision of an animated urban space, which found application, albeit in often watered-down fragmentary ways, in new projects during the later part of the 1960s. One of these was the *grand ensemble* of Bures-Orsay, designed by Robert Camelot and François Prieur.[88] The proj-ect renounced the idea of zoning in favor of a formal complexity that was thought to evoke a lively sense of place. "We cannot add the unexpected," the architects contended in an article accompanying the project's publication in the journal *Urbanisme.* "It needs to be provoked: the basic scheme needs to engender fortunate coincidence, that of volumes or spaces, as much as

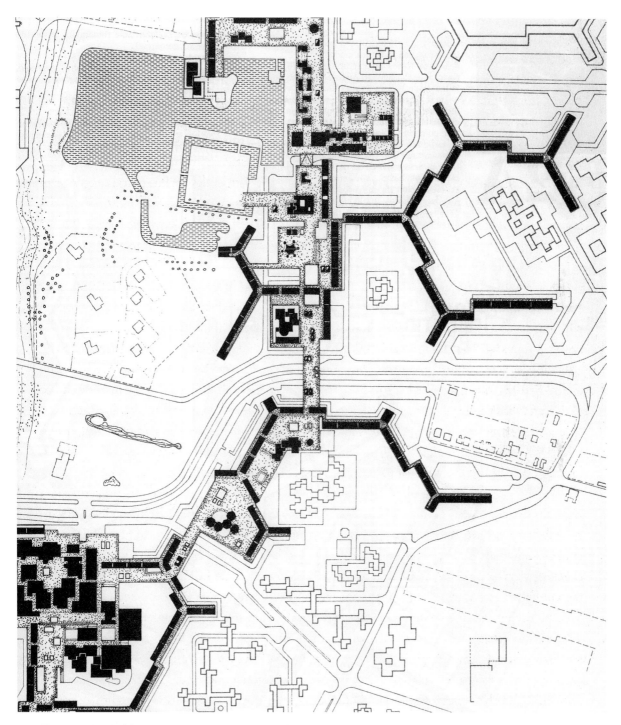

Figure 3.9. Detail of the street conceived as a raised platform that connects the hexagonally laid-out housing slabs. Candilis-Josic-Woods for Toulouse-le-Mirail, 1961–71. From Candilis-Josic-Woods, *Toulouse le Mirail—El nacimiento de una ciudad nueva* (Barcelona: Gustavo Gili, 1976), 29.

that of spontaneous activities."[89] Concretely, their plan consisted of two separated networks of circulation: a basic layout of roads and a network of pedestrian pathways. The housing blocks were placed alongside these paths so as to create an enclosed, intimate streetscape.

The publication featured a series of diagrams that aimed to represent the future "density of *animation*" of one of its neighborhoods by visualizing the imagined everyday movements of future inhabitants (Figure 3.10). According to the architects, calculations were based on the estimated power of attraction of individual amenities at different times of the day. The image they depicted was an idyll of street life, one in which cars were absent, children would play freely, adults would stroll and meet spontaneously, and the elderly would sit in the sun to distract themselves with the pleasure of seeing others. This kind of *animation urbaine*, they argued, was inscribed in the plan itself. Embracing spatial and formal complexity was part of their strategy to assure that the project would have "an organic life in which the different organs are imbricated and live in symbiosis."[90]

The layout, however, reiterated the concept developed by Candilis-Josic-Woods for their 1961 competition entry of Caen-Hérouville and subsequently used in Toulouse-le-Mirail: while the architectural form differed substantially by abandoning the hexagonal pattern of housing slabs, the basic diagrams were followed faithfully (Figure 3.11). Prieur and Camelot also added a "principal urban center" in the middle of the new development (at the western side of the first phase) that linked up with surrounding neighborhoods via overpasses. Schools, shops, and other collective amenities were no longer morphologically detached from this structure as they were in older *grands ensembles*. They were now inserted in the pedestrian areas in order to assure a "natural" liveliness, and their entrances, as well as those of the residential units, gave out onto this space for the same reason.

The designs for Surville in Montereau and that of Nîmes-Ouest by the brothers Xavier and Luc Arsène-Henry exemplified other directions for *animation* as an architectural concept. In the eyes of the architects, *animation* entailed not only spatial complexity, an increased urban density, and more public amenities, but, most important, an attention to the temporal and ephemeral qualities of the built environment.[91] Following the spatial trajectory of the inhabitant—the gradual transition from the intimacy of the dwelling to the publicity of the street and the urban center—they proposed a corresponding increase in the density of *animation*. This elusive quality was represented with a map of what were called "iso-densities." To realize such gradual qualities, attention needed to be given not only to the architectural design of urban streetscapes but also to a range of other environmental features. One of these was advertising. Rather than ignoring or trying to ban it, the architects were aware of the positive value of public advertising, displays, posters, and other kinds of urban graphics, which "accompany, underline and valorize the lively, attractive, colored, and changing character of facades, pedestrian passages, or urban perspectives" and give pedestrians and car drivers focus and

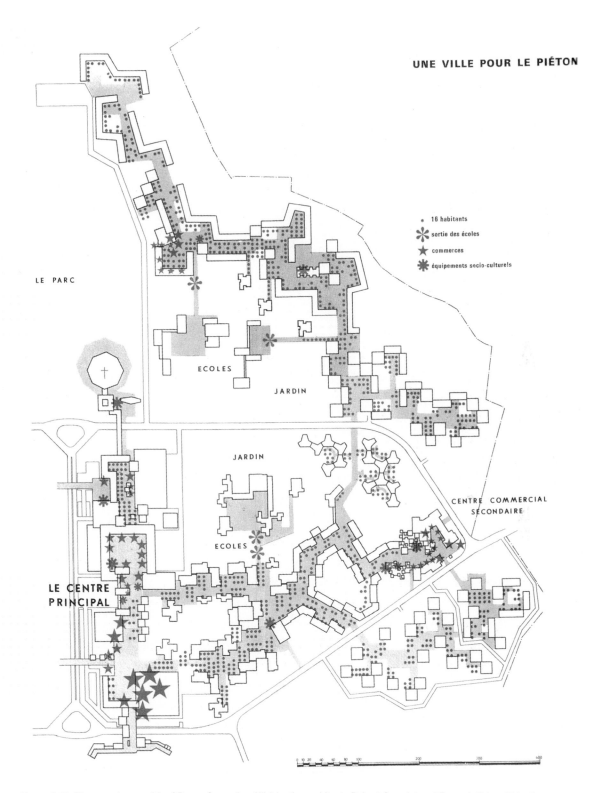

Figure 3.10. The *grand ensemble* of Bures-Orsay (Les Ulis) by the architects Robert Camelot and François Prieur. This diagram from 1967 depicts the density of people in the neighborhoods' public space, clustered around school entrances, shops, and sociocultural facilities. From *Urbanisme* 102–3 (1967): 68.

Figure 3.11. Diagram submitted by
Candilis-Josic-Woods for the 1961
competition for Caen-Hérouville.
Shadrach Woods Collection, Drawings
and Archives, Avery Architectural and
Fine Arts Library, Columbia University.

eventfulness in the urban spaces they traverse.[92] To the architects, the ultimate form of *anima-tion* seemed to be the open-air market, suggesting a temporal approach to programming urban spaces that only decades later would really become popular (Figure 3.12). Yet another important aspect to which the architects drew attention was the nocturnal atmosphere of the urban development: public lighting of facades, monuments, and trees, light displays, street signs, and shop windows—in their eyes, all contributed to "the wonderful, the unreal, and the poetic" elements of the urban landscape, and should be taken into account in the design process.

Animation thus seemed to have an increasingly wide range of possible applications to architecture and urban design. But, perhaps most important, it became an increasingly widespread concern that fundamentally affected the mainstream of mass housing production. Even in the design of Sarcelles—archetype of the heavily criticized first generation of *grands ensembles*—there was a marked revision of urban concepts, the most obvious one being the return to the street. With their "Entrance to the City" plan of the late 1960s, the architects Jacques Henri-Labourdette and Roger Boileau proposed a central avenue articulated by a series of identical towers and a parallel pedestrianized boulevard at their backs. The avenue was designed as a traditional commercial axis with galleries on each side that led pedestrians on to the cascading landscape of the parallel strip (Figure 3.13).[93]

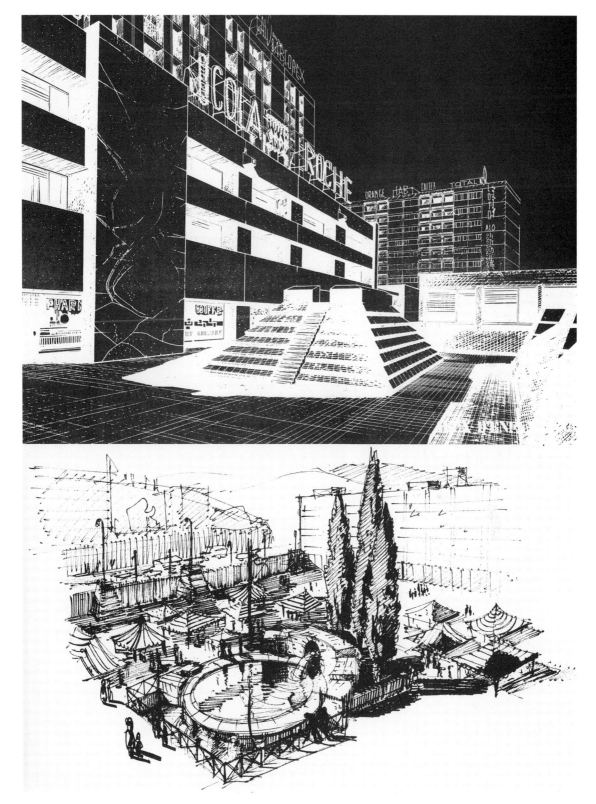

Figure 3.12. Sketches by the architects Xavier and Luc Arsène-Henry for the Quartier Sud in Nîmes, 1967. From *Urbanisme* 98 (1967): 37.

Figure 3.13. The phase "Entrance to the City" for Sarcelles by the architects Henri Labourdette and Roger Boileau, late 1960s. Located at the western side of the development, this later phase was conceived as the grand urban entryway to the *grand ensemble,* leading directly to the new urban center that was designed at the same time. Model photograph from Caisse des dépôts et consignations, CDC 1-B-010; copyright Jean Biaugeaud. Street photograph by the author.

Concomitant with this shift was a novel preoccupation with public art: no longer limited to the realm of "high culture," art was incorporated into urban design as one of the many applications of *animation*. Referred to as "urban aesthetics" in the 1965 *grille* publication, this new focus was proffered up in Xavier Arsène-Henry's article "L'art dans les villes nouvelles," and registered in the work of Émile Aillaud.[94] Government planners understood public art increasingly as a vehicle to express "the intimacy, mystery, and poetry of the city," and Aillaud's housing project of La Grande Borne in Grigny became exemplary to that ambition. The project featured the architect's signature design of playfully curving housing slabs—first built more than a decade before in projects such as Les Courtillières—as well as a series of small rectilinear housing blocks on a raised platform and a casbah-inspired "mat" of densely packed single-family homes. The master plan consisted of seven architecturally distinct neighborhoods built around public spaces that were connected by pedestrian pathways. The triangular development was delimited by two highways and a busy road, and parking was located at the edges to keep the neighborhoods free of cars (Figure 3.14).

To Aillaud, architecture "does not need to create juxtaposed buildings, but instead, landscapes."[95] Many *grands ensembles* as this time began to include art in their public spaces, but

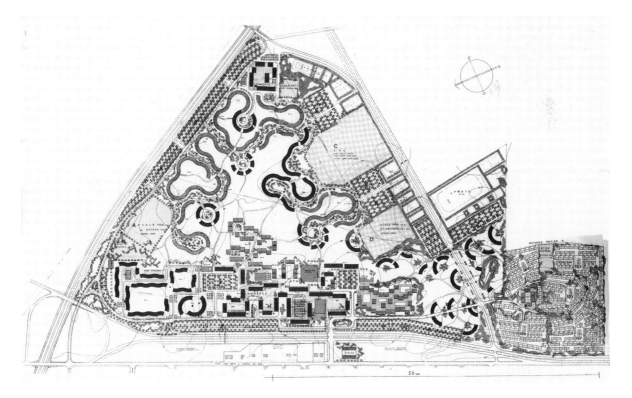

Figure 3.14. Plan of La Grande Borne (Grigny, near Paris) by the architect Émile Aillaud, 1963–74. Fonds Aillaud. Service interministériel des Archives de France/Cité de l'architecture et du patrimoine/Archives d'architecture du XXᵉ siècle.

at La Grande Borne it was elevated to the same level as the architecture and urban design. The architect's goal was complexity, mystery, and poetry—those cherished characteristics of the traditional city to be reproduced in new housing projects. Many of the squares and open spaces were dotted with gigantic sculptures to exude themes such as "The Astrolabe," "The Pond of Sand," or "The Ellipse." Gigantic murals and sculptures of animals and pieces of fruit figured prominently (Figure 3.15 and Plates 4 and 5). Combined with sandboxes, patterned paving, street furniture, and other landscaping elements, the sculptures functioned as playful devices for children and adults alike. The buildings' side facades were used as gigantic canvases for works of art executed in colorful mosaics. The comprehensive color scheme by the artist Fabio Rieti not only gave the housing blocks diversity and variety but also altered their haptic experience by decreasing the perceived scale and uniformity of the buildings.[96] These artistic interventions, which were to make La Grande Borne "the city of a painter as much as that of an architect," ultimately aimed to encourage inhabitants to use public spaces more intensely and to appropriate them as they pleased.[97] As much as planners were keen on stimulating people to participate in this sense, the awareness of how they actually did appropriate the spaces provided for them would nevertheless only emerge later.

What these *grands ensembles* projects had in common was the decidedly architectural strategy to evoke participation and social life more generally. *Animation* was the key concept that allowed the designers to do so. It invoked a simple physiological metaphor ("life") but also expressed human personality ("soul") and qualities of character, such as charm or vibrancy. This naturalism and anthropomorphism in the image of the animated city was the motor behind its success as a sociotechnical means to re-create urbanity in the French suburbs. In the context of mass housing provision, *animation* was a fundamentally ambiguous concept: it referred to the liveliness of the new neighborhood as much as to the organized recreational activities meant to integrate new inhabitants into their new community. And while the concept acknowledged the active participation of inhabitants as a crucial agent in the success or failure of mass housing areas, it did not do away with urban design or the authority of the architect. On the contrary, social concerns were translated into spatial interventions and informed architectural experimentation—not only with collective facilities but also with the design of the urban landscape at large. These initiatives brought forward alternative models, often cast as a clear revision or critique of existing *grands ensembles*.

In many ways, urbanism of the *grands ensembles* during the 1960s thus revolved around the intention to *animate* them. Meant to overcome the perceived ills of mass housing, the techniques of *animation* manifested the growing reach of French welfare as much as the ambitions of postwar architectural modernism. State administrators and designers assumed responsibility not only for the efficient production of mass housing, but also for its "happy consumption." The first strategy to translate these ambitions into concrete programs and urban interventions

Figure 3.15. La Grande Borne (Grigny, near Paris), by the architect Émile Aillaud. Color scheme by Fabio Rieti. Pigeon sculptures by François Lalanne. Fonds Aillaud. Service interministériel des Archives de France/Cité de l'architecture et du patrimoine/ Archives d'architecture du XXᵉ siècle.

was the "grid of facilities." But, despite the fact that such an approach transformed the institutions of community life into a bureaucratic series of requirements, its accompanying research brought more complex understandings of social life to bear on design. Eventually, novel urban and architectural design strategies were to bring newly built neighborhoods to life. At least, that was the aspiration of many French architects, planners, and policy makers faced with the problem of mass housing in the 1960s.

At a relative distance from Team X, the urbanism of the *grands ensembles* thus entailed a gradual change of mind-set: under the banner of *animation,* inhabitants were increasingly conceptualized not only as passive beneficiaries of dwelling units, but as active subjects of the urban environments provided for them. This mind-set was neither the sign of a decidedly emancipatory transfer of power to the inhabitant nor the disingenuous mirage of a user who was in reality nothing more than an alienated automaton of state capitalism. Instead, it was part of a complex power dynamic in which the freedom of inhabitants and state-led orchestration were not necessarily antithetical, but in fact part and parcel of the same project: the making of successful neighborhoods. This required not only the incorporation of sociological expertise in urban planning, but also the importance of more diverse approaches to architectural design, and thus, the gradual transformation of modernist doctrine as it was embodied by the first generation of *grands ensembles.*

Rather than being set in stone by the interwar CIAM or invented during Reconstruction, blueprinted by Marcel Lods and Eugène Beaudouin in the Cité de la Muette in Drancy or by Le Corbusier at the Unité d'habitation in Marseille, the *grands ensembles* constituted a gradually evolving and experimental form of urbanism: not only on a social or sociological level, but also in terms of architecture and urban design. The expansion of state welfare and the growing awareness that inhabitants' active participation was a key factor in the success of mass housing led architects, urbanists, state administrators, social scientists, and civil society representatives to collaborate at the intersections of architectural modernism, sociology, and social and urban policy making. Contrary to the assumption that a single and fixed model was simply repeated, the urbanism of the *grands ensembles* thus evolved during the time of their proliferation over the national territory in the late 1950s and throughout the 1960s. This evolution remained nevertheless within the purview of mass collective housing in large peripherally located estates—a paradigm that would only break down during the 1970s.

4

THE EXPERTISE OF PARTICIPATION

AFEW YEARS AFTER THE FIRST INHABITANTS had moved into the gleamingly new apartments of Sarcelles, their newly established local inhabitant association, the Association Sarcelloise, wrote that "the city of stone (or concrete) is built, now it is up to us to make it viable, to animate it to the best of our abilities."[1] The construction of many *grands ensembles* was not only accompanied by theories of *animation* that transformed—at least conceptually—inhabitants into active participants. Also, "on the ground" they engendered a particular kind of activism and associational life that would influence the course of French urbanization and help shape the ideology of participation in architecture and urbanism over the following decades.

The history of how people dealt with the new challenges of everyday life in the *grands ensembles* is transmitted to us only through the lens of what remains: television reportage, photos, written testimonies, social-scientific surveys, and here and there, local publications and periodicals (Figure 4.1). How did the first generation of inhabitants, often coming from rural settings or foreign cultures, understand their new urban environment, and how did they become part of a local community? How did social life take shape and transform? How did men, women, and children transform from a collection of migrants into new citizens of a minisociety that was taking shape as they settled in? These are not only questions for historians as they deal with fragments from the past; they were crucial to the inhabitants themselves, as well as to the planners, developers, and those managing these new environments. Everyday life was not only lived; it was also perceived, understood, criticized, and turned into a major concern at this time.

Figure 4.1. A sunny day at one of Sarcelles's commercial centers in the early 1960s. Photograph by Nabil Koskossi, Maison du patrimoine, Sarcelles.

Psychosociologist René Kaës, in the introduction to his popular study *Vivre dans les grands ensembles*, explained this concern as a logical consequence of the large-scale urbanization of postwar France: "How to conceive what will be the life in a *grand ensemble* built for twenty thousand metalworkers transplanted to the Moselle, massively and suddenly, with their families, coming from dozens of different departments, the majority of which are agricultural, with their own way of life, customs, and culture. Even if the question cannot everywhere be posed in these terms, it begs for a novel response, which supposes acquired and familiar notions of urbanism, regional planning, and social and cultural animation, and a lot of other things, of which at the least is a humble attention to everyday life."[2] He concluded that the *grands ensembles* were "the hearth of a new way of life," one of activism and participation.[3]

The architecture of many *grands ensembles* hardly strikes the contemporary observer as a nurturing site for the development of such a participatory neighborhood life. And yet, that development was not only an explicitly articulated goal for many planners and architects; it also turned out to be an ambition of many inhabitants. Participation operated at once as a promise, a discursive device, and a concrete reality in the planning process. It grew not only out of social contestation "from below" but also "from above," out of the initiatives and institutions of the centralized state apparatus itself as it was engaged in developing, projecting, building, and amending its urban policies and actions. Despite its notoriety, the history of Sarcelles in particular suggests a fundamental interconnectedness between political elites, high civil servants, experts, local activists, and inhabitant associations in the development of what would later be termed participatory urbanism.

Pioneer Worlds

Despite the persistent impression that the construction of postwar France amounted to a steamrolling of the national territory with standardized, monotonous forms of architecture, the urbanization process did not go unchallenged or unchanged. Apart from negative press reactions, doubts from experts, and the government's efforts to address emerging problems, as described in the preceding chapter, the implementation of *grands ensembles* gave rise to a complex of local reactions that would soon turn out to have national implications. Many observers at the time explained the vibrancy of inhabitants' reactions to their new surroundings by what they called a "frontier mentality." The first inhabitants, "this 'bastard race'—not urbanites, nor suburbanites, and villagers even less,"[4] were forced to organize their everyday lives in an environment that was often neither finished nor accommodating to their way of life. Whether they arrived from poor housing in Paris's thirteenth arrondissement, from a small village in rural Bretagne, or were "repatriated" from Algeria after its independence in 1962, they had to make do with what they found in their surroundings, often at the very borders of the existing city. Confronted with the construction site that was their new home, they had to find a place in a society still largely in the making.

This pioneer condition was shared by a new generation of French people, from the new Le Havre to the suburbs of Marseille, and from Rennes to Strasbourg. More than any other place, it was Sarcelles that came to epitomize the rewards and especially the challenges of this novel kind of living. The *grand ensemble* of Sarcelles was an exemplary, if not notorious, case. Although it was not the first mass housing project to appear on the outskirts of Paris, it was proclaimed "Europe's largest construction site" (Figure 4.2). From the late 1950s onward, Sarcelles became a staple of popular criticism and public opinion about the *grands ensembles*: when newspapers wrote about them as "a concentration camp universe," "silos for people," "rabbit

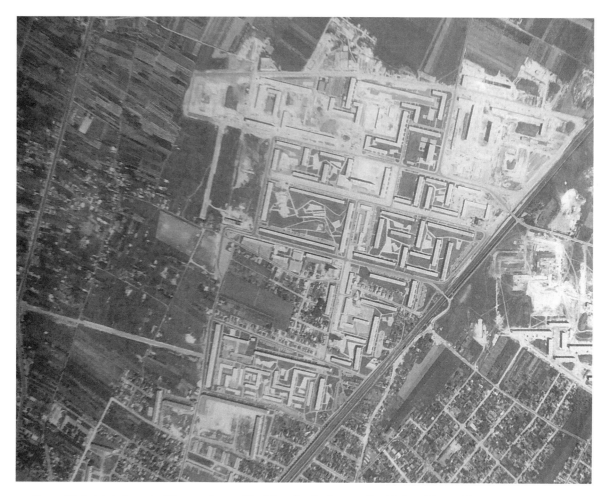

Figure 4.2. Aerial photograph of the *grand ensemble* of Sarcelles, by Jacques Henri-Labourdette and Roger Boileau, 1960.
The four housing slabs at the bottom of the image comprise another SCIC housing development designed by Jean Dubuisson.
Archives municipales de Sarcelles.

cages," or "dormitory suburbs," they often made explicit reference to Sarcelles.[5] The neologism
sarcellite—coined in the early 1960s to describe the various social and psychological ills the
grands ensembles were believed to cause—channeled the growing panic about France's enormous building boom through Sarcelles. It was not unlike what the term *brasilite* at this time
did to describe the traumatic impact of the modernist city of Brasília on its residents: the city's
negation of familiar urban forms and its architectural monotony were considered generative
of social anonymity and the lack of public life.[6]

     The *grand ensemble* of Sarcelles was built incrementally between 1955 and 1976 and not
according to a comprehensive plan drawn up at the outset. That is certainly surprising given
that France was in the middle of a love affair with planning, and even more so because Sarcelles

has always been the poster child of postwar planned housing. In his 1966 book *Vivre à Sarcelles?*, Jean Duquesne, a civil servant at the finance ministry and a locally active inhabitant of Sarcelles since he moved there in 1958, sketched the construction of Sarcelles as "decided piece by piece," concluding that "the result suffers from it." Proof of this was in the everyday experience of inhabitants, who saw "the tracing of certain streets being changed multiple times" and "neighborhoods that everybody considered finished witnessed the construction of additional buildings in their green spaces."[7]

The disjunction between the theory and reality of planning Sarcelles was a consequence of the difficulties of land acquisition during the 1950s. Sarcelles's developer and landlord was the Société centrale immobilière de la Caisse des dépôts (SCIC, or Central Real-Estate Company of the Deposits and Consignments Fund), established in 1954 by the state financial institution Caisse des dépôts et consignations (CDC, or Deposits and Consignments Fund) to boost the construction of mass housing.[8] An indirect arm of national housing policy, SCIC initially built in the suburbs of Paris but soon expanded to the provinces and abroad. By 1974, SCIC had erected more than 250,000 housing units. Sarcelles was one of its first large-scale developments. It was decided almost randomly. In 1954, a local group of self-builders associated with the Castor movement contacted the CDC for financing after buying a piece of land for the construction of single-family homes.[9] The terrain, just large enough for an allotment of a few dozen new homes, was located in an agricultural area surrounded by three old villages, now suburban communities of Paris—Sarcelles to the north, Stains and Pierrefitte to the south. When it got involved, the CDC's newly established subsidiary SCIC immediately saw the opportunity for a much larger development in the area, known as Bois de Lochères. A year later, it had already obtained enough land for a first phase of about 440 housing units in four four-story slabs placed rectilinearly around a large green space (Figure 4.3a). The plans had been drawn by Beaux-Arts architects Jacques-Henri Labourdette and Roger Boileau, who remained in charge of future phases as well.[10] A second phase of 1,180 units was already begun in 1956. Unlike the earlier phase, plans for the second included an impressive collection of collective amenities—including a market, a commercial center, and several schools. Some of those would never be built and others only much later (Figure 4.3b). As the developer hurriedly purchased additional land, subsequent phases followed at a rapid pace. The Castor allotment, located just north of the first phase, was quickly surrounded by collective housing blocks (Figure 4.3c).

Only in the early 1960s, when SCIC was finally able to purchase the necessary land, was an overall master plan drawn. The plan indicated subsequent phases of development and set out a grid of roads delineating "neighborhood units" of around 400 m square (Figure 4.4). The plan was meant to be a direct translation of the principles set out in the *grille Dupont*, to which Labourdette had contributed in the preceding years as a consultant for the Ministry of Construction led by Pierre Sudreau.[11] Housing construction only halted in 1975 when SCIC

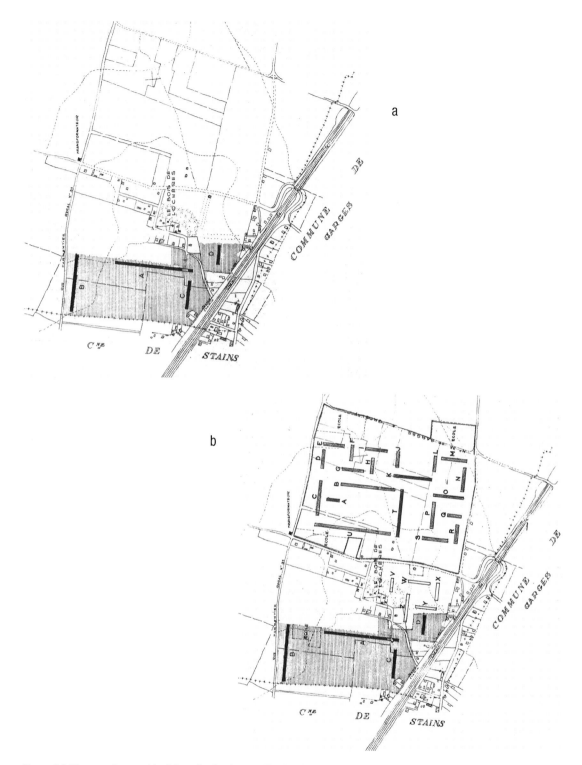

Figure 4.3. The *grand ensemble* of Sarcelles by Jacques Henri-Labourdette and Roger Boileau. (a) The first phase, built in urgency between 1955 and 1957 (plan from 1955) after land was coincidentally obtained, did not contain any collective facilities. The Castor allotment is located immediately north of this first phase. (b) A second phase, plan from around 1958. (c) Subsequent phases were laid out soon after the second phase. The existing allotments and single-family homes are black dots on the plan. Archives municipales de Sarcelles.

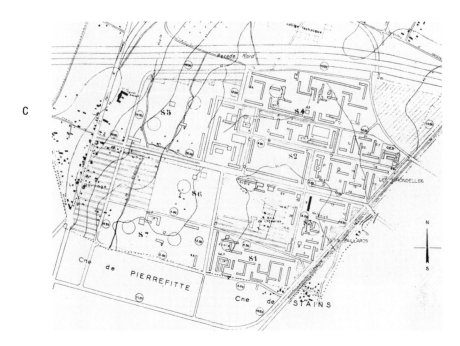

had built a total of more than twelve thousand housing units in eleven phases, all designed by the architects Boileau and Labourdette. While the architects later claimed that the absence of a detailed master plan for Sarcelles was "intentional," history demonstrates how the strictures of private property and messiness of expropriation got in the way of even the most ambitious government projects.[12] Aware of these challenges in the first generation of *grands ensembles,* policy makers subsequently revised expropriation laws to facilitate large-scale projects and curb private land speculation.

The social makeup of Sarcelles was the direct result of national policies prioritizing young working families. According to Duquesne, the "right to housing" in Sarcelles was the result of two criteria: "employment, and thus it is the employer who disposes of dwelling units for those who work for him, and the number of children. In a situation of shortage, the units go first to the largest families. . . . These origins of Sarcelles's population shape its physiognomy: the families are young, the adults fully employed, and the children many."[13] Sarcelles's population was indeed very young: a 1962 survey showed that only 8 percent was older than forty-five. Its first inhabitants were predominantly workers and employees. There was only a small minority of upper-middle-class people such as business owners, executives (*cadres supérieurs*), doctors, and lawyers. The first inhabitants were thus remarkably homogeneous in terms of both age and class: predominantly white French nuclear families with young children, a mix of blue- and white-collar workers, with a significant number of civil servants among them (Figure 4.5). There were almost no poor, adolescents, or elderly and few non-French people among them, and many came from the same factories and companies.

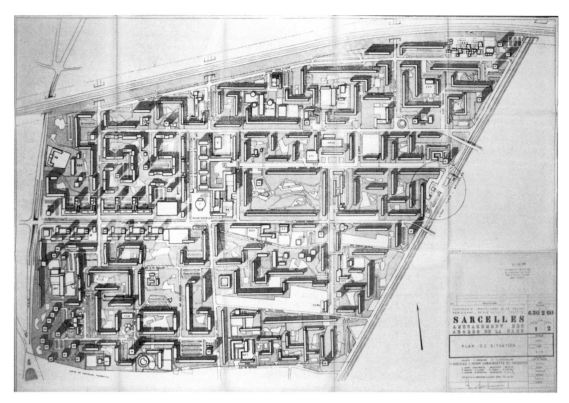

Figure 4.4. Plan of Sarcelles around 1964, showing how earlier phases were integrated into a more or less comprehensive plan. Using a grid of roughly 400 m by 400 m, the development was now conceived as individual neighborhood units, each with its own commercial centers. A "principal center" serving the entire community was to be situated in the middle of the development. Archives municipales de Sarcelles.

The majority of housing units in the first phases of Sarcelles were allocated to personnel from the companies that helped finance construction.[14] Only 10 percent of the units were available for the municipality to attribute to its employees and to those in slum housing, and another 10 percent were for SCIC's own personnel, caretakers, and those with liberal professions deemed necessary in the new development, such as medical doctors. The fact that in Sarcelles only families had access to housing was clearly reflected in its housing stock. F4 apartments made up the bulk of Sarcelles during its first decade, suggesting the new town would only house midsized nuclear families. There were practically no studios or very large apartments in the first phases. What further exacerbated the initial feeling of social homogeneity was the allocation of inhabitants to the buildings. While most buildings were allocated to a mix of families from different companies, some contained up to 80 percent families from the same factory, company, or organization.[15]

The first inhabitants lived in a neighborhood of numbered streets and buildings until street names were given in 1961. Apart from the "normal" blocks for white nuclear families,

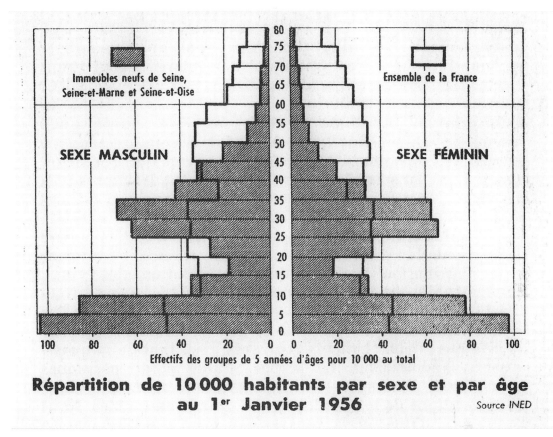

Figure 4.5. Demographic histogram of 1956, representing the distribution of the population according to age. The population of new housing areas in the Paris region (shaded bars) is characterized by a very high proportion of young adults (age 20–40) and children (age 0–15) relative to the national distribution (white bars). From René Kaës, *Vivre dans les grands ensembles* (Paris: Éditions ouvrières, 1963), 76.

some were allocated to specific groups and quickly stood out. Inhabitants spoke of "the block of the cops," "the block of the Africans" (housing interns from sub-Saharan Africa), and "the Citroën block" (housing Italians, Spanish, and provincials, often separated from their families and living in groups of four, to work in eight-hour shifts for the car manufacturer of the same name).[16] And then, there were also the blocks built for the *pieds noirs*, French nationals born in Algeria who migrated to mainland France after Algerian independence in 1962. Decolonization generated a considerable influx of repatriates, who were often tenuously situated in between two worlds. The government targeted the *grands ensembles* as their new home. At Sarcelles, more than three thousand of them, many of whom were Jewish, arrived in the mid-1960s from Algeria, Tunisia, and Morocco—often after temporary stays in Marseille. Some were housed in two especially designated blocks, but many purchased their own apartments across the *grand ensemble*.[17] Planners and housing managers considered organized forms of residential segregation increasingly a mistake and changed the allocation policy during the 1960s to increase social mixing.[18] Nevertheless, Sarcelles's families continued to be separated from others, who as special social categories were housed in specific typologies such as the *foyer des jeunes travailleurs*—an institution for young male workers—and the *résidence des personnes agées*—the home for the elderly.

Despite the fact that for the majority of first inhabitants the *grands ensembles* did not constitute their first urban experience, the new social world they entered did not have much in terms of a shared urban culture or tradition.[19] The only things to bind inhabitants were the sameness of their new dwellings and the sheer novelty of the modern world outside their doorstep. The emergence of social life in such estates was shaped as much by their particular social makeup as by their physical characteristics, their unfinished nature, and their often isolated location. The *grand ensemble* of Sarcelles was again emblematic. In the national press it was persistently portrayed as a new city sprung up in the middle of nowhere, among the fields of cauliflower and beets that were so typical for this agricultural region that once supplied Paris with food. On one side, this was true: the new development was located at a considerable distance from the existing village of Sarcelles, with which it had little in common apart from its denomination and a mayor. On the other side, however, the housing estate immediately bordered the suburban allotments of the adjacent municipalities of Stains and Pierrefitte. In fact, Sarcelles's first phase followed the orthogonal grid of an earlier, much smaller SCIC housing project situated right next to it and to which it was added like an extension (see Figure 4.2). This adjacent housing development, designed by Jean Dubuisson, was an infill project in the existing suburban fabric of interwar allotments. Subsequent phases of Sarcelles followed the orthogonality set out by Dubuisson but were also grafted onto the existing structure of rural roads and agricultural parcels.

The pioneering nature of the housing estate that was to become the new Sarcelles was thus shaped less by its "isolated" location than by its sheer size and urban form. Many *grands ensembles*—surrounded by suburban allotments—were isolated from their surroundings in exactly this sense. Their standardized architecture and modernist urban form simply negated the surroundings. The rigidity of their grid composition and the reversal of traditional urban form opposed them to the city center, while the scale of their housing slabs negated the suburban fabric in equally strong terms. The architectural language of social modernization did nothing less than condemn these unmodern contexts. While the construction of Sarcelles, especially during the 1960s and 1970s, included a variety of different materials and techniques—from traditional stone masonry to heavy concrete prefab and steel curtain walls—the initial results were the same facades, the same avenues, the same perspectives and window views, the same apartment layouts, and the same interior finishings; but also, the same modern technologies and appliances, and, especially, the same problems and aggravations when these did not function as they should. Defined in such a way, the *grand ensemble* was a brave new world, entirely onto itself.

Tenants, Users, and Consumers, Unite!

Perhaps not surprisingly, the new world of the *grands ensembles* engendered a particular climate of neighborhood solidarity. When in 1956 the pioneers of Sarcelles moved into their newly finished apartments, they were confronted with an unwelcoming outdoor space of construction dust, noise, and mud. Without nearby train or bus connections, post office, or shops, in a landscape of fields and shabby allotments, the inhabitants were stranded. Only in the next year were the nearby train tracks electrified and trains actually stopped at Garges-Sarcelles. For a proper train station, residents had to wait until 1966. In this climate of pioneering, "a spontaneous form of mutual aid emerged, as during the war, from these shortages: to avoid two neighboring mothers having to queue at the store, one of them would look after the children together, while the other did the groceries."[20] A culture of interpersonal "making do" thus developed in an urbanism of impersonal, state-aided provision. At the Garges-Sarcelles stop, where trains dropped tired commuters in batches during the evening, street vendors lined up to supply households that lacked local grocery stores (Figure 4.6). In response to the absence of basic amenities, other forms of unplanned, provisional kinds of intervention thus emerged. The deficient and unfinished character of their everyday environment stimulated inhabitants to find company in common goals: pavement instead of mud, shorter commutes to work, the opening of local shops and a post office. When they complained, inhabitants did so as a group.

In an area with predominantly leftist political leanings, this kind of solidarity soon shaped associational life.[21] The various inhabitant groups and local organizations that emerged in the *grand ensemble* were often separate and different in nature from those of the surrounding villages and suburban allotments. At Sarcelles, the social distinctions between the existing village and the *grand ensemble* could not have been more stark. During the first two decades after initial construction, there was marked tension between the two areas, each of which had its own social life, demographics, politics, interests, and, especially, local identity.

While some of the associations in the *grand ensemble* were typical for that time in France—sports and leisure clubs, for example—others were of an entirely new kind. Most remarkable was the Association Sarcelloise, a voluntary association established right after the arrival of the first inhabitants at the end of 1957. The association's explicit aim was to "defend the material and moral interests of the inhabitants, tenants, and homeowners of the housing groups in Sablons, Bois de Lochères, and Barrage," the three areas the *grand ensemble* would eventually cover. The association was not initially recognized by the developer, but that did not stop members from standing up to both the developer and the centralized state. Through insistent

Figure 4.6. Street vending near the train station of Sarcelles during the early 1960s. Photograph copyright Jacques Windenberger/VAGA, New York.

letter writing, the association complained about the many technical problems and lack of amenities of the housing areas—the lack of schools, public transportation, postal services, the insufficient sound insulation, and problems with heating.[22] It also contested the developer's rent increases, collective charges, and insufficient maintenance. Via a monthly newsletter, titled *L'A.S.*, the association updated its members about these struggles and reported about similar situations in other *grands ensembles* (see Figure 4.7).

The sense of solidarity here was perhaps particularly strong when compared to other *grands ensembles*. It was certainly intensified by the public stigmatization of Sarcelles, which encouraged inhabitants to defend it vigorously against often ill-considered critiques "from the outside." The different interpretations of *sarcellite* exemplified this. While the national press focused on the monotony and dehumanizing aspects of its architecture, medical doctors focused on its repercussions for inhabitants' mental health and sociologists on the boredom of women and on youth delinquency. Inhabitants, however, tended to interpret *sarcellite* very differently. They cast it, facetiously, as an infectious form of passivity, the remedy for which was to become an activist and fix the often mundane problems of the *grand ensemble*. The local

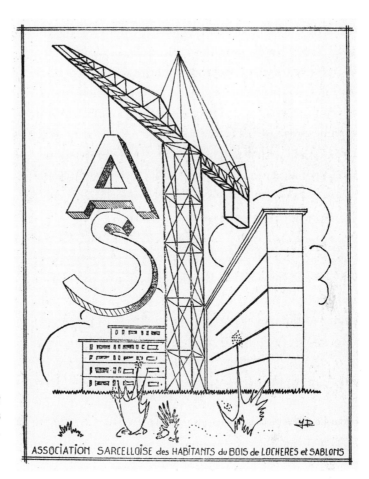

Figure 4.7. Cover of the monthly bulletin *L'A.S.*, 1958. Archives municipales de Sarcelles.

periodical *En famille* thus reported in satirical tone about the emergence of *sarcellite* as a virus that "incubated slowly" to "make the head empty." The actual disease then was described as a nervous breakdown, diagnosed by the fact that "in 60 percent of the cases, they buy a TV because the neighbor owns one." The remedy "consisted first of all to be member of the Association des familles" and boiled down to "an active life and a brain that functions."[23] During a public demonstration of the local associations in 1965, *sarcellite* was dismissed with a similar sense of humor: one of the decorated cars in the festive street procession was adorned with giant medicine tablets of "*sarcellomycine.*" Each of the tablets was inscribed with the name of a local association, making the visual argument that activism and associational life would deter the reputed disease.[24]

Regardless of Sarcelles's uniqueness, its associational life was characteristic of the *grands ensembles* more generally. Groups similar to the Association Sarcelloise were established in housing estates all over the nation.[25] While many of them remained unknown, others were fervently scrutinized. Local associational life was closely examined in Mourenx by Henri

Lefebvre and in Lyon-La Duchère by André Trintignac in a study for the Ministry of Construction.[26] Surely, not all of these associations were equally vibrant or successful, but just as in Sarcelles, they demanded more shops and schools, contested rent increases, and fought for the improvement of public transportation and street furniture. Even smaller housing developments, by social housing organizations or private developers, witnessed the emergence of such movements. Some would remain focused solely on the management of their apartment blocks, in particular when they were inserted in an already urbanized municipality with sufficient amenities and local political representation. In these kinds of developments, the associations were often less ambitious and their goals formulated less in terms of urbanism, but they were not necessarily less active.

This kind of associational life was unprecedented in the fact that it reacted to an entirely new entity. Almost all complaints of the Association Sarcelloise were directed against SCIC—which was not only the developer, but also the landlord, financier, builder, and manager of inhabitants' everyday environment. Moreover, the public nature of SCIC was inconsistent and changed dramatically during the 1960s. Initially established as an arm of the centralized government to provide low-rent housing using state loans and subsidies, SCIC soon began to develop a mix of housing units, including more generously sized and luxuriously equipped condominiums. In Sarcelles, the first condo blocks were erected in 1961. They began to predominate during the later phases of construction from the mid-1960s onward. While the *grand ensemble* of Sarcelles was not exactly a company town, SCIC as the monopoly holder was nevertheless ambivalently positioned: it represented the state but increasingly behaved like a large private corporation. SCIC soon went into private housing development through some of its many subsidiaries. But even in the 1980s, after having branched out further into the private sector, the company continued to define itself as a "social" and not a regular developer. In one of its bulletins, executives proclaimed that "SCIC is not and cannot be a company like all others. Its history, the source of its capital, and the role the State has given to it make it serve first and foremost the local communities and national housing policy as defined by the government."[27]

Despite its rhetoric of serving the public interest—supported by the widespread ideology that identified the centralized state unquestionably with the public good—the legal status of SCIC became the subject of debate during the 1950s and 1960s. The central focus was rent. To the distress of its tenant base, the company initially raised rents as it pleased. In July 1965, it announced a massive and sudden increase, purportedly to adjust rents to "current market rates." Inhabitants—given voice by associations such as the Association Sarcelloise and local branches of national family organizations such as the Union nationale des associations familiales—contested the increase and called for rent regulation. The government responded negatively. It declared SCIC a private company and thus free from rent regulation: "We need to insist on the fact that the developments of the CDC are not subject to HLM (Habitations à bon marché) legislation and regulation. The CDC is considered, from this point of view, a private owner and it is private law that reigns in the relations between tenant and landlord. When HLM norms are concerned, they pertain only the construction norms, and not those for management."[28]

In some respects, conflicts between tenant and landlord in the *grands ensembles* were similar to those of the interwar period and went back to the nineteenth century.[29] Rents constituted one of the most common domains of contestation, and in this sense inhabitants' activism in the *grands ensembles* was hardly new. Yet, with the development of mass housing during the postwar period, such struggles became less locally specific and appeared on the national political arena in novel ways. Many of the local associations in the *grands ensembles* were linked to existing national civil society organizations, tenant organizations such as the Confédération nationale du logement (CNL, or National Confederation for Housing).[30] Like trade unions, some of these were represented in the government's Conseil économique et social (Economic and Social Council) and helped shape national policy. At the same time, because they operated through departmental and municipal branches, they also engaged in local activism. Sarcelles's Association des familles, which was affiliated with the Union nationale des associations familiales as one of its local branches, had since its inception advocated for child care. Between 1962 and 1967, it managed the area's first and only nursery.

In 1963, the government had first instituted and then immediately eliminated tenant representation in the administrative councils of social housing organizations. The purported reason for ending the measure was to avoid the politicization of these councils and to make them more "efficient."[31] This only incited the national tenant and family organizations, who found a common goal in what they called "syndicalisme de l'habitat." This buzzword united national and local associations in the *grands ensembles* and informed the formulation of demands far beyond conventional domains of contestation, such as those focused on the legal relationship between landlord and tenant. Advocates of "housing syndicalism" were inspired by the larger social movement of *autogestion* or self-management, which had originated in Yugoslav workers' management practices and became an increasingly popular notion in French leftist movements during the 1960s and 1970s.[32]

In Sarcelles, such militancy led local associations like the Association Sarcelloise to demand participation in the management of the entire housing area and the provision of collective facilities corresponding to their own perception of what was needed. They called for the construction of schools—secondary schools in particular were urgently needed because of the rapid increase in the average age of children—as well as better roads and a greater range of shops offering less expensively priced goods. At the same time, Sarcelles's associations became increasingly concrete in defining their goals in terms of urban planning. In 1959 already, the Association Sarcelloise contested the expropriation and demolition of individual homes in

Barrage, an area cleared for future development.[33] A year later, the association formulated a counterproposal for this area in the form of a dedicated zone for single-family homes: "We are convinced it is in the interest of everybody, both tenants and home owners, to maintain at the western edge of the estate a zone of individual homes with their gardens, flowers, and trees."[34] Concretely, they proposed one part of the area, which was already scattered with cottages, to be densified with new individual homes, leaving the other part for collective housing. In 1962, when the association published its list of inhabitant needs, including the provision of a train station and a central market, it also included its own plan for the area.[35] By that time, however, SCIC had already obtained the land and the plans had been drawn. The company did build a few prefab individual homes—designed by the same architecture firm—in the area of the Castor allotment, for unknown reasons, but the Barrage area was built just as originally planned: in the form of dense collective housing.

SCIC's general response to inhabitants' demands was initially, if not hostile, lukewarm. The company did not deem inhabitants' demands and suggestions very valuable. The architects were the experts and, with the modest input of sociologists, they would know best what to build and where. While the company's managers were aware that some of the collective facilities were only built years after they were first needed, their planning was considered a matter of expertise, for which no input from users was necessary. Despite its neglect of inhabitants' demands, SCIC nevertheless undertook its own initiatives to improve their everyday lives, in large part because managers were increasingly aware that Sarcelles had become the company's public billboard.[36] Around 1960, the company built a pavilion for local exhibitions in the central park of the *grand ensemble* (Figure 4.8). It served as an advertising tool that allowed the developer to showcase the latest phase of development to local inhabitants and potential home buyers. At the same time, it also hosted various art exhibitions, including a show of van Gogh replicas that enjoyed popular success. Yet, the developer's key strategy for trumping inhabitant dissatisfaction was urban design. In the later phases of Sarcelles's development during the mid-1960s, commercial functions were located on the ground floor of residential buildings in order to create more lively urban spaces.[37] The principal urban center, planned around 1960 but only finished by 1972, was another gesture to this effect, and led local observers to conclude that "SCIC had the ambition to sensibly transform the general appearance of the estate and to a large extent the everyday environment of its inhabitants."[38]

Regardless of the developer's initiatives, the local associations were convinced they could improve the *grand ensemble* themselves, based on their own knowledge of everyday life. The library, for instance, now in its own purpose-built facility across from the principal urban center, grew out of a personal initiative that began with a makeshift installation inside a family's apartment. The Grosso family, who were active members of the Association Sarcelloise, moved in together with many other first arrivals in 1958. Appalled as they were by the lack of nearby

Figure 4.8. The Exhibition Hall of Sarcelles, located in the central Parc Kennedy, featuring a large model of the *grand ensemble* in the early 1960s. Caisse des dépôts et consignations, CDC 2-C-019. Copyright Studio Martin.

amenities, they decided to open an informal public library inside their own apartment, furnished with books borrowed from the existing library of the village of Sarcelles. The initiative was so successful that in 1960 the library was moved into the new municipal administration building just completed in one of the local commercial centers. In 1964, the library moved again, temporarily to a larger space, but farther from the center, and in 1969, finally, it was installed permanently in the building it still occupies today. Such anecdotes were far from unique. René Kaës described several examples of successful activism in his 1963 study. One was in Palente-lès-Orchamps (Besançon), where inhabitants established their own cultural center.[39] The initiative was started in the late 1950s by members of the local family association, which organized a movie club and book club in the gathering hall of a local café. Despite difficulties in financing, the initiative led to the creation of a Popular Cultural Center, which would shape local culture in the following decades.

If there ever was a utopian side to the *grands ensembles*, it was most likely located in the minds and intentions of small but very active groups of inhabitants such as these. They understood their activism as one of "completing" the modernity of their built environment. They did so by bringing it to life, literally. Yet the recorded sentiments were often less heroic. In the local periodical *En famille* of the Association des familles in Sarcelles, activists did not in fact describe their housing estate as a utopian world: "Sarcelles has not been conceived to develop the society of tomorrow, but to overcome the housing crisis. Sarcelles is therefore unfortunately not more than a dreary hybrid between bedroom suburb and rational urban center."[40] *L'A.S.* wrote that it was "neither hell nor paradise," but simply needed their initiative in order to work: "Sarcelles, a model city? Yes, but in five or ten years!"[41] Duquesne drew similar conclusions: "It is the task of the local inhabitants, with the help of time and the will to participate in social life, to humanize their city."[42] Many residents, not just the activists, would have agreed that its unfinished, halfhearted modernism could be brought to success only by their collective efforts.

Social life in the *grands ensembles* during the first decades was dominated by a culture of local activism that was predicated on notions of collective consumption as much as social militancy. The Association Sarcelloise defined itself as "at once a syndicate of tenants, an association of users, and a grouping of consumers."[43] What is crucial here is the unique way they asserted themselves: no longer just as tenants of housing blocks, but as citizens of a new kind of city. Local activists tended to describe the environment in which they lived (and sometimes worked) as a new city ("une ville neuve, ville nouvelle") more than as a housing area ("une nouvelle cité"). Compared to the housing projects of the interwar period, it was a new kind of place, a "welfare state city" with its own governance and, consequently, its own political struggles. These struggles were defined not only by its monopolistic ownership structure and the specific ambitions of SCIC to turn Sarcelles into a "real city," but also by its enormous scale and physical form. In many other *grands ensembles*, the emphasis on the autonomy of the development might have been less pronounced, perhaps resulting in a less lively associational life. Nevertheless, *grands ensembles* across the nation were characterized in similar ways by this fundamental ambiguity between housing and city. This was reflected in the confusion about their denomination: while the term *grand ensemble* was most often used, other expressions, such as "villes nouvelles," "nouveaux ensembles d'habitation," "ensembles urbains," "grands blocs," and "cités neuves" remained common throughout the period.

Sarcelles offers both a unique and an exemplary case for the *grands ensembles* and the particular social life it gave rise to. Its notoriety, scale, isolation from its urban surroundings, social composition, incremental construction, and social and ethnic diversity made it more of a real city than some other—especially smaller—housing estates. Yet, it was still a city built around the government-led provision of housing, and in that sense it expressed the fundamental ambiguities that characterized urban citizenship and belonging in the *grands ensembles* more generally: that between housing and city, private and public, and, most important, between tenants, users, consumers, and citizens as the basic condition of everyday life.

Management or Politics?

Just as Sarcelles served as an example, both positive and negative, for how to design mass housing, so it became exemplary in efforts to *manage* it. The activism of Sarcelles's first generation of inhabitants would ultimately inform new approaches to urban management and planning, both locally and nationally. This began with the involvement of social science. From the late 1950s, Sarcelles had not only been at the center of public celebration, outcry, and government concern; it had also begun to catch the attention of a growing number of journalists, medical doctors, and especially sociologists. Throughout the 1960s, researchers flocked to Sarcelles to gauge the future of urban France. Their studies were not only useful to politicians and opinion makers but also to the observed themselves.

Already in 1960 the Association Sarcelloise had suggested that the municipality involve an external research institute in a sociological survey of Sarcelles. Its explicit goal was to find ways to "adapt the architecture to its users."[44] Out of concern with the quality of their built environment, its members visited other *grands ensembles* in the Paris region, notably that of Massy-Antony. Soon after, an article published in its periodical dismissed the architects, "who think they don't need to listen to inhabitants and their needs."[45] The association then decided to organize its own survey by mailing questionnaires to all four thousand households of the *grand ensemble*. More than 1,200 forms were returned and the results published in *L'A.S.* in 1962. The survey showed that inhabitants were relatively satisfied with their apartments and content with "the rectilinear conception of the *grand ensemble* and the importance given to green space." It also showed, perhaps surprisingly, a relatively low participation of inhabitants in the available facilities such as the library and the social center. But, most important, it demonstrated the lack of other facilities. Especially grocery stores and other shops were deemed insufficient in both number and variety. Although it did not find a direct application, the survey demonstrated the growing faith in hard data to guide planning. *L'A.S.* was enthusiastic about the survey because it provided "a sense of the inconveniences, the shortages, the imperfections, and the deficiencies of one of those new towns, and as such, we can inform the technical expert [*technicien*] about the needs of the inhabitants of the homes he will be building or who already live in a city that needs to be improved."[46]

Local activists continued to harness social-scientific study. When the Ministry of Construction, with the support of SCIC, commissioned another research firm for a sociological survey in 1963, Sarcelles's local associations organized a public presentation of the study in the Exhibition Hall that had recently been completed.[47] And Sarcelles was hardly the only place where such initiatives took place: in Bron-Parilly, for example, the local associations also commissioned sociological surveys in the hope of using its results to legitimize their demands.[48] Such initiatives soon blurred the distinction between management and politics. As Sarcelles grew exponentially, so did its associational life. Tensions rose quickly between these associations, SCIC, and the municipality (Figure 4.9). When the Association Sarcelloise submitted a petition to stop the next phase of development, SCIC decided to organize a national conference to address what it saw as the "problem of the management of the *grands ensembles*." No doubt its executives were aware of the potential danger these tensions represented—especially since inhabitant groups elsewhere also began to protest, and with an increasingly loud voice.

SCIC's management was extremely centralized: while it had established more than two hundred subsidiary development firms for the execution of local projects, all its real estate was managed in its Parisian headquarters. The company's real-estate management was divided into a hierarchical series of services just like a French ministry. Most likely, managers themselves were becoming aware of the mismatch between this highly centralized operation and the task of controlling an immense collection of buildings and projects distributed all over France. The goal of the conference was not only to smooth relations with residents but to reform the company's management system altogether. While it might have been a harbinger of participatory decision making in the eyes of inhabitants, the conference was undoubtedly also a strategic move on the part of the company. The company's housing stock had grown exponentially since its inception and had simply become too large for direct management.[49]

The conference took place in Sarcelles on January 11, 1964, under the direction of François Bloch-Lainé, head of the CDC and exemplar of France's political elite. Not only for researchers but also for those in charge, Sarcelles, again, constituted the perfect site of study:

Figure 4.9. Local demonstration against the developer SCIC in the early 1960s. Photograph copyright Jacques Windenberger/VAGA, New York.

"Sarcelles was a privileged site for two reasons: Sarcelles was already very well known, the symbol of the *grands ensembles,* and thus everything we did there would be exemplary. If we would find something interesting in Sarcelles, it was known and could be done elsewhere. Sarcelles was large enough to launch interesting experiments."[50] Following the conference, SCIC commissioned the National Foundation of Political Sciences (Fondation nationale des sciences politiques) to pursue a social-scientific study of the possibilities for participation in housing management. The foundation created a working group of jurists, sociologists, and leaders of civil society organizations. Its report proposed to distinguish two domains for the question of participation, "that of the housing as such, where it considers that the decision of the landlord needs to remain sovereign, with nuances depending on whether it concerns rents or charges; and that of the sociocultural facilities, for which it recommends comanagement."[51]

Concretely, this implied informing and consulting with inhabitants in some domains and shared decision making in others. To realize this, the report proposed the creation of an Association of Residents of the *grand ensemble* (Association des résidents du grand ensemble), which would operate via a Residents' Council (Conseil de résidents) composed of representatives elected by the inhabitants and delegates of local associations. After long negotiations with the various organizations representing inhabitants—national family organizations, tenant associations, and some local associations, including the Association Sarcelloise—all parties agreed.[52] Signed on June 24, 1965, the agreement instituted a Conseil de résidents in twelve *grands ensembles*, ten of which were in the Paris region.[53] Each council would work to negotiate between developer and residents in three particular domains: rents, charges, and sociocultural facilities. The agreement would initially last for two years and be tacitly renewable. First elections were in 1966. Two years later, new elections were held—this time for three years—and in 1969, eleven new councils were created in other *grands ensembles*, bringing the total to twenty-three (Figure 4.10). SCIC embraced the agreement and the family organizations were also relatively positive, regarding it as at least the beginning of a democratic policy. The more militant tenant organizations were critical of the results.

During the following years, the councils in most *grands ensembles* were remarkably active. Sarcelles's council demanded that SCIC legitimize all its rent increases by providing more information to inhabitants and won a struggle over the establishment of a new three-year

Figure 4.10. Election day for *Conseil de résidents*, 1966. Photograph copyright Jacques Windenberger/VAGA, New York.

rental contract guaranteeing protection from sudden increases. It also made proposals to modify the collective utility bills and charges, at least some of which were taken into account. With respect to the sociocultural facilities, the councils did not appear to be very motivated at first—perhaps detracted by the complexity of financing and management. However, during the following years they demanded a more powerful voice in the social, youth, and community centers, many of which had been centrally managed by SCIC's Animation, Loisirs Familiaux, Action Sociale, a nonprofit subsidiary established to address social problems in housing areas. Some of the councils gradually broadened their goals and began to demand direct participation in issues of urban planning. Even SCIC itself was initially an advocate for such an approach.[54] *Ville-nouvelles*, the new local periodical of Sarcelles's council, which united the Association Sarcelloise, the Association des familles, the Union des copropriétaires, and other local associations, was a mouthpiece for these ambitions (Figure 4.11). The council saw the local knowledge and actions of inhabitants as the perfect tools for a new "intelligent urbanism."[55]

Figure 4.11. Sarcelles's *Ville-nouvelles* periodical, December 1968. The front-page article, titled "With the Detailed Master Plan . . . the Last Chance of the Grand Ensemble," speaks of the need for inhabitants finally to sit at the planners' decision-making table, as illustrated by the cartoon captioned "Pass me the high school, please." Archives municipales de Sarcelles.

Meanwhile, the municipality of Sarcelles assumed an increasingly strong role in the process—often bypassing the Conseil de résidents and dismissing its legitimacy to represent the inhabitants of Sarcelles. Initially, the mayor's office was both ill-equipped and ill-prepared for the arrival of the *grand ensemble* "from Paris," and remained practically silent during the first phases of construction. However, during the early 1960s it began to develop a more active policy for the *grand ensemble*, partly as a result of the growing concerns of local associations. In 1962, after an address by Noël Lemaresquier, the architect of La Dame Blanche in the neighboring municipality of Garges, the municipal council agreed that a program of studies for the future development of their community was needed. It thus established an advisory committee to foster participatory decision making in matters of urban development but was unable to bring the often mistrusting representatives of Sarcelles's many local associations around the same table. In 1963, the council voiced concerns about SCIC's plans for future development, in particular their high density and purported lack of collective facilities. It began to obstruct further development by putting building permits on hold and decided not to approve any construction until a detailed local survey was done to assess the current situation and inhabitants' "real" needs.

The municipality initially lacked the necessary leverage to really obstruct the powerful developer.[56] That situation only changed when the energetic Communist Henri Canacos took over as mayor in 1965.[57] Under his direction, the municipality challenged the developer more resolutely and in more specific terms. In a letter to SCIC, the municipal council again criticized plans for future development: in the council's eyes, the housing program was too dense, the new neighborhoods did not include the necessary schools and commercial facilities, and when they did they were badly located. The secondary school was to be built on the other side of a future highway, cut off from the residential neighborhoods. SCIC replied drily that it had taken all points into account.[58] During the following years, the municipality systematically denied building permits. It demanded—now formally—in-depth social-scientific study preliminary to any future urban development. It also stipulated that sufficient land be reserved inside the *grand ensemble* for future collective facilities. And, most important, it hired its own experts for municipal urban planning. The expertise it needed was both sociological and architectural. The municipality hired ORGECO, a consultancy firm that specialized in sociological research, for two studies: one general urban and administrative study and another focused specifically on the collective facilities. At the same time, it also commissioned an architect-urbanist, Jean Bailly, to draw up comprehensive plans for future urban development.[59]

The plans aimed first of all at unifying the existing village and the *grand ensemble*. In between these two separated urban entities, Bailly proposed the construction of a new urban center containing administrative functions as well as housing and a connecting park. His plan also included the renovation of the existing village center, the development of an industrial zone to create local jobs, and a zone of low-rise housing on the yet-undeveloped northern side of the municipality (Figure 4.12). Bailly was subsequently commissioned to execute the village side of the plan while Henri-Labourdette remained in charge of the *grand ensemble* side. Henri-Labourdette used the ORGECO study to create a synthetic map of existing and future collective facilities, on the basis of which the municipality approached SCIC. The municipality thus succeeded in obliging the developer to provide land and funding for the collective facilities, in exchange for approving its building permit applications for the final phases of the *grand ensemble*, most importantly its final "Entrance to the City" phase (see Figure 3.13).[60] At the same time, the municipality spared little effort to convince inhabitants about the virtues of these plans (Figure 4.13).

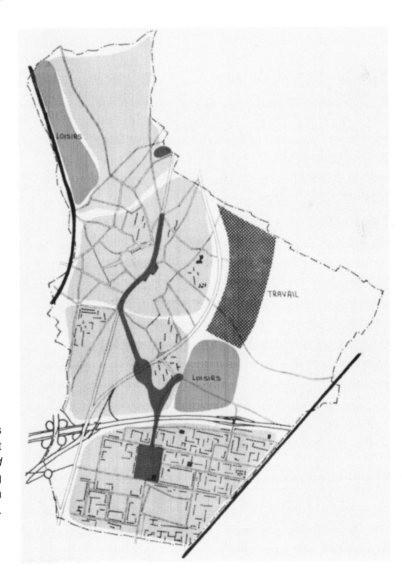

Figure 4.12. Jean Bailly's municipal urbanism project promised to bring the *grand ensemble* (bottom) and existing village (top) together. From *Urbanisme* 110 (1969): 35.

Il était une fois une calme petite ville du Parisis. Une grande cité vint à se greffer sur son territoire, et comme l'œuf du coucou voulut la supplanter. Le nom même de la petite ville ne servait plus à la désigner...

...elle, mais son énorme bourgeon. Mais la petite ville ne l'entendait pas ainsi et refusa que l'énorme cité écrasât toutes ses fleurs et bannit toute son harmonie de petite ville. Elle réagit et désigna ses délégués...

pour travailler à une heureuse conciliation. De cette élection naquit le plan d'urbanisme communal.

La petite ville et la grande cité, réconciliées, peuvent maintenant couler des jours heureux. L'avenir est riche de promesses.

Figure 4.13. A story of reconciliation between *grand ensemble* and old village. Cartoon from the *Bulletin Officiel Municipal*, December 1969. Archives municipales de Sarcelles.

Plate 1. Sarcelles Lochères. Postcard circa 1960. Lapie.

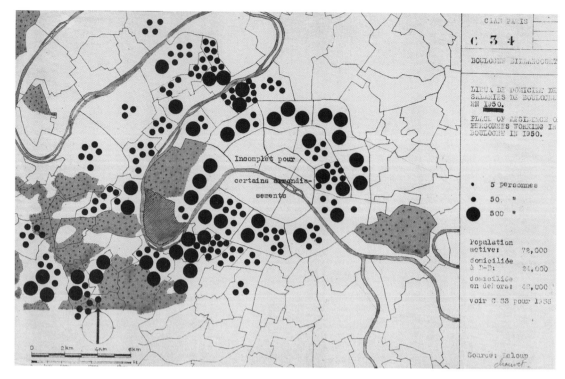

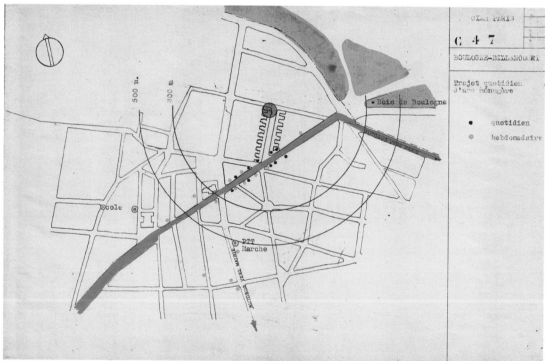

Plate 2. A selection of presentation boards from the Boulogne–Billancourt study by CIAM-Paris, 1953. (a) Map plotting the residences of workers in Boulogne–Billancourt, disproving planners' assumption that most workers lived close to work. (b) The daily and weekly trajectories and destinations of a housewife, whose residence is indicated with the red dot. (c) Map showing the uneven geographic distribution of neighborhood food stores, with some in clusters (the red ovals). Butchers and bakeries: 1 per 100 inhabitants; dairy and grocery stores: 1 per 285 inhabitants. (d) Analysis of a ground floor.

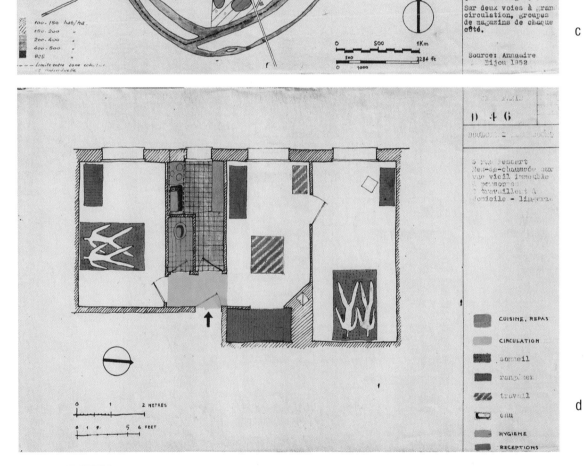

c

d

apartment in an old building, inhabited by four people, two of whom work at home in "lingerie"—presumably two females working as launderers or seamstresses. The red hatching shows where work takes place in the dwelling, refuting the strict separation of home and work upheld by most modern architects. Fonds Aujame. Service interministériel des Archives de France/Cité de l'architecture et du patrimoine/Archives d'architecture du XXᵉ siècle.

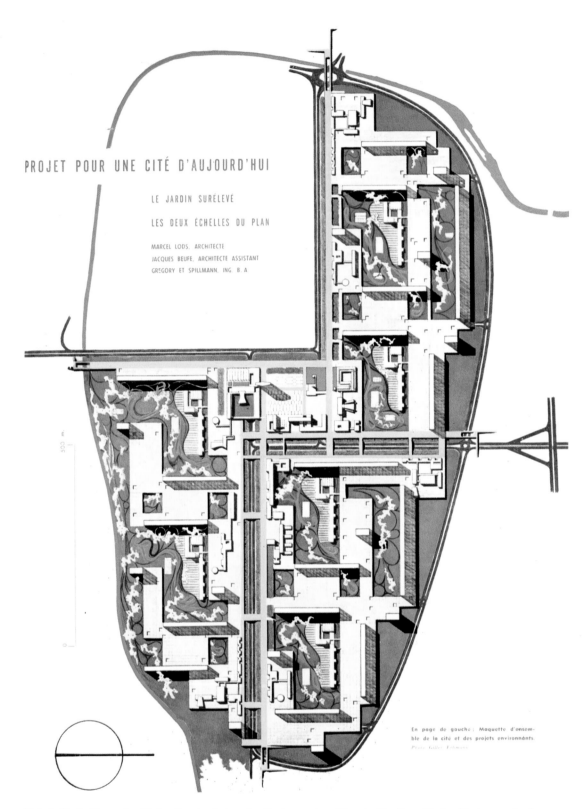

PROJET POUR UNE CITÉ D'AUJOURD'HUI

LE JARDIN SURÉLEVÉ

LES DEUX ÉCHELLES DU PLAN

MARCEL LODS, ARCHITECTE
JACQUES BEUFE, ARCHITECTE ASSISTANT
GREGORY ET SPILLMANN, ING. B. A

En page de gauche: Maquette d'ensemble de la cité et des projets environnants.

Plate 3. "Project for a city of today: the elevated garden, the two scales of the plan" by Marcel Lods with Jacques Beufe, assistant architect, and Gregory & Spillmann, engineers, 1960. From *L'Architecture d'aujourd'hui* 88 (1960): 15.

Plate 4. La Grande Borne (Grigny, near Paris), by the architect Émile Aillaud. Photograph by Eustachy Kossakowski, 1972. Fonds Aillaud. Service interministériel des Archives de France/Cité de l'architecture et du patrimoine/Archives d'architecture du XXe siècle.

Plate 5. La Grande Borne (Grigny, near Paris), by the architect Émile Aillaud. Fonds Aillaud. Service interministériel des Archives de France/Cité de l'architecture et du patrimoine/Archives d'architecture du XXe siècle.

Plate 6. Rendering by Henri Ciriani for the gallery space at Villeneuve. Promotional brochure, vertical files at Loeb Library, Harvard University.

GRENOBLE - VILLENEUVE

Plate 7. Postcard of Villeneuve Grenoble, 1970s. SPADEM. Courtesy of David Liaudet.

Plate 8. The 1965 master plan for Paris. Unlike previous plans, it locates major urban centers (black squares) outside the existing center of Paris; marks large swaths of land for future suburban development (light orange hatch); and ties together city and hinterland with major highways (red) and railways (black). The surrounding agricultural and forested zones (various shades of green) are now reconceptualized as recreational spaces in the service of the capital. From District de Paris/ Premier Ministre, *Schéma directeur d'aménagement et d'urbanisme de la région de Paris* (Paris, 1965).

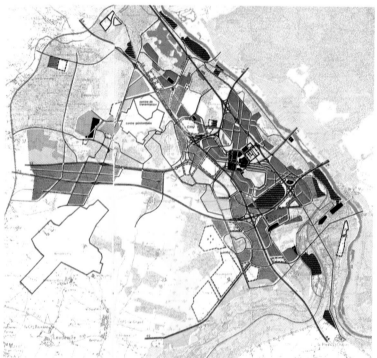

Plate 9. The structural plan for the New Town of Évry in 1969. The new urban center (black) is only a small part of the plan, which earmarks areas for future development such as high-density housing (crimson) and business (grey hatch), located amid existing housing areas (dotted patterns), housing developments under construction (crimson hatches), and agricultural and forest land (green). From *Urbanisme* 114 (1969): 14–15.

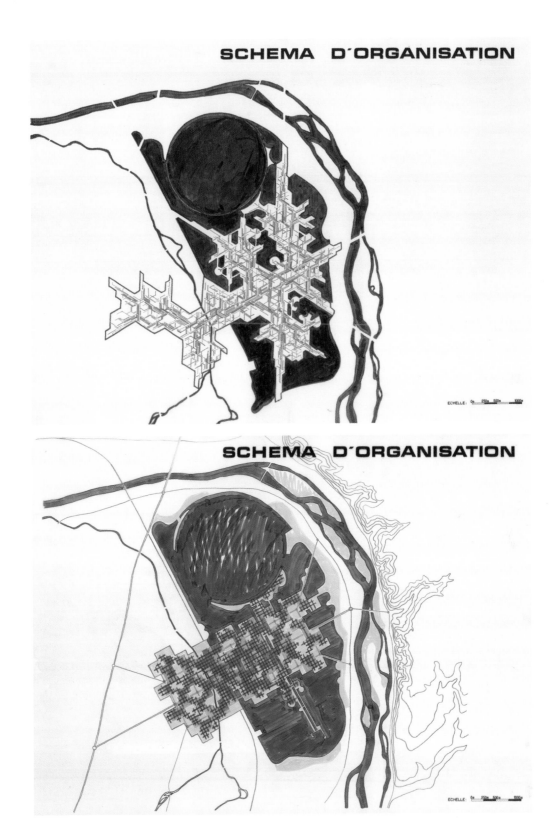

Plate 10. Atelier de Montrouge, two of three initial proposals for Le Vaudreuil, 1967–68. Fonds ATM. Service interministériel des Archives de France/Cité de l'architecture et du patrimoine/Archives d'architecture du XXᵉ siècle.

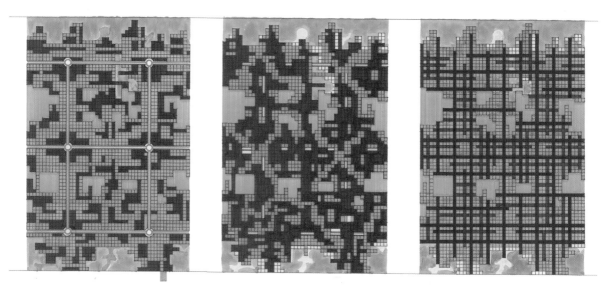

Plate 11. Atelier de Montrouge, organizational schemas for Le Vaudreuil, 1967–68. Fonds ATM. Service interministériel des Archives de France/Cité de l'architecture et du patrimoine/Archives d'architecture du XXe siècle.

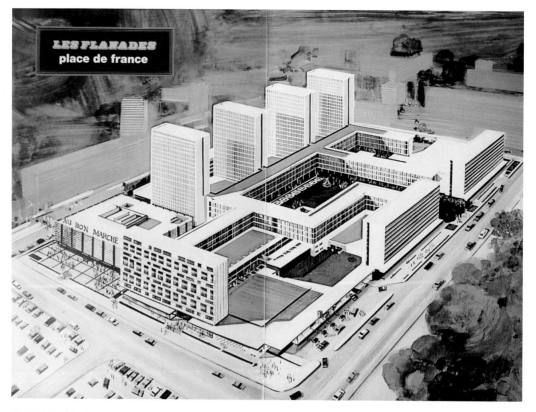

Plate 12. Principal urban center at Sarcelles by Roger Boileau and Jacques Henri-Labourdette. Promotional renderings for the center, now called "Les Flanades," early 1970s. Archives départementales du Val d'Oise, Bib D620.

Plate 13. Yona Friedman, Spatial City, 1958–59. Copyright 2012 Artists Rights Society, New York/Société des auteurs dans les arts graphiques et plastiques, Paris/MOMA. Licensed by SCALA/Art Resource, New York.

Plate 14. Rendering of Parly 2, late 1960s. Archives nationales, France, CAC 199110585/011.

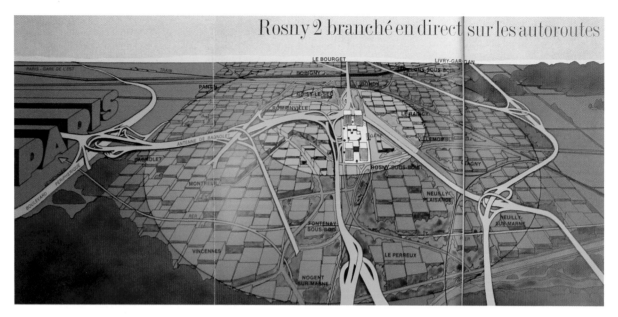

Plate 15. The strategic location of Rosny 2, plugged into the highway network, as illustrated in a promotional leaflet of the late 1960s. Archives nationales, France, CAC 199110585/011.

Plate 16. A postcard of Évry I upon completion. Raymon Publisher. Courtesy of David Liaudet.

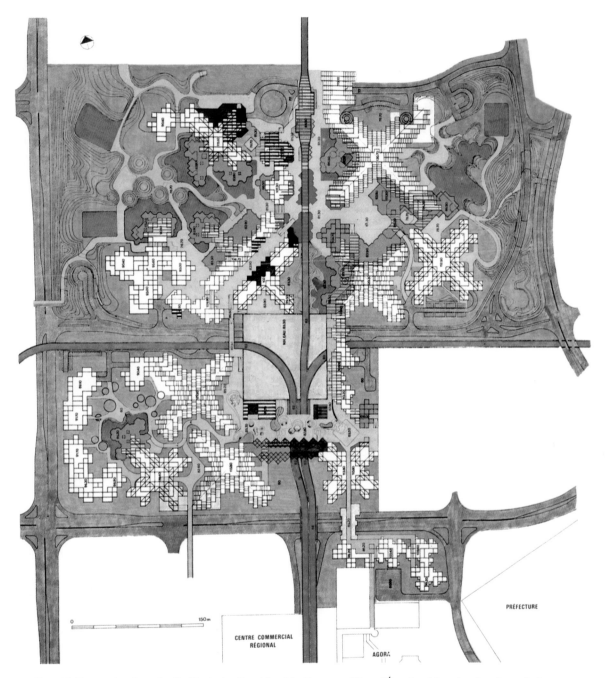

Plate 17. The master plan submitted by Andrault and Parat for the competition of Évry. Apart from housing, the project includes schools and sports and socioeducational facilities (blue); service functions (purple); administrative facilities, police station, and church (black); recreation grounds (brown); commerce (red); a bus line (orange); and a large water mirror in the center. From *Cahiers de l'IAURP* 31 (1973): 55.

Plate 18. Model of the Évry I project circa 1973, showing the project's treatment of public space. Archives nationales, France, CAC 197803179/001.

Plate 19. Promotional brochure for Évry I circa 1973, claiming that "At Évry I, gardens in terraces change the look of the city." Planners resorted to glossy brochures like these to entice prospective inhabitants, particularly home buyers. Archives nationales, France, CAC 197803179/001.

Plate 20. Jean Renaudie's housing project for Ivry as seen from one of the surrounding towers in 2009. Photograph by the author.

Plate 21. Hexagonal system for housing projects, nominated as 1974 "Modèle innovation," by Dominique Beau, Laszlo Feber, and Michel Orluc. Archives nationales, France, CAC 19840342/324.

The Conseil de résidents was kept out of these negotiations and had not been informed about the decision, either by SCIC or by the municipality, despite an earlier agreement. Although some of its recommendations had been taken into account, many of its adherents still felt disillusioned and betrayed.[61] They remained faithful to their militant position, but they did not ultimately succeed in getting a real voice in urban planning decisions. The agreements between municipality and developer had cut them off from further involvement, and one of their remaining goals, the construction of a second community center, was delayed. In subsequent years, the Conseil de résidents lost its vigor and the periodical *Ville-nouvelles* was discontinued in 1971.[62] Subsequent elections of the council drew fewer and fewer crowds, and the percentage of inhabitants actively involved diminished continually.[63] Ultimately, it was not the Conseil de résidents but the municipality that gained an important role vis-à-vis SCIC.

A 1975 social-scientific study of Sarcelles outlined three phases of this political evolution (Figure 4.14). In an initial period, from around 1954 until 1965, the various inhabitant associations—first informally led by the Association Sarcelloise and then officially by the Conseil de résidents—functioned as outside pressure groups attempting to intrude on the closed decision-making process of the developer. Then, in a second period, until around 1971, the developer accepted inhabitants' input, first mainly from the Conseil de résidents, but increasingly also from the municipality, which had launched its own process of negotiation independently. Both the Conseil and the municipality represented inhabitants and claimed to be the legitimate institution to do so. The council eventually lost out to the municipality, inaugurating a third period in which the inhabitants could participate in decision making via the

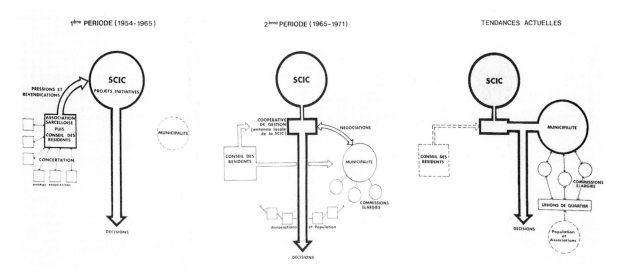

Figure 4.14. Diagram of the evolution of political negotiations in Sarcelles from a sociological study commissioned by SCIC, 1975. CDC/SCIC, Dossier Sarcelles-Lochères, 1954–74.

municipality through "neighborhood unions" and "enlarged committees." This political evolution inspired Manuel Castells and his colleagues in their well-known study of social movements in the Paris region; they in fact published an almost identical diagram with a similar periodization.[64]

When activists at the beginning of the 1970s made the balance sheet of this experiment, they acknowledged the modesty of the achievements. Concrete results included a long-term lease contract offering better conditions to tenants, a system of accountability with regard to communal charge and maintenance, and an evolution toward the comanagement of socio-cultural facilities. Some observers also referred to "a certain rehabilitation of the *grand ensemble*" and "the improvement of the built environment."[65] The Conseil de résidents of Poissy was able to slow down the extension of an industrial zone that it considered detrimental to the *grand ensemble*. In Sarcelles, it diverted plans for the construction of a car-park building away from the area's central park. Despite these successes, there was also disappointment, especially within the more militant organizations. The CNL concluded that "the councils do not offer the possibility for a veritable participation."[66] And yet, despite such criticism, there was certainly not a simple status quo. The experiment of participatory management in the *grands ensembles* might not have delivered on all of its promises but it did give local municipalities a voice in matters of urbanism. While SCIC constructed most of Sarcelles from the 1950s onward, the municipality was now in charge of its own urban planning projects. The politics resulting from the *grands ensembles* thus set an important precedent for the political decentralization of the 1980s.

Less discussed at the time was how the political struggles in Sarcelles were influenced by residential mobility patterns with not just class but also racial characteristics. The moment when the Conseil de résidents lost its importance coincided with the departure of many of Sarcelles's first generation of activists. Immigrant families from peripheral *bidonvilles* (shantytowns) moved into many of the older, less desirable flats left behind by white middle-class families, who could now afford to buy apartments or single-family homes elsewhere in the Parisian suburbs. The arrival of the *pieds-noirs* from North Africa and Spanish, Portuguese, and Italian immigrant workers in the mid-1960s was only the beginning of a process of social and ethnic diversification that has continued up until today. The newly arriving inhabitants created a different landscape of community, which weakened the kind of solidarity at the basis of many initial inhabitant associations. Contrary to the perception of first-generation activists, associational life continued to flourish, but it was increasingly organized around a multitude of small groups with culturally, religiously, and ethnically defined interests.[67] As Sarcelles became a major center of France's Jewish community, kosher butchers began to open up, synagogues were built, and a Jewish school opened in the early 1970s. Vietnamese and French Caribbean associations developed during the 1970s and especially the 1980s, as did

Muslim organizations such as the Association des musulmans d'inspiration sunnite, which established Sarcelles's first mosque in a small room at the back of one of the commercial centers in 1986–87.[68]

In class terms, the *grand ensemble* also changed. Later phases of construction in Sarcelles often included areas of relatively luxurious middle-class condominiums. The changing housing stock altered relative definitions of the poor and led to the increased concentration of working-class families—often immigrants—in the older, smaller, and less desirable apartments. While it initially served largely as a homogenizing and standardizing force, both socially and architecturally, housing in France now became an explicitly differentiating consumer product. For Sarcelles, this evolution was aligned with the construction of more generously sized apartments, which targeted middle-class home owners often with luxurious fittings, underground garages, and marble-clad entrance lobbies. These new developments also had a greater diversity in apartment units and included studios and one-bedroom apartments, generating more options for prospective residents to choose from. Surprisingly, the Communist municipality explicitly encouraged SCIC to diversify its housing stock and to attract middle-class home buyers in order to create the diversity of a "normal city."[69]

In 1972, Sarcelles inaugurated an internal public transport line connecting the old village with the *grand ensemble*. This line was the first of its kind in the Paris region—another sign that Sarcelles was now a city in its own right. The *grand ensemble* neared completion, and the relatively homogeneous character of the initial population gave way to social and ethnic diversity. In the early 1970s, the census already revealed more than a hundred ethnicities living in Sarcelles. At the same time, income levels were higher than the national average, contradicting the stereotype of the *grand ensemble* as the "place of the poor."[70] Yet, just as in other new developments, the concentration of a homogeneously undesirable housing stock led increasingly to problems of social segregation.

Sarcelles shows not only the conflicts, but especially the interrelations between those operating "from above" and those operating "from below." Political elites, high civil servants, experts, local activists, and inhabitant associations crossed different spheres by working on multiple levels, oscillating between national and local domains of action. Claude Neuschwander, the first leader of Sarcelles's Conseil de résidents, for example, was not only a local inhabitant and activist but also an influential figure on the national political scene. A graduate of the École centrale des arts et manufactures, he had made a successful career at Publicis—France's preeminent advertising and public relations firm—and was an influential member of the Parti socialiste unifié.[71] Figures such as Neuschwander saw participation as both a positive contribution to national development and an absolute necessity for local life.

Participation grew out of social contestation, but also out of the initiatives and institutions of the centralized state apparatus. It was not a purely emancipatory device at the hands of inhabitants faced with an all-powerful state; it also entailed opportunities for a more efficient way of dealing with housing, opportunistically seized by those in charge; and it proved useful in satisfying inhabitants' demands and avoiding conflicts. The history of Sarcelles thus confirms the importance of mediation as the precondition of participation—not only because of the involvement of associations or an elite group of militants, but because of the crucial role of expert knowledge about inhabitants and their everyday lives. Already in 1970, observers warned about the dangers of an "elitism of militancy" that would deny the very fundamentals of citizen participation. Considering the fact that less than 10 percent of inhabitants were part of any activist associations, this warning was not far-fetched.[72] From the early 1960s, inhabitants themselves began to understand the role of the social-scientific survey as a mediating instrument that could translate their needs into a concrete program for improving the built environment. At the same time, experts galvanized the idea that sociological inquiry was a necessary preliminary to planning, and that planning was therefore a matter of the social as much as of the physical fabric.

Municipal Brutalism

Despite growing emphasis on the social dimension of urban planning, calls for participation continued to emerge in direct response to the material and architectural qualities of mass housing in 1960s France. Therefore, not just social action or sociological study but also architectural design could be mobilized for a more participatory dwelling environment. A unique experiment in this regard was the making of Villeneuve in Grenoble during the late 1960s and 1970s. Just as in Sarcelles, inhabitants' contestation in Grenoble against what was increasingly perceived as a callously imposed urbanism gave rise to municipal-level planning processes and collaboration between different local and national professionals and experts. Unlike at Sarcelles, this situation arose before the buildings had been built. Grenoble's participatory urbanism could thus be developed "from scratch" and architecture and urban design could play leading roles.

Grenoble, a provincial city at the foot of the French Alps, had been growing rapidly since World War II. In 1960, in response to the housing shortage, Henri Bernard—a Prix de Rome architect known for his work in the reconstruction of Caen and Rouen—was asked to draw up plans for large-scale state-led housing developments at the edge of the existing city, known as Villeneuve.[73] The municipal elections of 1965 changed these plans fundamentally. The ruling Gaullist party was overthrown by a left-leaning coalition led by Hubert Dubedout from the Groupes d'action municipale, a movement that had emerged out of the city's local neighborhood unions. Unique to Grenoble, these unions had been established in the interwar period to organize local community events but had become increasingly powerful and challenged municipal authority during the early 1960s. The rise of Hubert Dubedout and the Groupes d'action municipale to municipal power was thus a victory for the neighborhood unions. The movement quickly spread across the nation, making Grenoble the icon of a new participatory municipal politics in 1960s France.[74]

Hubert Dubedout and his chief of urbanism, Jean Verlach, put urbanism at the center of their municipal politics. Favoring social housing organizations over private developers and collaborative design teams over Prix de Rome architects, the first thing they did was to reject Henri Bernard's existing plans.[75] "Not based on a study of actual needs," the Bernard plan had become the embodiment of all the problems of centralized state urbanism increasingly decried by the mid-1960s. The municipality's ambitions for Villeneuve were shaped in direct response to such discontents. As opposed to the monotonous "bedroom suburbs" mushrooming seemingly randomly all over France, the new municipal urbanism would create lively new neighborhoods by providing carefully designed public spaces and public amenities built at the same time as the housing units; it would foster social mixing by providing both rental social housing and middle-class condos in close proximity; and it would create urbanity by building in high density and providing ample employment opportunities. Most important, the new urbanism would be guided by the central principles of dialogue and participation: "As opposed to the secret urbanism, or in other words that of the bureaucratic system, the point is to incite debate and confrontations with the users about the goals of urban planning and the proposed solutions."[76]

In 1966, then, the municipality put together a planning team that included experts from a variety of disciplines. Most important, it engaged a new type of architect, the young collaborative agency Atelier d'urbanisme et d'architecture (AUA). This office in fact already constituted a collaborative multidisciplinary team in and of itself. Established in 1959 by the urbanist Jean Allégret with interior designers Jean Perrottet, Jacques Berce, and Valentin Fabre and architects Jean Tribel and Georges Loiseau, AUA was an explicitly left-wing critique of the Beaux-Arts tradition.[77] Its collaborative model of practice, which negated the artistic authority of the singular architect and was soon adopted by dozens of offices throughout France, was particularly well received in the new political climate of Grenoble. It allowed the urbanist Jean-François Parent, the architects Jean Tribel and Georges Loiseau, the landscape architect Michel Corajoud, and the sociologist Annick Dottelonde-Osmont to collaboratively design one of France's largest urban developments of the late 1960s.[78]

Exceeding this professional collaboration, the degree of participation in Villeneuve's planning and design was unprecedented. Not only the municipality, the planning team, and delegates from the Ministré de l'équipement were involved, but social workers, teachers, and some future inhabitants were as well. They first participated informally in the conception of Villeneuve, through meetings that were not publicly announced. Then, at a later stage, larger public meetings were organized to prepare future inhabitants for the new kinds of collective facilities that had been planned. There was thus participation in both the conception and the execution phase. At the same time, it was limited to a small segment of the population: a left-leaning, activist middle class intent on bypassing the existing establishment and institutions. In a charter published in 1971, the self-organized inhabitants declared that "the will to transform the human relations in the city is what characterizes the project of Villeneuve. The essential goal is to have users take charge of the diverse sociocultural and socioeducational facilities that have been put at their disposal."[79] Participation, in other words, went hand in hand with a remarkable ideological consensus about how to make Villeneuve the example of an alternative, new kind of urbanism.

Inhabitant participation did not preclude architectural expression. In fact, at Villeneuve it fostered a particular kind of formal language. The designers' response to the municipality's brief was to focus on the public realm as an organizing device for the neighborhood. The result of what they called "the unity of the overall urban structure" was a continuous mega-structure composed of brutalist concrete slabs between six and fifteen stories, which separated roads and parking on one side from a large park on the other (Figure 4.15). With its sixty-degree angles on a honeycomb pattern, this design escaped "the fatalism of the right angle" and allowed a formal diversity of architectures to be plugged in. It also generated direct relationships between different elements of the program—housing, collective facilities, and green space. The park was designed by Corajoud as an architectonic landscape of differently articulated atmospheres facilitating a multitude of public activities (Figure 4.16). The neighborhood's principal feature was its double-height pedestrian gallery space, which ran continuously underneath the linear housing slabs. This was the neighborhood's mile-long trunk line, connecting all apartments via mezzanines with the collective facilities, the park, the parking structures, and the surrounding neighborhoods (Figure 4.17). Neither a nineteenth-century passage nor a "street in the air" à la Alison and Peter Smithson, this covered public space was imagined to be the architectural vector of Villeneuve's community life, providing ample opportunity for *flânerie* and encounter.[80] With its plethora of urban signage and advertising, Henri Ciriani's design for this space acknowledged the street as a vehicle of communication and visual consumption. In some ways, this was the belated arrival of Anglo-American pop in French architecture (Plate 6).

Social ambition and architectural form came together particularly successfully in the design of the project's collective facilities. Supported by recent sociopedagogical theory, the basic approach for the neighborhood was a radical continuity between education, *animation*, and sociocultural life. The planning team dismissed the conventional quantitative approach: in order to be effective and socially inclusive, collective facilities needed to be resolutely integrated with each other and with the surrounding neighborhood more generally.[81] The public

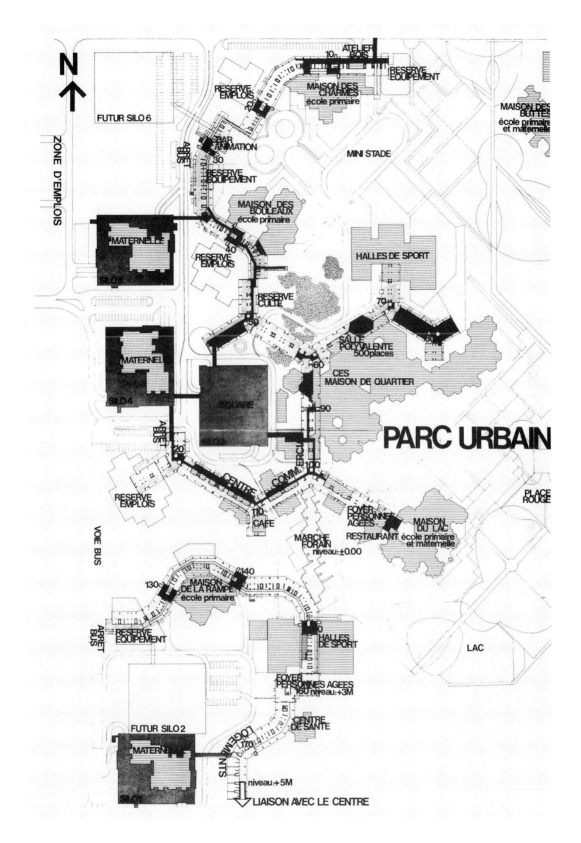

Figure 4.15. Plan of the Quartier de L'Arlequin, Villeneuve. From *L'Architecture d'aujourd'hui* 174 (1974): 29.

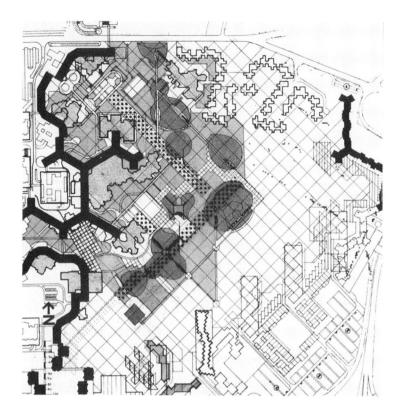

Figure 4.16. Park design by Michel Corajoud. Antipastoral and focused on maximizing the possibilities for active recreation, this plan combined an orthogonal grid and different types of hard surfaces with tall round grassy mounds offering visual relief and relative intimacy. Archives municipales de Grenoble.

Figure 4.17. Photographs of the public gallery space. Archives municipales de Grenoble.

gallery space provided the architectural structure to graft these on. Of all the required facilities, the school was most radically rethought as an institution: it became a pedagogical experiment in mixing secondary school education with youth and permanent education programs. This approach found spatial translation in interconnected, multiuse spaces and the radical opening up of interior spaces to the public space of the gallery.[82] Villeneuve's experimental school housed a public library, a sociocultural center, exhibition rooms, workshop spaces, and a restaurant, all of which opened up directly to the covered street of the main trunk line (Figure 4.18).

The neighborhood, envisaged to be only the first phase of the future Villeneuve, was baptized l'Arlequin—the harlequin—because of its multicolored facades. The architects had been keen on avoiding the repetitive, monotonous look of earlier *grands ensembles*. Working within the limits of standardized concrete prefabrication, they visually broke up the slabs by applying brightly colored strips and accentuating their bays volumetrically. They also introduced variety by means of loggias, unsystematically distributed over the facade. In their effort to visually diversify the facade, however, it was important to avoid making legible any distinctions between the different housing units behind it (Plate 7). Such articulation of the facade was only the easy part of a larger strategy to generate diversity. The mixing of different housing categories—an ambition shared by the municipal council, the planning team, and the participating middle class alike—proved to be the project's most formidable challenge. Local private developers as well as the semipublic developer SCIC showed little interest in the idea of putting social and market-rate housing close together.[83] The city and the department then decided to take on the role of developers themselves and build the bulk of the desired mix. The ideal combination of half condos and half social housing was not achieved: eventually, only 350 of the almost two thousand units were market-rate condos.[84] Despite planners' intention to also provide housing for the poorest and most marginalized, very low-cost-housing was eventually left out and only a small portion of housing was built for students, the elderly, and the disabled.[85] The private developers that were eventually taken on board in the project built housing separately. That of the developer Arc foncière, for instance, was located at the far opposite side of the park, and its lower density and urban form were a clear indication of its divergent social status (Figure 4.19). The mixing of other programs was equally challenging. Because planners feared that the complete dispersal of commerce would not generate enough customers and thus revenue, it was grouped in two clusters, one of ten and another of fifteen stores. The types of shops were first defined by the planners and then sold off to selected candidates.[86] This strategy did not allow for long-term management or the continued engineering of diversity. Despite good intentions, planners also failed to attract employment, just as they did at other mass housing developments. Of the five large spaces they provided, only one was occupied.

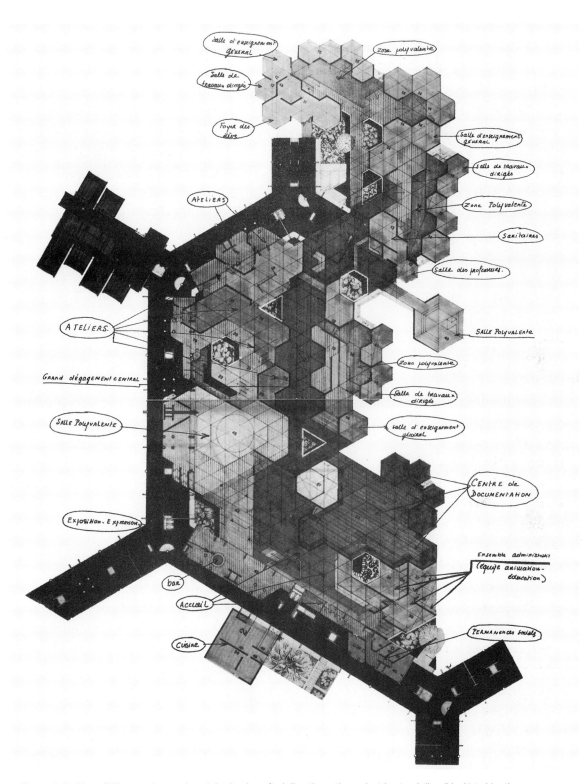

Figure 4.18. Plan of Villeneuve's experimental school, grafted directly on the pedestrian trunk line (black) to blur the distinction between the public space of the covered street and the interior spaces. The school featured an impressive mix of programs, including classrooms, workshop spaces, a documentation center, a bar, a reception desk, a kitchen, an exhibition space, and many undefined "polyvalent spaces." Archives municipales de Grenoble.

Figure 4.19. Aerial photograph of Villeneuve in the late 1970s. The private housing development of Arc Foncière, described as "horizontal collective" in type, is visible on the bottom right of the photograph. Archives municipales de Grenoble.

The first inhabitants arrived in 1972. They were generally young, more diverse than in the average social housing project, characterized by a relatively high proportion of intellectuals and the upper middle class, and with an about-average percentage of immigrants, predominantly working-class North Africans.[87] Long after the inhabitants had settled in, sociologists remained in Villeneuve to gauge the project's successes and failures. Eva Radwan in particular studied meticulously how exactly inhabitants used the spaces designed for them. The public gallery, their reports concluded, worked more or less as envisaged, at least in the first years after completion. Some inhabitants complained of its windswept character and lack of *animation*, and many found it alienating. But surveys also reported people appreciating the spatial complexity of the public realm, which allowed them to choose their own paths and discover places. The design of the park was generally considered too harsh. Corajoud's scheme, which aimed to incite active participation and opposed what he called "fake naturalism," did not ultimately meet inhabitants' desire for more trees, less concrete, and fewer rectangles.[88] Observers were most struck by the social segregation as a result of the different ways inhabitants appropriated the neighborhood. The North African immigrants, mainly of lower economic class, hung out in particular corners of the public gallery while the white middle class was most present in the collective facilities. Upper-middle-class inhabitants did not seem to have a particular spatial pattern because "their realm of action is the city at large rather than the neighborhood."[89]

Associational life was vibrant in Villeneuve's first decade, but again largely a left-leaning middle-class affair. Facilities were generally ample, and in domains where they were not, inhabitants took the initiative. Some had organized the production of a local newspaper (Figure 4.20). Another group of families organized their own informal child day-care center because insufficient care facilities had been provided by planners. Such initiatives were run by the "militant professionals," as sociologists categorized them, and subscribed to the "myth of Villeneuve" as a post-1968 activist project. The project had effectively increased inhabitant participation, but it seemed that only a small segment of the middle classes really benefited from it. Radwan described how the others "either ignore these facilities and do not feel concerned, or they have a certain curiosity but refuse involvement because of timidity."[90] Despite designers' attempts to design a socially diverse environment, she also concluded that "the exterior spaces (the gallery and the commercial center) do not favor the social relations outside the dwelling, which are characteristic of the way of life of this social class [the working class]."[91] Planners had not provided enough traditional meeting spaces—especially bars and cafés. When asked to make the balance sheet for Villeneuve a couple of years after its completion, planners concluded that, ironically, "the constitution of a professional group with the mission to engender social life in the neighborhood creates, in some cases, an obstacle for the direct dialogue between inhabitants and those in power, as well as for users to take control over certain parts of their everyday lives."[92]

The social group experiencing the most hardship was, not coincidentally, the one that felt most excluded by Villeneuve's participatory experiments. Often described simply as "the foreigners" in official reports, they were predominantly working-class North African immigrant families.[93] Nothing was really provided specifically for them. A familiar pattern seemed to appear to sociologists: "The North Africans already have the tendency to regroup in order to overcome their insecurity and find their cultural and ethnic origins." The establishment of a Comité culturel des Maghrébins was seen as an important factor in this process. But it was also fostered by housing allocation policies, which led immigrant families to cluster in specific hallways and blocks. Sociologists considered such community formation as threatening the integration of the neighborhood at large. The only really public space immigrants used in the neighborhood was the "bar-animation," an initiative initially set up by Villeneuve's social animation team specifically for adolescents. When they made it "too rowdy," the bar was closed down. It was subsequently reopened by people in the North African community and renamed "Bar-bu"—a play on "bar" and "bearded." The bar became the primary meeting spot for the North African community over the following years.[94]

Despite at times alarming reports of the purported dangers of social segregation—especially in a neighborhood explicitly designed to foster social mixing and participation—there were intense moments of social mixing. These had both positive and negative effects. In

Figure 4.20. *Le manteau de l'Arlequin,* a self-published local newspaper in the early 1970s. This front cover shows a festive Harlequin, the mascot of the neighborhood, putting his best foot forward for the camera—just like its inhabitants, who wanted to present their new neighborhood in the best light possible. Archives municipales de Grenoble.

interviews, many inhabitants spoke of the pleasures of living in a lively, mixed neighborhood. Noise, however, remained a constant complaint, as it had been in the first *grands ensembles*, but now for different reasons. The technical quality of sound insulation had increased dramatically since the mid-1950s, but now the cause of nuisance was programmatic. With the ambition of small-grained social mixing, small one-bedroom apartments had at times been placed right next to very large ones, and this meant single people, often elderly, living next door to large families with young children.[95] At the same time, perceptions of class-based segregation were certainly an important source of social friction (Figure 4.21). The successes and failures of Villeneuve, as reported by sociologists, city officials, planners, architects, and inhabitants themselves, were thus mixed and many.

The ultimate goal of much sociological research was clear: to improve for the future. Half a decade after the completion of Villeneuve's first neighborhood, a second one baptized "Les Balladins" was envisaged. Based on their careful observations of social life at l'Arlequin, sociologists recommended new ways to ensure social integration against the odds. This included informal meeting spots catering to the needs of immigrants and the working classes and exterior spaces that "allowed the urban practice of immigrant men and children who live predominantly outside of their apartments."[96] But too much had changed for designers to prioritize these suggestions. The later part of the 1970s posited severe economic challenges. Private developers were even harder to convince of proposals that worked against their conventional logic, state support for extravagant experimentation with collective facilities had practically vanished, and politicians were less inclined to embark on ambitious new projects. Any new urban development had to be divisible into small, isolated phases. Public and private programs needed to be clearly split. And overall planning was challenged by the uncoordinated development of private housing developments in the immediate surroundings. The result was an entirely different neighborhood. Les Balladins would take until the early 1980s to be finished. By this time, l'Arlequin's massive slab composition was clearly out of fashion. It was no longer praised for its architectural diversity but criticized for its megalomania. For Les Balladins, designers had given up on the idea of a unified urban structure.

Formal differences aside, the ambitions of social mixing remained the same. To attract the middle class, more condos were provided, but home owners were now more clearly separated from renters.[97] But the challenge was ever more steep: by the 1980s, the retreat of the middle classes from collective housing projects had become undeniable.[98] The intention to learn from one project for the next was broken by larger social and economic changes, on which neither architects, planners, nor sociologists had a definitive grasp. The importance of l'Arlequin thus lies in the brief historic moment in which the rhetoric of participation gave rise to a new municipal-level urbanism within essentially the same regime of housing production that had shaped the previous decades of French urbanization. In 1975, local member of the French

Figure 4.21. Graffiti in the public gallery of l'Arlequin, mid-1970s. When planners placed an information poster announcing the proposal for the placement of a public toilet, inhabitants reacted in writing: "The 50 [building number 50] = the ass of Villeneuve = concentration of social housing, large families, immigrants, poverty, dirtiness. The toilets are added to this, a symbol, no?" Archives municipales de Grenoble.

Communist Party Jean Giard vehemently denounced Villeneuve and its "so-called participatory" urbanism, pointing out that its rhetoric of participation corresponded exactly with the language of the developers and the "technocratic capitalist system" at large.[99] Villeneuve's municipal brutalism was brutal after all.

Participation from Above

In the wake of the student and workers' revolts of 1968, the ideology of participation in the realm of the built environment had transformed in two directions. On the one hand, intellectuals from the Left—empowered by a renewed Marxism—launched more fundamental critiques at the state apparatus and its role in the built environment. Manuel Castells's 1974 *Monopolville* used the case of Dunkerque to reveal the complicity of mass housing provision with the logic of industrial capitalism. Édmond Preteceille's 1973 *La production des grands ensembles* described them as expressions of capitalist contradiction. And other researchers at the Centre de sociologie urbaine—which at that time brought together some of France's most fervent Marxists—followed suit.[100] On the other hand, participation was steadily adopted by government institutions in a series of initiatives meant to overcome social critique and contestation during the 1970s. While these two directions seem utterly divergent, they were in fact intimately linked.

Sociological analyses preliminary to urban planning had gradually become standard practice within the institutions of the centralized government during the second half of the 1960s. Before 1968, however, many of these studies were purely instrumental to preestablished methods and goals of planning, and thus hardly allowed for a critical position: their aim was to better know "user needs" in order to increase satisfaction levels.[101] The *grand ensemble* remained a dominant model in practice, despite mounting evidence of its problematic consequences. One of the big changes precipitated by the political turbulence of 1968 was the development of new modes of urban research funded by the government. More theoretically informed, more critical, and more closely related to the development of academic sociology and other disciplines, this new wave of contractual research focused in particular on the social consequences of state-led urban planning. While relatively independent, the government still intended this new vein of research to eventually influence policy making. Critique and reform were thus more closely entangled than the rhetoric of many leftist intellectuals—vigorously critiquing a state apparatus that often supported their livelihoods by financing their research—would appear to suggest.

The experiments with participation during the 1960s had gradually brought together social militants and local activists, politicians and civil servants, local associations and civil society organizations, academics, urban planners, state research institutions, and contractual research firms. Although they did not make up a "movement" within a single milieu, they shaped participation as a loose arrangement of theories, individuals, and institutions in a variety of professional and ideological contexts. Supported by the critical and activist momentum of 1968, and amplified by the availability of public money for urban research, this network found its ultimate expression in the government-led program Habitat et vie sociale (Dwelling and Social Life) during the 1970s.

To assure the application of new urban policies, the Ministère de l'équipement organized a series of regional seminars in 1972 with the help of the Foundation for Social Research (Fondation pour la recherche sociale). Culminating in a national conference in February 1973, the initiative led to the creation of a coordinating group charged with the "development of social life" in housing estates all across the nation. The fact that activist groups such as the Association Sarcelloise could be seen as clear proof that social life was pretty well developed—if not overdeveloped—in urban France did not appear to cross the minds of the administrators.

Under the title "Habitat et vie sociale," the coordinating group was the place where many advocates of participation in the early 1970s found common ground. The group's main goal was to study key precedents in all social aspects of housing and urban planning: participation, consultation procedures, *animation*, the development of associational life, and so on. Trintignac, the civil servant at the forefront of housing sociology within the ministry since the 1950s, was one of the key members of the group.[102] He was in charge of coordinating meetings and local initiatives. He also worked closely with regional administrators who were in charge of developing exemplary projects. Paul Rendu, director of the Centre de sociologie urbaine, was in charge of the research division.

The group's main public outlet was a periodical with the same name. It featured analyses of existing cases that could serve as "best practices" for future planning policies. The by now well-known experiments of the Conseils de résidents and the Groupes d'action municipale, with Sarcelles and Grenoble as exemplars, figured prominently.[103] Based on such studies, novel experiments were launched all over the country through collaboration with regional administrators. In the Bouches-du-Rhône region, for instance, following the regional seminar that was organized there in 1972, the prefect of the department established a study group to develop participatory planning projects. These included new housing developments, such as at La Rousse in Miramas, where six hundred new HLM dwelling units were designed by a team of architects and sociologists after an architectural competition. It also included projects to improve existing *grands ensembles*, such as the ZUP (Zone à urbaniser par priorité) no. 1 in Marseille, and social projects to welcome inhabitants to new housing developments.[104]

Often modest in scale and scattered all over France, these projects reveal the contradictions of creating local participation by means of a centralized governmental think tank. And yet, while the Habitat et vie sociale initiative was in itself not very successful, it did set the scene for the next decades of urban policy in France. In 1977, the group's initiatives were further expanded to include actions focused on the rehabilitation of the first *grands ensembles*. In 1982, the Quilliot law and the National Committee for the Social Development of Neighborhoods (Commission nationale de développement social des quartiers) further institutionalized the participation of local associations in urban planning procedures.[105] Over the following decades, this direction of urban policy, known as "politique de la ville," became increasingly focused on the rehabilitation of what were coined "quartiers sensibles" or problem neighborhoods. Scholars have demonstrated how such well-meaning programs and projects reduced national-level social problems to locally defined issues and in doing so have been instrumental in the stigmatization of the *grands ensembles* up until today.[106] Equally striking about these urban policies was the way they instituted sociological study, social work, and a bureaucratized procedure of local participation as unquestioned elements of any urban development project. The state-sponsored research and experimentation with participatory planning of the

1960s and 1970s would thus lead to the dominance of participation as a subject of expertise in planning rather than a direct transfer of agency to individual inhabitants. The history of Alma-Gare in Roubaix, in which local contestation led to the creation of a public workshop for urbanism, is another staple of urban participation in 1970s France. While it was in many respects a unique and isolated example, it showed similarly how local and national levels of activism were closely related, and how this precipitated the professionalization of activists and the development of an expertise of participation.[107]

Sarcelles again suggests the consequences of this evolution. More than a decade after the establishment of the Conseil de résidents, the large-scale project to restructure the commercial center of Les Flanades addressed inhabitants again in unprecedented ways.[108] During its long period of planning and construction, the center had been a beacon of hope for the municipality and local associations in their ambitions to improve Sarcelles. After its grand opening in 1972, however, the center went into a steep decline—consumers stayed away, stores closed, and maintenance flagged. Already by the end of the decade the developer and city government had launched a "revitalization" project. Planners and local activists alike cast the project as an ideal opportunity for the direct participation of inhabitants in the built environment. Pressured by the municipality, planners began by organizing a "public consultation" project. This was paid for by the developer (a subsidiary of SCIC) and executed by a team of experts, including ORGECO, the private consultancy firm COFREMCA, and Larry Smith & Co., the American consultancy firm that had become famous for shopping-mall development in collaboration with the architect Victor Gruen. Designed by Bailly, the new center was to be more open and multifunctional, offering "well-being, conviviality, and urbanity" in contrast to the "hyperconsumption and functionalism" of the previous center.[109] The design itself amounted to an aesthetic postmodernization of Les Flanades: it covered the open plazas with pergolas, created elaborate landscaping, added exotic decoration, and expanded the parking scheme drastically. More than the aesthetic shift, the project revealed how expertise was invested with the social as much as the physical. Most important, it demonstrated how planning continued to conflate citizenship and consumerism by promoting participation—in this case, for what was in essence a shopping-mall refurbishment. Despite disagreements between the developer and the municipality, market research and participation had become no more than different varieties in the same planning regime.

The origins were in the inhabitant activism of France's *grands ensembles* during previous decades. The production of French mass housing had given rise to a complex series of local negotiations between inhabitant associations, developers, the centralized state, and municipal government. Sarcelles—which served at once as the national model of the *grands ensembles*, the focus of national public outcry, and a key object of urban sociological study—was most visibly situated on the crossroads of such local contestation and national policy. More generally, associational life in the *grands ensembles* was often a factor in their spatial ambivalence between housing and city, a condition that addressed the inhabitant at once as tenant, user, consumer, and citizen. Between the late 1950s and early 1970s, social belonging in the *grands ensembles* shifted from an isolated question of participation in the (efficient, fair, humanized) management of housing to a contextual question of urban politics. During the 1960s, a number of local associations working toward participatory housing management instigated a national debate in which state officials, national-level organizations, and social scientists took part. Their initiatives aimed to smooth conflict by developing new participatory procedures of planning and management. Such ideas of participation quickly transformed into more fundamental critiques with the social movements around 1968. Shaped at once "from above" and "from below," the emergence of participation shows how activists' initial enthusiasm for completing the "utopia" of the *grands ensembles* gave way to an increasingly fundamental questioning of large-scale development in general, and the vocabulary of modern urbanism in particular.

This evolution—shaped by the policy of the *grands ensembles* as well as by the changing culture of French society more broadly—in turn influenced the course of French urban development. During the early 1970s, exceptional instances of political mobilization in response to the state-led urbanism of the *grands ensembles*—as in Sarcelles and Grenoble—were harnessed as "good practice" in national attempts to develop a different urbanism. Rather than implying a wholesale shift from the national to a more local level of decision making, this led to a new kind of ambiguity: while remaining a national affair, experts increasingly acknowledged the need to treat inhabitants not as universal users but as differentiated actors locally embedded in social life.

Despite its brief success in infusing new architectural experiments, the advent of participation in planning ultimately strengthened the legitimacy of sociological expertise and the increased mediation between design and use. The study of social life in new housing estates and the gradual validity given to local inhabitant associations as sources of knowledge for planning were key steps in the context of a broad reordering of expertise in postwar France. Contrary to the rhetoric of participation, state-sponsored research and experimentation—both before and after 1968—did not entail a more direct participation of inhabitants, but instead the intensified involvement of experts ambivalently positioned between civil society and the state. Despite sociologists' proclamations after 1968 that urbanism was essentially political, sociological expertise more than citizen participation thus became entrenched in urbanism. Inhabitants were increasingly spoken for not only by organizations aiming to *politically* represent them, but also by the neutral, often explicitly "apolitical" studies by sociologists and other government-sponsored experts. Despite their recommendations for inhabitants' direct involvement, initiatives such as Habitat et vie sociale thus contributed to the further institutionalization of expertise.

5

PROGRAMMING THE
VILLES NOUVELLES

From the 1960s on, the approach will change. The necessity to conceive of the city in its totality is increasingly pressing: each large new operation needs to be studied and built according to a conception of the urban development as a whole. Furthermore, what is at stake is no longer only to house the inhabitants, but also to create their everyday environment: the *grands ensembles* show the inconveniences of an urbanism lacking in good architecture and in facilities for local social life. This orientation leads to an urbanism of New Towns.[1]

WHEN THE POLITICAL SCIENTIST PIERRE VIOT sketched this evolution in 1969, he had Charles de Gaulle's official *villes nouvelles* or New Towns project in mind. Launched in 1965, two decades after the first British New Towns, the project was closely tied to a new master plan for the capital called the Schéma directeur d'aménagement et d'urbanisme de la région de Paris. This plan resolutely abandoned what was called the "Malthusianism" of earlier plans—the acceptance of a relatively fixed footprint limiting urban development (Plate 8).[2] Instead of decongesting the center and densifying the suburbs, planners felt they needed above all to facilitate economic development and accommodate exponential urban growth far beyond the bounds of the existing city. The massive economic and demographic growth that had thoroughly reshaped the Paris region in the two decades since World War II was extrapolated into the long-term future: by the year 2000 Paris would count no less than fourteen million inhabitants and would double its existing footprint, planners contended. The plan was characteristic of the optimism of the 1960s but also of the leadership of Paul Delouvrier, the charismatic "man of action" who at the side of de Gaulle was to modernize the nation and give it back the grandeur it deserved.[3]

To accommodate such unprecedented urban growth, Delouvrier and his team needed a new approach, one that could envision "the city in its totality," from the concreteness of the everyday to the abstract structure of the urban territory at large. Motivated by the desire to break with the monotonous scale of the *grands ensembles* as well as with the capital's "suffocating" radio-concentric structure, their strategy was to channel future urban growth along two major "preferential axes." On these axes large New Towns could then be developed to absorb anticipated growth (Figure 5.1). Compared to existing urban development such as Sarcelles or Toulouse-le-Mirail, and to the British New Towns, the *villes nouvelles* would be up to five or even ten times the size.[4] Above all, they needed to be "real cities" rather than bedroom suburbs. With the ambition of an all-encompassing approach to people's "cadre de vie" (living environment),

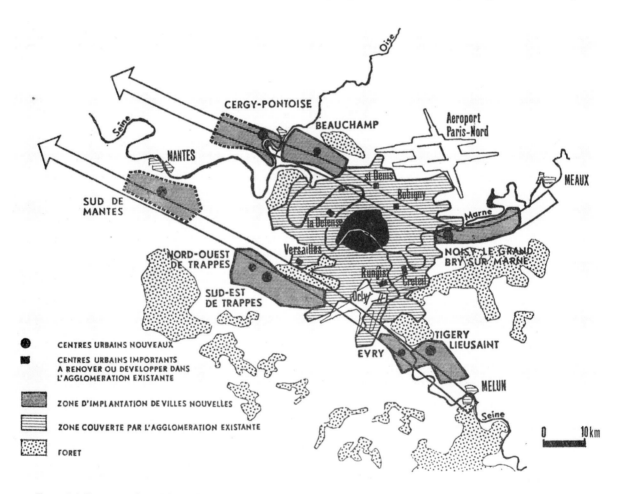

Figure 5.1. The two preferential axes for Paris guide the location of the New Towns in a diagram based on the 1965 regional plan. Ultimately, five New Towns will emerge from this initial plan: Cergy-Pontoise, Évry, Trappes, Marne-la-Vallée (initially called Noisy-le-Grand/Bry-sur-Marne), and Melun-Senart (initially called Tigery-Lieusaint). From Pierre Merlin, *Les villes nouvelles* (Paris: Presses Universitaires de France, 1969), 262.

planners promised a dramatically new way of city building. Up until then, New Towns internationally had been shaped essentially by an antiurban ideal—from the Anglo-American suburban communities inspired by Howard's garden city to the Russian plans for remotely located New Towns around heavy industries. In the eyes of French planners, this antiurban agenda applied even to the tabula rasa condition and vast empty spaces of Brasília and Chandigarh. Locating many of their *villes nouvelles* in or close to existing suburbanized areas, French planners faced an almost opposite challenge. In order to effectively decentralize the capital and the nation, these suburbs would have to be infused with an urbanity of their own. But how could such urban character be created? If, as Viot suggested, housing had proven insufficient and the *grands ensembles* were now the problem more than the solution for urban France, what tools, programs, or methods could be used to produce urbanity itself? If the city was made up of more than the four functions postulated by interwar modernists, how could its complexity, diversity, and dynamism be developed from the drafting board?

New Cities, New Questions

In the gulf of ambition and expectation accompanying the *villes nouvelles* project, one thing was clear to those in charge: existing models and methods were by definition insufficient. Inhabitants, journalists, and other observers had long rung the alarm bell about the monotony of social life in many new housing estates and the lack of urban amenities in the suburbs more generally. The *villes nouvelles* planners agreed and pointed their fingers univocally at the *grands ensembles*—even if some had been designed explicitly to facilitate social life and inhabitant participation. It was an easy blame to place. While the *villes nouvelles* were just as much a product of state intervention, they were the work of a different set of government actors and institutions. Instead of HLM organizations or public development companies that tended to commission Prix de Rome architects for housing projects guided by the technical norms of the Ministry of Construction, the *villes nouvelles* were developed by a new type of planning team. These teams would be locally installed but guided by centralized think tanks, including the Central Group of New Towns (Groupe central des villes nouvelles) and Delouvrier's Institut d'urbanisme et de l'aménagement de la région parisienne (IAURP, or Institute for Urbanism and Planning of the Paris Region). Because of their distance from the bureaucratic production of the *grands ensembles*, the *villes nouvelles* planners were quick to dismiss these "unorganized" and "underequipped" developments as being no more than bedroom suburbs that had made "comprehensive planning" impossible (Figure 5.2).[5] Newspapers reported that "to repeat Sarcelles" was people's number one fear, and planners were well aware of this.[6]

The *villes nouvelles* would thus be shaped in direct relationship to the *grands ensembles*—albeit primarily in opposition to their perceived failures. If the *grand ensemble* was the city

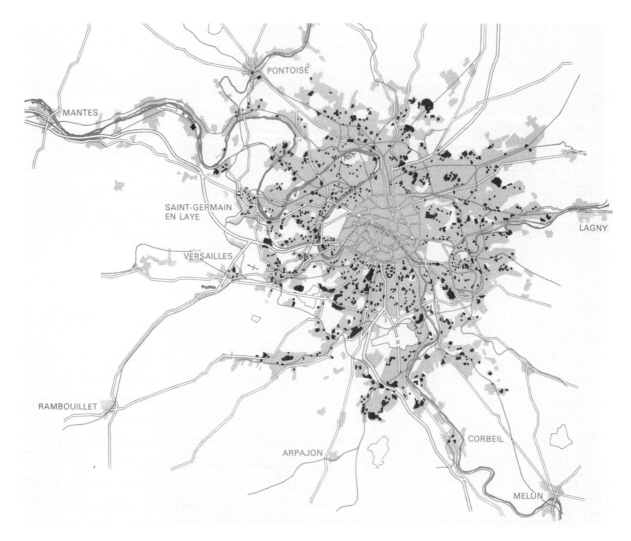

Figure 5.2. A map from 1965 of housing developments built in the Paris region between 1939 and 1964, meant to show the disorganized character of urban growth. From District de Paris/Premier Ministre, *Schéma directeur d'aménagement et d'urbanisme de la région de Paris* (Paris, 1965), 56.

taken apart, the *ville nouvelle* ought to be the city put together. That conviction informed the official denunciation of the *grands ensembles* with the famous Guichard directive of March 21, 1973. Signed by Olivier Guichard, who had worked under Delouvrier and had enthusiastically supported the Gaullist modernization of France before he became minister in 1972, the directive was motivated by growing evidence of social problems in the *grands ensembles* and effectively terminated any further development of such large-scale housing projects. The *villes nouvelles* not only escaped the legislative condemnation; in fact, their presumed antithesis helped Guichard to further endorse them by stating that "the *grand ensemble* opposes the center, while the *ville nouvelle* re-creates a center. The *grand ensemble* is without moorings. The *ville nouvelle* becomes the node in a network of connections."[7] By the time of this speech, the reactions to and critiques of the *grands ensembles* had already informed specific design strategies for the *villes nouvelles*. And these had not remained in the realm of thought, as large swaths of land around Paris and in provincial locations had been earmarked, infrastructure works had started, and the first buildings had appeared on the horizon.

In the face of a nation beginning to show the growing pains of the rapid urbanization associated with large-scale state-aided projects, the *villes nouvelles* project was acceptable only insofar as it appeared to be something radically new. Casting the *ville nouvelle* as anti–*grand ensemble* was a productive myth: a strategy as old as Baron Hausmann, of separating the project of modernization from the troubles of the past. The only challenge was that the *grands ensembles* were not yet in the past: they continued to be massively constructed until well into the 1970s, despite mounting critique. The temporal coexistence between two purportedly opposite models of urban development within the same centralized state apparatus was certainly confusing, and not only to the planners themselves.[8] To the general public, the role of the state in the built environment appeared increasingly contradictory between the mid-1960s and the mid-1970s—simultaneously endorsing and criticizing its own actions. More important, public surveys showed that the vast majority of the French did not often see the difference between a *ville nouvelle* and a *grand ensemble*.[9] Both terms were in common use to describe a variety of large-scale urban developments built or planned at this time. Some large-scale urban developments, including Mourenx, Créteil, Toulouse-le-Mirail, and Grenoble Échirolles, had been explicitly branded by their developers as *villes nouvelles*. Even Sarcelles, the most typical counterexample for Delouvrier and his New Town planners, tried to obtain the official status of *ville nouvelle* when the municipality found out about the project.[10] *Grands ensembles* and *villes nouvelles* were thus vulnerable to the same criticism of large-scale, state-led urbanism mounted by the public media.

In fact, much of the logic behind *villes nouvelles* planning was indebted to, rather than in opposition to, that of the *grands ensembles*. First of all, they shared the same rhetoric of radical change.[11] In 1956, Pierre Sudreau had envisaged the *grands ensembles* as "veritable transplants on a sick body." In addition to solving the housing shortage and facilitating economic development, they were also instruments "to tidy up the Paris region."[12] Just like the *villes nouvelles*, so were the *grands ensembles* thus cast as solutions for the existing suburbs, their unorganized development, and their lack of amenities. Gérard Dupont, the administrator behind the *grille Dupont*, had described the *grands ensembles* around Paris in remarkably holistic terms: "To the conception of the Parisian agglomeration as having a single center linked via umbilical cords to dormitories further and further removed, needs to be substituted a polycentric development around *grands ensembles*, poles of new growth representing balanced and complete

residential units—that is to say, containing centers for employment, commerce, administration, social protection, recreation, and culture."[13] A decade later, the planners of Évry
explained the future New Town in very similar terms to Sudreau's and Dupont's. Only now,
their project was an opportunity to address not only the problems of existing suburbs but also
those of the *grands ensembles*, which had not lived up to their promise:

> The programming of a New Town thus corresponds to an urgent need to structure an urban
> fabric marked by the proliferation of housing, insufficiently compensated by the development
> of employment sites, means of transportation, and offering the inhabitants of the 14 munici-
> palities—that will soon amount to 200,000 people—not more than very mediocre possibilities
> for social life and exchange, a function that the center of Paris—saturated and far removed—
> can no longer really assure.[14]

The dominant perception of the *grands ensembles* as "silos for people" devoid of social life and
amenities—whether this was a reality or not—informed the conception of the *villes nouvelles*
in quite specific ways. One consequence was the exacerbation of planners' interest in making
lively urban environments, which was in fact a continuation of earlier strategies centered on
animation. Only this time, planners realized that they needed to fundamentally alter the mix.
Rather than a substrate of housing with collective facilities and public spaces as the icing on
the cake, less than a third of the *villes nouvelles* should be made up of housing.[15] An important goal would be employment. At the onset of the New Town of Cergy-Pontoise, planners
realized that "the *ville nouvelle* will be a failure if the jobs do not follow: 46,000 jobs need to
be created before 1975."[16] But housing and jobs were not enough to create "real cities."

What other kinds of program they should be made up of, and how those would come
together spatially and architecturally, was central to the *villes nouvelles* over the following
decades. This question would bring architecture and social science together in novel ways,
leading to new methods of planning and urban design. The challenge was not just to find the
right mix of ingredients for city building, as the *grille Dupont* had attempted, but how these
elements could be integrated into an urban system. It was a *system* rather than whole—or
ensemble—because interrelations now mattered more than just things by themselves. All of
the city's functional elements needed to be integrated into a system that allowed them to be
interconnected. Complexity, which sociologists increasingly emphasized in their studies of the
existing urban condition and planners saw lacking spatially and architecturally in dominant
models of urban development, became a goal unto itself. The *grand ensemble* was identified by
its self-contained nature, despite recent attempts by Dupont and his colleagues to overcome
the *grille's* enumerative approach to facilities. The *ville nouvelle*, to overcome these shortcomings, needed to be more than the sum of its parts.

The relationships between different programs and their spatial integration also begged new ways to take into account the factor of time. Instead of the projection of an urban plan frozen in time, planners began to emphasize planning as a *process*. This shift was again inspired—at least in part—by a critique of the *grands ensembles*. Their perceived (and often real) failure to provide urban amenities led planners to attend first and foremost to the construction of public infrastructure and institutions and only later to housing. At the New Town of Cergy-Pontoise, one of the first buildings to go up was the prefecture. In order to provide facilities for the first inhabitants that would soon arrive, the building contained a large public atrium, a cinema, a restaurant, a bar, an art gallery, and about fifteen shops, including a hairdresser, a shoemaker, a travel agent, and clothing shops (Figure 5.3).[17] The building was conceived as the urban nucleus of a much larger city to come. Such approaches to city building often responded to very mundane problems associated with the *grands ensembles*, including the arduous experience of first inhabitants who had to tread through muddy construction sites for years. Some planners thus felt inclined to promise a city "without construction sites" (Figure 5.4).

In short, the *villes nouvelles* were no longer about a given set of programs but became a question of programming. In 1960s France, programming or *programmation* emerged as an elusive notion and set of techniques in response to the critiques of mass housing projects and the ambitions of the *villes nouvelles*. In the United States, programming seems to have entered into the field of architecture as a "second functionalism" centered on flexibility in institutional architecture and fostered by the development of corporate practice.[18] And in Britain, programming became perhaps most prominent as an architectural approach through the collaboration of Cedric Price and the cybernetician Gordan Pask in the Fun Palace, an unbuilt participatory cultural center whose architectural technologies aimed to organize flexible forms of social activity.[19] By contrast, *programmation* in France emerged at the intersection of architecture, planning, and sociology, by virtue of a centralized state that orchestrated a significant part of urbanization through large-scale intervention and acted as the central platform for the knowledge production that accompanied it. Yet, the approach of programming in French New Towns would also be prompted by forces outside the government, more precisely by the dynamics of a rapidly changing consumer society.

Volition and Volatility

What shaped the course of French urban planning most profoundly during the 1960s was an economy that seesawed between state invention and free-market principles. Contrary to the lasting perception of French authoritarianism and the legacy of the Vichy government, the Plan Monnet was already based on an idea of planning whose method would continuously adapt to changing market conditions. During the presidency of de Gaulle, economic planning

Figure 5.3. Prefecture building of Cergy by the architect Henri Bernard, 1965–70. Exterior view: Fonds H. Bernard. Académie d'architecture/Cité de l'architecture et du patrimoine/Archives d'architecture du XXᵉ siècle. Copyright 2014 Artists Rights Society, New York/Société des auteurs dans les arts graphiques et plastiques, Paris. Interior view: *Techniques et architecture* 32, no. 5 (1970): 60.

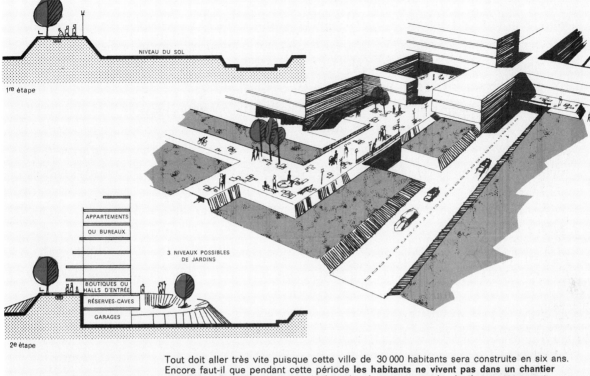

une ville "sans chantier"

Tout doit aller très vite puisque cette ville de 30 000 habitants sera construite en six ans. Encore faut-il que pendant cette période **les habitants ne vivent pas dans un chantier permanent.** Pour les quartiers résidentiels, c'est assez simple : les logements seront construits par îlots avec leurs écoles, leurs rues, leurs pelouses. Pour le **centre** c'est plus difficile puisque les réalisations seront progressives en fonction des demandes et des besoins.
En conséquence, on commencera par construire des **digues** pour les piétons et des voies en tranchées pour les voitures et les camions. Sur ces digues les canalisations seront enterrées, les arbres seront plantés et les piétons pourront circuler à l'abri de la circulation des chantiers qui deviendront un spectacle au lieu d'être une gêne.

Figure 5.4. "A city 'without construction sites'" promised by a promotional brochure for Cergy-Pontoise in 1969. Archives nationales, France, CAC 19910585/009.

was increasingly understood in terms of an *économie concertée* or mixed economy, rather than being based on direct state intervention. This notion, initially espoused by François Bloch-Lainé, had gained widespread acceptance throughout the upper levels of state administration as a way to conceptualize the relation between state and market.[20] The state would no longer be an essentially reactive arbiter of competing private interests; it should now actively encourage private economic development.[21]

Perhaps it was the continuity of this kind of economic planning throughout the *trente glorieuses* that obscured the momentous changes wrought by a steadily advancing consumer culture infiltrating the country's economic and social fabric. Although its disarranging repercussions remained hidden to most observers until the escalating protests by students and workers in May 1968, mass consumption had been enthusiastically embraced at least since

Liberation. Even if "private interests" often meant an oligarchy of large industrial companies, especially in the first postwar years, consumers became increasingly central in the understanding and management of the economic realm. Consumer culture did not have the same weight in French economic life as it did in the United States, but, as elsewhere on the Continent, it still gained increasing dominance over economic and social affairs—in part under the influence of American entrepreneurs.[22] The changing rhetoric of national economic planning was a clear reflection of this evolution. During the 1960s, its goals were increasingly described in extraeconomic terms: planning now aimed at social and cultural development focused on "individual happiness" and "quality of life," concepts translated from the world of consumption and marketing rather than that of macroeconomic quantification.[23]

French suburbanization showed increasing signs of consumer-driven development. Commercial and real-estate developers were particularly important in placing the figure of the individual consumer at the center of urban planners' concerns. At the beginning of the 1960s, planners' prevailing attitude was still that commerce needed to be planned "top-down" by grouping it in commercial centers in concert with the neighborhood unit—a method for which the *grille Dupont* was the manual.[24] By the mid-1960s, however, planners opened the door to "modern, American solutions" for commercial development. These were focused mainly on suburban mall development, which, despite its late arrival in France, was an instant success.[25] Realizing that developers simply ignored their logic, planners began to question the virtues of top-down planning as it seemed to impede the freedom of commercial developers and shop owners to choose the best location for their business—and hence, that of individual consumers. Increasingly, it was no longer the state official or the urban planner, but the developer and the consumer, who were recognized as the bearers of economic rationality.

Just as private companies could choose where to locate, so individual consumers had an increasing ability to choose where they wanted to live, work, and shop. Car ownership had radically increased the geographic mobility of middle-class French families, and as they became increasingly central to French society, they became more powerful—not in the least through their purchasing power. The number of privately financed housing units had risen sharply during the 1960s and was further encouraged by the 1963 legislation promoting private instead of public financing for housing.[26] This evolution was all the more remarkable considering the lack of a mortgage policy, forcing home buyers to put down deposits approaching half of the total cost of their new homes.[27] Despite the absence of proper condominium legislation, developed only in the late 1960s, many of these new homes were apartments. Modern single-family homes, a rare sight before the mid-1960s, slowly began to find their way into French urban development, and, while still largely catering to the upper echelons of the middle class, they functioned as a powerful tool of social distinction in a society increasingly driven by consumerism.[28]

Whereas the early postwar projects took place in the near absence of a private housing market, and the *grands ensembles* initially filled this vacuum by producing mass standardized housing, state action during the 1960s would necessarily be defined by the way it took into account the dynamics of a differentiated housing market in which private developers and consumers had an increasingly powerful voice. More than any other initiative, it was the *villes nouvelles* project that demonstrates the way in which this evolution, which led individuals to be identified as consumers in search of distinguishing options more than as citizens bearing the right to housing, shaped French urban planning.

This was all the more surprising considering the intellectual tradition out of which the *villes nouvelles* had emerged. Despite the transnational exchange of ideas during the "golden age" of the New Towns globally, the *villes nouvelles* project was closely tied to the specific notion of *géographie volontaire* or volitional geography.[29] Despite the influence of François Gravier and Eugène Claudius-Petit during the late 1940s and 1950s, the idea of comprehensive territorial planning had stayed largely within the realm of political rhetoric. With Delouvrier, however, it seemed closer to reality than ever. Before being in charge of the district of the Paris region (1961–69), he served as a member of Jean Monnet's national planning committee during the late 1940s, moved in the highest ranks of the French government during the 1950s, and became general delegate for the Algerian government during its war of independence.[30] The troubles of French decolonization further reinforced the will to modernize, partly as a result of the insertion into the state administration of a generation of former colonial administrators. Together with Delouvrier, their appetite for strong rule and visions of bringing order to France's suburban "wilderness" helped to further focus state policies on modernizing the metropole.[31] Geographers such as Jean Labasse translated their ambitions into an increasingly realistic theory of *géographie volontaire*, in which entire geographic regions would become the object of rational yet flexible organization by the state.[32] In other words, the *villes nouvelles* project, drawn up behind closed doors by an elite of state planners and high-level politicians and adopted regardless of its brief "public consultation," was a perfect embodiment of *géographie volontaire* and the authoritarian nature of French planning more broadly.

The extraordinary sense of volition, however—and the accompanying belief in a "makeable society"—was bound to confront the growing economic dynamism of French society in the 1960s. In planners' early discussions about the *villes nouvelles* emerged the acute awareness that the private market could no longer be neglected, in particular in the way it shaped and was shaped by individual consumer choice: "The urban expansion obeys to imperatives born out of the notion of profit: a certain region is urbanized because it is known that it will be sought by a potential clientele of homebuyers. Can the objective of the plan be to substitute a different logic for this development? Can it impose, in the name of a rational urbanism, different solutions than those born from the market? We are touching the limits imposed on the plan here."[33] Pierre Merlin, an academic geographer and *villes nouvelles* consultant, would later write that one of the central objectives of the project was to "restore the freedom of choice for citizens, and in particular those of the second zone who were the suburbanites: choice in employment, choice in the type of dwelling and its surroundings, choice in shops, choice in recreation, choice in friends, choice in love."[34] Colored at the time of writing by the liberal aspects of the project, such statements nevertheless show how the nature of French planning was slowly changing during the 1960s. While it was still to be *volitional*—defined by resolute leadership and expert decision making—planning also needed to be *realistic,* taking as its basis the dynamics of the market and thus consumer choice in the urbanization process. The *villes nouvelles* project thus implied at once more freedom and more planning: it would be fundamentally consumer-oriented but remained closely directed by centralized state institutions, at least until decentralization in the 1980s.

Unlike the mass housing of the *grands ensembles,* the *villes nouvelles* needed not only to satisfy housing needs or economic development but also to attract and entice future inhabitants. The key place given to recreation and leisure in the *villes nouvelles* project was an indication of this shift. Many planners saw the New Towns first and foremost as consumer products that needed to be sold to the public. The 1968 advertising brochure for Cergy-Pontoise no longer promoted dwelling units, shopping centers, or office buildings but "a new way of life." The New Town lifestyle was "to work in proximity of one's residence, to slide down the hills to bathe in the lake, going to the countryside or the coast on Sundays without the nightmare of traffic, to go out in the evening without needing to reserve tickets weeks in advance, to enjoy the liveliness of an urban center without suffering from its noise, to drive or leave your car as you please, to leave the children to go to school by themselves without risk."[35]

Lifestyle was itself a relatively young notion in France. The older notion of *mode de vie* or "way of life" had been central to French geography from the time of Paul Vidal de la Blache, but its meaning shifted fundamentally during the postwar period. *Mode de vie* no longer had the essential connotation of timeless regional tradition, but instead began to be explicitly related to notions of modernity and newness—in other words, the term approached the English notion of lifestyle. This specific understanding, signaled in the replacement of the term by *style de vie,* was a factor in the rise of middle-class consumer and leisure culture and thus the advent of a new "postindustrial society" founded on a radical diminution of working hours, paid holidays, and other welfare state benefits.[36]

The notion of lifestyle found its way into French urbanism during the 1960s. In a 1961 press conference about the goals of the plan, Delouvrier had stated the vaguely defined aim of "improving everyday life" as part of his larger ambitions to "design the Paris of 1975" and "think that of the year 2000." In the plan's publication in 1965, the concerns were described with the simple term *le bonheur* or "the happiness" of the French. While this notion expressed the ambition to transcend the quantitative provision of housing or facilities, it still lacked the specificity of the concept of lifestyle, more particularly its diversity, differentiation, and, essentially, freedom of choice. *Espace et loisir dans la société française d'hier et de demain*, a study by sociologists Joffre Dumazedier and Maurice Imbert, was crucial to the import of lifestyle as a preoccupation in urbanism.[37] The study took as its starting point Jean Fourastié's optimistic outlook of economic growth and its direct consequence, the spectacular development of leisure culture—proven by things such as the sales of pop music LPs and the popularity of *bricolage* (do-it-yourself) and *ciné-clubs* (movie clubs) or the construction of holiday resorts and second homes. While still indebted to a quantitative concept of use based on *grilles d'équipement*, the authors understood the evolution of leisure as a radical expansion of people's freedom and aspirations. This, they argued, prompted a rethinking of urbanism to encompass "the planning of the living environment in its entirety."[38] Most important, the study emphasized not just the increase of individual consumption, but the radical *diversification* of needs that this evolution entailed. By suggesting that urban development should center on leisure—such as recreational lakes—the authors of the study articulated the design strategies of *villes nouvelles* such as Cergy-Pontoise. Here the concept of a new urban lifestyle was based on the transformation of a nearby river bend into a massive recreational environment serving as the backbone for the New Town (Figure 5.5).

In the wake of the 1968 protests and the departure of de Gaulle, consumption and lifestyle entered more explicitly into political programs and policies. Urban planning ideology, still fundamentally shaped by a belief in expert leadership, gradually opened up to focus on the citizen as a dynamic consumer with the right of mobility and individual choice. The new administration of Georges Pompidou thus circumvented the authoritarian origins of the *villes nouvelles* project. Some of this was personal: Pompidou did not seem to like the project and did not get along with Delouvrier, who remained a Gaullist at heart. But the ambivalence about the *villes nouvelles* was more fundamental. The new government, engrossed with restoring calm after the violent eruption of public discontent in 1968, openly questioned the expensive and increasingly unpopular large-scale state interventions of the past decades. Minister of housing and infrastructure Albin Chalandon called to "vigorously suppress this excessive interventionism."[39] But it was too late to abandon the colossal state project altogether. It thus needed to be reframed. The official strategy was now first of all to "limit the intervention of the public authorities in terms of both conception and construction, by concentrating it on the key structuring elements," to "allow the largest possible flexibility to the intervention of the developers," and to "engage the public authorities only insofar as financial means allow."[40] Many state officials were aware that private corporations and developers would not obey a government considered far too centralized, interventionist, regulatory, and normalizing. By the close of the decade, Jean-Eudes Roullier, head of the *villes nouvelles* think tank, articulated the new role for

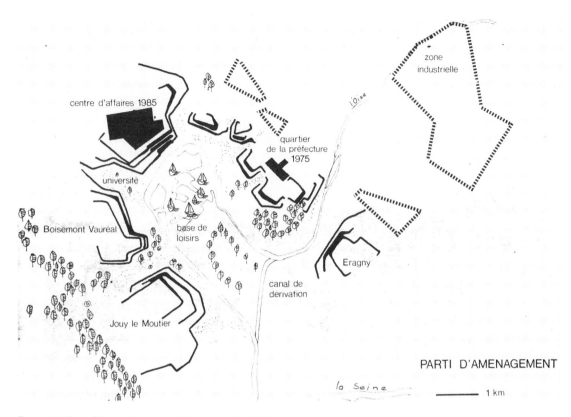

Figure 5.5. Plan of Cergy-Pontoise with the recreational lake in the center, illustrated in the promotional brochure for the New Town, 1968. Archives nationales, France, CAC 19910585/009.

government-led urban planning: no longer to regulate the private sector but just to mobilize and incite it.[41]

While this new political ideology did lead to a more careful elision of interventionism and a stronger reliance on private development, the *villes nouvelles* project continued to be based on a centralized state defining not only the location of the New Towns but also their urban conception. Government control over land use was at the basis of French New Town planning. Yet, because of their enormous scale—they were initially projected to occupy an average surface of around 5,000 hectares compared to an average of 100 to 200 hectares for the *grands ensembles*—the *villes nouvelles* could not be built using the same legislative mechanisms. The government thus intervened in ways at once more "soft" and more decisive. It developed acquisition methods that would increase control over land prices while minimizing direct investment. This meant maximizing private investment while minimizing speculation. State purchase of land was limited to the strategic elements of the plan: the urban centers, major amenities, and public infrastructure, for which development required direct government intervention. The majority of land was subsequently planned in collaboration with the private sector through a new set of legal procedures. Yet the *villes nouvelles* project precipitated more than just a new strategy for controlling large-scale development. The volition of French state planning and the volatility of a flourishing consumer society engendered a new kind of city building—which required a new type of city builders.

Professionalizing Programming

The *villes nouvelles* project was part and parcel of a significant reorganization of expertise in France. The project precipitated but also relied upon new relationships between the professions and professionals of the built environment. Government officials were aware of private developers' increasing power and activity, which often went without government oversight. Those in charge of the *villes nouvelles* project thus realized that planning could no longer be centered on the design of a static master plan, as the *grands ensembles* had been. It required a more flexible approach of programming zones and activities in a larger territory that was in ongoing (sub)urban development. The New Town of Évry, for instance, was meant to steer rather than freeze the development of the surrounding region, which had undergone rapid suburbanization in the previous two decades.[42] Planners cast the New Town as an "open structure" that would adapt to its surroundings while allowing planners to mold and structure them by means of strategic development (Plate 9). Despite this flexibility, the plan was centered on a rather idiosyncratic cross-shaped figure, meant to allow green space to penetrate into the center while keeping main roads away from the residential neighborhoods (Figure 5.6).[43] The *schéma des structures* or structural diagram for the New Town of Cergy-Pontoise included not only the areas marked for development but also the existing village of Pontoise and the forests and lakes that were being reframed as recreational zones (Figure 5.7). This was a plan of relations and connections, an urban network rather than a set of hermetic boxes. With buzzwords like "urban framework" (*trame urbaine*) and "urban armature" (*armature urbaine*), the need for large-scale structures that would efficiently reorganize large swaths of suburban land while facilitating the mobility of an increasingly demanding population was at the forefront of planners' concern.[44] Roullier contended that the vast new scale with which planners were confronted prompted a shift from "rigid French-style master plans or the city of an architect" to an approach focusing on "the problems of the center, the force lines, leisure, and transportation in a flexible and living diagram."[45] The *villes nouvelles* were thus cast as the results of a "better" kind of modernism, focused on a consumer imbued with individual mobility and the right to choose.

The ideas were in line with the work of University of California, Berkeley planner Melvin Webber. In a paper published shortly before, he had argued that urbanization in the era of the automobile gave rise to "communities without propinquity." Planning consequently should be

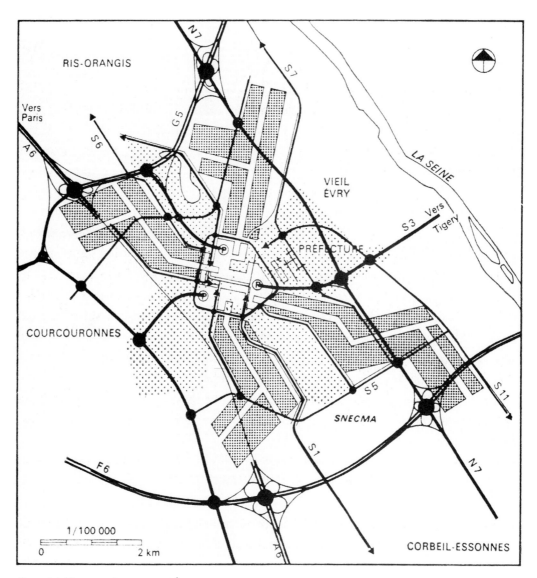

Figure 5.6. The new urban center of Évry in 1969, based on the idea of a cross of four *trames urbaines,* more densely built-up urban spines (hatched areas) separated by open space (lightly dotted areas). From *L'Architecture d'aujourd'hui* 146 (1969): 46.

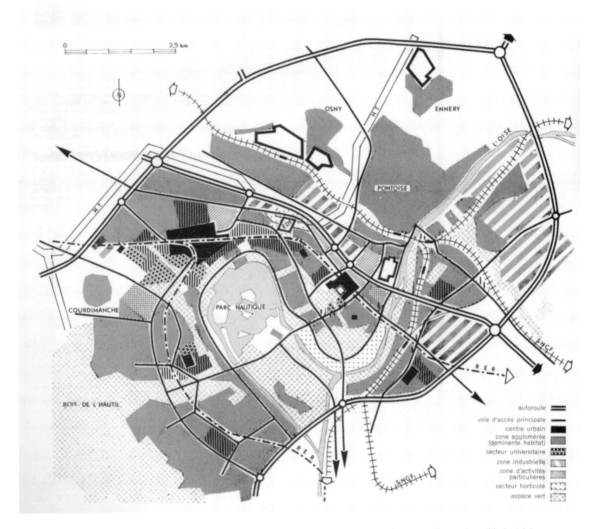

Figure 5.7. Structural plan for Cergy in 1970, with the urban centers (in black), housing areas (in gray), and industrial zones (in diagonal hatch) all connected by a network of circulation. From *Techniques et architecture* 32, no. 5 (1970): 46.

not in rigid neighborhood units but should flexibly respond to the "non-place urban realm."[46] His ideas were crucial to the latest phase of British New Town plans, in particular Milton Keynes.[47] The planning of this New Town radically defied centrality in favor of a flexible urban grid of highways. Without giving up centrality, in fact vigorously reinforcing it, French planners were influenced by the flexibility of this approach and the redefinition it suggested between structure and program.

French planners went so far as to cast the *villes nouvelles* as a paradigm shift, from *urbanisme* to *programmation*. The first term referred to a particularly architectural approach to the city in France at this time: urbanists were generally trained as architects, and the dominant approach was one of urban form and composition. *Programmation*, in contrast, was thought of as starting from the content rather than the form. For Évry, for instance, planning began with a geographic comparison of different French cities based not on their morphology but on the mix of urban activities they contained. This programmatic analysis of reference cities was then extrapolated for the New Town based on a projection of future needs in the surrounding region. The method led to a great variety of urban programs, which no longer had much to do with the four functions of the Athens Charter.[48] With such scientific, or at least methodical, operations, planners aimed to do away both with the dogmatic approaches of interwar modernists and with the approach to urbanism as an "art urbain" based on Beaux-Arts composition or the artistic ideas of individual designers more generally.

During the 1960s, the promise of science remained particularly appealing to planning professionals in France and beyond. The attempt to reframe urbanism as a rigorously scientific and technically exact endeavor was in part prompted by the social status of science and technology. Engineers were both a source of anxiety and an inspiration for French urbanists. The French centralized state had been cultivating an elite corps of state engineers for centuries, and their role was only further strengthened in the postwar decades. In 1963, the Direction à l'aménagement du territoire (Territorial Planning Department), initially a division within the Ministry of Construction, was placed under direct command of the premier. This led to the creation of a new, powerful planning institution, the Délégation à l'aménagement du territoire et à l'action régionale (DATAR, or Delegation for Territorial Planning and Regional Action).[49] The ministry remained in charge of urbanism but saw part of its responsibilities taken away by the engineers at DATAR, whose approach was geared first of all toward regional-scale economic development. The fusion in 1966 of the Ministry of Construction and the Ministry of Public Works into a large and powerful Ministère de l'équipement led by Edgard Pisani further galvanized the position of engineers in state-led urban planning. It was also a sign of the government's ambition to gain a more comprehensive understanding and control over the urbanization process. Rather than to a more technocratic kind of urban planning, however—at least in the sense of a predominance of technical and engineering aspects—it led to a more "scientific" approach in which the comprehensive view became key.[50]

What such a comprehensive view required first of all was the fusion of multiple kinds of expertise. As such, the social sciences gained a prominent place in the planning process.[51] In the face of the growing complexity of French urbanization, the *villes nouvelles* could no longer be the work of a single author. They required more than just the masterly hand of a Beaux-Arts–trained architect-urbanist, the technical expertise of engineers, or the norms established by a ministry; their planning entailed intense collaboration between architects, urbanists, engineers, economists, sociologists, geographers, and so on. The more, the merrier, it seemed, in the optimism of the 1960s. The new method of city building was thus that of a large team of experts creating long-term, scientifically grounded visions, diagrams, reports, and studies. These multidisciplinary teams promised an exciting new way for *villes nouvelles* planners to overcome the challenges of marrying ambitious state-led planning with the uncertain dynamics of private development.

Some French architects and urban planners had been calling for multidisciplinarity since the early 1950s. A decade later this was no longer a suggestion at the margins; multidisciplinary teams were quickly becoming a dominant mode of practice. Sociologists such as Paul-Henry Chombart de Lauwe, as discussed in chapter 2, had been at the forefront of this trend as they promoted the inclusion of their expertise into urban policy during the 1950s and 1960s. The Centre de recherche sur l'urbanisme (Center for Research on Urbanism), jointly established by the ministers of construction and of national education in 1962, became a key platform for interdisciplinary exchange.[52] Meaning to create "a direct relationship between applied and fundamental research," it brought together architects, planners, and policy makers with academics from a wide range of social-science disciplines, including Robert Auzelle, Pierre George, Jean Stoetzel, and Fourastié.[53] The center's director, Jean Canaux, described the growing dialogue as a result of a proactive sociology, which "begins to surpass the description of the existing condition, in order to reach a new phase in its history. It becomes capable, bit by bit, of discerning the formative currents of the future society, and maybe even of acting on these in order to attain a desired future."[54]

The authors gathered together for the 1966 *Urbanisme* journal issue on urban sociology argued in similar terms that sociologists were "in the process of passing from the role of spectator to that of actor" and that "the intervention of the sociologists cannot be limited to the sphere of reflection," but instead must "be constantly associated on all levels to the creation of the destiny and all transformative phases of the city." Unlike previous calls, they envisaged a particular kind of sociology, "freed from general and abstract notions, transcending the level of the family unit or the housing unit," one that would "engage at the level of the city or the agglomeration considered in its entirety."[55] Just as urbanism itself needed to be rethought—away from the drab housing estate and toward a conception of the city at large—so the purview of sociology was to change in scale. When the government incited new forms of social-scientific research through a range of different institutions, the focus was increasingly on large-scale urban regions. This was the case not only for the IAURP in Paris, but also for new organizations in the provinces, such as the Regional Organization for the Study of Metropolitan Areas (Organisme régional d'étude de l'aire métropolitaine) and the local Urbanism Agencies (Agences d'urbanisme). While they remained the hallmarks of the *villes nouvelles* planning, multidisciplinary planning teams became standard practice in all of these institutions.[56]

Multidisciplinarity was in fact written into the basic procedures of New Town planning. Concretely, upon the decision for the definitive location of each New Town, the prime minister created a local study team (*mission d'étude*). This multidisciplinary team was charged with all preliminary studies and plans. Once a preliminary plan for the New Town was created, it would be transformed into a Public Planning Institute (Établissement public d'aménagement) charged with the detailed execution of the plan. In 1967, the team of Évry was made up of around twenty-five professionals divided into four groups: administrative and financial tasks, technical aspects, urbanism, and *programmation*. Whereas the urbanism group was largely made up of architect-urbanists, the latter group entailed not only straightforward economists or experts in public administration, but also a new breed of planning experts.[57]

However central *programmation* became to French New Town planning, it remained ambivalently defined as something in between a new planning method, a new type of expert knowledge, and a new profession of *programmateurs* or "programmers." With a background in political science, sociology, or architecture, these programmers were primary carriers of the belief that social-scientific research was fundamental to a better kind of urban design and planning. During the initial phase of the *villes nouvelles*, between the late 1960s and the mid-1970s, the hopes were high: although in some cases it was not clear what *programmation* meant, it was considered an essential element in the planning process, in particular for that of the New Towns' public facilities.[58] *Programmation* owed much of its success to the general appeal of hard science and exactitude in planning. At the same time, it was seen as a way toward a more user-centered approach to the built environment. Many of the new research and consultancy firms emerging during the 1960s harnessed programming as a crucial method of adapting architectural production and urban planning to people's needs and desires.

Of these consultancy firms, Centre d'études, de recherches et de formation institutionnelles (CERFI, or the Center for Institutional Studies, Research, and Formation) was perhaps most radical about the emancipatory potentials of programming. The group, founded in 1967 by psychotherapists, pedagogues, architects, and urban planners under direction of the psychoanalyst Félix Guattari, developed a uniquely theoretical approach that was heavily influenced by Guattari's collaboration with the philosopher Gilles Deleuze at the time. That collaboration had led to *L'Anti-Œdipe*, a philosophical treatise on desire under capitalism and a fundamental critique of Freudian psychoanalysis, published in 1972. Inspired by this work, and specifically by Friedrich Nietzsche's *Genealogy of Morals*, the group's critiques and proposals were based on a "genealogy of collective facilities."[59] They started out by analyzing the conventional way of programming such facilities, which was based on the quantification of need per housing unit in a given area. Subsequently, they demonstrated how need was anything but natural and in fact resulted from deliberate social engineering. Historically speaking, collective facilities were instruments of domination, they concluded, constituting "the nonfamilial territory where the sovereignty of the State is directly exercised."[60]

Instead of the predefined calculation of need, they proposed a "global, integrated approach" based on needs as they were "actually expressed." Programming consequently was "a complex social function not departing from a social demand that is already given but determining its formation."[61] In a study for the establishment of mental therapy facilities in the New Town of Évry, they argued that what was at stake was "not a sort of science of programming, made up of a range of abstract models," but that "the essence of a program lies in its particularity, in its original way of intertwining the different constraints of the project," and that "the users are the only ones in the position to mark, determine, and formulate these specific constraints."[62] Following *L'Anti-Œdipe*, the study argued against the dominant understanding of desire as a lack and instead theorized the productive capacities of the unconscious as a factory, a production machine.[63] The work's emphasis on the singularity of desire directly informed its approach to programming, which was concretely tested in Évry's new child day-care center.[64] The application signified the formidable traction of often rather arcane and abstract theories by French intellectuals such as Deleuze, Michel Foucault, or Jean Baudrillard in urban expertise at this time.[65]

That terrain was heterogeneous, to say the least, and *programmation* was no different. Despite planners' embrace, its concrete role remained often unclear. Was this new form of expertise meant to inform the public, to consult future inhabitants, or to engage them in participation? Were programmers to intervene in specific urban problems or only pursue research? Or were they perhaps merely to coordinate the multidisciplinary team itself? The planning process of Cergy-Pontoise, the first New Town to be developed, brought these fundamental ambiguities to the surface. The first plan was drawn up by the Prix de Rome architect Henry Bernard, who proposed a representative, symbolic center with administrative buildings bounded by dike-like structures. Both the appointed urbanist Jean Coignet and the prefect of the department opposed the plan for its lack of openness and attention to social life. Coignet then suggested consulting children, "because it was them, more than adults, who would be directly concerned by the *ville nouvelle*." With the help of the Ministry of National Education, he organized a drawing competition in primary schools of the region. It was lauded as a big success and received national attention. The Musée de l'homme even proposed to analyze the drawings ethnographically. But beyond what was expected, it did not lead to immediate guidelines for planning.[66]

For Cergy-Pontoise, a team of urbanists led by Coignet was installed in a temporary office on the location of the future New Town in order to allow a more intimate knowledge of the terrain and give inhabitants the chance to serve as local interlocutors. A year later, when this team was turned into an official planning mission under the direction of Bernard Hirsch, it was substantially enlarged both in number and in diversity of professionals involved.[67] Sociologists, both internal and external to the team, were intensively involved now. Planners initially believed that because of this involvement they would be at the cutting edge of their discipline; they were quickly disappointed. According to Hirsch, "the sociologists were unable to respond and practical recipes never entered into their preoccupations, which revolved entirely around an abstract discourse and esoteric language."[68] The inclusion of sociology nevertheless had some concrete repercussions. When a female sociologist, addressed simply as Madame Lévi, was hired directly to be part of the planning team, she was apparently charged to study the immigrant construction workers. Her involvement led to the construction of emergency housing for single men and an allocation policy to house immigrant families in the apartments of the New Town. Other sociologists visited Hirsch's team to study the planning process itself. During one visit, Jean-Paul Trystram, professor of sociology in Lille, tried to convince Hirsch that sociologists needed to take a more central role by contributing to "more general ideas" in the conception of the New Town. Alain Touraine, by that time a well-known sociologist, was given a research contract to study the mechanisms of decision making in the planning process. The planning team found his work too theoretical to be of any concrete use. Hirsch then suggested that a sociologist come and observe for a longer period. Touraine sent his assistant Jean Lojkine, who, in the eyes of Hirsch, remained a quiet observer and disappeared "without exchanging his findings with the team."[69] The involvement of sociology in New Town planning was thus ambivalent, to say the least; it was often enthusiastically engaged, yet increasingly critical and often resistant to instrumentalization.

The Productivity of Critique

While sociology became increasingly central to French planning during the 1960s and 1970s, it also became progressively more critical. The conference Urbanisme et sociologie, held during the first three days of May 1968 in the quiet settings of the Royaumont Abbey outside Paris, was—not surprisingly, perhaps, considering its historic timing—a landmark for this critical turn. Four years earlier, the Ministry of Construction had commissioned a team of academic sociologists to study provincial cities, including Lille, Bordeaux, Strasbourg, and Toulouse.[70] The question of how exactly such studies could contribute to urban planning was what led the administrator Françoise Dissard and the academic Trystram to organize the Royaumont conference.[71] Apart from a wide range of sociologists—including Henri Coing, Raymond Ledrut, Henri Lefebvre, and Chombart—the conference gathered state officials such as Paul Cornière, architects including Marcel Lods, Gérard Thurnauer, and Hubert Tonka, urbanists such as Auzelle, and representatives of various civil society organizations. It was the veritable culmination of a decade of discussions about the virtues of linking sociology and urbanism. In retrospect, it also was the sign that a strictly consensual relationship between sociologists and urban planners was no longer possible.

The heated discussions at the conference centered on increasingly fundamental critiques of state-led urban development and the role of expertise. The new generation of critical sociologists that had emerged during the 1960s radically opposed the simply instrumental use of sociological data in such urbanism.[72] They no longer understood planning as just a neutral form of expertise in the name of the common good and aimed instead to unveil its fundamentally political nature. The social unrest that was unleashed soon after the end of the conference that same month of May further precipitated this shift in mind-set. Not only Lefebvre, but many of the other young academics and planners were in fact involved in the protests or otherwise identified strongly with the protesters. As much as it had changed the face of urban France over the past decades, state-led urbanism was now increasingly criticized for its complicity in maintaining a classist capitalist society. Influenced by the writings of Lefebvre, whom he served as an assistant at the Institut d'urbanisme de l'Université de Paris (IUP, or Urbanism Institute of the University of Paris), Tonka concluded after the conference that "the urban question is not innocent in the global strategy of class power, because our society—according to the latest news—is a class society." Consequently, he argued, "urbanism is not an issue in itself, exterior to class struggle," but has a "coherent repressive rationality": its expertise is thus a direct instrument of class power.[73] The year before, Tonka had helped establish Utopie, a collaboration among architects, urbanists, sociologists, and theorists who criticized mainstream architecture and urban planning practice through their magazine, exhibitions, pamphlets, and posters.[74] Unlike Architecture Principe, the contemporary group established by Claude Parent and Paul Virilio, which augmented its theoretical work with (often paper) design proposals published in a similar "little magazine" format, Utopie conceived of its critique as a form of "theoretical practice."[75] No matter how destructive, its critique was still a fundamentally productive endeavor.

Such critique also reverberated within the very governmental institutions that the protesters held responsible. And it was quickly internalized. As not only the *grands ensembles* but also the *villes nouvelles* had become a primary target of critique around 1968, Michel Mottez, one of the planners of Évry, recounted the period with ambivalence: "It is a fact that the wind of 1968, of which we made use in our approaches and reflections, was often turned against us by many inhabitants for whom we were the slaves of big capital and of a technocratic government."[76] The "events" of May 1968 in fact engendered a new self-critical culture within the state administration. Rather than fundamentally negating the legitimacy of the state, this culture was still wedded to the idea of pragmatic improvement. Just as the government had an obvious interest in understanding the reasons for the popular and intellectual unrest of 1968, so it had an interest in sociological expertise, however condemning or critical it was. Quantitative studies and standardized opinion polls had failed to predict May 1968, so such uncritical approaches were now invalidated. New types of research were required: more independent, fundamental, in-depth, and critical. Exactly such approaches, often highly theo-retically inclined and qualitative in method, were thus cultivated by the French government during the following decade.

The ground for this evolution had been laid before 1968 in state-sponsored urban research programs and institutions. At mid-decade, the Délégation générale de la recherche scien-tifique et technique (DGRST, or General Delegation of Scientific and Technical Research), a premier government research institution, launched an ambitious series of open calls for urban research projects, indicating administrators' desire to get a better sense of the social repercussions of their urban interventions.[77] A similar call came from the recently established Central Technical Service of Planning and Urbanism (Service technique central d'aménage-ment et d'urbanisme). Its collapse in 1968 after internal contestation was emblematic for the widespread upheaval in government hallways and institutions as a result of the protests that year.[78] The institution's mandate was taken over by the DGRST, where from then on government-funded urban research was to be coordinated. Under the leadership of Michel Conan, the DGRST promoted a new type of research.[79] The application of research findings was de-emphasized and government calls were radically opened up. Entering researchers thus enjoyed more freedom to be explorative and critical, even if their conclusions often veered back toward the realm of policy.[80]

This new opportunity for financial support engendered a veritable research "market," which benefited a range of research offices and institutions, from the Centre de sociologie urbaine (Center for Urban Sociology) and CERFI to new teams such as that around Bau-drillard or the Institut d'urbanisme de Grenoble.[81] Some of these were offshoots of large semi-public economic research institutions; others were entirely new and claimed novel forms of urban expertise. Situated on the borders of the university, the public sector, and the private consultancy sector, they were a wind of change in the research landscape otherwise dominated by the schism between "ivory tower" academic studies and the "applied" research directly com-missioned by the government. Many of these offices were on the political Left, and their work was specked with references from a renewed Marxism and emerging poststructuralism.[82] As fervent as they were in their criticism of the state, many owed their livelihoods to it.

The new generation quickly extended its criticism from dominant state-led urbanism to those who had facilitated it. In contrast to Chombart, who, as Amiot has put it, "did sociol-ogy for planners," they "did sociology *of* planners and planning itself."[83] Despite Chombart's attempts to address the diversity of people's needs, his research was thus dismissed as com-plicit with the oppressive forces of state capitalism. The time of Chombart was clearly over: instead of an objective study of material needs, urbanism was now understood to be a politi-cal practice. Yet, despite the radical nature of this new critical apparatus, sociological exper-tise continued to find its way back into planning, albeit with the necessary detours and translations. Critique and intervention were closely tied, not only for the avant-garde but also at the level of state bureaucracy.

The architects seemed to have joined in rather late but made up for that with their vigor and enthusiasm. After a time of conspicuous silence, architectural culture was front and center during May 1968.[84] A younger generation had almost imperceptibly emancipated itself from its elders by dismissing what it saw as stale ideas derived from Beaux-Arts academicism or a regurgitation of the Athens Charter. This older generation was, after all, responsible for designing and building now widely despised *grands ensembles* such as Sarcelles. French architecture education, epitomized by the elite École nationale supérieure des Beaux-Arts (ENSBA), was crucial in this shift. Contrary to the perception of the school as a bastion of resistance to change, many educational reforms took place during the 1960s and these effectively prepared the ground for architects' involvement in the protests of 1968.[85] Such changes included the establishment in 1963 of an atelier by Georges Candilis and Alexis Josic, who had their students attend the lectures of Lefebvre, then teaching at Nanterre. Whether the administration willfully resisted or promoted such intellectual renewal, May 1968 sped up change in architectural culture to the level of a revolution. And what positioned itself as a direct vehicle of that revolution—and initially filled the vacuum left by the collapse of the Beaux-Arts system—was an approach to architecture mixing social critique, sociology, and architectural research.

Until 1968, architecture at the ENSBA remained in the hands of the "mandarins," as its leaders would later be referred to. In this regime of white gray-haired men, the development of urbanism in the curriculum, which introduced a novel sensibility toward the urban, figured as a harbinger of change. Urbanism at the school was synonymous with the Atelier Tony Garnier, founded by André Gutton, who also taught at the IUP. Originally a professor in architecture theory, Gutton had developed courses in urbanism based on his own interpretation of the Athens Charter and the French ambitions of territorial planning. When Auzelle joined in 1961, the course was transformed into a seminar and workshop, whose briefs were informed by the "real-world" demands of private developers and the state.[86] Not just the teachers, but much of the student body in fact crossed over between the ENSBA and the IUP at this time. Following Auzelle, the workshop was not only indebted to modernism but also inspired by the "human sciences" as they transpired in the work of Gaston Bardet, George, and Chombart, among others. Rather than looking at "the building itself," Gutton argued, the Atelier Tony Garnier was the only studio to study "the building in the city." This, for him, entailed a shift from *form* to *program*, or, in other words, "the architecture of the building was no longer only linked to its function, the building in itself 'had a goal' in the social life of the city."[87] Architectural program, in other words, was sociologically understood. For actual courses in sociology, students had to wait until 1968, though such a curriculum change was in fact planned the year before.

Meanwhile, at the IUP, the country's oldest institution for urbanism, students did have such courses. "Introduction to Urban Sociology" had been taught by Jean Margot-Duclot since the early 1960s, based on the work of Georges Gurvitch, Georges Friedman, Maurice Halbwachs, Max Sorre and George, and Chombart.[88] The school however seemed intellectually more dominated by Auzelle's "Théorie générale de l'urbanisme." This course explicitly promoted an "urbanism of applied social science," which included economics, biology, sociology, demography, geography, and history.[89] Despite his focus on the social dimension, he dismissed opinion polls demonstrating the desire for single-family homes, following the argument of many modernists and intellectuals that such polls strengthened traditional views and obstructed innovation. And despite the embrace of social science, the school lacked the institutional strength to create an environment conducive to academic research.

Sociology as a form of practice-oriented research was thus present in the curriculum but seemed relatively inconsequential. The protests of May 1968 changed that dramatically. At the ENSBA, the open workshop Atelier populaire employed poster art to radically question the role of architecture and urbanism in society at large. Its posters featured statements such as the famous "Motion of 15 May," which read:

> We want to fight against the conditions of architectural production that submit it to the interests of public or private developers. How many architects have agreed to carry out projects like Sarcelles [des Sarcelles], large or small? How many architects take account in their project specifications of the conditions of information, hygiene, and security of the workers on their construction sites and would do it if not a single developer responded to their call for tender?[90]

The contestation at the IUP was not all that different.[91] The only thing that could save architecture and urbanism, therefore, seemed to be a deeper understanding of its social use and consequences. And what else had already provided architects such critical insight but sociology? Young architects' embrace of radical social critique was accompanied by a devotion to sociology. While teachers and students at the ENSBA had more than occasionally received it with hostility, after 1968 sociology came into heavy demand from all sides.[92] Despite the highly politicized climate, its inclusion in architectural production continued to be based on an ideal of scientific rigor. Such an approach was posited as opposite to the strictly formal or normative approaches with which the architectural and urban production of the preceding decades was now identified.[93]

Many of the "pedagogical units" (*unités pédagogiques d'architecture*) created after the educational reforms of 1968 offered a prominent place to sociology and "scientific" research more generally. These units, which often brought students and teachers with similar political ideologies and pedagogical interests together, strengthened the position of sociology in architectural education during the following decade. Many students and young architects still hoped this social science would supply them with in-depth knowledge about user needs and aspirations, even though a strictly instrumental use of sociology was increasingly discredited.[94] The functionalist theories of modernist architecture and planning were replaced by critical approaches such as that of Baudrillard, who proclaimed that "A theory of needs has no sense: the only thing that can exist is a theory of the ideological concept of need."[95] In a mass consumer society, he argued, needs were invented rather than given. More generally, sociology and anthropology were central at this time in redefining need from a mere physiological or biological given to a complex of cultural, psychological, and social factors, and confronted architecture with considerable challenges.[96] Sociology in particular assumed such an overwhelming position that some saw it increasingly as a threat and spoke of an "imperialism facing architecture."[97]

To sociology and critique was soon added architectural research. Not surprisingly, the government was key in the development of a research culture in French architecture after 1968. Conan, who was heavily inspired by the architectural doctrines of Christopher Alexander at this time, had already provided many architects with the opportunity to pursue urban research projects funded by the DGRST. In 1969, then, the Ministry of Cultural Affairs established an official committee for architectural research. Heated policy discussions in which prominent sociologists including Philippe Boudon, Bernard Lassus, Nicole and Antoine Haumont, as well as Henri Raymond, took part, resulted in the establishment of a Comité de la recherche et du développement en architecture (Committee for Research and Development in Architecture) two years later. This committee supported architectural research in early 1970s France, and collaborated with the DGRST to encourage and evaluate experimental architecture projects. With advocates such as Bernard Huet, journals such as *Urbanisme* and *L'Architecture d'aujourd'hui* functioned as a sounding board for this novel branch of the discipline, "research."[98] Ambivalently situated in between professional ideologies and the academy, being scientific would remain an obsession for many architects throughout the 1970s. To a large extent, the emergence of architectural research in France mirrored what was going on elsewhere in Europe and the United States. At a moment when architecture was going through a fundamental crisis, architects from John Habraken to Alexander turned toward research. They temporarily formulated a productive alternative to both the "business as usual" of the older generation and the radical negativity of critics such as Manfredo Tafuri and Massimo Cacciari.

This ambivalence was also reflected in the societal position of the French architect at this time. While architecture was still largely shaped as a liberal profession, the overwhelming role of the state during the *trentes glorieuses* had radically overturned architects' identity. In the eyes of the critical public, they were often seen as accomplices of the centralized state and thus equally responsible for its purported mistakes—especially the *grands ensembles*. The combination of such external critique with increasing self-critique shaped the intellectual universe of young architects in the years around 1968 and placed them in often contradictory situations. The opportunities for young collaborative offices such as the Atelier d'urbanisme et d'architecture (AUA) often existed by virtue of the very same institution they criticized so fundamentally: the centralized state. In the proposal submitted for the *ville nouvelle* of Évry, the AUA explained that contradiction as follows:

> As long as sociology and town planning continue to serve a system where urban functions are restricted to the storage of the manpower necessary to the development of capitalism, theoretical choice shall be restricted to either the utopia of a testimony concealing impotence or the search for experimental spaces, while awaiting a liberated social practice that shall come at the proper time. . . . The city is not a free space for the accumulation of functional envelopes, it is an experimental support for intercourse. Our mission is to imagine its mechanisms and processes of development. While waiting for an adult society capable of constructing its own environment, we willingly accept the role of Demiurges ascribed to us, limiting our ideology to DIDACTISM and COMPLEXITY.[99]

The AUA was held together by its commitment to Communism at a time when the French government was decidedly liberal but a vigorous neo-Marxism shaped the dominant intellectual mind-set. In this climate, the AUA continued to submit proposals for large state-led planning projects, as for the New Towns of Évry and Cergy-Pontoise, the Villeneuve project of Grenoble, and La Défense (Figure 5.8).[100] Some of these were not the kind of projects that constituted a radical break from the large-scale capitalist state-led urbanism of the preceding decades; quite the contrary. Yet that contradiction was not perceived as such by many of the young, often collaborative architecture offices that would be increasingly patronized by the French state during the 1970s. The *villes nouvelles* were a central playground for this kind of architecture, which, as Tafuri would note, spoke the language of contradiction remarkably well.

Combinatory Urbanism

The reorganization of urban expertise, to which French New Town planning was crucial, was driven by a certain sociological sensibility more than by the direct insertion of sociological data. Le Vaudreuil, one of the official New Towns launched in 1965 and one of the first to be conceptualized in architectural detail, was exemplary of how a concern for the user and a social critique of the planning process moved sociology into design. The New Town was part of the first regional planning study outside the Paris region, but despite being developed in concert with local politicians and the private sector, it still fit the centralized mold of a Gaullist

Figure 5.8. Proposal for the New Town of Évry from the competition for Évry I, 1971–72, by Paul Chemetov, Georges Loiseau, and Jean Tribel (AUA), together with Taller de Arquitectura—Ricardo Bofill, Jean Ginsberg, and Martin van Treeck. Archives nationales, France, CAC 19840342/324.

France in the thrall of national modernization. Optimistic forecasts legitimized a projected size of one hundred thousand inhabitants for the New Town, located in the middle of a still largely rural region. The plan was drastically scaled down in the mid-1970s, and all that remained of the ambitious plans thirty years later was a small municipality of 13,500 inhabitants with a new name, Val-de-Reuil. Despite this failure when compared to large French New Towns such as Cergy-Pontoise, its architecture and urbanism—some of which got built—still embodied high hopes for the creation of a better kind of city.[101]

These aspirations began with the very first proposals for the New Town, developed by the young collaborative architects' office Atelier de Montrouge.[102] The office was created in 1958 by Pierre Riboulet, Thurnauer, Jean-Louis Véret, and Jean Renaudie, graduates from the ENSBA who shared leftist political affiliations. The office, whose collaborative nature was itself already subversive in the reigning architectural climate, was at the forefront of the younger generation of French architects who eventually overturned the Beaux-Arts system.[103] Atelier de Montrouge was first commissioned for Le Vaudreuil in 1967, when the team still included Renaudie. After his departure the following year, the three others continued to work on the New Town plan (until 1972), now in collaboration with the official study team, the Mission d'étude de la ville nouvelle du Vaudreuil.

The architects proposed not so much a master plan as a series of theoretical arguments about the nature of the future city (Plate 10). Their drawings channeled some of the utopian concepts in Constant Nieuwenhuys's New Babylon and Yona Friedman and Nicolas Schöffer's "spatial urbanism," in particular their assertion that freedom, change, and spontaneity were the basic ingredients of urbanism.[104] They also took inspiration in megastructures such as those proposed by Alison and Peter Smithson for the Golden Lane and Berlin Hauptstadt competitions and the concepts further developed by Candilis-Josic-Woods, who replaced the rigidity of functionalist space with a complex, flexible, and open structure that gave some form of agency to its users. In the late 1960s, such modernist technological utopias escaped the total condemnation that hit the *grands ensembles*, but they were nevertheless increasingly faulted for their social irresponsiveness. In the proposal for Le Vaudreuil, such utopian ideas were meshed with heightened social concerns and sociological theorization. The architects suggested a networked urbanism that encouraged individual mobility and flexible forms of sociability. At the same time, they envisioned an alternative kind of urbanity in which the intimacy of social life would be fostered by the structure of an all-encompassing environment.

After the official establishment of Le Vaudreuil's multidisciplinary study team in 1968, the work of the architects was subsumed within this group. Led by Jean-Paul Lacaze, the team included some architects and planners (for executive work and technical detailing), a geographer, a landscape architect, an economist, and several sociologists, with whom the Atelier de Montrouge worked most closely.[105] The preliminary studies were primarily economic, demographic, and geographic. Rather than to pursue studies geared toward urbanism, the sociologists were mandated to reflect on the methodology of the planning process itself. According to Gérard Héliot, this encouraged them to think outside of their special expertise and reflect more globally, "almost philosophically," on the project. As such, their role quickly changed and they began to synthesize the team's reflections on the city and its goals for the project. And as planning ideas became more concrete at later stages, their responsibility became increasingly focused on *programmation*.[106] Across this changing involvement of sociology, there was a strong alliance between the sociologists and the architects of the Atelier de Montrouge. Both parties insisted that the whole team sit together to "theorize the project globally" before detailing any plans.[107]

The urbanism of Le Vaudreuil was thus developed in close collaboration between the sociologists and the architects. As Héliot later recounted in an interview, "To me, it seems that the role of the human sciences, in Le Vaudreuil, has been fundamental during this whole study period. I repeat: human sciences, that is to say, a certain state of mind that was a certain way of reasoning and willingness to pursue studies that were prevalent as much with the human sciences properly speaking as with a group of architects who were particularly sociologized, if I may say so."[108] Rather than a master plan that would set the New Town in stone, the architects and sociologists proposed to provide only "the conditions of its birth and its development."[109] This led to their concept of a *germe de ville* or "embryo of a city." Instead of a normative procedure of discrete phases of development, the city could be programmed as an "organic" process in which each subsequent phase of development was to be "complete in itself" (Figure 5.9).

Le Vaudreuil was no less than a manifesto. At the basis of the team's theoretical reflection was the ambition for a radical alternative, which they described as the "choice to make a new kind of city." With a diverse and open structure that would allow freedom of choice in both lifestyle and future planning, it was to be "a combinatory, complex, and evolving city."[110] By combinatory, they meant that the sum would be greater than its individual parts and that all parts of the city would be linked to each other in a complex whole: "In the city, there are no simple objects; there is undoubtedly not even an object at all. Each element takes meaning only in combination in a much vaster whole that is itself implied at the very heart of the element."[111] This idea—both biological and structuralist in inspiration—was a direct critique of dominant French urbanism and its lack of attention to the "indispensable linkages" that make up a city (Plate 11).[112]

The notion of "combinatory" was inspired by systems thinking and computer science and directly evoked Norbert Wiener's cybernetics, not surprisingly, at the height of an architectural culture heavily attracted to such "hard sciences." It led the designers of Le Vaudreuil to develop a theoretical conception of urbanity as one of communications, patterns, elements, relations, structures. Their job, therefore, was not to design but to *program* the city. Just as

Figure 5.9. The "embryo of a city" concept for Le Vaudreuil, 1973. Rather than building the shoulder, the arm, the head, and then the other arm of the city (left), planners proposed to build an embryo that would grow into a mature city "naturally" over time (right). From *Cahiers de l'IAURP* 30 (1973): 23.

cybernetics analyzed life scientifically with the aim to eventually reproduce it, so architecture was believed to have the capacity to duplicate the ephemeral qualities and liveliness of the city. Unlike the borrowings of some other architects lured by science at this time, those of the Atelier de Montrouge were ultimately moved by the poetic and the social. Like Aldo van Eyck, they responded almost philosophically to the dominant mind-set of structuralism during the 1960s, a time that some would later refer to as "the Foucault, Lévi-Strauss, Barthes, and Lacan years."[113] Believing in the possibility to transpose such social analyses onto the structure of space, they commissioned Habraken and his Stichting Architecten Research group for a study on the patterns and "rules" for the urban organization.[114] The eventual result of such collaborations was a three-dimensional urban mesh (*maille*) that could be filled in at random to create a diversity of different dwelling conditions and public spaces. In some ways, the proposal reflected the concurrent shift in structuralism from closed to open systems as a lens of analysis. In urban planning, this meant a shift away from the hierarchy of the neighborhood unit and toward the kind of complexity for which the design of Le Vaudreuil was quickly becoming exemplary (Figure 5.10).

More than by cybernetics or structuralism, Le Vaudreuil's conception was informed by specific sociological concepts that had been circulating over the previous decade. The concrete design proposal for the New Town, as it was published in the *Cahiers de l'IAURP* in 1972, abundantly cited sociological studies such as Ledrut's "L'espace social et la ville" and Alexander's "A City Is Not a Tree." But it was the work of Lefebvre that constituted the primary source of inspiration for the architects. As pointed out earlier, Lefebvre was a key mediator of sociological concepts and critiques in the domain of architecture. His "The Right to the City" of 1968 had rapidly become a classic for the younger generation of French architects and urban planners (Figure 5.11). The ambition of the Atelier de Montrouge to design what it called the "right to architecture" was a direct transposition of Lefebvre's notion of the "right to the city." For Riboulet—who became somewhat of a regular contributor to *Espaces et Sociétés,* the critical urban sociology journal established by Henri Lefebvre and Anatole Kopp

Figure 5.10. The proposal of a three-dimensional woven structure by Atelier de Montrouge for Le Vaudreuil, 1968–72. Model photograph: Fonds ATM. Service interministériel des Archives de France/Cité de l'architecture et du patrimoine/Archives d'architecture du XXe siècle. Drawing from *Cahiers de l'IAURP* 30 (1973): 54.

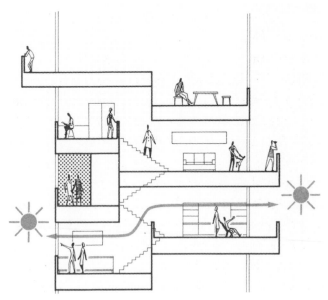

Fonctionnement d'une équipe pluridisciplinaire non hiérarchisée.

Figure 5.11. Cartoon from 1973 illustrating the "nonhierarchical" working of the multidisciplinary design team of Le Vaudreuil (top), compared to that of a hierarchical one (bottom). It also demonstrated how central Lefebvre's *Le droit à la ville* was in this new way of planning (top right). From *Cahiers de l'IAURP* 30 (1973): 8.

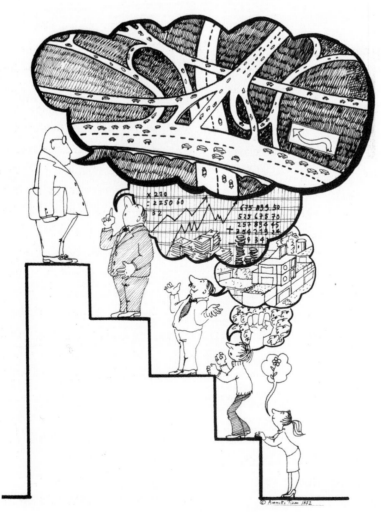

Fonctionnement d'une équipe pluridisciplinaire hiérarchisée.

in 1970—"the city is architecture," and thus the "right to architecture" was understood as the right of inhabitants to freely create their everyday urban environment.[115] One of the more famous phrases in Lefebvre's book read: "The right to the city manifests itself as a superior form of rights: the right to freedom, to individualization in socialization, to housing [*habitat*] and dwelling [*l'habiter*]. The right to creative work (participatory activity) and the right to appropriation (clearly distinct from the right to property) are all implied in the right to the city."[116] It was this concept of appropriation that the architects of Atelier de Montrouge and the planning team of Le Vaudreuil adopted most emphatically.

The notion of appropriation was not a novelty in French sociology. Chombart had employed it already during the 1950s in his analyses of suburban housing estates. He spoke about inhabitants' use of interior decoration in new apartments as a way to appropriate or personalize them. Although they recognized the importance of such processes, researchers such as Chombart and René Kaës did not emphasize the spatially transformative aspects of appropriation. For Lefebvre, however, appropriation was first of all a critical and creative response to the functionalist concept of need at the basis of the *grands ensembles*. Two sociological studies had provided him with the concrete inspiration for this understanding. The first was a government-funded research project on dwelling culture in French suburban single-family homes. Published as *L'habitat pavillonnaire* in 1964, with a preface by Lefebvre, the study revealed inhabitants' practical and symbolic markings of space, and demonstrated the creative possibilities and changing uses of attics, basements, garages, and front lawns as a form of spatial and social flexibility.[117] A second landmark study, by Boudon, analyzed the process by which the inhabitants of Le Corbusier's suburban housing estate in Pessac had altered their homes over the years since its construction to adapt to changing needs and popular tastes. The study resulted in his 1969 book *Pessac de Le Corbusier*, again prefaced by Lefebvre.[118] The findings of these two studies were instrumental to Lefebvre in the development of his concept of appropriation, which was "at the same time analytical, critical, and prospective."[119] Appropriation was understood as a set of creative practices that substantially transformed a given spatial setting or model without destroying it. It was this understanding that architects readily adopted at the end of the 1960s. The collective research project on "the functional needs of man" sponsored by the DGRST and in which many French architects and sociologists collaborated—from Lefebvre to Georges-Henri Pingusson—marks the impact of this adoption. The study was directly founded on the dichotomy between "architectural space" as conceived by architects, and "users' space," which was the result of "the praxis of space by its users, considering that they build their personal space by marking and appropriating it."[120]

In an explanatory text for Le Vaudreuil, titled "La mobilité dans l'architecture en tant que moyen d'appropriation," Riboulet cited Lefebvre's concept of appropriation as he had formulated it in *La vie quotidienne dans le monde moderne*.[121] The essay, written in 1968, celebrated the creative and transformative characteristics of appropriation in architecture. At this time, the Atelier de Montrouge was also explicitly inspired by Boudon's study of Pessac.[122] The architects thus linked appropriation directly to the architectural conception of Le Vaudreuil as an open, free, and mobile urban space. Freedom and structure were reconciled in a similar way as they had been in Yona Friedman's "spatial urbanism," namely, by means of an overarching structure that would allow the free and adaptable montage of elements and thus changing activities or functions. Only, and importantly, the overarching framework was eliminated here. The solution the architects sought would "need to allow for 'mounting' and 'dismounting' the structure of the city; it will thus need to allow inhabitants to act on this structure, in fact to create it within a [certain] language so that the coherence and cohesion of the city is maintained in all possible configurations."[123] What was needed instead of a megastructure was *programmation*: a set of rules that would allow fixed elements—necessary because of technical demands—to remain as constraints but would in turn facilitate mobile elements as the tools of individual appropriation.

The planning team and the architects of the Atelier de Montrouge explained that one of their official goals was "to allow as early as possible the appropriation of the city by its inhabitants."[124] As such, in the eventual plan for Le Vaudreuil presented in 1972, Lefebvre's notion of appropriation found formal expression in architectural flexibility and complexity. But these formal characteristics were only the visible manifestation of an underlying principle, which was to conceive of the city the way computer scientists designed programs: not as fixed zones of activity, but as a set of rules allowing games to be played with indeterminate outcomes. This principle was the crux of a radical critique of dominant planning methods, denouncing the belief in a determinate, linear relationship between users' needs, architectural form, and function.[125] Structural openness and architectural complexity were seen as facilitating qualities for the participatory game of urban life, in all its unfinishedness, indeterminacy, and spontaneity. For Renaudie, architecture was "the physical form which envelops human lives in all the complexity of their relations with their environment," and therefore it needed to be as complex as the life inside it.[126] And by "giving the city 'to make' to its inhabitants," it would be naturally *évolutive*, continually transformable by social use.[127] In short, while formal complexity became the symbolic carrier of intentions to create a new kind of city, *programmation* was the underlying rationale.

This wealth of cybernetic, sociological, and philosophical ideas remained to some extent in the eventual planning of Le Vaudreuil when the study team was officially transformed into a planning institute charged with execution in 1972.[128] The official planning credo included one crucial point: "to make possible the appropriation of the city by its inhabitants by means of their participation in the conception of their living environment, as such breaking with a taken-for-granted urbanism." Consequently, planners contended, "in the domain of relationships with the inhabitants, it has been deemed essential to abandon traditional urban planning methods and to recommend a collective practice between designers, specialists, and users."[129] Nevertheless, instead of a direct transfer of agency toward the individual, this "collective planning practice" first of all entailed novel ways to entice people as consumers in search of a lifestyle. With the 1972 advertising slogan "Change life, come live at le Vaudreuil!" ("Changez de vie, venez vivre au Vaudreuil!"), the New Town located itself at the center of a growing environment-driven debate about the need for new, alternative urban lifestyles.[130] As such, the "socioarchitectural utopia" of the Atelier de Montrouge's project for Le Vaudreuil—despite not being executed as planned—was exemplary of how social critique, heightened by sociology and smoothed by consumerism, entered into French planning. The development of state-led urban sociological and architectural research and methods such as *programmation* had fundamentally contributed to this kind of experimentation, which would quickly peter out over the following decade.

1970s

CONSUMING CONTRADICTIONS

6

MEGASTRUCTURES
IN DENIAL

I N A C O U N T R Y S H O C K E D B Y E C O N O M I C C R I S I S, the inauguration in March 1975 of the urban center of Évry was the antidote to any call for austerity. Yet, more even than by the exuberant opening events, reporters were taken by the peculiar nature of the New Town itself. Without irony, newspapers announced that "in a utopian landscape of plowed land spiked with pink and pistachio-colored pyramids, just opened the commercial center and the agora, the stomach and brains of the New Town. For ten days, there will only be games and spectacle in the enormous fifty-five-thousand-square-meter souk—half-open and half-covered, partly amusement park and partly administrative and social center—where all the services of the city are assembled as in the ancient agora."[1] Whether they approached the complex from the elevated walkways that linked it to the surrounding housing areas, arrived by bus or train from the station underneath, or left their cars on the vast parking lots surrounding the complex, visitors found an urban machine they had likely never experienced before. In this "oasis in the middle of the desert," as *Le Figaro* headlined,[2] the new inhabitants of Évry and its surrounding suburban population were treated to the most unlikely smorgasbord of activities under one roof: a department store, a hypermarket, cafés, bars and restaurants, a bowling hall, a nightclub, a cinema, a skating rink, a sports hall, a swimming pool, a theater, a library, an information center, a family care center, a center for maternal and child protection, and a kindergarten, a meeting center, an ecumenical church, a broadcasting studio, a national employment agency, creative workshop spaces, a police station, and much more (Figures 6.1, 6.2).[3]

While Évry remained one of the most elaborate and perhaps well known, it was far from the only new urban center being built in France at this time. Many *villes nouvelles* and other

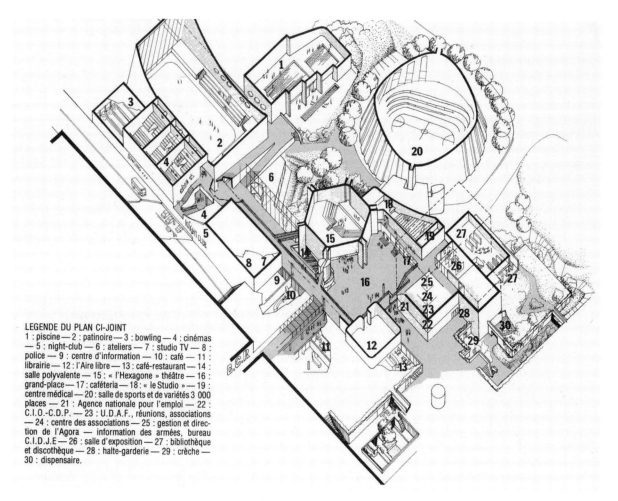

Figure 6.1. The diversity of functions at the Agora of Évry. Fonds Le Couteur. Service interministériel des Archives de France/Cité de l'architecture et du patrimoine/Archives d'architecture du XXᵉ siècle.

large-scale urban developments had planned a version of this new (sub)urban type. Almost all of them combined a vast range of new private and commercial amenities with public state-funded facilities. Widespread enthusiasm, resulting from their promise to produce a lively city from scratch, provided the momentum that allowed many of these colossal new "palaces of the people" to be built. The moment was nonetheless short-lived. Only a week after the opening of Évry's center, newspapers had already reported on its possible closure because of a lack of public funding.[4] By the end of the decade, such state-sponsored megaprojects had come to embody a governmental hubris no longer affordable or desirable. But why did so many of their underlying principles suddenly seem as illogical and ill-founded as they had been rational and self-evident less than a decade earlier?

Figure 6.2. Aerial photograph circa 1975 of the new urban center of Évry, with the Agora in the middle. Fonds Le Couteur. Service interministériel des Archives de France/Cité de l'architecture et du patrimoine/Archives d'architecture du XXᵉ siècle.

The megastructure urban center was the expression of a unique entanglement of citizenship and consumerism in France at this time. On the one hand, these projects were intensely consumer-oriented: planners seemed to take consumer freedom and satisfaction as the basis of their urban principles, translating happiness unproblematically as profitability. On the other hand, they are the ultimate megaprojects of a centralized welfare state on the verge of a radical withdrawal from such large-scale engineering of the built environment. Their complex architecture—the result not of a playful single genius but of hardworking collaboration and constant negotiation—speaks of that fragile hybridity. Yet, as much as these projects signify the decadent culmination of an era—France's thirty years of unprecedented prosperity—they constitute the beginning of another. These megastructures-in-denial are also the first generation of interiorized "total environments" in which so much of contemporary urbanity now takes place. Critical observers have continued to cast shopping malls as signs of the corporate takeover of public life. Yet the Agora of Évry and its cousins suggest that the welfare state may have had an important, if momentary, stake in the making of such environments.

The Center in Question

During the initial conception of the New Towns in the 1960s, one goal stood out from planners' ambitious list. More than because of the expansive infrastructure system or employment opportunities, the *villes nouvelles* would be groundbreaking because of their "markedly urban character." As one of the official reports proclaimed, the point was to "substitute 'a city in pieces' with that which constitutes the soul of the city: the ordering of spaces and neighborhoods, the variety of densities, the landmarks for the inhabitant, mixing and integration of the 'urban functions' (housing, commerce, offices, culture, recreation, and so on), mobility, and communication. This objective needs to be realized in the first instance by means of the creation of veritable urban centers that are dense, varied, attractive, and radiating onto a zone larger than the New Town itself while giving the latter its individual character."[5] How had urbanity and centrality become such overriding concerns in French New Town planning?

As in many other parts of Europe, the magnitude of postwar suburbanization in France had thrown the city center into question. On the other side of the Atlantic, suburbanization had certainly run an older and more dominant course. By the 1950s, many American observers agreed about the crucial impact of postwar suburbs on inner-city decline. In France, the upheavals were different, but no less dramatic. Frantic construction in the suburbs of many French cities during the 1950s had begun to radically transform a country that until recently had understood itself as predominantly rural outside of Paris. Nevertheless, Paris was still Paris. While postwar calls for decentralization—following Jean-François Gravier's influential 1947 thesis that there was only Paris and beyond it "the French desert"[6]—had to some extent informed the process of industrial relocation, they had effectively failed to decentralize Paris. Until the late 1960s, shopping, apart from the everyday necessities for any suburban housewife from suburban Gennevilliers to Créteil, still required a lengthy excursion to the *grands boulevards* in the heart of Paris. Universities, hospitals, and other large public institutions were hardly to be found outside metropolitan city centers. Paris was still the prototype for all things urban, and in the French "urban system," large provincial cities such as Bordeaux or Marseille were imagined to be not more than smaller versions of the capital.[7] If centrality thus became a key concern for French planners during the 1960s, it was not because its validity was questioned—there was no Melvin Webber in France—but on the contrary, because it remained the yardstick for evaluating two decades of unprecedented suburbanization.

In contrast to the United States, where the city center had more often been considered the problem and the suburbs the solution, France had long deplored the state of its poorer suburbs. Yet, during the 1960s, a curious convergence occurred when New Towns on both sides of the Atlantic were propped up as miracle solutions for suburban malaise. As American critics increasingly bemoaned the mass-produced American suburbs for their monotony and conformity, social critics, citizen activists, and enlightened businessmen joined forces to create privately developed New Towns such as Reston, Columbia, and Irvine during the 1960s.[8] In France, that same critique of suburban monotony and conformity targeted the country's mass collective housing estates. By the 1960s, many parts of the country had undergone chaotic suburban growth, leading to fragmented landscapes of sprawling housing estates in a sea of substandard single-family home allotments divided by highway and rail infrastructure (Figure 6.3). Many intellectuals, from their "bohemian" neighborhoods in central Paris, regarded this landscape with condescension, underestimating the profound cultural shift it embodied in the way the French increasingly lived their lives. No longer the sediment of long-standing traditions, cities were looking more and more like careless collections of disposable products, they argued. Inhabitants were less concerned with such distanced appraisals than with the basic lack of shops and amenities in their new suburbs. Yet, from whichever angle it

Figure 6.3. Aerial photograph of *grands ensembles* projects in the context of the southern suburbs of Paris, early 1960s. From Jean Bastié, *La croissance de la banlieue parisienne* (Paris: Presses Universitaires de France, 1964), 384.

was perceived, the "suburban problem" rallied planners and policy makers in 1960s France, and their most convincing solution was the New Towns.

Unlike their American counterparts, the French New Towns were government-initiated instruments for managing uncontrolled suburban growth through the insertion of large-scale urban figures that would be able to structure their surrounding suburbs by giving them identity and a new form of concentration. The cornerstone of this strategy was, of course, the urban center itself. For Évry, there was only one such "heart of the city." Some other *villes nouvelles*, like Cergy-Pontoise, were to contain two centers, which would allow planners to control the urbanization process more carefully. A first center would be built to fit the needs of a New Town still in development; a second, larger center would then be added to complete it. At Marne-la-Vallée, another New Town around Paris, a linear sequence of four centers on a new commuter rail line would structure its vast outward development.

The notion of the new urban center enjoyed considerable symbolic power: sometimes referred to as "the antisuburb," planners and policy makers projected it as the antidote and solution to all perceived suburban problems.[9] To build the opposite of a bedroom suburb meant first of all to create a place with a "soul." What could be more suitable for the sprawling suburbs than to give them a lively urban center? Such convictions were in large part shaped by the appraisal of modern state-led urbanism, which had so fundamentally transformed the country since World War II. Observers from different corners had pointed their fingers at the *grands ensembles*, as they were often underequipped and plunked down irrespective of their surroundings. The government's primary focus on housing had led to the neglect of many other needs and urban programs, experts argued in unison. Legislation had created an economic reality in which housing could be more easily financed by developers than by the urban facilities it required; but the urban form of the *grands ensembles* themselves—and thus architects' designs—had also played a role. Whether the architects were simply too busy keeping up with their profitable commissions for large-scale housing projects or too embedded in modernist dogma, they had marginalized the notion of the city center together with that of the traditional street, so the verdict stood. Just like the country's innumerable mass housing projects of the 1950s, the Athens Charter's four functions of living, working, recreation, and circulation had neglected the innumerable activities of the traditional city center: shopping, civic functions, social encounter, strolling, symbolic representation, and so on.

These convictions neglected not only the many revisions of *grands ensembles* architects as discussed in chapter 3, but also the postwar discourse of CIAM itself, to some extent. Its 1949 meeting, organized by Josep Lluís Sert and the Modern Architectural Research Group, had already proposed a crucial revision of the Athens Charter by focusing on "civic centers" and "the core."[10] The only French project presented at this meeting was Le Corbusier's plan for Saint-Dié, and the fact that it was never built—and his Unité d'habitation became the key reference instead—seemed to further emphasize the French lack of interest in urban centers (Figure 6.4).[11] The key projects that inspired French urbanists during the 1950s—such as Marly-les-Grandes-Terres or the Cité Rotterdam in Strasbourg—were based on deconcentration and negated traditional centrality. In many ways, the first generation of *grands ensembles* were still built with the idea to "ventilate" the city—hence the low-density, large green areas separating the housing blocks, and wide boulevards from which the buildings were set at a distance. Yet, as much as the *villes nouvelles* planners saw their urban centers in diametrical opposition to the urban form of the *grands ensembles,* their conception was in fact directly embedded in the ideological and formal revision of that modernism during the 1960s.

Even the urbanism of Sarcelles, "exhibit A" in the vilification of the *grands ensembles,* revealed a marked evolution toward a different kind of thinking, one in which urban density and centrality became paramount. When the first overall plan for Sarcelles was drawn up around 1960, it was a schoolbook example of the *grille Dupont.* Each of its different neighborhood

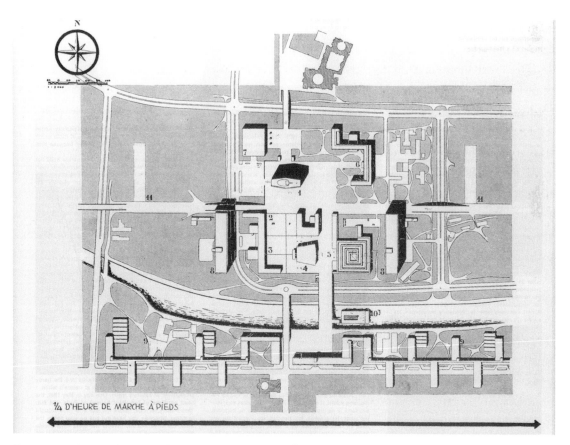

Figure 6.4. Le Corbusier's proposal for reconstruction of Saint-Dié, 1945, focused on a pedestrianized civic center. Fondation Le Corbusier. Copyright 2012 Artists Rights Society, New York/Société des auteurs dans les arts graphiques et plastiques, Paris/Fondation Le Corbusier.

units was equipped with a small commercial center. In the middle of the entire development, then, a "principal center" would rise up (see Figure 4.4). A mix of Le Corbusier's Saint-Dié center and Victor Gruen's early shopping-mall designs, this center was conceived in relatively low density, as if to mimic the dispersed layout of housing blocks around it.[12] The center featured an outside promenade sided by small shops and terminated by a large supermarket and department store on either side. It also included some housing, a municipal administration building and town hall, a church, a cultural center with cinema and theater, and a social center—all distributed spaciously over a vast pedestrianized surface (Figure 6.5). Funding delayed the execution of this project, and its plans were modified several times over subsequent years. The density was continually increased and the center became more enclosed (Figure 6.6). As the *grand ensemble* grew around it, the need for a well-equipped city center increased. By the end of the 1960s, then, the developer added a regional-scale commercial center meant to serve the larger population of Paris's northern suburbs. Baptized "Les Flanades," this multifunctional complex would transform the housing estate into a real city in its own right (Plate 12). Apart from commerce, the project also contained a hotel, a restaurant, and luxury condominiums when it was finally completed in 1973.[13]

The most important change across these revisions was the introduction of the *dalle* or plinth.[14] The final project for Sarcelles offered several floors of parking space and a large covered marketplace underneath a vast public plaza linking all other elements of the program. The *dalle*, which the architect Raymond Lopez referred to as "vertical zoning," emerged in the early twentieth century as a solution to adjust the future city to the automobile. It became a staple of modernist architecture and urban planning in later decades, when separating functions was elevated to the primary organizational principle for the city. During the postwar period it was enthusiastically promoted by traffic engineers who needed to accommodate the exponential rise in car ownership and individual mobility. The concept of the *dalle* shaped projects internationally, from Lincoln Center in New York and the New Town centers of Vällingby and Cumbernauld to the Parisian projects of Maine-Montparnasse and La Défense. Moving transportation and parking down below allowed planners to provide the large-scale pedestrianized public spaces prescribed at CIAM 8. Vertical separation allowed horizontal integration: one of the reasons for its particular success in French urbanism was its ability to create controlled yet lively public spaces and integrate a mix of different programs. Condemning the deadening functionalism of an earlier modernism without abandoning its basic premises, architects thus counted on the integration of once-separated functions to accomplish this new kind of urban space.

The idea of an architectural structure that would foster sociability and urban interaction resonated with a generation of visionaries in 1960s France. Michel Ragon's "prospective architecture" and Yona Friedman's "spatial urbanism" might at first sight seem far removed from

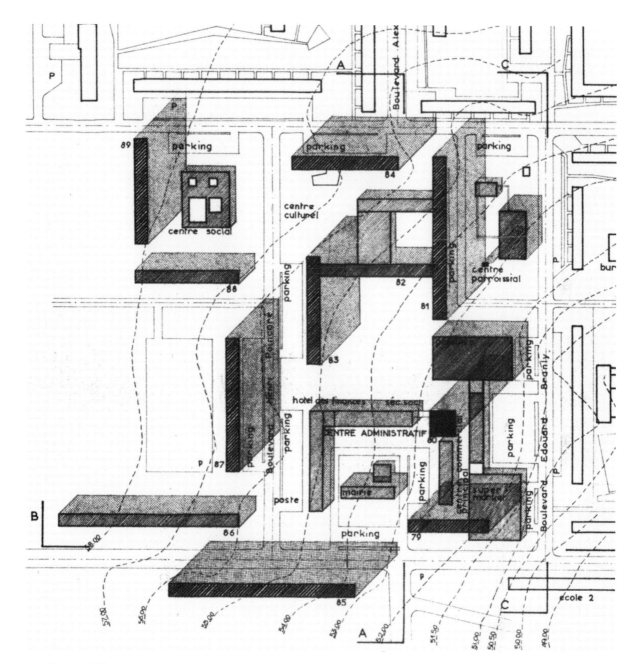

Figure 6.5. Plan by Roger Boileau and Jacques Henri-Labourdette for Sarcelles's principal urban center, submitted by SCIC for preliminary agreement in 1959. Archives municipales de Sarcelles.

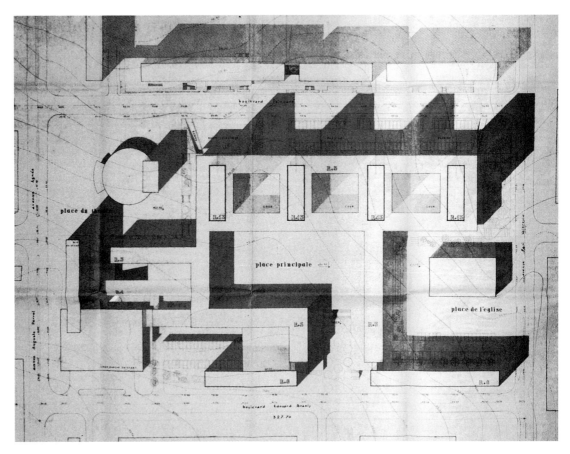

Figure 6.6. Plan by Roger Boileau and Jacques Henri-Labourdette for Sarcelles's principal urban center, submitted by SCIC for building permit in 1963. Archives municipales de Sarcelles.

such "pedestrian" concerns with enlivening the suburbs (Plate 13).[15] If such visions did address the concept of the center, it was rather to explode it altogether: an element of the past rather than the future, so it seemed. Well-known projects such as those of Friedman or David Georges Emmerich celebrated the advent of a new urbanized world in which freedom of movement, unlimited individual consumption, appropriation, and spontaneity would directly shape urban space. In this new "total environment," the solid forms and distinctions of traditional urbanity had evaporated. As these visions suggested how a new mobile subject would produce a new kind of architecture and city, they also extended the Corbusian city of circulation into a feverish world of networks and communication.[16] Despite being worlds apart from the concrete concerns of French state planners, such ideas nevertheless percolated into the gradual reorientation of New Town planning principles in the 1960s and found direct translation in the architects' ambitions for new urban centers across France.

While celebrated for their apparent libertarianism, these visions in fact affirmed the role of a strong state in the production of the built environment: they left little doubt as to who the singular, rational actor would be to provide the overarching framework facilitating individual appropriation. This peculiar blend of state provision and personal freedom was considered by many contemporaries as radically progressive, but also fitted surprisingly well within the Gaullist modernization project of the 1960s. During these years, visionaries and state planners were not worlds apart—both understood the city through the lens of an optimistic future made possible by technological progress—and were in fact linked by a network of intermediaries including Jean Fourastié, Gaston Berger, and Ragon.[17] Despite the fact that most of the utopian urban visions of this period dismissed traditional notions of centrality, they helped to expand the ambitions and strategies of state-led planning and its associated modernist architecture. The avant-garde's focus on architecture's stake in what Reyner Banham called "urban spontaneity" and the British avant-garde group Archigram simply "fun" mirrored state planners' confidence that urbanity was something that could be *produced*.[18] Rather than shaping the spatial structures of social organization, as Robert Auzelle would describe the task of urbanism in the 1950s, it no longer needed to be about order: urbanism could effectively generate the very dynamism and unpredictability of the contemporary city, rather than merely providing its physical support. As that ambition became central to the *villes nouvelles* during the 1960s—whether they were to be inserted in the messy suburbs around Paris or on farmland in the provinces—planners built upon the visionary ideas of the avant-garde. Sometimes the inspiration was direct, such as at Le Vaudreuil. More often it was implicit.

Politicians and policy makers often hailed the *villes nouvelles* as privileged sites for architectural and urban experimentation. Maurice Doublet, Paul Delouvrier's successor, called them "testing grounds open to all innovations."[19] During the late 1960s and early 1970s, experimentation was focused on the new urban centers, which figured as trigger projects for future development. Numerous studies and debates were organized on the theme of urban centers. Contributors to the themed issue on centrality of the journal *Urbanisme* in 1970 considered the demise of the traditional city center a fact, but they were also enthralled by its urban atmosphere and asked themselves how it could be reproduced.[20] While the *dalle* remained the main principle for the first generation of urban centers in Évry, Cergy, and Marne-la-Vallée, planners were keen to distance themselves from a modernism considered too brutal and alienating to an increasingly sensitized French public.

Like that of other *villes nouvelles*, Évry's multidisciplinary planning team—a mix of architects, urbanists, engineers, economists, geographers, and sociologists led by André Lalande, who had made his career at the ministry—was keenly aware of the public critiques of modern urbanism during the late 1960s.[21] When these planners imagined the urban center to be an intensively sociable, mixed-use urban place, the traditional city was in the back of their minds: "An important part of visiting the center is 'nonfunctional' and responds to motivations that escape the notion of quantifiable services, amounting in particular to the need for animation, intensity of life, social affinity, and cultural ubiquity—in short, sociability."[22] French architects and planners were more generally driven to a reappraisal of the traditional city at this time. In a 1967 article in *Urbanisme*, Maurice-François Rouge had already emphasized what he called "the logic of the nonquantifiable" of the city center, which included not only social, psychological, and affective dimensions but also the worlds of individual memory and collective history.[23]

These changes in urban thinking were directly inspired by regained attention to France's old city centers, Paris in the first place. That inspiration, however, was necessarily ambivalent: during the 1960s, traditional urban spaces were at once in a moment of crisis and one of rediscovery. While old neighborhoods such as that around Place d'Italie in the thirteenth arrondissement of Paris were being torn down for modern high-rise housing projects, other areas such as the Marais were being revalued as the focus of historic preservation shifted from isolated monuments to entire neighborhoods.[24] While inner-city inhabitants increasingly resisted large-scale urban renewal, planners sought to extract the essential qualities of traditional Parisian neighborhoods and to insert these in their New Town plans (Figure 6.7). The director of Évry's planning team, Lalande, literally stated such an ambition when he described the future of Évry as "a medium-sized Latin city that will be the beacon of a region."[25] The term "Latin" here stood for a series of desired urban qualities associated as much with Paris's vibrant *quartier latin* as with traditional cities of southern Europe: urban density, social and functional mixing, and an active street life during the day, but especially in the evenings. The idea of Latinness had, in fact, shaped the design of Évry's urban center since its initial conception.[26] The planners of Le Vaudreuil emphasized their overall goal in similar terms, namely, to "reconcile the characteristics of scale and animation of a Latin city with the qualities of the contemporary world."[27]

One of the organizing principles of the French New Towns, therefore, was a pedestrian network of paths, squares, and boulevards—much like any traditional city plan. As one of Évry's planners recounted, its new center was conceived first of all as a "pedestrian experience" filled with "possibility for exchange, for spectacle, permanently offered to all people." Consequently, he continued, "our spatial organization, the placement of buildings, and the programs needed to depart from a pedestrian network." Accessibility was another issue, however: "The center only has the possibility to function if its accessibility is the best of the whole surrounding zone. It is thus necessary that the center be served by public transport and by car."[28] The new centrality thus meant complete pedestrianization—and was defended as the European, culturally superior response to American car-dominated suburban space—yet it also had to

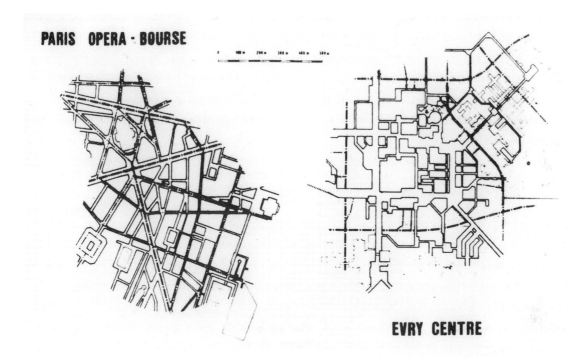

Figure 6.7. A comparison at the same scale of the New Town of Évry and the central area of Paris around the Opéra and the Bourse, 1972. From Secrétaire général du Groupe central des villes nouvelles and Institut français du Royaume Uni, *Centre et centralité dans les villes nouvelles françaises et britanniques.* Archives nationales, France, CAC 19840342/335.

be easily connected to the highway and public transport networks. Vast plinths and parking lots connected via overpasses were thus the counterpart of allusions to an organically grown historic urban fabric.

Where did the new urban concept leave mass housing, that old fixation in the *grands ensembles?* Despite fear of committing the same mistakes, planners still saw housing as crucial to the success of their new centers. In a 1972 government report, researchers contended that "all urbanists insist on the absolute necessity to build housing in the urban centers in the nearby future, whatever their financial difficulties (higher price of infrastructural investment), juridical problems (renting and not reselling of the land), and technical issues (difficult provision of green space, underground parking, stacking of housing, and collective facilities)."[29] In the case of Cergy-Pontoise, the center was meant to be more than a concentration of shops and collective facilities. With 1,500 planned housing units in dense urban typologies, it was designed to become a lively residential neighborhood in its own right. A similar rationale guided the proposal to include a diverse array of nighttime activities in the program. If the desired ideal was the vibrant nocturnal atmosphere of Parisian boulevards, the obvious counterimage was the deserted landscape of many housing estates after dinnertime. That the

French state would now actively plan for bars, cafés, and even nightclubs in new residential areas was not considered especially bizarre. Yet, only a decade earlier, it would have been impossible to imagine even a brasserie that served alcohol in many housing estates. In this sense, the *villes nouvelles* did open their doors to unprecedented architectural and social experiments. Their architects and planners were influenced at once by modernist visions testifying to an expanded definition of architecture as "total environment" and by the growing desire for the traditional city.

The Mantra of Integration

For an architectural vision of the New Town center, planners could have relied on Team X's well-known revisions of international modernism. But their strategies to create a new type of urban center to overcome the dreaded condition of France's modern suburbs were more directly shaped by the experiments of *équipement intégré* or integrated facilities. The provision of collective facilities in new neighborhoods—social centers, youth centers, schools, cultural centers, and local community centers—had long been on planners' agenda.[30] But by the 1960s, an increasing number of policy experts and social workers considered their discrete provision to be insufficient. Only drastic reconfiguration and radical integration could promise success, and the New Towns offered unprecedented opportunities to achieve it.

The initial testing ground for these ideas, however, was not New Town plans but public school buildings. The Cultural and Educational Center of Yerres outside Paris, inspired by British school reform and its development of community colleges, was one of the first projects in France to attempt such integration. The project combined a secondary school, a sports center, art studios, a music and dance conservatory, a social center, and a library, all under one roof. Launched by local politicians and experts in social work, this initial experiment informed a government-sponsored program for ten such centers. All of them would transform the school into a new, more effective type of social facility. The projects informed the gradual development of an official doctrine for *équipement intégré* during the second half of the 1960s and culminated in the establishment in 1971 of an overarching committee derived from a variety of ministries—National Education, Équipement (Planning and Housing), Cultural Affairs, and Youth and Sports. The initiative was officially abandoned in 1975, but by this time it had already left a lasting imprint on the architectural conception of the *villes nouvelles* and French late-modernist urbanism more generally.[31]

The underlying conviction was that the integration of collective facilities would more effectively foster personal and community development. Although some policy makers had previously argued that collective facilities "constitute perhaps the only means to democratize culture," the impetus of integration transcended André Malraux's cultural policies.[32] His new cultural centers of the 1960s were an important instrument of institutional reform, and democratizing culture certainly had a social dimension. But advocates of integration had a more specifically social agenda, summarized in a 1973 directive on *équipement intégré* as "a veritable transformation of social relations and civic attitudes, offering each individual animation structures that allow to better situate oneself in society and to participate more actively in community life, an approach of a new living environment by means of the creation of urban entities that are understandable and controllable by their inhabitants."[33] Aside from lofty goals of personal development (*épanouissement*), officials went so far as to cast the integration of collective facilities as nothing less than a cure for "cities without a soul." Such facilities should thus "encourage the creation of veritable hearths of social life, playing the kind of role, in newly urbanized zones, of the old village common."[34] As the institution operated far beyond its walls, people's participation in such facilities thus stood for a more encompassing practice of local citizenship: "The integrated facilities encourage not only the participation of the population in artistic creation, but also (and especially) the participation in a real community life."[35] The agenda of *équipement intégré* thus linked personal fulfillment and development directly with citizen participation, social encounter, and community building.

These noble goals, which marked the expanding ambitions of French welfare provision, went hand in hand with a rhetoric of efficiency. The integration of facilities promised to "increase the efficacy of state and municipal investments by reducing double use and dead time."[36] In other words, the same public spending would allow more people to be served. Increasing accessibility to social and cultural "services" would thus imply a more intensive use of their physical infrastructure. As part of a general aim to make the state administration more transparent to the public and improve public services, the impetus of integration was also shaped by the desire for a more efficient collaboration between different state institutions. Advocates of integration warned about the dangers of "compartmentalization" and saw the New Towns as ideal opportunities for developing interministerial collaboration between Planning and Housing, Health, Social Action, Cultural Affairs, and Youth and Sports.[37]

Beyond efficiency in provision, the integration of collective facilities was guided by a fundamental shift in what kinds of needs were to be fulfilled. Moving away from the functional, divisible, and quantifiable understanding of people's needs, planners and policy makers made increasing reference to a vaguely defined "global social need."[38] Encouraged by some of the critiques of May 1968, the integration of facilities was part and parcel of the desire for a more holistic conception of both the individual and his or her environment. When taken up by planners and policy makers during the 1970s, this shift informed a new discourse around "quality of life" for which the built environment became a primary arena. This is what explains the particular urban agenda of integrating facilities: just as a holistic understanding of people's complex needs exceeded any "functional enumeration," so would *équipement intégré* overcome the dispersal of isolated and disconnected amenities over the French territory, particularly as such discrete distribution was calculated for the *grands ensembles*.

Meanwhile, the emphasis on integration—with all its social goals of participation and community building—crossed over to architectural discourse and became crucial to the design of an entire generation of public facilities in France. Calls for participation, such as Joseph Belmont's manifesto for architecture as a collective creation, were common after 1968 but often remained vague about what such an architecture would look like or how it could be produced. Beyond by then tired suggestions of multidisciplinarity, his book *L'architecture, création collective* did not offer any concrete design strategies.[39] More fruitful was the concept of *polyvalence*—polyvalence, multifunctionality, or adaptability. It inspired formal innovations that were specifically endorsed by the government for new integrated facilities built all over France during the early 1970s. Particularly inspired by Dutch and British public architecture, not in the least Aldo van Eyck's famous orphanage in Amsterdam, *polyvalence* found architectural expression in constructive modularity, spatial fluidity, and formal transparency.[40] In contrast to the clear-cut orthogonality of postwar French school architecture, which essentially went back to André Lurçat's Karl Marx school in Villejuif of the early 1930s, the design of the new integrated facilities emphasized pattern over function and thus complexity over simplicity.[41] Public institutions needed to be "closer to the citizen," and their design was instrumental to this ambition. They could no longer be rigid, abstract, honorific, removed from everyday life, or divorced from their physical surroundings. Instead, they should be convivial, intimate, inviting, and surprising, and their design should lower the psychological threshold for visitors while improving accessibility. The community center of the New Town of Saint-Quentin-en-Yvelines by the architect Pierre Venencie was only one of the many French projects with these ambitions. It used an interlocking hexagonal structure (Figure 6.8) similar to AUA's experimental school at Grenoble Villeneuve.[42] As such, architectural form not only signified but was intended to actively produce sociality, following Henri Théry's idea that "to the complexity and fluidity of the contours and interactions of economic and social life corresponds a complexity and fluidity of space."[43]

In the architectural conception of these new facilities, the critiques and proposals of radical movements such as the Situationists clearly reverberated. *Espace global polyvalent*, Ionel Schein's book about the integration of collective facilities, was prefaced with Raoul Vaneigem's famous quote "We do not want a world where the guarantee not to die of hunger is exchanged for the risk of dying out of boredom."[44] Despite the inspiration he found in some contemporary developments, including shopping malls, Schein remained committed to a certain utopianism in contending that "the real polyvalent space has not yet been materialized. Motive: it disrupts too many habits, it disorients those habituated to these habits; it implies the invention of new rhythms of life, it prevents routine, it prevents most of all the transformation of

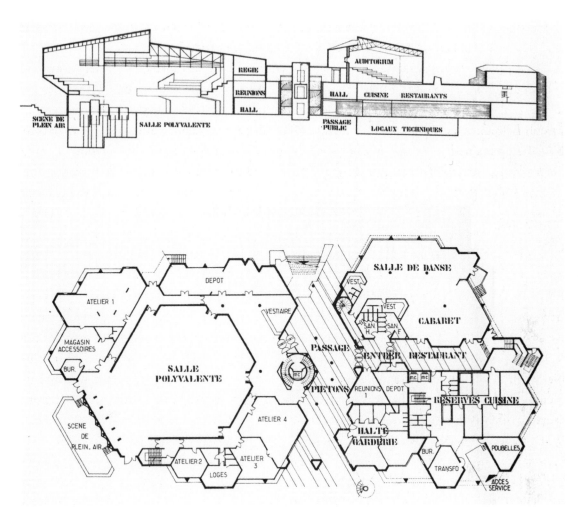

Figure 6.8. The center of "Les 7 mares" at Saint-Quentin-en-Yvelines, with the large "polyvalent hall" on the left. Architect: Pierre Venencie, 1971–72. From *Recherche & Architecture* 35 (1978): 40.

this routine in an act of construction."[45] His concept of polyvalent space was fundamentally anarchic and qualified by the freedom of spatial appropriation.

One precedent was key to New Town planners as they adapted the social and architectural ambitions of *équipement intégré* to their own plans: the Agora of Dronten. This large multi-functional community center for a New Town in the Dutch polders, designed by the architect Frank van Klingeren, appeared time and again in French architecture journals and government reports.[46] Opened in 1967, the project essentially consisted of a large hall that was transparent toward the outside and covered by a giant space-frame roof. The only specific functions formally articulated in this large open space were a theater, a restaurant, and some office space (Figure 6.9). The Agora could thus be used for an impressively wide range of cultural and

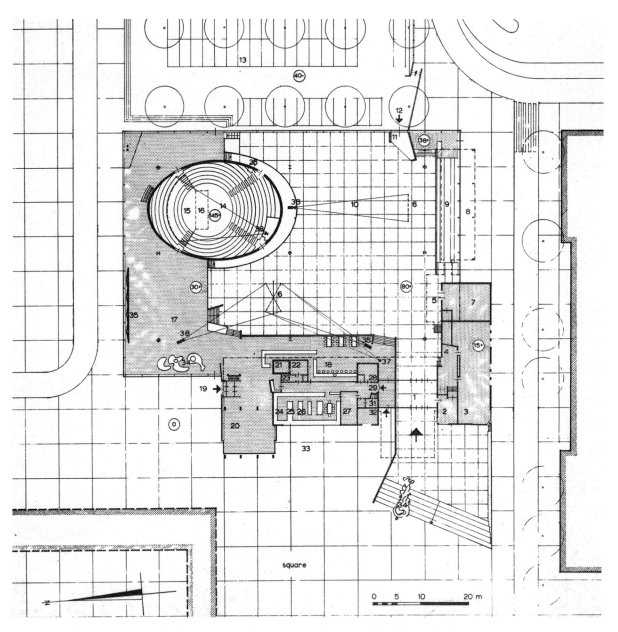

Figure 6.9. Agora in Dronten, the Netherlands. Architect: Frank van Klingeren, 1966. Plan by NAi. Photograph by Jan Versnel/MAI, Fotoarchieven Amsterdam.

sports activities, games and shows, from small gatherings to large public events. When a delegation of the Central Group of New Towns (Groupe central des villes nouvelles) led by the French premier visited the center in 1968, they were particularly impressed by the participation of the local inhabitants in the management of the center and its public activities.[47] Van Klingeren, who was trained as an engineer and thus somewhat autodidact in architecture, was well known at this time and built similar community centers in the Netherlands.[48] He was invited to participate in multiple French conferences about collective facilities in the early 1970s.

Schein acknowledged the Agora's crucial role in his own conception of polyvalent space: "The Agora of Dronten, starting point of our study, needs to be considered as a first step toward a global-anarchic space." At the same time, he pointed out how exactly its design fell short: "the intelligent and intelligible polyvalence of the volume of the Agora, while being flexible in its internal use, remains, in terms of urbanism, far too isolated. There is a separation between the internal dynamism and the exterior fixity: no organic link with the housing, the school, or the work in the city, one has to come there!"[49] Schein might have been unaware of the fact that soon after its completion, the Agora had begun to house the weekly market of the New Town of Dronten, and thus effectively blurred the distinction between public institution and public square. His ultimate call was exactly for this kind of spatial blurring between cultural production and everyday life: "Polyvalence—this liberty of actions, functions, approaches, incidents, and so on—needs to be expanded to all of the urban space, to all its inhabitants, regardless of their socioprofessional category."[50]

These ambitions were directly inspired by the radical deinstitutionalization called for after 1968 and so cogently formulated by Ivan Illich: existing institutions needed to be dismantled in order for the street to become the democratic space of direct action and animation.[51] Such ideas had quickly gained currency in French architectural culture at the time. In its 1970 theme issue "The places of spectacle," *L'Architecture d'aujourd'hui* emphasized the everyday life of streets and squares as a form of theater. Its contributors analyzed the scenographic qualities of urban spaces and the temporary architecture of markets, processions, festivals, street fairs, and mobile theater performances. They mapped urban spectacles and protests, including the "events" of 1968 themselves, but also examined the new cultural facilities planned for the *villes nouvelles*.[52] If there was one message to the publication, it was that just as culture and social life needed to be diffused, everywhere available and accessible, so could the architecture that facilitated them be mobile, flexible, and adaptable. This would entail a radical blurring of the distinctions between exterior public space and internal institutional space. In order for collective facilities to be integrated in the everyday lives of inhabitants, therefore, their architecture needed to be "molten in its surroundings" and "in osmosis with the animation of the street."[53] Despite the lofty aspirations, many designs for collective facilities during the following decade remained in tension between the desire for total flexibility, openness, and communication and the adherence to conventions of monumentality and architectural symbolism.

The idea of integrating facilities resonated in multiple ways with *villes nouvelles* planners during the early 1970s.[54] Because they were the centralized government's main statement for creating a better quality of life during 1970s France, the *villes nouvelles* were home to many of the experiments with *équipements intégrés*. And just like the New Towns themselves, these facilities were cast as social restructuring devices for the anarchic urbanization of postwar France and as beacons for a new urban lifestyle, alternative to the dreariness of its modern suburbs. Integration appealed to many New Town planners because it provided a concrete strategy for developing the much-needed animation and social life in the New Towns, through the mixing of programs and activities. When they laid down the basic options for their new urban centers, integration was thus considered on at least three levels: the combination of commercial with noncommercial programs; the spatial integration of the urban center itself understood as a large multipurpose complex; and the blurring of the new urban center with its surrounding neighborhoods.[55]

The integration would henceforth not only be spatial (by combining different programs or functions) but also social ("the intermingling of generations and social groups") and urban (by making the new facilities part of every life through careful implantation in the neighborhood). In some cases, the impetus of integration directly shaped the architectural conception of the New Towns. This was most pronounced at Le Vaudreuil, where the Atelier de Montrouge had translated the idea of integration into a three-dimensional urban lattice. At Cergy-Pontoise, the idea to mix a wide range of urban functions on the *dalle* and to fuse interior and exterior spaces also followed earlier, already built examples of integrated facilities. Yet it was at Évry's new urban center that integration would be perhaps most rigorously pursued. The result would be a thirty-thousand-square-meter state-sponsored complex of social, cultural, sports, and recreation facilities, baptized "The Agora of Évry" after the Dutch project by van Klingeren. But this megacomplex was only one part of the new city; the other part was a shopping mall more than double its size.

Shopping-Mall Fever

In late 1960s France, the most prominent suburban phenomenon generating the liveliness and crowdedness of something like a traditional city was undoubtedly the shopping mall. The success and proliferation of suburban commerce vexed New Town planners as much as it fascinated them. Big-box stores and malls popping up at the outskirts of Paris and other large French cities generated the crowds they imagined for their urban centers. State-commissioned studies for these centers acknowledged the crucial role of commercial development: "It is true that the commercial function is a driving force of the urban centers because it generates a considerable inflow of people (clients) whose presence assures animation (movement) and serves as a pretext, in a fluid way, for extra- or para-commercial events (exhibitions, shows, fashion shows, and so on). . . . We can consider that the commercial center is an anchor point from which we can envisage different planning programs."[56] Yet shopping was more than a simple programmatic element. Despite many intellectuals' denunciation of the shopping mall as a tasteless product of Americanization, which destroyed the French way of life, it became a rich object of inspiration for the planning and architecture of new urban centers. A history of New Town centers in postwar France would thus mean nothing without an account of the shopping mall.

The first self-service supermarkets emerged in French suburbs during the second half of the 1950s.[57] Despite their relatively small number and modest size, they enthusiastically inaugurated a U.S.-inspired consumer culture for French households. At the same time, neighborhood-level commercial centers were planned in the first generation of *grands ensembles*, following the *grille Dupont*, which detailed the required numbers and types of amenities per housing development.[58] Often built only years after the housing blocks were finished, these centers remained very small: a clustering of rarely more than ten shops supplying everyday necessities—a grocery, a bakery, a launderette, the odd café, and at times a small supermarket (Figure 6.10). Both these planned commercial centers and the privately developed supermarkets catered to a local, mainly pedestrian clientele.

When Carrefour opened the first *hypermarché* or hypermarket in Sainte-Geneviève-des-Bois outside Paris in June 1963, it launched a revolution not only in shopping but in French suburbanization more generally.[59] With its 450 parking places and total surface of four thousand square meters—four times the size of the average French supermarket—its adjacent gas station, and its variety of nonfood offerings in addition to the conventional supermarket goods, all at lower prices and all under the same roof, it was a huge success. Attracted by cheap land at a considerable distance from Paris, Carrefour's developers were inspired by American sales methods. They had made their "obligatory visit" to the American Bernard Trujillo, then the world's leading supermarket guru.[60] The hypermarket was nevertheless a French invention of sorts: at a time when American big-box malls were essentially chain stores specializing in specific products, the French hypermarket formula kept the diversity in offer of the supermarket while adding new products and services.

In France, the hypermarket was the first type of shopping experience that was exclusively suburban. Its premise was that customers would travel considerable distances by car to buy large quantities beyond their daily necessities. Thanks to the widespread democratization of the car and the refrigerator, that is exactly what young suburban households did as they swapped grocery trolleys for car trunks. Eager to consume, but also to save money and time

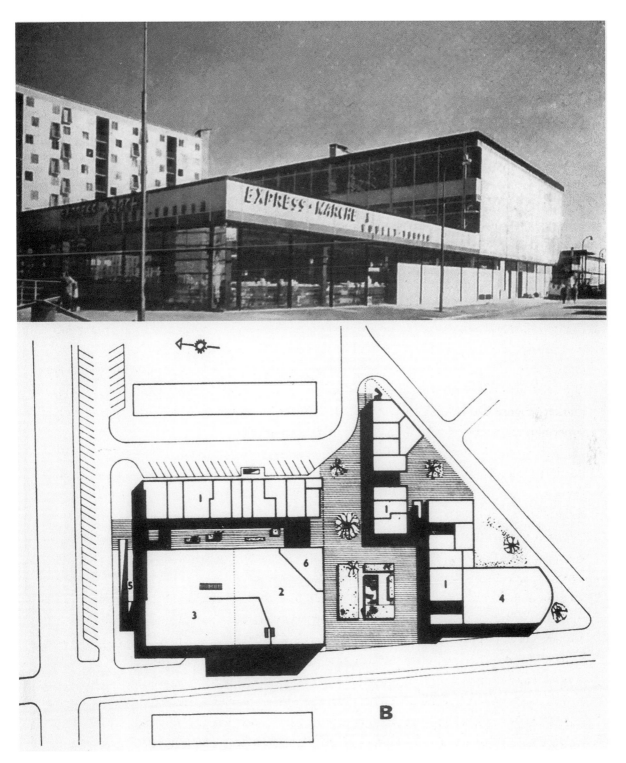

Figure 6.10. Planned commercial center of Reuil near Paris by Sonrel and Duthilleul with Claude Parent, late 1950s. From *L'Architecture d'aujourd'hui* 83 (1959): 32–33.

by getting all their groceries in one and the same store, the new consumers of the baby-boom generation made the hypermarket an immediate and unprecedented success. Competitors quickly imitated Carrefour's new formula, and during the 1960s hypermarkets proliferated across the country. To limit investment and offer cutthroat prices, they were often not more than expediently built hangars on cheap, peripherally located land (Figure 6.11).

By the late 1960s, France counted more than a thousand supermarkets and more than two dozen hypermarkets.[61] Their rapid proliferation enraged France's declining number of small shop owners for decades to come. As unregulated private developments, they constituted a sea change for the French suburbs and soon rendered the planned commerce of the *grands ensembles* obsolete. Of the around six hundred planned commercial centers in new housing estates by the mid-1960s, the majority were relatively small in size, and only one in five actually contained a supermarket.[62] Despite claims to rationality and efficiency, they were never very successful. Customers often complained of exorbitant prices owing to monopolies, and shop owners reported poor business.[63] Commercial distribution experts were the first

Figure 6.11. Carrefour hypermarket in Annecy, Rhône-Alpes region, 1968. From *Urbanisme* 108–9 (1968): 116.

to recognize these problems and instead suggested larger shopping malls directly at highway intersections—something that was unacceptable to the makers of the *grille Dupont* and many other French planners. Yet, other state officials with an eye on rationalized commerce considered larger developments such as the hypermarket to be the key to a more efficient mass production and distribution system.[64] By the end of the decade, the approach to link commercial facilities directly to housing development was officially abandoned, as was the *grille Dupont* itself.[65]

A second revolution in suburban shopping—equally important for the *villes nouvelles* but rather short-lived—was the import of the American dumbbell mall. It arrived with the opening in 1967 of Parly 2, "the first regional commercial center in France."[66] Located at a major highway intersection, this private development contained several hypermarkets and supermarkets in addition to more than a hundred boutique stores, banks, a movie theater, a gas station, an art gallery, and a travel agent. It featured the first suburban outposts of the Parisian department stores Printemps and BHV. The developer had gone to great lengths to promote the advantages of the complex's controlled environment: the stores all benefited from the "spectacular ambiance of the mall," its "careful management of collective provisions," and the branding of their collective identity (Plate 14). The ultimate ambition of Parly 2 was to offer an alternative to the commerce offered by the existing city center: this explained the "2" in its brand name. More centers soon followed. With names such as Grigny 2, Vélizy 2, and Rosny 2, they all claimed to offer a second, interiorized city center, even better than the real one.

Parly 2 was an unabashedly American product.[67] It was designed by Lathrop Douglass, the American mall architect who had at that time already designed more than seventy shopping malls in the United States and Europe. It was developed by the commercial developer Société des centres commerciaux (SCC), but not without the help of the famous American consultancy firm of Larry Smith, coauthor with the Austro-American architect and urban planner Gruen of *Shopping Towns U.S.A.*, a bible for commercial developers worldwide.[68] At the head of SCC stood Jean-Louis Solal, who was the first Frenchman to join the International Council of Shopping Centers and had met Gruen during his studies in the United States.[69] He emphasized that Parly 2 was not just an isolated shopping experience but that it would function as the center of a new residential neighborhood of more than five thousand dwelling units. Located at a major highway intersection in the municipality of Le Chesnay, the large-scale development drove up land prices in the surrounding region and contributed to its accelerated urbanization.[70] Many of Solal's other commercial center projects had an equally extensive program. Rosny 2, which also featured a dumbbell mall layout designed by American architects with the consultancy of Larry Smith, featured four office towers at the corners of the site and similarly incited the urbanization of surrounding areas (Plate 15).[71] Like many other commercial entrepreneurs, Solal believed in a radical liberalization of commercial development and saw little reason to collaborate with government planners.

Not surprisingly, state planners perceived such private developments as chaotic and "wild." Local and central government officials had no grip on the private developers who reinvented suburban commerce.[72] They often found themselves running behind. The official 1965 plan for the Paris region did not even contain specifications for commercial development, until the publication later that year by the Institut d'urbanisme et de l'aménagement de la région parisienne (IAURP, or Institute for Urbanism and Planning of the Paris Region) of a special report on "regional and intermunicipal commercial centers."[73] The study was one of the first attempts to plan comprehensively for large-scale commerce. Adopting the shopping mall as their basic unit of development, the planners proposed an implantation strategy that confirmed the crucial role of both commerce and the New Town centers in suburban restructuring. Meanwhile, the private malls and hypermarkets mushrooming around Paris at this time did not at all correspond to their plans. Parly 2 and many other developments were located in the richer, western suburbs of Paris, whereas planners envisioned a more equitable distribution of commerce, including in the eastern, less rich, and less populated suburbs.

Consequently, state planners called for direct consultation with developers to "rationalize" the location and planning of commercial developments.[74] They hardly entertained the idea that their prescriptions were not necessarily logical to the developers or to some of their prospective customers—and that what they saw as "chaotic" development actually had its own logic. The large state-led developer SCIC warned that shopping malls "killed urbanism" because they were impossible to integrate into their surroundings and encouraged uncontrollable urban growth.[75] Similarly, French architects were quick to criticize them for their "anti-urban" character. Yet, while such air-conditioned boxes surrounded by large parking surfaces did isolate their clientele from the surrounding urban fabric, they still tended to function as the de facto urban centers of their rapidly urbanizing and often ill-equipped suburbs.

State officials tended to react with a mixture of fascination and condemnation, following the judgments of many intellectuals. For Jean Baudrillard, commercial centers such as Parly 2 confirmed the advent of a new, dystopian society based on individual consumerism. This development was based on the dominance of a new type of space, the essential characteristics of which he saw manifested in the *drugstore*. This French Anglicism was imbued with meanings of modernity and American-style consumer culture. However, the French phenomenon did not exactly correspond with the American drugstore, which was basically a pharmacy selling toiletries and soda drinks. The French *drugstore* was essentially an imaginary type. Apart from the two or three real *drugstores* in central Paris, located in busy pedestrian areas such as the Champs-Élysées or Saint-Germain-des-Prés where they could be open day and night, they did not in fact exist as a regular feature of the French urban landscape (Figure 6.12). In spite, or rather because, of this quasi inexistence, the *drugstore* earned mythological status in French postwar culture. Featured in Jacques Tati's 1967 film *Playtime*, the imagined type of the French *drugstore* not only sold medical drugs, cosmetics, tobacco, candy, and knickknacks, but also included a bar and fast-food restaurant, and sometimes even a dance and meeting hall, all of which were open day and night. In his landmark critique of consumerism, *The Society of Consumption*, Baudrillard introduced his analysis with a description of this ideal type:

> The synthesis of abundance and calculation is the drugstore. The drugstore (or the new commercial centers) realizes the synthesis of consumer activities, not the least of which is shopping, flirting with objects, playful wandering, and combinatorial possibilities. . . . it does not juxtapose categories of goods, it practices the amalgam of signs, of all categories of goods considered as partial fields of a consumerist totality of signs. [With the drugstore,] the cultural center becomes integral to the commercial center. . . . The drugstore can become an entire city: this is Parly 2, with its giant shopping center, where "the arts and leisure mix with everyday life," where each group of dwellings gathers around the swimming pool club that becomes its node of attraction. . . . We are at the point at which "consumption" encompasses all of life, where all the activities link up to the same combinatorial mode, where the channel of satisfactions is traced in advance, hour per hour, where "the environment" is total, totally climatized, designed, culturalized.[76]

For Baudrillard, the shopping center most emphatically embodied the target of critiques of mass consumption that had erupted with May 1968: with this environment's many consumer promises and engineered conviviality, it channeled the novel desires that had been left unexplored in two decades of rational state-led modernization. In the book's 1970 publication, the image of one of Parly 2's luxuriously decorated interior atriums was captioned with the following phrase: "On these beaches without paving stones, the class A and nonclass A people will come to get tanned in the sun of commodities."[77] The allusion was fundamentally ironic, referring to that famous catchphrase of 1968, "Under the paving stones, the beach." The architects and planners of the French New Towns did not escape from this new cultural condition—regardless of their political ideologies. They were aware that contemporary commercial space was a programmatic must for any large-scale urban development. For some architects, it was not so much a necessary evil as a fertile source of architectural inspiration. The architect Schein, in his efforts to develop a "polyvalent global space," went so far as to turn the *drugstore* into an architectural manifesto:

> The *drugstorian* space, as it has evolved in Paris and only in some points of high sociocultural density, like the Champs-Élysées and Saint-Germain-des-Prés, the Opéra, and Saint-Lazare, is a first approach to a polyvalent space, based only on the exploitation and encouragement of

consumption and founded only on commercial profitability. The *drugstorian* space only takes on the formal principle of polyvalent space, but the experiment is interesting on the social level, because it is the quality of the space—by means of the conglomeration of functions that it contains—that has provoked the social density of these places and their commercial profitability.[78]

The *villes nouvelles* planning teams were equally ambivalent about the commercial center. They were fascinated by its ability to create such a dense kind of urbanity, but they also decried the "antiurban" character of these "shopping-centers à l'américaine." Realizing that the large shopping center was an inevitable phenomenon, they set themselves the goal of incorporating it as primary programmatic elements in their urban centers. They believed such malls could be adjusted to fit their more noble goals. This attitude was almost too perfectly summarized in Prime Minister Jacques Chaban-Delmas's famous dictum "We need to master the society of consumption by providing it with a supplement of soul!"[79] By this time, planners had understood that their projects needed to take into account the forces of private development and their only chance was to work with rather than against them. Yet, how these "wild" private developments could be curbed into a carefully planned new urban center was less clear.

One response to this very French question came from the unexpected corner of Gruen, perceived by French planners as the very embodiment of the shopping mall "à l'américaine." His collaboration with Larry Smith was so successful that they soon became leading experts in shopping-mall development, and their 1960 *Shopping Towns U.S.A.* influenced mall development over the next decade. Yet, for Gruen, the mall was not about shopping or profitability alone: it was only the starting point for a whole array of civic and urban functions. Starting with his mall projects of the 1950s around Detroit, he had in fact reenvisioned the American shopping mall—which had first emerged in the 1920s—as a "regional commercial and civic center."[80] Gruen understood this kind of development as being in line with the Greek agora and the medieval market square.[81] Following this rather romantic view of the past, his malls featured interior plazas that were meant to facilitate civic participation. To a certain extent, these controlled public spaces did in fact allow for this: fashion shows, holiday celebrations, community events, and public spectacles were—at least initially—not uncommon in some of his malls. During the 1960s, Gruen continued to design malls but became increasingly frustrated with the way developers adapted his ideas and marginalized his civic ambitions.[82] Toward the end of the decade, when his interests expanded to urban planning and he got involved in the design of privately developed New Towns, Gruen distanced himself from shopping-mall development and criticized some of his earlier ideas and projects. Coinciding with his move from the United States back to Europe, he began to develop visions for an urban center that would play a more direct civic role and would be better integrated with its surroundings. It was during this time that he began working as a consultant on French New

Figure 6.12. The drugstores of central Paris, at Champs-Élysées (above) and Saint-Germain-des-Prés (below). From *Urbanisme* 108–9 (1968): 39.

Town projects. His initial proposals were based on the—by that time already tired—formula of a hierarchical cellular structure in which individual neighborhood cells were centered on public facilities and combined to form larger "villages" separated by green belts. A main center would contain the more specialized urban functions. Recalling some of his earlier projects such as that for Fort Worth, this city center would be entirely pedestrianized but easily accessible by means of multistoried parking structures on its periphery.[83] Although his proposals were not particularly convincing to some French New Town planners, the underlying issues—which Gruen had been grappling with on the other side of the Atlantic for more than a decade—proved to be remarkably similar.

When he spoke at a 1969 conference organized to find concrete solutions to the urgent design problem of the urban centers for France's nine New Towns, French participants still continued to find his ideas "too close to the American shopping-mall idea."[84] And yet, in his presentation Gruen had in fact confirmed the reigning idea that planners needed to engage with private developers but keep them at bay by resisting "standard recipes." And that was exactly the position French planners would soon take when they tried to convince private mall developers to include noncommercial programs in their projects. Moreover, Gruen's emphasis on the civic nature of the urban center was similar to that of many French planners. His high-density plan for Valencia's city center, proposed around the same time but never built, bore striking resemblances with the initial plans for Cergy-Pontoise. But perhaps most important, as a consultant at the decision-making table of the IAURP, Gruen encouraged planners to engage the types of expertise he had been tapping into for over a decade. And they did just that when they hired Larry Smith & Co for socioeconomic studies to guide several New Town plans, including Évry, Marne-la-Vallée, and Saint-Quentin-en-Yvelines.[85] Such unprecedented collaboration between government planners, developers, and private consultants would eventually define the course of France's new urban centers.

A Fragile Alliance

The construction of such vast New Town projects proved to be far from self-evident. In their search for suitable commercial developers, the *villes nouvelles* planners faced hurdles that seem remarkably pertinent today. Because much of the land for the future urban centers had been purchased by the centralized state, planners assumed they could easily exert sufficient influence on the developers. Their idea was therefore to set out the general lines of the plan and then submit it for tender to commercial developers. Yet, according to an intermittent report on several urban center projects currently under way, that process was less smooth than expected. Developers simply would not budge: "the similarities we can observe between the five projects [of the study] derive from the demands of the private developers much more than from a cooperation with planners or even from their reference to common models. The developers are in fact almost totally set on the American model (of the Shopping Center in particular), outside of which there is no point in negotiating."[86] In this conflict, the planners understood themselves to be defenders of the public good against the dangers of private interest and profit. Developers, from their side, experienced much planning policy as irrational, controlling, and unwarranted—in their view, market forces would be in the direct interest of consumers. Despite this seemingly irreconcilable opposition, a very productive alliance, albeit a fragile and temporary one, would eventually emerge.

French planners faced a poor track record in dealing with private commercial development. Mall developers usually worked behind the backs of government. Only in exceptional cases did state or local planners effectively control private developments. At Bures-Orsay, a suburb of Paris, they tried to convince the commercial developer to divert from their preferred location—at a highway exit—and instead to build their mall in the center of the new housing development that was under way. The architects, Robert Camelot and François Prieur, proposed a compromise between the planners and the developer, with the center ultimately located at the edge of the housing estate as close as possible to the highway.[87] For the new urban development of Créteil—not an official *ville nouvelle* but perhaps one of the first concerted efforts to avoid the *grand ensemble* model and create a "real" town with its own center—planners were successful in finding a private developer willing to build a shopping mall at the center of the development (Figure 6.13).[88] They considered the shopping mall to be the main "node of attraction," albeit a consciously temporary one: the supermarket giant Carrefour signed a contract with the developer for a period of only ten years, after which the mall would be demolished. The temporary nature of the shopping center was understood as rational and American and was expressed in the design of the facade, which featured a kinetic public art projection.[89] Yet this alliance was an exception that confirmed the rule. Generally, shopping malls had a logic that seemed incompatible with that of mass housing and New Town developments: cars versus pedestrians, the highway versus the urban center, cheap and temporary versus complex, integrated, and fixed.

Planners' formidable challenge was how to marry these opposites. At Cergy-Préfecture, as at other New Town centers, they refused to accept the developers' concept of the commercial center as a self-enclosed entity. Their main objective was to embed the mall in its urban surroundings and thus to integrate it with the other activities of the center. For the pedestrian, strolling the plazas and streets of the future Cergy, interior and exterior spaces should blend into each other, they contended. Similarly, conventionally separated urban functions should be merged into each other. This initial concept of a unified project in which the commercial program was practically indistinguishable from the other urban functions was repeatedly put to the test during the planning and construction phase. Planners were forced to compromise

Figure 6.13. Postcard of the commercial center of Créteil, date unknown. Courtesy of David Liaudet.

with the developers, and in the end the division between commercial and "civic" functions was still more articulated than planners had initially hoped.

While many young architects and critics of the "post-1968 generation" dismissed the project as too conservative and while its design would never become part of the French architectural canon in the 1970s, Cergy-Préfecture was no less than "revolutionary in the eyes of the commercial developers."[90] Instead of a shopping mall surrounded by parking lots or a typical modernist New Town center, the collaboration between planners and developers led to a startlingly complex and inventive hybrid. The final project for Cergy-Préfecture selectively adopted reigning shopping-mall principles while holding on to the formula of the *dalle*. Separating pedestrians from the main road and railway station underneath, this platform was intensely urbanized by dotting it with a variety of sociocultural facilities, shops and cafés, offices and governmental buildings. On its northwestern side it was flanked by a large L-shaped shopping mall, which the pedestrian zone gradually spilled into—thus blurring exterior and interior, and public and commercial space. On the back side of the mall were the required parking lots, directly visible and accessible from the highway running next to it (Figure 6.14). On its southeastern side, this complex blended into the surrounding office neighborhood and the urban

a

b

Figure 6.14. Diagrams for the urban center of Cergy-Préfecture, drawn in 1972 by the architect Aymeric Zublena, showing how car circulation and parking defined position and integration of shopping mall with other functions, with construction phased over time: (a) projection for 1975; (b) projection for final situation. From Aymeric Zublena, Patrice Noviant, and Xavier Triplet, *Les centres urbains des villes nouvelles françaises* (Paris: Ministère de l'équipement/Secrétaire général du Groupe central des villes nouvelles, 1972), 22–23.

park. Pedestrian connections and bridges on all sides linked it to the surrounding neighborhoods (Figure 6.15). With this hybrid form, the project successfully combined the logic of the car—easy access from the highway and ample parking space—with that of the pedestrian. In other words, it combined the logic of the mall developers with that of the planners. Or, perhaps most important, it combined the rationale of the suburbs with that of the city center. As such, the shopping mall became an integral part of the urban center. Not only had it become part of a larger urban fabric but, as some contemporaneous critics suggested, the urban center itself was now conceived of in terms of a shopping mall.

An equally unique form of hybridity took shape at Évry. The elaborate program of integrated facilities for the New Town's urban center promised planners a serious counterweight to the project's shopping-mall component. At the same time, planners—whose heart was with the social ambitions of the integrated facilities much more than the consumer heaven

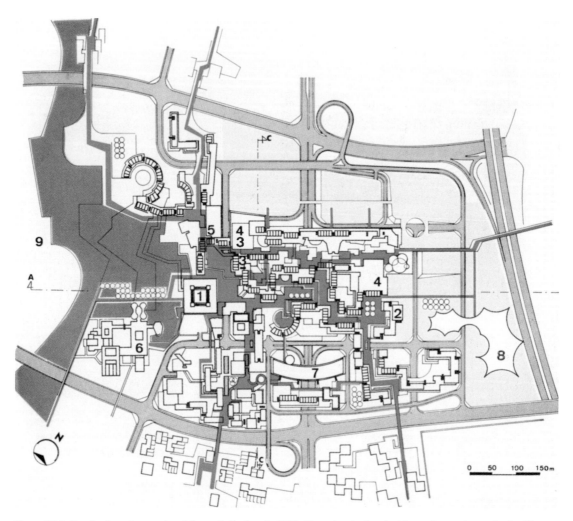

Figure 6.15. Plan for the urban center of Cergy-Préfecture in 1970. The network of pedestrian pathways is emphasized in shading. The park is on the left of the plan and parking lots are on the right, adjacent to the highways. Key: 1 = prefecture; 2 = city hall; 3 = cultural center (below the left 4); 4 = department stores; 5 = swimming pool; 6 = business school; 7 = parking and commuter rail; 8 = exhibition hall; 9 = park. From *Techniques et architecture* 32, no. 5 (1970): 55.

imagined by the developers—readily admitted that "if there had not been the commercial center, there would not have been the Agora."[91] Évry was the first of Paris's New Towns to be further developed after the launch of the ambitious project in 1965. The first proposal presented in 1966—by the IAURP because the local planning team had not yet been established—was still rather conventional (Figure 6.16). It featured a conglomerate of commercial buildings and courtyards organized around a main pedestrian boulevard and surrounded by parking lots and a ring road. Three large department stores were included in the program, and the entire compound was dotted by office towers and housing. This design was in line with some of

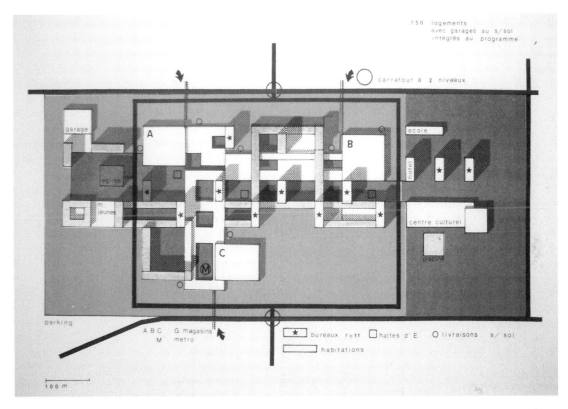

Figure 6.16. An early proposal for the urban center of Évry by the IAURP in 1966. Archives départementales de l'Essonne 1523W/638.

Gruen's projects—Valencia in California, for instance—as well as with new European shopping centers such as the NordWestZentrum near Frankfurt that was under way at this time.[92] Nevertheless, the inclusion of housing in the program, as well as the connection of the main boulevard to civic amenities outside of the ring road, already suggested a desire to transcend the idea of an entirely self-contained center surrounded by cars.[93]

The proposal was quickly modified when the local planning team took over from the IAURP in 1967. Around this time, planners also found out that Printemps, the Parisian department store, had plans to branch out into the suburbs, that Parly 2 was to be its first project, and that more suburban locations would follow. The planning team was keen on seizing this opportunity for their own project, in spite of economic studies that had already suggested that Grigny would be the perfect location for such a commercial development. In fact, planners faced the constant threat of other commercial developments being installed too close to the New Town, which would detract from the new center's liveliness and commercial profitability. Lalande described the role of such encroaching development as central to the planning process:

We had some good hypermarkets around, we were certain to have one at a few kilometers from the center, hence the permanent anxiety we had to realize the commercial center as soon as possible. Since we have been there, there has been the construction of a big Carrefour at Chilly en Bière, a big Inno four kilometers fom the regional center, a Euro-marché on the route to Orly, at four or five kilometers, and a commercial center at la Belle Épine. There was but one risk left and that was the construction of a forty-thousand-square-meter Carrefour on the land of M. Bouygues, which would have been catastrophic. It was thus high time that our commercial center was built.[94]

In other words, shopping was quite literally a matter of life or death for Évry's new urban center. But including a department store such as Printemps would imply a substantial modification of its overall concept, as planners realized. The basic logic of the department store was to serve as one of the key magnets within a larger commercial complex of boutiques and other stores. Despite their willingness to include such commerce in the urban center, planners vehemently criticized the design of shopping malls such as Parly 2 that had pioneered this logic in suburban France. The new center of Évry was to be "an embryo of an Urban Heart and therefore to avoid the American-style shopping center, antiurban by its very nature, with its desolate facades and sea of parking space."[95] Rather than simply rejecting this model, however, they insisted that it could be tweaked to fit their own ambitions. To this effect, the planning team hired the architect Jean Le Couteur to draw up plans that could be used to find a suitable developer.[96] This led to a significantly different project compared to the initial plans of the IAURP. Without giving up the desire to bring different programs together into a single development, Le Couteur's proposal consisted of two parts that were programmatically as well as spatially distinct. One part was coined the "regional commercial center"—adapted from the model of the American-style dumbbell mall, despite planners' aversion. The other part contained all noncommercial or civic functions and was baptized the "Agora." Only one pedestrian connection linked the two parts. In the most basic terms, the plan looked like a large community center stuck onto a dumbbell mall (Figure 6.17).

During their negotiations with developers, planners were confronted with some unshakable convictions. In the developers' eyes, American practice had proven that only an isolated, internally integrated mall worked efficiently. More important, the logical location for any commercial center was to be adjacent to a major highway intersection, not in the center of a New Town that was only at the beginning of its development and thus had few potential customers. Lalande described on multiple occasions how much developers resisted the idea of a shopping center at a distance from the highway, let alone integrating it with the social and cultural facilities of a publicly funded Agora.[97] Negotiations were based on two entirely different pools of expertise and forms of rationality. Private developers based their convictions on the

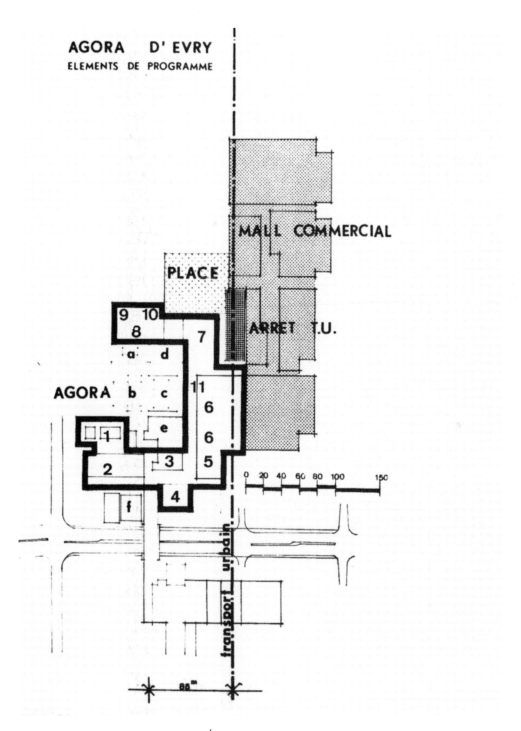

AGORA D'EVRY
ELEMENTS DE PROGRAMME

MALL COMMERCIAL

PLACE

ARRET T.U.

AGORA

transport urbain

Figure 6.17. Early proposal for the Agora of Évry by the architect Le Couteur, with the Agora on the left and the mall on the right, joined by a central plaza, a bus stop, and a public transportation line below. Key: 1 = pool; 2 = skating rink; 3 = drugstore; 4 = cinemas; 5 = recreation; 6 = shops; 7 = banks and insurance agents; 8 = bookstore; 9 = hotel; 10 = restaurant; 11 = café; a = library; b = theater; c = polyvalent hall; d = information hall; e = garden; f = foyer restaurant. Archives nationales, France, CAC 19780319/001.

studies of American economic consultancy firms such as Larry Smith & Co. Their reasoning was that of the market: action radii, accessibility, and the socioeconomic characteristics of target populations, which together defined profitability. Despite their relative openness to contemporary commercial development, planners' ideas were based on diametrically opposite foundations—most important, the belief that only the state could guarantee the public good and should guide the "uncoordinated" actions of the market in a rational manner. In the eyes of developers, however, the state was just an actor—and a slightly "irrational" one at that—in a market otherwise defined by private interest. Moreover, they proposed a clear model, as opposed to the sometimes vague or lofty ambitions of state planners. In one sense, planners' attempt to freeze commercial development in a fixed urban center was a sign of their inability to deal with the essentially dynamic nature of commercial development—and perhaps postwar urbanity and consumer culture more generally.

Despite these opposing rationalities, an alliance was ultimately forged. A common enemy proved useful in this respect: the hypermarket. During the 1960s, private mall developers faced fierce competition from hypermarkets. Despite markedly different audiences—developments such as Parly 2 included posh Parisian department stores and upscale boutiques while the hypermarket with its discounted products catered to a lower-middle- and working-class clientele—they competed for the same locations at highway exits and intersections close to densely populated suburbs. New Town planners preferred to work with mall developers such as SCC rather than hypermarket developers, supposedly because the latter were less reliable. But planners' elite backgrounds and middle-class bias undoubtedly also played a role in favoring prestigious suburban malls over "lowly" big-box stores—despite their ambition to assure social mixing and counter segregation.[98] The malls, in fact, coincided with the official New Town ambition to attract more middle-class families, exactly the clientele targeted by mall developers. In some ways, competition with the hypermarket thus helped to keep planners and developers at the negotiation table.

Évry's planners sought a developer willing to build and manage both the commercial center and the Agora. Two candidates remained in the final round: COREDIS-SACC, a relatively young firm but enthusiastic about both parts of the project, and SCC, more experienced but not interested in the Agora. Planners first decided to go into business with the first.[99] They suggested that "to preserve the unity in the conception," Le Couteur work closely with the developer's architects, Jankovic-Hardion. Gruen was also invited to collaborate because he had the trust of the department store owners. Although the developer was on board with the Agora, it ultimately failed to attract the desired chain and department stores.[100] Accomplishing this would mean the end of the urban center. The planners were thus forced to hire another developer, and the sole one they found was only interested in the commercial part of the program.[101]

To prevent the commercial part from predominating, the planners focused attention on the design of the Agora. The celebrated projects by van Klingeren built in the Netherlands were proof to them that a complex of this kind could be a strong enough counterweight to the commercial program. They devised an elaborate program, divided into six categories: the "library function," which included books, music, video, and so on; the "studio function," which allowed for creative workshops, youth meetings, and so on; offices for management and for the various local associations; the "information function," which included an information point and temporary exhibitions; the "shows and recreation function," comprising, among other things, the sports hall and the swimming pool; and, finally, social services such as child care.[102] The Agora was seen as the instrument to bring all of these functions together and make Évry a really urban place.

It became gradually clear to the planning team that both parts of the center needed autonomy, and that realization was not only a consequence of developers' relentless pressure.[103] Planners had their own anxieties about commerce encroaching on the public services and functions of the Agora. They went out of their way to dispel fears that a far-reaching integration of commerce would mean a commercialization of civic functions: "To accept the existence of commercial activities linked to the cultural activities does not mean that we accept a 'commercialized' culture. In short, it is a matter of making the sociocultural and sports facilities, which suffer from being underutilized, benefit from the more spontaneous trips of the population to the commercial centers."[104] The fear of commercialization was legitimate: during the negotiations, the developer had gone so far as to propose to name the urban center "Évry 2," after the success of malls such as Parly 2.[105] Relinquishing their ambition to have the Agora shape the overall urban center, planners were happy if they could simply prevent its being swallowed by the commercial center. Making the Agora spatially autonomous was one way of doing so.

Yet, throughout the design process, planners continued to advocate for a radical integration of facilities within the Agora itself as well as with its immediate surroundings. The architects responded by increasing the transparency of different programs toward the central public atrium of the Agora (Figure 6.18). The formal gesture of the cantilevered space-frame roof, reaching out over the main entrance at the public square, was meant to express the direct relationship between atrium and exterior. Ironically, the most fruitful architectural strategy for spatial and programmatic integration was to *disintegrate* the Agora formally. The decomposition of the Agora as a single, monolithic volume and the articulation of different programs in iconic forms and sculptural volumes—in particular the swimming pool and the sports hall—generated a certain blending between exterior and interior space (Figures 6.19, 6.20, 6.21). What obstructed a more radical blurring of the complex with its surrounding neighborhood were the vast parking lots required for the commercial center. Planners worked hard

Figure 6.18. Interior plaza of the Agora of Évry, circa 1975. Space-frame roofs became common features of the public architecture of French New Towns. Fonds Le Couteur. Service interministériel des Archives de France/Cité de l'architecture et du patrimoine/Archives d'architecture du XXᵉ siècle.

to have these lots hidden underneath the complex or stacked in parking structures dotted around the urban center. In the end, three sides of the center were surrounded by asphalt.

The final product of the intensive negotiations between developers, planners, and architects at Cergy, Évry, and many other places was nothing less than a megastructure in denial. Unified by a plinth underneath which parking and public transport was organized, the elements of the program were far more imbricated than the initial proposal had suggested. For the visitor, the experience of this unprecedented mix of functions was certainly overwhelming, if not disorienting. At the same time, the final project expressed a clear architectural distinction between Agora and commercial center: the communication between commercial and noncommercial programs was limited in the plan and the Agora's sculptural volumes and formal expression contrasted with the simple big box of the mall. This fundamentally hybrid architecture was not the result of individual genius but of negotiation and compromise. Its

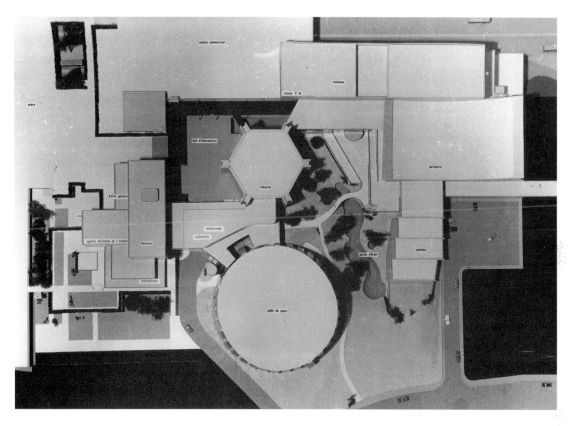

Figure 6.19. Model of final project for the Agora, by Le Couteur. Fonds Le Couteur. Service interministériel des Archives de France/Cité de l'architecture et du patrimoine/Archives d'architecture du XXᵉ siècle.

unique complexity was the result of a process of pursuing "and" instead of "or." Its forms and spaces spoke of an architectural agency embedded in a complex mix of private and public interests and a multitude of actors and ideas. It comes as no surprise, then, that these projects would be ignored in the canon of postwar architecture: they begged fundamental questions cutting to the core of the discipline's unspoken assumptions about genius and authorship.

Suburban Monuments

Despite their sturdy looks, the life of these megastructures-in-denial turned out to be as fragile as the planning process that had given rise to them. The same newspapers that had triumphantly announced Évry's festive opening in March 1975 soon reported on its inhabitants' disappointments. Despite initial praise to have given Évry a "real urban heart," the journalists suggested that its inhabitants were still merely *hoping* not to live in a bedroom suburb. Most visitors were initially content with the facilities of the Agora itself, but everyday life in Évry

Figure 6.20. Exterior view of the Agora, circa 1975. Fonds Le Couteur. Service interministériel des Archives de France/Cité de l'architecture et du patrimoine/Archives d'architecture du XXe siècle.

ultimately seemed all too similar to that in Sarcelles two decades before: housewives complained of boredom, inhabitants' participation in decision making was practically nonexistent, and taxes, well, they were still too high.[106] When the Agora opened, its central plaza and covered walkways had the legal status of public streets and were thus open day and night. That changed after local inhabitants complained about the presence of homeless people and drug addicts who "had a negative impact on the popularity of the Agora with families." In the 1980s, then, one of the walkways was eliminated and the interior secured and closed off at night.[107] This obviously limited the public uses of the Agora and precipitated its failure to perform as the "real urban center" of the New Town. A similar downward spiral befell such urban centers elsewhere in France and abroad.[108] Their historical moment was a brief one.

Economically, the French urban centers simply lost against the big-box stores and the hypermarkets. While a few of the hypermarkets inserted themselves into dumbbell malls as one of their magnets, their low-end "discount" identity generally clashed with the image of "luxury" that these malls aimed to exude.[109] Instead, the hypermarket adopted some of the strategies of the dumbbell mall—such as the inclusion of independent boutiques—but with a decidedly less upscale character. Whereas the shopping mall was a risky and complex undertaking, these

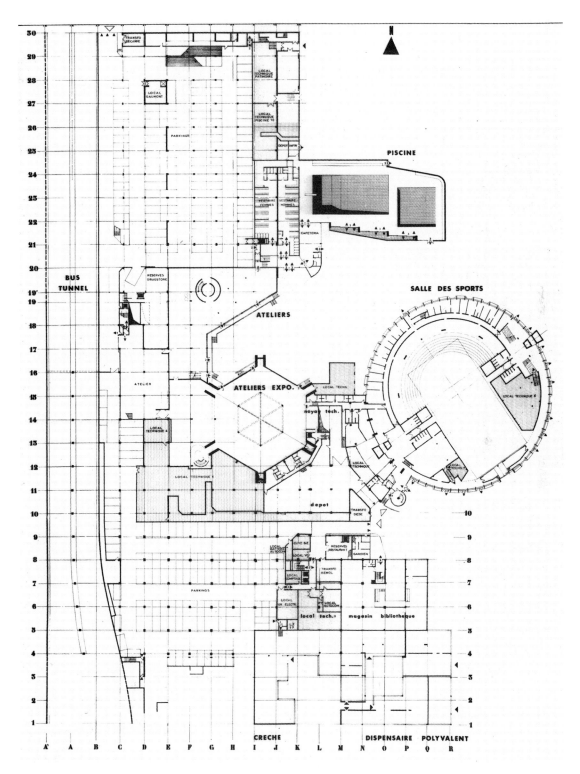

Figure 6.21. Plan of the Agora's lower level, showing the common base shared by the programs and volumes above. Fonds Le Couteur. Service interministériel des Archives de France/Cité de l'architecture et du patrimoine/Archives d'architecture du XXe siècle.

second-generation hypermarkets were directly developed by the chain stores themselves. They seemed better adjusted to the social makeup and everyday needs of the French suburbs and were hugely successful—in stark contrast to the upscale shopping malls. The department stores were quick to realize this: soon after their initial expansion into the suburbs, they retreated again to focus solely on city-center commerce.[110] And with this experiment, so waned the new urban centers based on them.

The mid-1970s also marked the end of the experiment with integrated facilities. Critiques about their inherent contradictions ran parallel to their emergence and development, in fact, but were initially smothered by Agora-mania. Already in 1973, experts had concluded that "the stubbornness of the planners to realize from day one complex spatial organizations is a purely static and unrealistic view. We even ask ourselves if, in certain cases, it is not contradictory to the goals they envisage, namely, the appropriation of facilities and the everyday environment by the users. We can show—and it is not the famous and often-invoked example of the Agora in Dronten (in the Netherlands) that will allow to prove the contrary—that the heavier the investments, the more complex is the organization and the more the operation eliminates the users, together with their ability to invent and appropriate."[111] Management and coordination remained a key obstacle for the integrated facilities because they required the participation of an unwieldy number of state institutions and actors. The disparity between people's needs and the complex and often monumental architecture of integrated facilities became increasingly clear. By 1976, the interministerial committee for *équipements intégrés*, which had been the primary promoter, was dismantled.[112] And when soon after the Left came to power and dismissed these kinds of facilities as the product of a technocratic state, it was already beating a dead horse. The idea of an integrated supersized facility in fact no longer corresponded to the altered economic conditions after the oil crisis of 1973. Such welfare-state extravaganza seemed ill-considered, if not simply economically and bureaucratically impossible. The rescaling of the welfare state and the growing importance of political decentralization and local government suggested other approaches to public service. By the end of the decade, the new model was that of a distributed network of facilities rather than architectural integration.[113]

Did the sudden demise of these urban centers signify the end of a belief in architecture's social agency, as is so often assumed in light of the postmodernist architecture that followed it? French "urban postmodernism" or neotraditionalism certainly did not lose all hopes of creating a better quality of life—and this may be a crucial difference with the dominant reception of postmodernism in the United States.[114] But at least something was lost. Together with the megastructure, the conviction waned that architecture could serve as a *direct* instrument in the realization of a social project. In 1972, Banham had suggested this change in mind-set as he proclaimed the megastructure dead.[115] The history of the movement that he ultimately published in 1976 as *Megastructure: Urban Futures of the Recent Past* called the phenomenon "a fossil future that was not to be," and with it, he proclaimed the end of "'Modern' architecture as we have known it."[116] The movement of mobile cities and visionary megastructures had in fact already been denounced by many critics during the 1960s. Manfredo Tafuri, who had previously supported such proposals, denounced them in his *Theories and History of Architecture* of 1969.[117] Utopie, an influential French group of architects and sociologists of which Baudrillard was a key member, argued that same year that the megastructure ultimately represented nothing more than a "luxury good, blinding us with its splendor."[118] Yet, at that time, the megastructure movement was hardly dead. Especially in France, its results had yet to appear on the horizon of French cities, as a mushrooming of Parly 2's and New Town urban centers.

What was at stake in megastructure mania was the desire to reclaim architecture's importance in the contemporary city—a thread running through the history of modernism but which came to a head in the chaotic development of the postwar city. Its corollary was the imaginary of a new kind of urbanite and user—spontaneous, mobile, and creative. By accommodating this new figure, architecture would be able to transcend the uncontrollable nature of the city, or, in Banham's words, "to resolve the conflicts between design and spontaneity, the large and the small, the permanent and the transient."[119] Although Banham presented the megastructure movement as an architectural and essentially *academic* pursuit—especially in France, for which he limited the discussion to the 1960s paper projects championed by Ragon—the widespread construction of French new urban center projects during the 1970s suggests otherwise. These megastructures-in-denial are the "banal late modernisms" of the postwar French city just as the *grands ensembles* are the banal products of an earlier modernism less than two decades earlier.

For a first-time visitor to Évry or Cergy today, the inevitable lens is that of an urban archaeologist exploring an unfamiliar yet recent past. Among the multitude of well-known global chain stores are spaces so incomprehensibly different that they may well have been built by another civilization. In a single decade, from the mid-1960s to the mid-1970s, French planners created suburban monuments of an unprecedented scale and complexity. Their aim was to transform suburban life with a new, animated kind of environment bursting with liveliness and social encounter. Offering a counterpoint to the postwar suburbs, as well as to the perceived failures of an earlier modernism embodied by the *grands ensembles,* they created pilgrimage sites for a new consumer culture. The enormous success of suburban commerce in France was both a lightning rod and an eyesore for those in charge. The urban centers embodied their desire for a consumer cum welfare society: a playground for middle-class consumers that could at the same time be a radical instrument of social-democratic engineering. This late-modern urbanism was faithful to the ideology of the French welfare state while incorporating the new ethos of private consumption.

The Agora of Évry was a poster child of this far-reaching integration of private commercial development and public services and facilities. Despite its uniqueness, it exemplified the widespread but short-lived experimentation with such new megastructure urban centers in France at this time. As modern public services and facilities were to speak the language of contemporaneous consumerism—accessibility, availability, efficiency—so they could converge with private commercial developments in the creation of a city-under-one-roof in which architecture was elevated to become the main social animator. Even if more recent commercial developments have outdone them by far, in creating experiences at new scales and intensities without much government engineering, these urban centers still embody that peculiar, momentary amalgamation of citizenship and consumerism in postwar France.

7

THE ULTIMATE PROJECTS

THE SPECTACULAR OPENING of the Agora of Évry in 1975 left its adjacent housing project somewhat in the shadows. Yet the recently completed neighborhood, simply coined "Évry I" because it was the New Town's first housing area to be completed, would turn out to be of at least equal significance to the final incarnation of the production regime that had shaped France over the previous decades. Its makers cast it as the prototype of a new kind of urbanism that would fundamentally transform France's suburban condition. Policy makers enthusiastically agreed. Pierre Hervio, a director in the Ministère de l'équipement, wrote that same year that "a new type of dwelling is born, intermediary between the collective and the individual. Multiple models confirm a return to an urbanism of human scale where the voids count as much as the volumes, where the monotony is systematically resisted, where a veritable urban life can develop itself."[1]

The project's unconventional massing, a series of cross-plan pyramids of stacked cubic volumes, allowed each dwelling unit not only plenty of light and orientation but also a private room-sized terrace. Its architecture of prefabricated concrete spoke of combining economies of scale with a diversification of form, space, and type. Its close-grained mix of dwellings, including social housing units and luxury condos, was meant to encourage the integration of diverse social groups. And its panoply of public amenities and carefully designed public spaces would facilitate neighborhood life unlike any other housing project before it (Figure 7.1 and Plate 16). Some connoisseurs contested the formal originality of the project, which immediately recalled the famous Habitat project at the Montreal Expo of 1967. But to grasp the project's significance would require more than a formal resemblance or the stated intentions of its architects, Michel Andrault and Pierre Parat.

Figure 7.1. Évry I "Les Pyramides" by Michel Andrault and Pierre Parat, 1971–74. From *L'Architecture* 403 (1977): 92–104.

Évry I was perhaps the most iconic of its kind, but it was hardly the only one. During the 1970s, the French suburbs were flooded with housing developments just like it. Despite their diverse provenance and formal differences, the crucial thing they had in common was that they attempted, above all, *not* to be "projects." Yet, this ambition was fundamentally contradicted by the fact that they were products of the same centralized state apparatus that had built the *grands ensembles*. The convergence of a post-1968 architectural culture bent on research and a self-critical government eager to improve the quality of its housing production intensified large-scale experimentation, the physical products of which can still be found across France. These projects tried to combine the economies of scale of government-funded mass housing production with the logic of the individual home as a consumer product. They embodied France's ambiguous shift away from public housing production and toward liberalized consumption in the realm of dwelling. In that sense, these were France's ultimate projects.

The increasingly scathing critiques of state-led urbanism—only fueled by the contestations of May 1968—had engendered a new ethos. Quality of life had become the central political concern and crossed over into architecture and urbanism during the 1970s.[2] Policy makers were acutely aware of public discontent and keen on reversing it. Sociological surveys spoke of social segregation, the need for choice in housing, and the desire for a "beautiful and varied architecture." Architects and policy makers responded to newly asserted hopes for a better quality of life by using new industrial methods of construction that allowed formal and typological innovation. Without giving up centralized planning—and actually expanding its ambitions to shape everyday life—the government channeled such experimentation into ambitious new housing projects, until the economic crises of the mid-1970s forced another direction. In some ways, that other direction had already emerged on the horizon during the 1960s.

Mass Housing after the *pavillon*

The 1960s was the heyday of the *grands ensembles*. By the beginning of the decade, their legislative, financial, and construction machinery was well oiled, and they were erected all over France at a rate unprecedented and unparalleled ever since. A large portion of the more than half a million dwelling units built each year was in the form of collective housing estates—not only massive ones such as Sarcelles, but also a multitude of smaller ones inserted into existing urban and suburban fabrics. And yet, at the same time, the 1960s also harbored entirely new residential trends that would come to define the radically changing landscape of French housing in subsequent decades. Two concurrent forces explain that change: the surge in individual home ownership and the popularity of the modern single-family home. Both of these had a direct impact, not only on the fate of the *grands ensembles*, but also on the direction of future housing policy and design.

The brief but intense enthusiasm for the *grands ensembles*—solutions to the housing shortage, vehicles of national development, and emblems of modern living—went hand in hand with an equally categorical dismissal of the single-family home. Between the mid-1950s and mid-1960s, it was hardly mentioned in professional or policy-making circles, or otherwise identified with the shabby cottages of the interwar period. And in their celebration of modern domestic comfort, advertisements often depicted homes as interiors only, suggesting apartments rather than single-family dwellings. Most important, few single-family homes were built during this time. For the exceptional development of La Haie Bergerie (Figure 7.2), the developer felt compelled to explain that "there is no suburban cottage [pavillon de banlieue] in the common sense of the term at la Haie Bergerie but individual homes [maisons individuelles], which is not the same thing."[3] There appeared to be insufficient demand, too many legislative obstacles, and almost no construction firms with adequate experience. Whereas in 1964, 61 percent of new housing construction in the United States consisted of single-family homes, such construction counted for only 21 percent in France, and half of this percentage consisted of traditional construction in rural areas.[4]

Figure 7.2. The single-family home development of La Haie Bergerie, early 1960s. From Jacques Riboud, *La maison ndividuelle et son jardin dans la ville nouvelle: Un récit sur la création de La Haie Bergerie à Villepreux* (Paris: Mazarine, n.d.).

That same year, William Levitt—attracted by what he saw as a fortuitous gap in the market—came to France to expand the business that had earned him the titles of "the father of modern American suburbia" and "the Henry Ford of the construction sector."[5] Kaufman & Broad, another American home builder, followed suit. These entrepreneurs understood that in an increasingly prosperous France, a growing number of middle-class families would be interested and able to purchase individual homes, even in the absence of supporting mortgage legislation. Whether the French actually desired such suburban living was not in question, as opinion polls since the 1940s had demonstrated. Coined "new villages," Levitt's first French subdivisions were a huge success. The homes were modeled on their American counterparts but also featured some "typically French" styles and a more intricate overall layout that attempted to take into account some aspects of the local context.[6] Yet, in contrast to inexpensive American tract homes, the higher land prices and absence of an industrial production method made them affordable only to the upper echelon of the French middle class.

At the same time that American home builders traveled across the Atlantic, the French government became interested in the single-family home—albeit independently and for different reasons. In 1964, the District of Paris organized a competition to encourage designers to focus on single-family home typologies. Its goal was to increase the possibility for the French to choose their preferred type of dwelling: "it is indefensible that 84 percent of new housing in the Paris region since 1955 has been collective while 66 percent of Parisians prefer individual," argued the organizers.[7] The competition was only the beginning of a long series of state-sponsored initiatives to encourage single-family home ownership. Particularly important was the Villagexpo exhibition of 1966 because it gave the single-family home broad national exposure (Figure 7.3).[8] It comprised the construction of an entire "village" in the suburbs of Paris, showcasing various models by internationally selected home builders. Some of the prototypes were subsequently endorsed by the government for large-scale construction. In contrast to Levitt—who participated in the competition but was excluded from endorsement

Figure 7.3. A selection of modern single-family homes at Villagexpo. From Anne M. Meistersheim, *Villagexpo* (Paris: Dunod, 1970), 170–71.

because his project surpassed cost limits—the state focused first and foremost on affordability. In his inauguration speech, the director, Roland Nungesser, referred to the single-family home as an instrument of social mobility, prioritizing home buying over renting. Industrial production, he contended, would make them affordable to the lower classes.[9] Moreover, democratization had to be accompanied by careful urbanism: instead of standard subdivisions, homes were grouped in various patterns and densities together with the necessary collective amenities. As such, the modern single-family home was not considered the antidote, but rather a complement, to the *grands ensembles*, which still dominated French policy.

With the political liberalism of Minister Albin Chalandon after 1968, the single-family home began to take on a more central role in housing policy. Casting himself as the sensible opponent of a "technocratic urbanism," Chalandon organized an international competition in 1969 to promote the single-family home.[10] The philosophy was simple: "a home needs to be able to be a consumer good like a car," in other words, a turnkey product (Figure 7.4). But the French also needed flexible dwellings that could be customized depending on changing needs—an extra room for the children, a garage for the car, or a hobby room—so that "everybody can occupy not just a house, but his or her home."[11] The single-family home could thus be both a ready-made consumer product and an essential attribute of inhabitants' identity. It was, in other words, a matter of lifestyle. The competition instigated the construction of sixty-five thousand homes. The "Chalandonnettes," as they were called, had a clear target group: instead of the managers and businessmen targeted by private home builders, they catered to young French families of workers and employees. Despite inhabitants' criticism of their small rooms and shoddy construction, they remained popular alternatives to collective housing. Yet the initiative's most enduring impact was on the French development and construction sector: the competition promoted a new kind of developer who could master all parts of the production process—financing, marketing, conception, and construction—similar to what U.S. builders had been doing for decades.[12] Other competitions soon followed, but by the mid-1970s the single-family home needed no further incitement.[13] It had become the new norm for middle-class living in France, albeit not in the neatly planned communities envisaged by the government. The large majority of new homes were built one by one, by small companies using mainly artisanal techniques of construction.[14]

The rise of the single-family home was directly linked to the demise of the *grands ensembles*. Inhabitants and the general public had criticized housing estates ever since their construction and for an almost infinite list of functional and technical deficiencies. But experts and policy makers focused their growing concerns on one particular consequence of such discontents: social segregation. While initially the *grands ensembles* housed large segments of the French middle class and the sociologist Alain Touraine even labeled them "quintessentially petit-bourgeois," residential mobility patterns during the following decades legitimized that

Figure 7.4. Advertisement from 1975 by the home builder Balency-Briard for its single-family home type, with the slogan "I am called Freedom." From *Urbanisme* 151 (1975): 30–31.

concern. Housing production at a rate of half a million or more units a year during the 1960s dramatically altered the housing market. Together with a lowering birthrate and negative net immigration during the 1970s, this caused the housing supply to begin to exceed demand. The rapid increase in standards of comfort and often low quality of prefabricated construction made much of the housing stock of previous decades now relatively undesirable. When they could afford to do so, many middle-class families moved out of *grands ensembles,* often into suburban single-family homes. Consequently, the remaining housing stock became the home of an increasing number of working and nonworking poor, young families, senior citizens, and others who were unable to attain home ownership. This evolution was particularly pronounced in the mid-1970s and coincided with the influx of minorities after family relocations of especially North African, Turkish, and sub-Saharan African "guest workers."[15]

As early as the late 1960s, experts and policy makers recognized the departure of middle-class residents—and consequently, the concentration of the working classes and the poor—as the fundamental problem of mass housing. The "expulsion" of the lower classes out of Paris, in large part by means of slum clearance projects that required rehousing in collective housing estates on the periphery, was a common theme of critique after May 1968. Government intervention had certainly played its role in this process. But the role of middle-class families gradually moving out of housing estates—a dynamic at least equally responsible for social segregation—was less often mentioned. Rather than focusing on this unplanned residential mobility pattern, the political Left—some of whom undoubtedly lived in such new suburban homes—focused instead on condemning government and big business for their complicity in concentrating the poor. And that critique was quickly internalized. The ministry's urban sociology think tank addressed the problem of the *grands ensembles* in exactly such terms when it published an internal report in 1970 deploring "the increasing difficulties of everyday life for those 'exiled to the suburbs' that need to resolve tiresome problems of transport and isolation."[16] The imaginary of urban crisis was never far away, and a key reference for French commentators was American urban segregation: the presence in France of what were termed "little Chicagos" needed to be avoided at all cost.

Abundantly quoted in the report was an academic study published that same year by sociologists Jean-Claude Chamboredon and Madeleine Lemaire. Titled "Spatial Proximity and Social Distance: The *grands ensembles* and Their Inhabitants," it was key in overturning existing housing policies.[17] The study railed against the utopian assumptions and spatial determinism underlying the bulk of existing sociological studies of mass housing estates. Instead, the sociologists demonstrated that the spatial proximity of social classes in such projects in no way guaranteed social mixing. They exposed not only the falsity of ideals such as the neighborhood unit but also the dominant sociological readings of these environments once built. Against what they called the "populist utopia" of Paul-Henry Chombart de Lauwe, the study encouraged planners and policy makers to let go of the idea of the *grand ensemble* as social melting pot. Widely read by planners and policy makers, it made them aware of the role of housing in social polarization and conflict.[18]

Racial identity was not a focus of sociological analysis and has become so only recently in France. The absence of detailed census data on racial and ethnic background, implicitly part of the French citizenship ideal, contributed to this state of invisibility. Demographic studies often suggested race through the inappropriate and inaccurate categories of foreign citizenship and "socioprofessional category." If cloaked terminology was any indication, planners and policy makers were well aware of growing racial tensions in the *grands ensembles*. Their analyses were generally normative: social segregation was the problem, local integration the solution. The underlying assumption was often straightforward: if there were too many foreign workers—North Africans in particular—in a given neighborhood, there would be racial conflict.

Thus followed the rationale to deconcentrate and to forge a "sociological balance" of French middle classes and foreigners—by definition assumed to be of lower economic class.[19]

Whether social and racial segregation was in fact as dangerous a tendency as policy makers stressed is not really the question. What mattered more is how their alarms came to lead a life of their own. As reports warned that "the expulsion of the 'rehoused' to the periphery of cities can lead to a fundamental social instability," social segregation became an increasingly dominant reality to experts and policy makers, as well as to Parisian academics and intellectuals.[20] The diversity of suburbanites' everyday problems was increasingly gathered under this rubric. Yet, segregation was more than a register of perception. Government reports also set in motion a range of initiatives that left their imprint on the production of the built environment in subsequent decades—unfortunately, without averting France's deepening suburban crisis.

In 1970, the ministry's urban sociology think tank issued a report that assigned social segregation to the increasing distinction between renters and home owners and the growing social stigma of public rental housing.[21] Architecture played a role in this regard, the researchers concluded. The rapidly decaying facades of the first *grands ensembles* and their aesthetic homogeneity, ignoring the expression of individuality, were symbolic carriers of social demise. The researchers observed that "because of mobility, the oldest buildings gather little by little the fraction of the population whose income is the lowest."[22] Differences in social housing categories were all too often visible in the facades, noted the Commissariat général du Plan (CGP) in a subsequent report.[23] Apart from better maintenance and changes in allocation policies, it stipulated specifically architectural solutions. First of all, "new architectural forms and collective spaces capable of expressing the individuality and the diversity of the social groups within the same housing group" were needed. The underlying idea was that architectural differentiation would foster social diversity. Second, architects and planners needed to "take into account specific inhabitant needs in the conception of new housing areas."[24] Such ideas became crucial to subsequent design experiments in mass housing.

Experts and policy makers were aware that housing was directly associated with personal identity and lifestyle. A CGP working group concluded in 1970 that "the increasingly direct link between housing and environment—in actual fact and in users' perception—leads to an increasingly direct relationship between the type of dwelling and the lifestyle. Hence, the possibility to lead the lifestyle of one's choice—expression and condition of personality—appears to be an increasingly recognized demand, and claimed as the social groups reach a sufficient economic and cultural level."[25] Subsequent reports analyzed the repercussions in the realm of housing of a consumer society in which commodities were directly aligned with lifestyle. As developers increasingly "sell lifestyle," the report argued, "in the long term, the dwelling conceived like a consumer good and the transformations of the urban environment will tend to merge."[26] Most important, researchers identified two novel options that would shape future development: the semirural lifestyle "close to that of the United States" that catered to the desire to be in closer contact with nature; and the urban lifestyle of the revitalized city centers. Collective housing in the suburbs was no longer an option.

When Minister Olivier Guichard delivered the death stab to the *grands ensembles* with his famous directive of 1973, he did so explicitly in terms of their role in engendering social segregation: "The city and the society, like life, are diversity. The *grand ensemble* opposes the social diversity of the city. It is the physical aspect of a policy that tends to organize the social segregation in our cities."[27] The minister used sociological expertise to legitimize the policies that abandoned the *grands ensembles* as a development model. Fighting social segregation through housing, he explained, found its political parallel in fostering local democracy. What bound such ideas together for him was Henri Lefebvre's concept of the "right to the city," which had quickly become a key reference for policy makers after 1968. Guichard placed it unequivocally at the heart of his policies when he proclaimed:

> At the basis of all the reasons that inspire the change in policy that I propose is what has rightly been called "the right to the city." Right to the city because the city is a value, because the city, work of civilization, is civilizing in return. Right to the city rather than to the four walls of a dwelling: that is to say, right to a certain type of social life where the exchange is richer. Right to the city for all, because urbanization is a generalized phenomenon that incorporates the rural world. Right, finally, to be responsible for his or her city.[28]

Guichard called the French urbanism of the past decades "poor, and therefore impoverishing for Man" because it was built only to be "functional, forgetting almost always that the beauty of the everyday decor is also a function that architecture needs to fulfill."[29] But he did more than criticize the past; he also formulated concrete principles for future policy guided by what he called a shift from quantity to quality. He prohibited the construction of *grands ensembles* by quantitative thresholds for development: a maximum of 1,000 units in cities with fewer than 50,000 inhabitants and 2,000 for larger cities. He launched a panoply of policies to promote the architectural quality of collective housing. And he supported the encouragement of the single-family home and of city center revitalization—perhaps not realizing that such middle-class projects might only accelerate the very residential mobility patterns that had engendered segregation.

As the planning of the French New Towns and their urban centers has already shown, the French government after 1968 embraced self-criticism and a renewed leftist sociology— Lefebvre being only the proverbial tip of the iceberg—at the same time as it championed liberal approaches to consumerism.[30] Fueled by the political liberalism of Georges Pompidou's government, that ambiguity also characterized housing policies throughout much of the 1970s. After two decades of public investment in mass housing, the government focused on mobilizing the private capital of an increasingly prosperous French middle class. The approach corresponded conveniently with the political goal to "restore" home buyers' and renters' "freedom of choice." As choice in terms of housing became the key concern, the government attempted to radically diversify national housing production. But, despite promoting the single-family home and slowly abandoning the *grands ensembles*, the government did not give up on mass housing altogether or all at once. On the contrary, during the early 1970s it effectively intensified experimentation with new types of housing—alternative to the *grands ensembles*, but also to the single-family home.

Another Industrialization

An alternative approach to housing would have to begin by rethinking its industrial production. How could the despised monotony of mass housing be avoided without giving up its achievements in terms of economies of scale, efficiency, and cost effectiveness? Or, in other words, how could those same goals be attained with different architectural qualities? That question brought policy makers, engineers, and architects together as they sought for a new approach to industrialization, one with opposite formal qualities: diversity instead of uniformity, flexibility instead of rigidity, complexity instead of transparency.

Architects and policy makers increasingly dismissed heavy prefabrication methods such as those employed by Camus for being incompatible with other construction methods and too limiting in architectural terms. The use of load-bearing partitioning walls, often less than five meters apart, imposed an extreme rigidity on the interior organization of dwelling units. It also made postoccupancy layout alterations practically impossible—soon one of the main challenges in rehabilitating the first generations of *grands ensembles*. The development of dimensional co-ordination promised new possibilities for the flexible assembly of a variety of components allowing the creation of multiple assemblages. This shift to what was called "open industrialization" would spur new formal possibilities, architects hoped. In contrast to heavy or closed prefabrication, the new systems could be light, flexible, more geographically mobile, and more open to formal manipulation. Around the mid-1960s already, technological research into heavy prefabrication was being gradually abandoned in favor of such new systems.[31] But a market-driven construction sector would not in and of itself evolve in this direction, state administrators believed.

Just as the government had played a key role in developing a large-scale construction sector founded on heavy prefabrication techniques in the decade after World War II, it should now steer that sector in another direction. And that was exactly the goal of the Plan Construction.[32]

Launched in May 1971 under direction of Paul Delouvrier, this ambitious agency aimed to encourage innovation in the construction industry by incentivizing architectural and engineering research, supporting experimental programs, and developing new housing prototypes. For Delouvrier, who had moved on from the *villes nouvelles* project to head the Plan Construction for the next decade, the problem was simple: architecture during the 1960s had "lacked imagination" and thus government was to promote "architectural quality."[33] Nevertheless, the motivations were far more complex: aesthetic concerns with industrialized building hid implicit and at times contradictory social and economic ambitions.

The Plan Construction was definitely not the first attempt to encourage innovation in housing production, despite being presented as such. It was as if the influential experimental competitions during Reconstruction, which had similarly been concerned with technological innovation and architectural quality, were erased from memory. The formal celebration of infinitely repeatable elements in the competitions' resulting projects, such as the Cité Rotterdam, were simply anathema to new ideas about architectural quality that had emerged during the 1960s. While aesthetic expectations had profoundly changed in the span of little over a decade, the underlying regime of housing production was essentially the same: until well into the 1970s, housing would be built in bulk on large estates by large developers and construction companies in concert with the central government. The search for alternative architectural approaches to housing would thus necessarily be mired in contradiction.

The idea to go beyond the expression of repetition or uniformity in mass housing design was first officially suggested by a CGP working group in 1965. Presided over by Eugène Claudius-Petit and including Chombart as well as modernists including Jean Prouvé, Jean Le Couteur, and Bernard Zehrfuss, the group railed against the "ugliness" of the *grands ensembles*, which it saw as one of the main problems of contemporary architecture. Members argued for a series of government programs to encourage architectural experimentation. Such programs would attack both the "supply" and the "demand" side of architecture: they would promote architectural research and the realization of experimental projects as well as initiatives to educate the general public and influence public opinion.[34] Even SCIC, the large semipublic developer responsible for the much-loathed monotony of Sarcelles, blew the wind of change. From the early 1960s, the company had already begun to diversify its housing production by commissioning architects to design grouped single-family homes and more-upscale apartment buildings, as at Val d'Yerres.[35] In 1969, then, it established its own research program and launched a series of pilot projects explicitly meant to improve architectural quality and develop novel housing typologies and technologies. SCIC would become a close partner of the Plan Construction, just as it had been of earlier state initiatives.

At the same time, the government's agenda clearly transcended architectural aesthetics. An equally if not more important goal was to boost the French construction industry through what was considered "American-style" technological innovation. Already in 1968, the Consulting Committee for Scientific and Technical Research (Comité consultatif de la recherche scientifique et technique) had proposed an experimental program addressing technologies of housing production, not only because existing French housing "engendered social tensions" but also because its "technological backwardness" threatened to obstruct economic growth.[36] Yet the Plan Construction was unprecedented in the boldness and combination of its ambitions, which were at once economic, industrial, architectural, and social. The goal was not only to consolidate France's position in the international construction industry, to reduce the global cost of housing, and to create more affordable housing, but also to "make a better dwelling environment possible, adapted to the present and future demands of our society."[37] Realizing the dangers of public discontents, the underlying logic was that a better architecture would mean a more satisfied end user.[38]

The first task of the Plan Construction was sponsoring research. This was an almost standard response for a state bureaucracy beguiled by the potentials of policy-oriented research burgeoning in a variety of fields at this time. The variety of research that administrators commissioned was certainly remarkable considering the agency's emphasis on technology. Initially, they supported predictable research topics including construction methods, materials, industrialization, renovation, insulation, acoustics, and so on. Yet, when the sociologists included in the committee, such as Nicole Haumont, called for the inclusion of social-scientific research, subsequent themes were extended to include a broader range of topics—from residential mobility and interior flexibility to pedagogy for inhabitants.[39]

These social themes were a clear expression of the peculiar ideology underlying the Plan Construction and the new approaches to industrialized housing construction more generally. Policy makers saw it as a crucial part of their mission to "gradually put the public in the position of intervening in the process of construction, so that the users are effectively associated to the conception and management of housing" as well as to "inform the diverse professions of the construction sector of recent development in the domain of the social sciences applied to housing." This would "eliminate blockages owing to the lack of information, which obstruct architectural or technological innovation."[40] Through the research it sponsored, the Plan Construction thus acknowledged the realms of use and inhabitation—at least theoretically—as a crucial part of architectural innovation. This implied a politics of participation focused on the relationships of developers and builders with tenants' groups, family organizations, and civic education associations. Yet it also comprised an implicit approach to the inhabitant as consumer. Administrators were well aware that for developers and many inhabitants themselves, housing was a consumer good and thus needed to be recognized as an expression of social distinction and individual lifestyle.[41] Despite its technocratic nature, the Plan Construction thus offered a surprisingly fertile platform for intellectual discussions about choice, participation, social distinction, and the expression of identity in housing. At the same time, administrators still aimed to operate with impeccably scientific standards. Research programs were established using structural analyses, multi-criterion methods, and corporate diagramming techniques such as Honeywell's Pattern method.[42] Such methods, originally derived from the U.S. military and industry but long adapted for civilian and commercial use, gave the Plan Construction scientific rigor at a time when science could still offer a practically unquestioned model of political legitimacy.

Apart from research, the second and most important task of the Plan Construction was to foster experimental building projects. Such experimentation was also defined in strictly scientific terms, as the testing of a "system of hypotheses."[43] In 1972, Robert Lion created a yearly nomination system for innovative models ("Modèles innovation") to promote innovative, industrialized housing prototypes by groups of architects, construction companies, and developers. The assumption was that a limited set of well-tested prototypes, subsequently built in multiple locations all over France, would improve the overall quality of housing while maintaining cost rationality and efficiency.[44] Three years earlier, the ministry had already launched a similar policy especially for social housing projects. Once approved, social housing organizations no longer had to go through the lengthy consultation and commissioning procedures—a streamlined process remarkably similar to the *Logéco* policy of the 1950s. After only three years, that program had already led to the construction of more than a hundred thousand housing units. When Lion took over as head of construction at the ministry in 1970, he gave the policy a new label and focused it more specifically on the "new" concern with architectural quality and innovation. This focus was prompted not only by economic or technological promises, but also by growing social unrest in mass housing estates.[45]

Apart from prototypes, the Plan Construction also directly supported experimental housing projects across the country.[46] Some of these had been launched by other state institutions but were deemed worthy of extra support, while others were instigated by the agency itself. In conjunction with the Programme architecture nouvelle, a national program to promote new architecture, the agency rewarded inexperienced but emerging architects to carry out large-scale innovative housing projects.[47] The flurry of projects ultimately realized with the help of the Plan Construction in the first half of the 1970s coincided with a momentous shift in French architectural culture.[48] In the wake of the social movements and protests of May 1968, a unique mix of social critique and interdisciplinary research in architecture, engineering, and the social sciences had emerged. Critics hailed it as the vehicle of much-needed renewal, for which the Plan Construction turned out to be an ideal sponsor.

Consequently, the alternative industrialization of housing was intensively theorized in both technological and social terms. In their government-sponsored study of 1971, the architects Bernard Hamburger and Gérard Bauer and the sociologist Philippe Boudon contended that a rethinking of closed industrialization could foster architectural diversity, and with it a new emancipatory dwelling culture. Their line of argument was first economic, focusing on the need for diverse architecture in the real-estate market, and then technical, claiming that "diversity is perfectly compatible with a significant reduction of work on the construction site and with the production of elements in large quantities."[49] Yet there was clearly a social agenda as well.

Just before, Boudon had undertaken a sociological study of Le Corbusier's housing project in Pessac near Bordeaux, in which he had concluded that its architectural modernism was a success not despite but *because of* the many adaptations and additions of its inhabitants over time.[50] Individual appropriation could thus be "written in the plans" themselves, he argued. And that assumption informed the subsequent study on industrialization in which the authors embraced architectural diversification for its social potentials. In their theoretical exposé, they cast the Athens Charter as a "progressive rediscovery of the complexity in architecture and thus of the variety it engenders."[51] Formal complexity was understood as part of a shift away from the belief in a uniform subject and toward the differentiation of lifestyles. Aware of the heated debates on closed versus open industrialization, the authors nevertheless continued to contend with modernist brio that industrialization was inevitable and that it required a new architectural theory. Closed industrialization, they argued, would allow for more architectural experimentation and complexity—despite the disadvantage, briefly mentioned, that it was less adapted to the housing market. Paul Chemetov, who worked with the Atelier d'urbanisme et d'architecture around this time, argued for industrialization in similar terms. To him, the main obstacle to progress was an ill-informed public and a lack of training among architects. The rationale for industrialization he laid out in his own government-sponsored study of 1971 was both architectural and social: demographic growth combined with increasingly complex urban needs made the flexible and multiple usage of space a necessity. The assemblage of housing complexes through a "free combinatory of industrial elements" was the best way to allow such novel use of space.[52]

In other words, for many of the young architects and administrators gathered around the Plan Construction, technological innovation was not a goal in and of itself: it was inextricably linked to a social agenda, however vaguely formulated. Similar to the industrialization of architecture that preceded them and to which they reacted so vehemently, the new proposals were deemed to be unquestionably benevolent. But while advocates of industrialization during the 1950s believed it would universalize access to housing, the proponents of alternative industrialization held up the dream of emancipation. The radical normalization and standardization of construction elements would thus no longer lead to uniformity in meaning and use but would instead generate spatial diversity and encourage appropriation and participation. Henri-Pierre Maillard, whose modular system became widely used in housing construction, promoted it as the basis for "collective creation" and participatory dwelling.[53] Developed in the context of his Centre de recherches d'architectures modulaires (Research Center for Modular Architectures), the system resulted between 1972 and 1978 in no less than ten thousand dwellings (Figure 7.5).[54]

Although in some cases this rhetoric of participation was too flimsy to convince critics and inhabitants, it was common currency in the political climate after 1968. During the mid-1960s, observers, planners, and activists had begun to cast participation as the panacea for mass housing. Robert Durand summarized this possibility as an almost logical consequence of mass housing itself, when he wrote that "in the domain of residential life, participation appears fundamentally like the complement and the corrective to the process characteristic of the last twenty years: institutionalization, professionalization, concentration, bureaucratization, or technocratization, on the one hand, massification, on the other."[55] Whether participation was really able to reverse such an evolution was questionable. Yet experts, professionals,

Figure 7.5. Rendering for an experimental housing project in Toulouse using the Maillard-SAE construction system, 1972. From *Techniques et architecture* 34, no. 6 (1972): 70.

and policy makers alike continued to uphold the promise that a fundamentally reconceptualized industrialization of housing could foster the emancipation of dwelling.

The Promise of Flexibility

The question of what forms and strategies could fulfill the renewed promises of industrialization brought architects, engineers, social scientists, and policy makers to what they called *habitat évolutif*—flexible, evolving, or adaptable dwelling. In 1972, when enthusiasm about the concept was at its peak, a team of state-funded researchers defined it as "a dwelling capable of assuring at once the different aspirations of the clients and the structural modifications of their family. To talk about *habitat évolutif* is to emphasize the diversity of construction techniques opposed to uniformity."[56] The assumption was that constructive diversity would engender a diversity of use. And the way to attain this was, perhaps paradoxically, standardization. Identical construction elements could be put together in a range of different assemblages, at least if they were designed as such. With the notion of *habitat évolutif*, the flexibility of dwelling and the participation of inhabitants were thus cast as matters of technological innovation and architectural design.[57]

The concept itself was hardly novel: design as facilitator of an environment transformable by its occupants had been one of the staples of the postwar avant-garde, from Constant Nieuwenhuys's New Babylon to Archigram's Plug-in City and Cedric Price's Fun Palace. Their celebration of a new leisure society was founded on an optimistic belief in the emancipatory power of technology. More particularly, they suggested that the virtues of social participation and the techniques of architectural flexibility were inextricably linked.[58] Despite claims to novelty and embrace of the latest technologies, these linkages were first forged in the interwar period. Precedents ranged from Le Corbusier's Maison Domino and his *plan libre* concept, realized in several residential projects in France, to Gerrit Rietveld's movable wall partitions at the Schröder house in Utrecht and Mies van der Rohe's open plan apartment block at the Weissenhofsiedlung of 1927. With his *Plan Obus* for Algiers, Le Corbusier had even taken these ideas up to the scale of the city at large.[59] Postwar modern architects built on these ideas as they promoted new construction methods as the tools of spatial and programmatic flexibility. Yet, pragmatic interests in the possibilities of modular construction during the 1950s, such as in the work of Ezra Ehrenkrantz, were often overshadowed by aesthetic concerns, such as the resurgent interest in proportion illustrated by Le Corbusier's use of the Modulor at the Unité d'habitation.[60]

Like many of their colleagues abroad, French architects left the potentials of flexibility largely unexplored, absorbed as they were in national reconstruction and mass housing production. International examples such as Sweden's flexible housing experiments would only really influence France during the early 1970s.[61] Before that, only a handful of French architects were interested in the idea of flexible dwelling. Auguste Perret's housing at Le Havre could be seen as a modest attempt. Claude Parent and Ionel Schein proposed a flexible interior for individual homes in 1953 but their proposal did not find broad reception.[62] The proposal of the architects' group Syndicat des architectes de la Seine, presented at the Paris household fair Salon des arts ménagers in 1960, did not either.[63] And then there was the more theoretical project of Candilis-Josic-Woods, whose distinction of what they called "determined elements" from "indeterminate elements" similarly promised a free organization of interior space. Their research on flexible apartment units and their placement within high-rise blocks was perhaps most promising but could not be fully tested in their subsequent large-scale projects owing to stringent cost limits and regulations (Figure 7.6).[64] At Bagnols-sur-Cèze and Toulouse-Le Mirail, the only concrete result was mobile partitioning.[65] Successfully built precedents were far and few between.

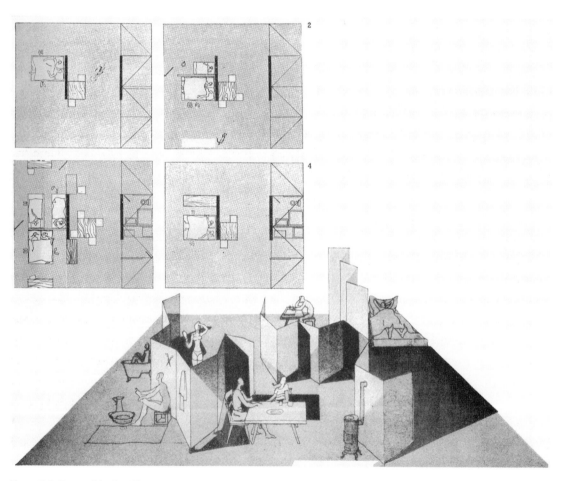

Figure 7.6. Proposal by Candilis-Josic-Woods for flexible dwelling, 1959. From *Techniques et architecture* 19, no. 2 (1959): 83.

France had to wait until the late 1960s before flexible dwelling really took off. But when it did, enthusiasm for it was fervent. A similar avidity caught Dutch architecture with the advocacy of Jan Trapman and Herman Hertzberger. The new enthusiasts saw industrialized construction methods as the only way to realize flexible dwelling on the kind of scale needed in the booming 1960s. In France, *évolutivité* now became almost interchangeable with the use of new technologies and methods of industrialized construction. The apartment building by the architects Xavier and Luc Arsène-Henry and Bernard Schoeller for the Surville housing project in Montereau, a small town in the vicinity of Paris, was the first significant realization. Completed in 1969 and closely studied by sociologists and the policy makers of the Plan Construction, it functioned as a prototype for subsequent projects. The architects' goal was to create an architecture that would allow inhabitants to individualize their apartments. They dismissed standardized architecture "in which the typical user would find everything, including his standard pajamas chosen by a computer." Far from political radicals compared to some of their peers at this time, the architects still cast their design as a direct critique of the "insidious alienation by way of materialism" in a society of mass consumption.[66]

Built by a local social housing organization on an existing estate, the nine-story apartment block featured thirty-six rental units whose layout could effectively be shaped by future occupants. Collective facilities were located on the ground and top floors. Each other floor was divided into four dwelling units of eighty-three square meters, organized around a central core. In every unit, the only fixed elements constraining interior organization were the entrance door and a utilities duct placed in the middle of the space and adjacent to which kitchen, bathroom, and toilet needed to be placed (Figure 7.7). Otherwise, future inhabitants had absolute freedom in the placement of walls and rooms. They could also choose out of five facade elements: a wall panel, a fixed glazed panel, a glass door panel, a fixed window panel, and an opening window panel.[67] This innovative approach to interior flexibility was not reflected in the facade. With massive balustrades in white concrete surrounding the entire perimeter, the building looked like a conventional modern apartment block to passersby.

Despite its experimental nature, the building was constructed just within the cost limits of social housing, albeit the uppermost bracket. The process of consultation with future tenants—families with a mix of lower-middle- and middle-class backgrounds—began with the distribution of a graphic board displaying possible options for apartment layouts as designed by the architects. On average, three meetings with future inhabitants were organized: a first one, without the architects, to explain the flexible system and set of choices; a second one in which the architect would sit together with the inhabitants to sketch possible layouts based on their expressed needs and desires; and a third one to finish the apartment plan (Figure 7.8).[68] The consultation process did not diminish the legitimacy of architectural expertise. On the contrary, the architects were now acting very much as they had in past decades: offering a

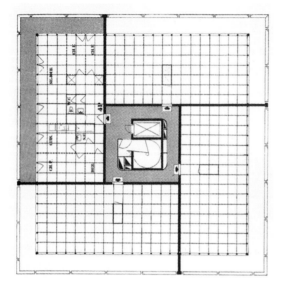

Figure 7.7. Apartment building at Montereau by Xavier and Luc Arsène-Henry. Photograph from 1973. From *Techniques et architecture* 292 (1973): 95.

service as liberal professionals to individual clients. That these clients were now tenants of a municipally owned housing project only implied a "more advanced" role for the architect as a provider of what was now termed "architectural assistance."

In the end, none of the nine layouts originally proposed by the architects was exactly adopted, and none of the eventual apartment layouts were the same.[69] Some families chose to separate the kitchen from the living room, others to integrate them, and still others preferred a separate dining corner. Some decided to pair up children's rooms to create a communal play area; others kept them separate. Some preferred entirely glazed facade elements; others opted for a more traditional setup with a limited number of windows. The process was carefully monitored by the Association d'anthropologie appliquée, a consultancy firm funded by the Plan Construction. The social scientists were motivated by what the experiment could offer their own field of inquiry. They carefully analyzed the plans and layout choices, monitored the consultation sessions with the inhabitants, and, most important, studied the actual use of the

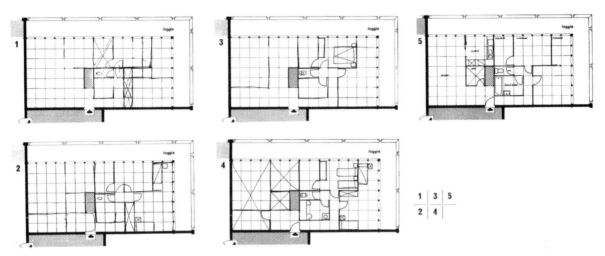

Figure 7.8. Apartment layouts drawn during workshop sessions with the architect and a future tenant of the apartment building at Montereau. 1 = after twenty-five minutes; 2 = after thirty-five minutes; 3 = after forty-five minutes; 4 = after one hour; 5 = final adjustments. From *Techniques et architecture* 292 (1973): 94.

dwelling units.[70] Their research interests—problems of parental authority, the symbolic role of the living room, the relation between apartment layout and family structure, and so on—did not exactly correspond to those of their sponsors. But the study's primary conclusion satisfied administrators and advocates because it pointed out that "the families have really created plans adapted not only to their needs, but also to their personality, as is proven by the variable degree of originality of the plans following the social characteristics of the sample."[71] Most plans were adapted again a couple years later, and some even multiple times.[72]

This success quickly led to a second, even more ambitious project, called La Clairière du Lauzun. After the selection of a new site at Bordeaux-le-Lac, the architects provided a fairly conventional massing: ten housing blocks, six slabs, and four towers were peppered over the terrain as at so many other *grands ensembles*. Again, just as at Montereau, the apartment layouts were drawn up individually in consultation with future inhabitants. The plans followed a flexible system of rules defined by a modular grid and a structure of movable partition walls that could be dry-mounted, both orthogonally and diagonally. The only constraints were the front door and the fixed utilities duct for kitchen, bathroom, and toilet, again exactly as at Montereau. The duct was load-bearing and held up the floors together with the concrete frame facades, so that the plan could remain free from columns. The standardized exterior wall elements among which inhabitants could choose were multicolored and given more visibility in the facade than at Montereau, which led to a facade that was more expressive of individual choices (Figure 7.9). The most important difference, initially neglected by the policy makers and sociologists, was that the project consisted of condos and not rental units. Considering

Figure 7.9. Bordeaux-le-Lac,
by Xavier and Luc Arsène-Henry.
Photograph from mid-1970s.
Fonds DAU. Service interministériel
des Archives de France/Cité de
l'architecture et du patrimoine/Archives
d'architecture du XXᵉ siècle.

the security of their tenure, the social housing organization was likely aware that home buyers would be more invested in the participatory design of their apartments than renters would be. Yet it was also a matter of social class, which experts only gradually recognized as a crucial factor in the success of participatory experiments such as these. In a 1974 survey sponsored by the Plan Construction, researchers timidly acknowledged that the social group "most resistant to architectural innovation" was "the poor and the working classes."[73] Those most receptive were "intellectual elites," "artists and teachers," and segments of the middle and upper-middle classes. They naturally became the main target group for these types of projects.

A simultaneous experiment in industrialized flexible dwelling—again sponsored by the state—was the system developed by the Groupement pour l'étude d'une architecture industrialisée (Group for the Study of Industrialized Architecture). An association of the architects Marcel Lods, Paul Depondt, and Henri Beauclair with the construction firms Aluminium Français and Saint-Gobain, the group proposed a construction system of lightweight prefabricated steel elements.[74] Purportedly only two workers were needed to build an entire apartment block out of this "giant Meccano," as the architects called it.[75] Not concrete but steel was the appropriate material for industrialized housing production, they insisted: "It is an 'adaptable' architecture that we need to create today. And for that, light construction, mobile elements, and modifiable forms are an absolute necessity."[76] The system allowed for large spans, creating columnless spaces that could be freely and easily partitioned. It was tested on a large scale for the housing development of La Grand-Mare in Rouen, where five hundred rental social housing units with strictly defined maximum surface and construction costs were built between 1967 and 1969 (Figure 7.10).[77] In contrast to Montereau and Bordeaux-le-Lac, the developer did not inform future inhabitants about the project's flexibility: some only found out about their apartment layout options after moving in.[78] The developer had carefully selected the inhabitants it considered best suited for such experimental apartments: the more upwardly mobile and "culturally attuned." After moving in, many eventually decided to modify their layouts, making the project a success in flexible dwelling after all.

Lods, Depondt, and Beauclair's continued interest in constructive systems led to a second, even more ambitious project. Resulting from a national competition for four thousand dwellings in the New Town of Le Vaudreuil, the project not only expanded the notion of flexibility to the neighborhood scale but also engaged more seriously the social sciences. Launched in March 1971, the competition guidelines had emerged out of the preliminary urban designs by the Atelier de Montrouge (discussed in chapter 5). Apart from industrialized construction and the "radical integration of functions," an important criterion for the competition was what the architects of the Atelier de Montrouge had called the city's *évolutivité*. By this they meant more than just a flexible approach to long-term planning; the housing and urban space itself had to be able to constantly evolve.[79] Their constructive and theoretical arguments were fundamentally interrelated: "A city cannot be created by the simple juxtaposition of disparate buildings. On the contrary, between all the elements that compose it, there need to be relations so that elements can form a system that is coherent and capable of evolving."[80] The system needed to harbor "spatial margins" fostering the mobility and growth of urban programs, and a "network of volumes" creating human-scale urbanity and the urban density "characteristic of a Latin city." Although such concepts had been applied to architectural projects across France since the late 1960s, the ambition to realize them with novel industrialized methods at such a large scale was unique.

The competition's winning proposal was developed by Lods, Depondt, and Beauclair in collaboration with the technical engineering firm Alpha-Ingénierie and the developer Bouygues. Their industrial construction system started from a simple module that could be assembled in multiple ways.[81] The module was centered on a slice of elevated pedestrian walkway around which different housing types could be developed through flexible assembly (Figure 7.11).

Figure 7.10. La Grand-Mare by the architects Marcel Lods, Paul Depondt, and Henri Beauclair. Fonds Lods. Académie d'architecture/Cité de l'architecture et du patrimoine/Archives d'architecture du XXᵉ siècle.

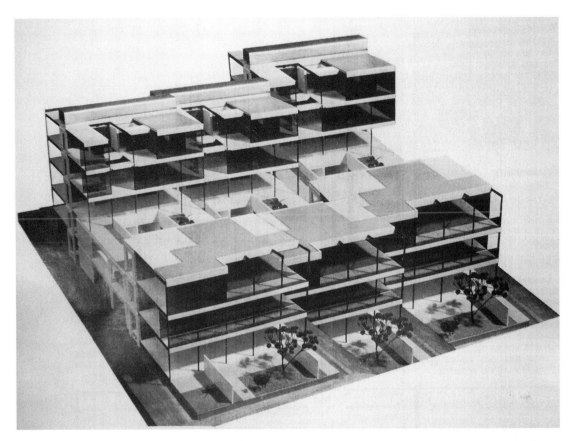

Figure 7.11. The project by the architects Marcel Lods, Paul Depondt, and Henri Beauclair for the housing competition of Le Vaudreuil, 1972. This model presented only one possible outcome of the flexible assembly system. From *Techniques et architecture* 34, no. 6 (1972): 52.

These ranged from two- to five-story blocks of apartments as well as terraced housing types (Figure 7.12). Technically, it was an open construction system on a 30-centimeter-square grid of four industrially produced "families of components" (structure, envelope, partition, and facilities/utilities) that could be dry-mounted. With its open floor plans lacking load-bearing partitions, the system was meant to enable not only flexible dwelling but also a new kind of urban environment, open and transformable by the inhabitants—purportedly not only before their arrival but also during their occupancy. Yet how that would be concretely achieved was not entirely clear.

The technical construction of such a uniquely flexible environment required an equally exceptional social process. Quaternière Education, an independent team of experts, was hired to organize the negotiations between architects and future inhabitants of the no less than 1,365 housing units. The team's sociologists, psychologists, and pedagogues developed a

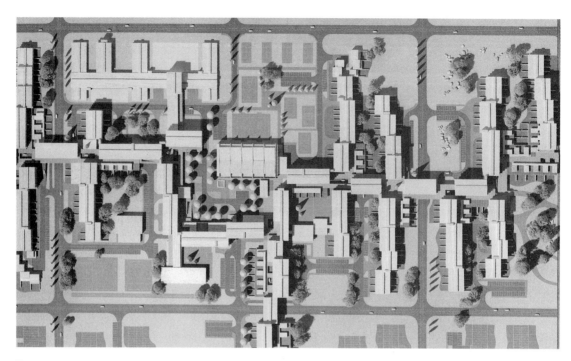

Figure 7.12. The project by the architects Marcel Lods, Paul Depondt, and Henri Beauclair for the housing competition of Le Vaudreuil, 1972. The model shows possibilities for the overall urban organization. Fonds ATM. Service interministériel des Archives de France/Cité de l'architecture et du patrimoine/Archives d'architecture du XXᵉ siècle.

systematic and elaborate procedure to assist families with the development of their apartment layouts. After a first meeting to discuss their needs and demands for future dwelling, they would sit together with a consulting architect to draw possible apartment layouts. Realizing that the families would not necessarily have the skills to make or even read such drawings, the social scientists then built a physical model, scaled one to one, to test out possible apartment layouts. Its lightweight partitions could be moved around instantly, giving future inhabitants the possibility to experiment with their spatial ideas "in reality" and in real time (Figure 7.13).[82] Only after this playful process would the architect come in to address potential problems or to suggest improvements.[83] Despite the success of this approach, tested with a small sample of families, the method was not systematically applied. Not surprisingly, it was considered too labor-intensive and was therefore not integrated into the eventual marketing procedure of the development.[84]

Such experiments with flexible dwelling—often at once rationalist and naive, radical and overworked—brought utopian modernism, state technocracy, commercial development, and hippy culture together with remarkable ease. They reached an almost logical conclusion in the concept of "total flexibility" promoted by the architects Bernard Kohn and Georges

Figure 7.13. Stills from the 1975 documentary *Logement à la demande* by Éric Rohmer, showing how the architect and pedagogue worked with future inhabitants to shape the apartment layout.

Maurios. Instead of partial flexibility—constrained, for instance, by the fixed utilities duct at Montereau—their goal was the complete independence of programmatic organization from physical structure. Maurios, who had gained experience working for Le Corbusier in India, had been interested in architectural flexibility ever since his studies at Harvard University with José-Luis Sert, Jezzi Soltan, and Louis Kahn. He had not found much support from the government until the DGRST ultimately funded his research in 1967. After a failed attempt to build in the New Town of Évry, the ministry and its Plan Construction helped realize their first large-scale flexible housing project at Val-d'Yerres.[85]

Called Les Marelles, the project's constructive innovation was the *poteau-gaine*, a hollow element that combined a load-bearing function with the distribution of utilities. A three-dimensional structure made out of such elements would provide access to utilities at any place within the building, and thus, "total flexibility" in organization, including the placement of kitchen, bathroom, and toilet (Figure 7.14). The system was industrialized by means of three prefabricated concrete elements.[86] Architecturally, it was very close to the approach of John Habraken, who also promoted flexibility as an alternative to mass housing: large-scale structures (*dragers* or supports) for dwelling would be maintained by the collective while their infill would be at the liberty of individual inhabitants (Figure 7.15).[87] That solution would address the principal shortcomings of mass housing as the architects perceived them: their monotony, lack of inhabitant participation, and failure to fully benefit from industrialized building. However, such a proposition meant that the occupant had to enter into the design process, which complicated the relationship between the architect and the institutional client. Inspired by the work of Habraken, the architects and sociologists at Les Marelles had taken on a similar postulate, namely, that "it is to the people to decide themselves about their dwelling," and their goal was therefore "to give to the users the power and the means to conceive themselves, if not their house, at least their inhabited space."[88] Although for someone like

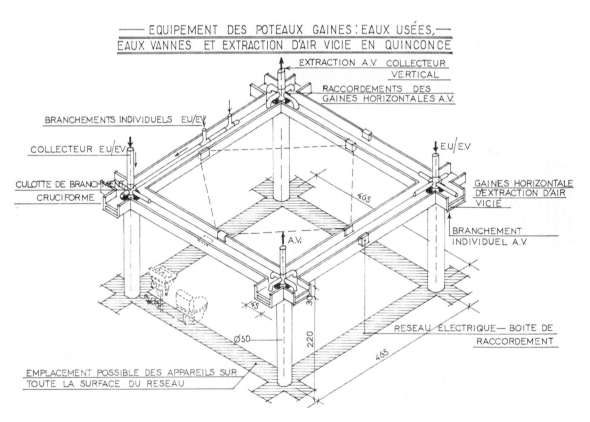

Figure 7.14. The three-dimensional construction system for the project of Les Marelles by the architects Bernard Kohn and Georges Maurios. Utility ducts are inserted into the hollow structure. From *Les Cahiers du Centre scientifique et technique du bâtiment* 167 (1976): 48.

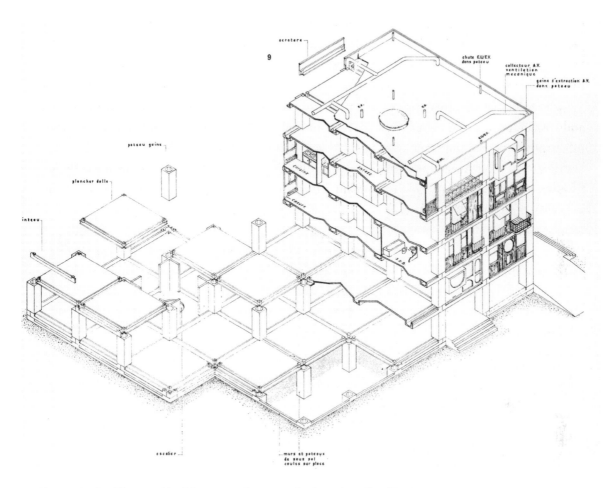

Figure 7.15. Possible assembly of the construction system for the project of Les Marelles by the architects Bernard Kohn and Georges Maurios. From *Techniques et architecture* 292 (1973): 55.

Nieuwenhuys such a goal still fell within the realm of an architectural utopia, the architects—who referred to future inhabitants ambivalently as both users and clients—acknowledged "the little real difference there is between a classic process of commercialization and that of Les Marelles."[89]

The developer SCIC signed off on an initial development of a hundred condo units built with the system. The consultation process with inhabitants was well-organized, elaborate, and particularly high-tech. Apart from a physical model at one-tenth scale that allowed inhabitants to envisage their future dwelling, there was a video display setup that could move the camera inside this model as if the viewer were actually located inside the apartment.[90] With the help of a psychosociologist appointed by Maurios, these techniques were meant to generate a smooth process of participatory design. Despite these whistles and bells, the project was a commercial failure. Of the one hundred available units, only fifteen found buyers who had effectively laid out their own apartments using this technique (Figure 7.16).[91] Whether it was because of a lack of advertising for the project or the economic slump at the time, the project discouraged the developer from venturing into experiments with flexible dwelling ever again.

The underuse of possibilities offered by flexible housing systems might have been most startling in the case of Les Marelles, but it was in fact a more general problem.[92] Transforming an already occupied apartment entailed a multitude of technical and logistical hurdles. Major transformations were perhaps only necessary once or twice in a lifetime, and the constant physical presence of what flexible systems required—rails, cores, ducts, and so on—was often experienced as hindrance rather than potential. Despite the flexible options available, inhabitants often reproduced conventional apartment layouts as they were comfortable with and used to them. Whether out of conformism or a lack of guidance by the developers, customized apartments did not necessarily seem to spawn the creative emancipation of dwelling some architects and social scientists had hoped for. In the 1976 issue of *Techniques et architecture* on flexible dwelling, the enthusiastic reportage on international projects such as Lucien Kroll's

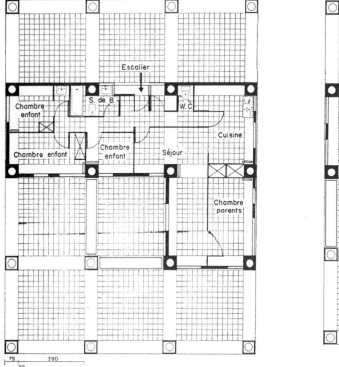
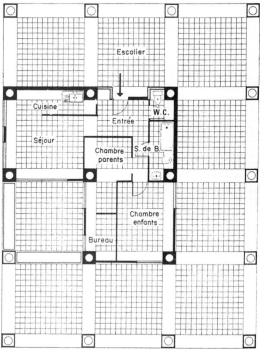

Figure 7.16. Two customized apartment layouts for Les Marelles, showing individual solutions following inhabitants' desires. From *Les Cahiers du Centre scientifique et technique du bâtiment* 167 (1976): 48.

participatory student housing projects in Brussels together with a wealth of French "Modèle innovation" projects could not conceal the sense that this was the end of an experiment rather than the beginning.[93]

The architectural concept of flexibility still relied on the old assumption that dwelling was a relatively neutral set of practices that could be subjected to rationalization. In everyday life, inhabitants experienced the architectural technologies of flexible dwelling not so much as neutral enablers but as anathema to the feeling of a stable home.[94] While architects and developers cast mobile partitions as liberating instruments, their very mobility posed an almost ontological obstacle for inhabitants in the process of homemaking. With his New Babylon project, Nieuwenhuys had come to exactly this conclusion via a different route: from a total environment of self-realization through the leisure of making one's own space, his imaginary world had evolved into a dystopia of melancholia and aggression.[95] More concretely, the mass provision of dwellings that would continuously adapt to the changing needs of their inhabitants did not reflect the realities of geographic and residential mobility in 1970s France. As one of the final gasps of France's mass housing regime, *habitat évolutif* was perhaps ultimately an architectural metaphor—in Cacciari's sense, of only being able to show architecture's impotence: a signifier of the exact opposite of flexibility and of the troubling lack of choice the French had in a housing market aiming to be consumer-oriented while still largely defined by two decades of state-led mass housing production. Rather than flexible apartments in collective housing blocks—as state planners, sociologists, and modern architects still believed—it was to be the private boom in single-family home building that would eventually change this condition.

Between Housing and Home

The single-family home was the elephant in the room in more than one way. It shaped the course of mass housing as a beguiling mirage—and a nightmare to the many policy makers and experts who continued until well into the 1970s to identify it with spatial chaos and with the worst kind of petit-bourgeois ideology. Architectural experimentation—still largely under the aegis of the state—remained focused on collective housing but was often drenched in guilty desire for the new lifestyle afforded by the modern single-family home. Obsessed by overcoming the opposition between mass collective housing and the single-family home, architects and policy makers promoted forms of "intermediary dwelling" or what was termed *habitat intermédiaire*. Like flexible housing, it would take into account the changing needs of inhabitants—not through adaptable apartment layouts but by offering "the advantages of both the individual house and the apartment building" in a single typology, "as far from the towers and bars as from the dreary suburban sprawl."[96]

The unrivaled poster child for this novel type in France was Évry I, the first new neighborhood for the New Town of Évry in the southeast suburbs of Paris. The project was the result of a high-profile architectural competition organized by the local New Town planners with the help of the central government.[97] With a program of seven thousand housing units including public amenities, the competition enjoyed the financial support of the Plan Construction, whose administrators also joined in the competition's jury. Cast as a vehicle for the much-needed renewal of French mass housing and urbanism, the competition called for projects that were "at once innovative and realistic, experimental and comprehensive." But the most important goal was to "revive the love of urban life" and thus to counter the predominant desire of the French middle classes for the suburban single-family home. The competition brief specified some concrete ways for reaching that elusive goal: not only the general conception of the neighborhood, the integration of its amenities, and the careful attention to its open spaces were crucial, but also the "variety and quality of the architecture" and the "nonsegregation of different housing categories."[98] Making explicit reference to Lefebvre's 1968 *Le droit à la ville*, which by then had become a standard reference for a whole generation of intellectuals, the brief spoke about "the AESTHETIC EMOTION . . . that exalts the symbolic value of places in harmony with their 'use-value,' and their potential for sociability."[99] To achieve such lofty goals, the brief encouraged participants to engage social-scientific expertise and pursue architectural research focusing not only on public art and landscaping, but especially on the "spaces of transition between the individual cells and the public space."[100] Housing design, in other words, had to take a more serious account of the complexity of dwelling and in particular the subjective world of domesticity—of coming home and feeling at home.

With its complex program including a diverse array of collective facilities, the competition prompted many of the entrants to collaborate with social-scientific experts, much as the organizers had proposed. After careful selection, the jury retained four proposals, and a second round left two (Figure 7.17). Both finalists had emphasized social-scientific reasoning in their entries. The team EUREVRY, which was led by the collaborative architecture office Atelier d'urbanisme et d'architecture, had the help of a consultancy firm from Grenoble, the Groupe d'architecture et pédagogie. The winning team, UCY, led by the architects Andrault and Parat, was consulted by Jean Ader, an expert in pedagogy who helped plan the school infrastructure, and by SCOOPER, which supplied the preliminary socioeconomic studies.[101] As in other large competitions at this time, architects were required to team up with developers and engineering firms to guarantee construction budgets and smooth implementation. The addition of social-scientific expertise to this mix was less conventional.

In the winning design, sociological sensibilities most clearly converged with the new ethos of industrialization. The project's cross-shaped pyramids were arranged so as to create intimate urban spaces between them and offered an unmistakable counterimage to the dreaded uniformity of "towers and slabs" (see Figure 7.1, Plate 16, and Plate 17). The stacking of cubic

UCY
architectes
GARP : michel andrault et pierre parat, pierre sirvin
et la SCAU, société civile d'architectes et d'urbanisme

promoteurs
sociétés et offices d'H.L.M. et société
de technique immobilière, regroupées autour de l'O.C.I.L.
(office central interprofessionnel de logement)

EUREVRY
architectes
A U A (atelier d'urbanisme et d'architecture)
cabinet van treek, bofill (taller de architectura)

promoteurs
FFF (le foyer du fonctionnaire et de la famille)
IFRA (société immobilière franco-allemande)
SACI (l'auxiliaire de la construction immobilière)

ICP . JCB
architectes
jean-claude bernard, jacques beufe,
paul ducamp, henri-pierre maillard.

promoteurs
sociétés du groupe
de l'immobilière construction de paris (ICP)
sociétés d'HLM adhérentes
à la cellule opérationnelle de l'essonne.

E 1
architectes
jean chedeau, gilbert guillemaut, maurice silvy. bertin et c^{ie}
coyne et bellier, équipe de conception dirigée par jean prouvé

promoteurs
SETIMEG - SGE

Figure 7.17. The finalists of the Évry I competition as featured on a leaflet for an exhibition in 1973. Archives nationales, France, CAC 19780319/001.

volumes generated an impressive diversity of housing units in different sizes and layouts, with each apartment enjoying multiple orientations and a luxurious, room-sized terrace. What made this possible was a constructive system with a small set of prefabricated concrete elements that could be variously assembled in three dimensions. The resulting architecture articulated the individuality of dwellings and terraces as expressive shapes and colors, but also celebrated the overall collectivity as an imbricated pattern (Figure 7.18).

In purely formal terms, the proposal was hardly new. It followed in a long tradition of modernist interpretations of the Mediterranean vernacular, in particular the hilltop village and the casbah. The first iteration of the modern pyramidal housing type had perhaps been André Studer's 1954 proposal of an "Arabersiedlung" in Casablanca.[102] Yet the most well-known built example was Moshe Safdie's project at the Montreal Expo of 1967. And even within France the project of Évry was no pioneer: various architects, including Andrault and Parat themselves, had been experimenting with pyramidal and stacked housing typologies since the mid-1960s. A first rendition was their competition entry for Villetaneuse of 1966, and the first large-scale realization was in Villepinte around 1970 (see Figure 7.19).[103] But to

Figure 7.18. Sketches for *habitat intermédiaire* by Michel Andrault and Pierre Parat. From Marc Gaillard, *Andrault–Parat Architectes* (Paris: Dunod, 1979), 234–35.

Figure 7.19. Housing project at Villepinte by the architects Michel Andrault and Pierre Parat, 1970. From *Architecture française* 391 (1975): 42.

grasp the significance of Évry I and its many kin spread over suburban France in the 1970s, formal precedents are easily outweighed by the complex motivations—social as much as architectural—behind the projects themselves.

How exactly was design harnessed to "revive the love of urban life," the competition's main goal as articulated in the brief? With its massing, the project substantially transformed, but did not fully invert, the figure–ground relationship of modernist housing. The dense composition of cross-plan pyramid-shaped volumes left a negative of "canyons," interconnected public spaces that held the middle between streets and squares. These canyons introduced human scale, variety, and playfulness—well-known ideals of the new urbanism for the French suburbs. Essential to this strategy was the decomposition of the conventional prismatic shapes of housing blocks into fragments. This created a visual landscape in which the end of one block seemed to fade into the beginning of another. The public realm was organized by a central pedestrian path linking all collective amenities, as specified in the brief. The architects distributed these facilities, commerce most importantly, on the ground floors of the housing blocks so as to generate more lively urban spaces and a density of social encounter. The ambition of creating new public spaces that made reference to traditional urban spaces such as streets, parks, and squares was prolonged in the careful landscaping, public art, and urban furniture by Jacques Simon (Plate 18). Many of these strategies to create "urban animation" had already been tested in a multitude of projects during the 1960s.[104]

What was pioneering about the proposal was its sociologically attuned approach to alternative housing typologies. The competition guidelines had prescribed a mix of private-sector and state-aided housing, and one of the explicit criteria of the jury was the "degree of imbrication of the different categories of housing" (Figure 7.20).[105] These categories included market-rate apartments, social housing rental units, social housing condos, and units financed by state loans for home buying. The competition organizers aimed to attract a mix of lower-, middle-, and upper-middle-class families and to have them live closely together. Clearly motivated by increasingly loud outcries of ghettoization, they contended that a policy of fine-grained mixing would avoid the dangers of segregation.[106] Still under the assumption that spatial proximity would engender social mixing, they seemed not to have taken Chamboredon and Lemaire's lesson to heart. And yet the competition's ambitions proved to be remarkably productive in design terms. Reacting to the dominant view that associated the mounting contestation in many *grands ensembles* to their "antiurban monotony," the architects' response was a formal language of "diversity and harmony." Translating social ambitions most clearly into architectural design strategies, the winning proposal successfully positioned architecture as a vehicle not only to express but to actively *facilitate* social diversity and peaceful coexistence.

Formal differentiation in a complex three-dimensional facade made it possible to distinguish individual dwelling units and thus fostered the visual identification of inhabitants

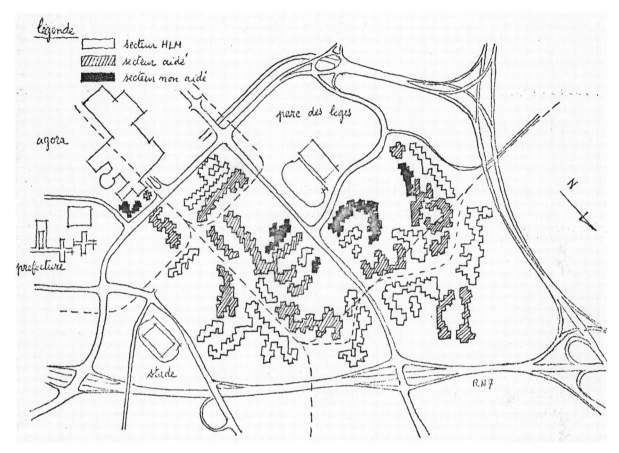

Figure 7.20. Work sketch by the jury to represent the distribution of different housing categories for each project. White: HLM housing; hatched: state-aided housing; black: private sector housing. Archives nationales, France, CAC 19780319/001.

with their own homes. That design strategy was quickly translated into real-estate language. Targeting France's new middle-class consumers, the advertising brochure read: "At Évry I, choosing an apartment is not a word in vain. For example, in building one there will not be two terrace apartments that are identical."[107] Even more important than their unique character were the dwellings' generous room-sized terraces, which were explicitly cast as alternatives to the suburban lawn (Plate 19). Despite the competition's commitment to create a decidedly urban neighborhood, the suburban single-family home on its lot was seen as the principal competitor. The architects thus asserted that the project's terraces, ringed with big plant holders to provide privacy, would offer prospective inhabitants a new domestic lifestyle that could parallel that of the single-family home.

By this time, a wealth of sociological reports on the popularity of the new suburban dwelling was available to architects, planners, and developers. The 1964 landmark study *L'Habitat pavillonnaire* had described that dwelling in terms of its feelings of intimacy, the possibilities

offered by extra space (storage, hobby room, and so on), the psychology of having an individual entrance, and the freedom offered by a private outdoor space.[108] More in-depth sociological studies such as these confirmed earlier opinion polls, which had demonstrated the
preference of many French families for single-family homes ever since the 1947 INED study.
But, as they examined in greater depth how people actually lived in single-family homes, these
qualitative sociological studies offered policy makers, planners, and architects much more
than quantitative opinion polls. Sociological expertise allowed them to launch a fundamental
critique of architectural functionalism in general and the monotony of mass housing in particular. In an attempt to learn from the single-family home, Évry I housing was organized in a
flexible constructive grid that would allow "changing uses of volumes and their transformation
in function of the unpredictable evolution of needs." Together with the project's terraces, the
innovative constructive system would facilitate "an appropriation of space by the inhabitants,"
in the same way that the single-family home allowed its inhabitants to live outdoors and adapt
their home to changing family conditions.[109] The image of vertically stacked homes, used ironically to illustrate the "irrational" desire for individuality in a 1975 *Urbanisme* issue, had thus
been the not-so-ironic rationale for Évry I and a dearth of similar housing projects built during the ultimate phase of the French construction craze in the early 1970s (Figure 7.21).

Despite its ambitions to curb social segregation and to sell a new urban lifestyle to French
consumers, the experiment of Évry I failed to escape the problematic residential mobility patterns of many other *grands ensembles*. Nevertheless, not all projects befell the same fate. The
housing project by Jean Renaudie for the center of Ivry, another southeastern suburb of Paris,
enjoyed a different course.[110] His design consisted of a startlingly complex series of stacked
star-shaped volumes that infiltrated the existing urban fabric (Figure 7.22). Even where the
volumes were not physically connected, their complexity created a strong impression of visual
interpenetration for passersby. At the center was a building no less than megastructural in
scale and ambition: it contained not only more than one hundred housing units but also a
range of urban amenities, including a supermarket, shops, offices, and sociocultural facilities.
Many of these were accessible from the crevices and openings that blurred distinctions
between public and private, and between inside and outside. The project not just abutted but
made a variety of functional connections to the existing fabric and surrounding housing projects. The intricacy of the urban design was matched by the absolute singularity of dwelling
units: each and every unit was different not only in size and layout, but also in form (Figure
7.23). Most of them had a large, private, outdoor space in common. What made this project
so exceptional was that, in large part because of its spacious apartment layouts and generously
planted roof decks, 90 percent of interviewed first inhabitants considered their dwelling
equivalent to a single-family home.[111] If real-estate values are an indication, the project is still
attractive to the urban middle class today (Plate 20).

Figure 7.21. Cartoon illustration by Paton, 1975. From *Urbanisme* 151 (1975): 64.

Sociological studies of the project, sponsored by the Plan Construction and including both pre- and postoccupancy evaluations, emphasized its design as the carrier of a shift in agency from architect to inhabitant.[112] Following Lefebvre and some of his colleagues, the concept of appropriation and its emancipatory power figured prominently in the sociologists' analyses. The dwellings' spatial complexity—their sharp interior angles, oddly placed pillars, and unconventional room shapes—forced occupants to become active and creative dwellers. "The absence of preexisting referents to the dwelling practice," in the words of the sociologists, was "exactly what allowed (and obliged) inhabitants to create or reconstitute their own referents for organizing their apartment and the life inside it, because the a-normal shaping of the space and its complexity did not induce a single predefined orientation for its interior fittings and use."[113] Despite the fact that many of the units were rental social housing, the occupants' profiles did not fit those of the average beneficiary. Many, even if they did not characterize themselves as having an "alternative" lifestyle, had higher than average cultural capital, in Pierre

Figure 7.22. Conceptual model of the renovation project of the urban center of Ivry by Jean Renaudie, 1969–81. From *Techniques et architecture* 34, no. 6 (1972): 79.

Bourdieu's terms. Like other experiments in flexible dwelling, Renaudie's complex design resulted in social housing of the highest cost bracket and thus a different target group.

Évry and Ivry were exemplary, but far from unique. Many similar projects were constructed under the aegis of the Plan Construction. Some resulted from architecture competitions, for instance, the housing project Pont-de-Bois for the *ville nouvelle* of Lille-Est by Alexis Josic (Figure 7.24).[114] Yet the majority of built projects was more conventional, less ambitious in scale, and did not always pay attention to the provision of collective amenities. Idiosyncratic in form, but less convincing in plan, was the honeycomb project by Dominique Beau, Laszlo Feber, and Michel Orluc (Plate 21).[115] The 1974 "Modèle innovation" prototype "Eurydice," by the architectural firm Bouchez, Morax, and Montès proposed a linear assembly of modules into linear blocks—a juxtaposition and superposition of maisonettes separated by a central

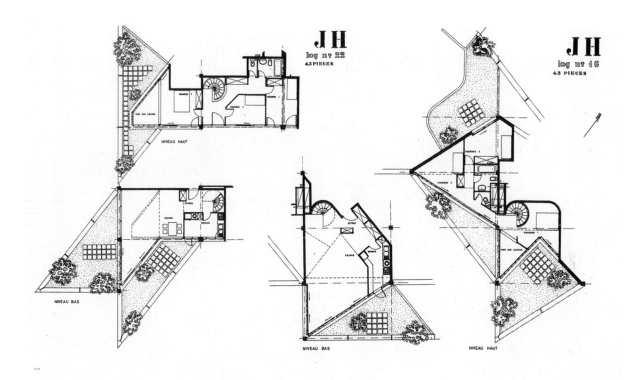

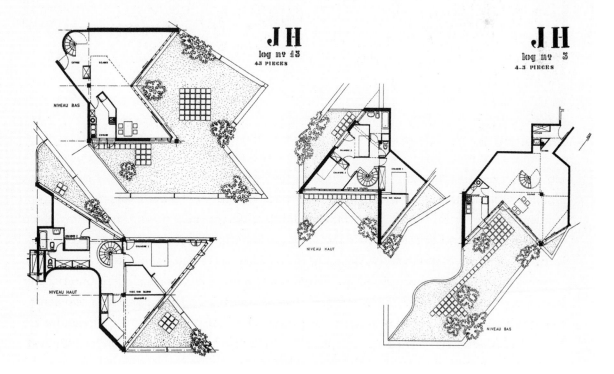

Figure 7.23. Various apartment plans of "Jean Hachette" project, Ivry, by Jean Renaudie. Courtesy of Serge Renaudie.

Figure 7.24. Model of housing project for Pont-de-Bois (Lille-Est) by Alexis Josic, 1973. From *Architecture française* 391 (1975): 58.

pedestrianized mall (Figure 7.25). With its intermediary floors and transversal units, the project offered dwellings reminiscent of Victorian terraced housing. Its units either had a sunken garden or a roof deck, extending the private realm to the outdoors. Such new housing typologies were akin to those developed at this time in Britain, particularly by Camden Council architects such as Neave Brown, and in New York City by the Urban Development Corporation under Edward Logue.[116] Despite their different contexts and constraints, these government-sponsored projects were united by the ambition to marry the advantages of collective housing provision with the virtues of the middle-class single-family home.

That ambition was short-lived but nevertheless spawned unprecedented typological and formal innovation. Whether interpreted as stacked housing units, maisonettes, semicollective, or semiurban housing, the concept of *habitat intermédiaire* was extremely productive for French housing design during the 1970s, in both qualitative and quantitative terms. Such enthusiasm was quickly curbed. The hopes of intermediary housing had already proven idle by the end of the decade: in the end, French middle-class home buyers literally did not buy

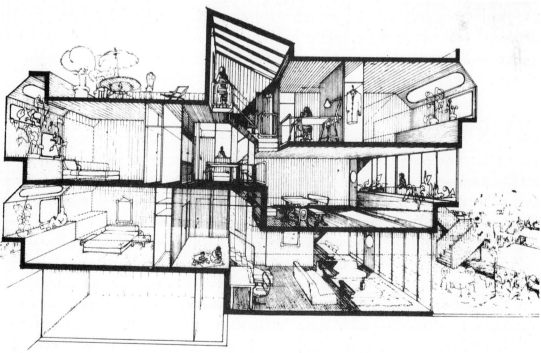

Figure 7.25. "Eurydice" project by Bouchez, Morax, and Montès, 1974. Fonds DAU. Service interministériel des Archives de France/Cité de l'architecture et du patrimoine/Archives d'architecture du XXᵉ siècle.

the concept. The private roof terraces were not enough to compensate for the absence of a basement or an attic, and despite all the promises, interior spaces often did not veer far from conventional apartment types. In a 1978 government report, the architect Christian Moley wrote that "the inhabitants of intermediary dwellings experience these as a second-best compared to the dream of the individual home. For them, this type of dwelling is good collective housing, but collective nevertheless."[117] These projects were ultimately not more than a stepping-stone to the single-family home—the annual production of which already exceeded that of collective housing at mid-decade.

Nevertheless, *habitat intermédiaire*—in particular the interspersing of suburban middle-class condos—brought significant novelty to French housing production. Despite being a product of far-reaching state intervention, this alternative housing type also marked an ideological shift toward liberalized consumption in the realm of dwelling—and thus a shift away from public housing. Yet its at times lofty sociological motivations did not entirely divorce it from the economic rationale of mass housing. In the words of the architect Jacques Bardet, who had built one of the first such projects at Val d'Yerres, such intermediary forms of dwelling were new in that they combined "the technical advantages of prefabrication, the economies proper to collective housing, and the independence attached to individual homes."[118] The economic rationale was to increase density and lower the cost of construction while creating a more desirable product. To state administrators, *habitat intermédiaire* was a way to expand housing choices for French consumers without giving in to the *pavillon* altogether. Under the influence of the centralized government, developers thus created what was effectively the last generation of mass housing projects. These were "projects" in disguise, in between housing and home.

Out of the Project

The housing projects of Le Vaudreuil, Les Marelles, Évry, and Ivry were only the tip of the iceberg: they represented a more widespread production of the built environment in 1970s France. The alternative industrialization of housing—so enthusiastically pursued in the late 1960s and throughout the 1970s—generated a new layer of urbanization of which traces can still be found all over France. More than just imitations of a few iconic designs, these projects made up a particular culture of building and dwelling. Complex volumes of stacked units, hexagonal prisms and pyramids, large terraces and roof decks, elaborate footprints, industrialized and prefabricated construction, architectural flexibility and modularity, inhabitant consultation and participation—all of these worked together as signifiers of a renewed social project for housing. Architects were particularly quick in asserting such principles as carriers of an emancipation of dwelling and a shift in power from producers to users and consumers. Social scientists, who in their postoccupancy studies monitored inhabitants and the spatial transformations of their dwellings, remained more ambivalent about whether these projects actually achieved such a transfer. Their work occurred in part under the aegis of the state and its many programs and agencies. But private builders and developers were in many cases equally keen to build alternative housing projects, because in their view they corresponded well "to the aspirations, needs, and habits of a clientele coming largely from collective housing blocks in urban areas."[119] The resulting housing projects were thus not just meant to emancipate their occupants but also to benefit developers and builders.[120] Soon after 1968, popular social concerns appeared to converge all too well with economic profitability. Whether the alternative housing types of the 1970s were a means for government to make mass housing work against the odds, for developers to make more money by targeting new consumers, or for inhabitants to have more of a say in how they lived, was a question that remained in many cases unresolved.

In opposition to the standardized cells of the first *grands ensembles*, the architectural diversification of housing in the 1970s was nevertheless the expression of a fundamental shift: housing was increasingly recognized as a highly complex lifestyle product of its distinguishing consumers rather than a mass provision for rights-bearing citizens. And yet, many alternative housing typologies were still a product of the same regime of mass production responsible for the first *grands ensembles*. This was the fundamental ambiguity shaping architectural and social experimentation during the 1970s. The social problematization of the *grands ensembles* had often been correlated with an aesthetic critique—monotony, repetition, scale, mathematical rigor, and emptiness—and this conflation of architectural aesthetics and social agency was at the core of the experiments. The resulting *architecture proliférante*, as Moley termed it, was ultimately as intense as it was short-lived.[121] The signs of change were already setting in at mid-decade, and by the end of the 1970s critics dismissed these projects as the final gasp of a naive but now decayed modernism.

The social project of mass housing was soon deflated. The slowdown of public investment and the reduction in scale of housing projects made such complex experiments simply unviable. After the economic downturn of the mid-1970s, the shift toward smaller development projects that could respond more flexibly to economic conjunctures called for a different material organization and a different architectural form.[122] But equally important was the agency of individual families to get housing through the market rather than the state. General discontent with mass housing projects now united groups as disparate as French economic liberals rallying against direct state intervention, leftist sociologists decrying segregation, young French architects denouncing mainstream modernism, activists fighting for direct participation in housing design, and much of the general public who codified them as places for the poor.

Industrialization—at least in the way modern architects had envisioned it—was increasingly recognized as a failure by officials and citizens alike. Economic downturn had caused a dramatic cut in the scale of construction sites and consequently a return to more traditional building techniques. Expensive, investment-heavy experimentation was the obvious first victim. The single-family home, by contrast, proved to be remarkably recession-proof: its economic flexibility was in reality far superior to the architectural flexibility of collective housing.[123] Sociological expertise, which had been the lionized corollary of architectural form-making and open industrialization, proved equally disappointing. After the intense cross-fertilization of architecture and urbanism with sociology in the period from the mid-1960s to the mid-1970s, the love affair was clearly over. Hopes had been too high perhaps, and there was a general feeling of disappointment about the role to which sociology had aspired in rejuvenating architecture and redeeming the societal position of the architect.[124] Sociologists—together with their calls for complicated participatory processes—would increasingly be cast as an obstruction to innovative design rather than an inspiration.

Despite their attention to urban form and collective space, the bulk of housing projects during the 1970s remained isolated from their context—Renaudie's Ivry being a rare exception. The existing site and surroundings of experimental housing projects mattered little to the policy makers in their Parisian offices. This would become an obvious critique by the end of the decade, when a new paradigm arose that explicitly revolved around place, context, and the historic city. Despite the rhetoric of *architecture proliférante*, it was the emergence of neo-traditionalism at mid-decade that would define the periodization of architectural history.[125] This was a break not only with modernism, but also with state programs and universal models. Instead, urban morphology, architectural type, symbolism, tradition, historicity, and the restoration of urban fabric became central concerns. They were especially hailed by a new set of actors entering the scene: a younger generation, trained at the reformed pedagogical units that had been established after the implosion of the Beaux-Arts.[126] Already in 1975, critical observers like Édith Girard vehemently dismissed the architectural experiments in the wake of 1968 as pretexts to further ignore the real socioeconomic issues of the French city:

> The bourgeoisie continues to reclaim the center of cities, the workers to be deported to the periphery in ZUP where people are among themselves, well delimited by the "functional" traffic system. There, what awaits you is "integration," "the re-created," the "past recovered in the architecture of tomorrow." While they gut the old city, where profitability and power demand replacement, they re-create—the way a "steak is reconstituted" (Baudrillard)—the past, the diversity, the continuity, the animated, the human, the power to the user by means of flexibility, and so on, in the ZUP. . . . Strict functionalism is renounced, laid aside the architecture and the urbanism by the proponents of flexibility. But is their problematic not fundamentally similar?[127]

At the cusp of what would become the "urban architecture" of French postmodernism, the denunciations were drenched in neo-Marxist theory, as propagated by French intellectuals such as Jean Baudrillard and institutionalized in government-sponsored research cells such as the Centre de sociologie urbaine. Some such critics went so far as to dismiss the government's ambition of expanding housing choice as just another way for capital to create surplus value. But these one-sided critiques were often contradicted by a more complex reality. Giving inhabitants "what they want" within the strict bounds of a production regime already set by the centralized state ultimately failed to stop the great leap forward of the single-family home—a result of the new capitalist development par excellence. Nor did it stop the residential mobility patterns as a result of which many collective housing projects moved in a downward spiral.

CONCLUSION

WHERE IS THE
SOCIAL PROJECT?

O N OCTOBER 27, 2005, TWO FRENCH YOUTHS of Tunisian and Malian descent
were electrocuted as they tried to escape from the police in the Parisian suburb of
Clichy-sous-Bois. Over the following three weeks, riots broke out in hundreds of
neighborhoods across the country and abroad. Journalists and observers related the widespread violence directly to the drab concrete housing estates, which often formed the back-
drop in images of burning cars and youths throwing Molotov cocktails. While the sheer
amount of media attention was unprecedented, the suburban riots themselves were not. Violent incidents and rioting had taken place in modern housing areas since the late 1970s, and
the "hot summer" of 1981 at les Minguettes in the suburbs of Lyon was the first to receive
national media coverage. Since then, postwar housing estates have increasingly appeared in
the popular imagination as no-go zones arrested by intractable violence, poverty, and crime.
At the same time, France's postcolonial youth have recast them both as the crucible of fran-
cophone hip-hop culture and as the symbol of their persistent exclusion from French society.
But media in fact shaped the public life of these areas from the very moment they were built.
In the late 1950s already, when newspapers reported the ecstasy of many French families at
the sight of their fully equipped bathrooms and kitchens, some journalists dismissed the new
projects as "rabbit cages" and "silos for people." During the 1960s, housing estates were the
proud face of modern France to some and the equivalent of a concentration camp to others.
While the content of media representation diverged and fluctuated, its historical role was more
consistent. Over three decades of construction, national and local media reportage not only
shaped the popular imagination but also prompted, if indirectly, small and large amendments
in policy and design.

These changes culminated in the mid-1970s, at the end of France's postwar economic growth. The architectural and social ambitions that had guided the country's frenzied urbanization over the previous decades were fundamentally questioned as citizens increasingly voiced concerns over segregation, the environment, and their "quality of life" more generally. This buzzword, which had become politically charged in the wake of May 1968, had gradually filtered into French state planning, architectural culture, and urban policy during the 1970s.[1] And so had calls for participation. By mid-decade, architecture and urbanism journals were flooded with articles and op-ed pieces on the topic. Even champions of 1960s technocratic futurism, such as Michel Ragon, turned into advocates for participation and the "democratization of architecture."[2] The planning process with local inhabitants in the renovation of Alma-Gare, a working-class neighborhood in Roubaix, was celebrated as a model, and the participatory housing designs of Lucien Kroll across the border in Brussels became a staple reference for architects.[3] In 1976, the involvement of local associations in planning was officially written into French law.[4] As elsewhere in Europe, participation was institutionalized and has been ever since.

The moment when participation reigned supreme was also the moment when the social project of architecture fell into crisis. With the end of three decades of state-led modernization for which it had been a primary ally, modern architecture lost much of its aura in the organization of social life. It no longer supplied the principles of urban development and ceased to act as a primary platform for the expertise of dwelling. While participation in the 1960s could still serve the utopian projects of late modernism, a decade later it had become nothing more than a palliative to earlier mistakes—a Band-Aid for modernism's crimes against the city—or worse, a convenient corollary of neoliberal urban development. Turning inhabitants into active participants now meant a shift of direct responsibility away from the centralized state, whose provisions even state administrators no longer considered superior to that of the market. Housing policy was instrumental in this shift, by replacing what was called "aide à la pierre"—direct support through housing construction—with "aide à la personne" and the further encouragement of individual homeownership.[5] In his work on governmentality written during this period, Michel Foucault pointed out that this seeming retreat of the state amounted to its restructuring.[6] With the decline of state-led housing provision, and its corollary of a universal recipient without history or memory, emerged a new regime of development. No longer reliant on an urbanism of national standards and models, it aligned notions of locality and self-responsibility with market-led home building. Consequently, the new, privately developed suburbs boomed while collective housing busted. Single-family home construction in France rose between 1970 and 1980 from around 200,000 units annually to nearly 300,000, while the production of collective housing declined from over 300,000 to less than 150,000 in the same decade.[7] The new era was that of the single-family home, whose industry largely bypassed the discipline and profession of architecture.

Modern architecture seemed no longer necessary. Its social project became a social problem. With the vilification of architectural modernism and state-led modernization, the social lost ground as a positive force for the organization of space. It remained a guiding imaginary, but an increasingly negative one. Social problems in France—rising poverty and unemployment at the end of three decades of phenomenal economic growth—were increasingly anchored to a particular type of space: the modern housing estates that were gradually becoming home to the immigrant poor. French social scientists and government experts played a crucial role in this process of stigmatization.[8] But the situation was not unique to France. By the mid-1970s, high-rise publicly funded housing was almost uniformly rejected across Europe and the United States. American public housing, which had been more controversial and often suffered from underfunding and a chronic lack of maintenance, was especially the subject of condemnation. The architect and planner Oscar Newman turned this into his career by harnessing an old belief in environmental determinism to "solve" public housing problems by design. His study of American public housing projects argued that their inherent material qualities and physical layout inculcated not community or social encounter, but instead violence and crime. The solution of what he called "defensible space" seemed so promising that his theories became accepted as fact and shaped policies all over the world—including in France, where the rehabilitation of housing estates came to be focused on privatizing its public spaces, a strategy known as *résidentialisation*.[9] Alice Coleman, one of Newman's fervent followers, became Margaret Thatcher's right hand in the radical reversal of British housing policy and organized massive amounts of social housing, which had similarly suffered from a downward spiral of residential mobility and lack of maintenance, to be privatized.

The turn, first against high-rise subsidized housing and then publicly funded housing altogether, fundamentally affected the discipline of architecture in Europe and the United States. Architects often found themselves peculiarly liberated after their profession was severed from a social project defined to a large extent by exterior forces. In the postwar decades, modern architecture had been much more than just an architects' cause; it had also been the working material of government officials, financiers, developers, engineers, inhabitant associations, social scientists, and many others. Architecture could now finally think of itself in explicitly *political* terms, some architects argued. And being critical or political was explicitly *not* to participate in the compromised real-world politics of building and planning controlled by capital. After the social project, the new dominion of architecture was that of critique. Despite the enduring conviction, even today, that radical critique (often accompanied by formal innovation) can only thrive when architecture is autonomous from social projects and concerns, the real terrain of architecture was a lot more murky. While architectural discourse in elite American universities shifted toward such disengagement shortly after the politicization triggered by civil rights movements in the 1960s, the emergence of postmodernism in Europe certainly suspends any easy judgment that architecture retreated from the social in subsequent decades. French architects in particular continued to work with state bureaucracies during the 1980s and onward, but their involvement shifted. No longer agents of national modernization, they were more often called on to interpret contemporary urban issues and rehabilitate the projects built by a previous generation.[10]

In France and across Europe, architectural postmodernism certainly opened exciting new terrains for thought while the stream of commissions for mass housing projects dwindled. But the French government did not immediately give up on building housing altogether, and neither did French architects. The *villes nouvelles* remained a fertile territory of experimentation over the decades to come as political culture embraced the arrival of architectural postmodernism.[11] Many state administrators and architects were quick to shore up their political and aesthetic orientations by vilifying modernism. *Pars pro toto* for decades of modern architecture, the Athens Charter became the enemy of the state. For President Giscard d'Estaing, the current state of architecture had been "in a global crisis since the 1950s."[12] Its principal cause was the loss of a sense of urbanity in the process of rapid urbanization and economic development of postwar France. Architectural postmodernism thus came in as the savior of urbanity. Neotraditionalist styles and forms were cast as part of a new urbanism—soon to be the New Urbanism, after transatlantic travel and the suburbanization of its concepts. In France, however, the primary ingredients of the new "urban art" of building were the morphology and typology of the historic city. The publication in 1977 of *Formes urbaines: De l'îlot à la barre*, in which the authors Philippe Panerai, Jean Castex, and Jean-Charles Depaule rehabilitated the traditional perimeter block as the basis for city building, symbolized the definitive denunciation of architectural modernism and the return to traditional urban form.[13]

In the process of effacing and reordering, this kind of postmodernism relegated the content of architecture's social project to its visual communication. The housing projects of Ricardo Bofill in French New Towns, such as Les Espaces d'Abraxas in Marne-la-Vallée, epitomize that shift (Figure C.1). The idea of using classical themes to create a "palace for the people" was not unlike the socialist architecture of Berlin's Stalinallee. And, like the monumental modernist housing slabs of Haut-du-Lièvre and La Duchère (see Figures 1.18 and 1.19), which meant to evoke a new "Versailles" for the average Frenchman, Bofill's was an architecture that aimed to represent the grandeur of collectivity. Similarly to its modernist predecessors, the project did not engage with the existing context and employed standardized prefabricated concrete elements to create an expressive facade. In other words, only its stylistic expression was directly opposite to that of an earlier modernism.

Figure C.1. Les Espaces d'Abraxas, Marne-la-Vallée, by the architect Ricardo Bofill. Raymon Publisher. Courtesy of David Liaudet.

A comparable move was articulated at the level of national politics, where an older political concept was conveniently realigned with the style of the day. Despite its origins in the *grands ensembles*, participation was discursively transformed into a panacea for the city's recovery from the violent interventions of modernism. The renovations and demolitions of modern housing, which began in the late 1970s, only strengthened this newly invented opposition between a now-reviled modernism and a participatory urbanism (Figure C.2). The role of the architect, newly stipulated in a 1977 law, was to respond to the "profound needs" of inhabitants and to become a "mediator" of their aspirations.[14] How fundamentally similar that task was understood by professionals and policy makers two decades earlier went unnoticed. The new postmodern cladding of French mass housing projects concealed not only the modern apartments behind it but also the social project of modern architecture at large. It effaced the complexity of three decades of experimentation, as much as it hid the unfulfilled promises and potential pitfalls of participation.

Figure C.2. The demolition of one of the towers at les Minguettes in 1977. Corbis Images. Photographed by Armel Brucelle.

To excavate that history has been the premise of this book. Contrary to the prevailing idea that the postwar urbanization of France was based on a single doctrine or an unchanging culture of architectural modernism, the study has demonstrated its fundamentally experimental nature. A changing network of professionals and experts from a variety of fields not only produced buildings and projects, but also scrutinized the life of what was built. The process of feedback between these realms—in which the social sciences played a preeminent role of mediation with the state as central platform—shaped the course of modern architecture, and with it that of the French suburbs. Sociology was more to architecture than just the provider of an imaginary or a fondness for social critique. While it proved impossible to fully instrumentalize sociological knowledge in architectural design, sociologists did provide architects with a productive entryway into the unknowable universe of architecture's reception, use, consumption, and change—in short, its social life. Despite being recast as harbingers of a novel mind-set, theoretical notions such as the production of space or the everyday are in fact in direct dialogue with postwar modernism, and accompanied rather than succeeded the rapid urbanization and state-led modernization of postwar France. But if there was one concept that allowed French architects and planners to address—but not necessarily access—this universe beyond the controllable process of design, it was that of the user. Originating in the social abstractions of the welfare state, that figure transformed with rapid urbanization, expanding social welfare, and a burgeoning consumer culture. As it evolved from a passive beneficiary of standard provisions to a creative consumer and participant, the user became a register for the increasing contradiction between state-led and market-based urban development.[15]

This study is not meant to redeem France's bureaucratic regime. The "good intentions" of many of the planners, social scientists, architects, and bureaucrats in this story are in no way apologies for, nor do they completely explain, the devastating reality of poverty and segregation in the resulting built environments today. In fact, an important aim of this study has been to counter the contemporary tendency of handing out easy blame. It has done so by moving away from a priori suspicion about the intentions of usual suspects, be they government officials or modern architects. By showing the complexity of actions and actors, and the contingent rather than determined nature of this history, the study demonstrates how much deeper the contemporary problems of suburban France cut than is usually assumed. They are a collective responsibility today and cannot be relegated to past "mistakes."

In the same way, this study neither redeems authoritarian modernism nor serves to denounce the promises of participatory planning. Instead of answering directly to the overwhelming rhetoric and critique, I place them in their larger historical context. That allows the study to examine the architectural making of postwar France beyond the master narrative of authoritarian imposition and reactive contestation. While architectural and urban historians have over the past decades begun to revise the canonical understanding of postwar modernism, one fundamental assumption has remained surprisingly intact: that of the opposition between "top-down" and "bottom-up." What seemed intuitively logical was the way in which participation breaks with the technocratic nature of modernist architecture and planning. But, as this study has shown, this shift entailed the development of sociological expertise and thus continuing involvement of experts. Seemingly opposed to technocracy—the belief that technology is independent from politics and can make it redundant by offering a neutral tool in policy making—participation is in fact part of a sociotechnical regime that fundamentally confounds clear opposition between expertise and emancipation, between top-down and bottom-up, and between architectural form-making and social engagement.

While the intellectual and practical terrains of architecture and urbanism have since shifted, many of these same tensions still haunt contemporary practice.[16] In the last decade or two, a range of user-oriented, participatory, and activist practices have emerged as the self-proclaimed inheritors of architecture's social project. From Architecture for Humanity's aid in poor and disaster-struck regions to temporary urban interventions—celebrated in exhibitions such as San Francisco's *DIY Urbanism* and Montreal's *Actions: What You Can Do with the City*—these vibrant subcultures of architecture not only blur disciplinary boundaries; they also operate without—and often explicitly reject—governments as sponsors or interlocutors.[17] Their protagonists help design user-driven mapping tools, build shelters in Burma, reclaim the streets of Seville, guerrilla-garden in London, and study the favelas of Rio de Janeiro. Privileging self-organization, activism, and alterity over what is perceived as a dominant culture of architectural formalism and celebrity, they aim to expand design from the manipulation of form and material to the development of procedures and the creation of models of engagement.[18] The fault line it revealed, between architecture as social process and architecture as formal object, profoundly shapes current debates.

If this distinction only became a disciplinary rift over the last decades, it is remarkable how much of architecture's activist subculture today is founded on the same theories and critiques that emerged during the heyday of postwar modernism and modernization. The work of Henri Lefebvre is only the tip of this theoretical iceberg. In the Anglo-American reception of this work—especially since the 1991 English translation *The Production of Space*—the concepts of the everyday, the right to the city, and the production of space have often been harnessed as harbingers of a novel mind-set.[19] This process of reinscription has been gradual and multilayered. Even when Michel de Certeau published *L'invention du quotidien* in 1980, its title ignored the fact that ever since Lefebvre's 1947 *Critique de la vie quotidienne*, the everyday had been a domain of investigation for postwar intellectuals.[20] De Certeau's interpretation privileged spatial practice over built form and the creative agency of consumption as production over that of another "controlling" production. This rendering effaced the everyday as a theoretical concept that accompanied rather than succeeded the rapid urbanization and state-led modernization of postwar France.[21] The preceding chapters of this book reveal instead that social critiques of urbanization—including Lefebvre's theories and the work of the Situationists in the 1950s—were quickly institutionalized by the bureaucratic state and selectively co-opted by entrepreneurs and corporations.[22] Not unexpectedly, then, they were also harnessed by architects in the service of, and against, both state and capital.

The fact that such critiques now guide architectural practices that privilege small-scale, provisional, and fringe actions over government-led intervention, mainstream building, and mass housing might speak not so much to an expansion of architecture's purview as to its retraction. A crucial weakness of many activist architectural practices today is not that they are divorced from the conventional tools of design but that they are often limited to demonstration projects and thus rarely sustain new forms of life. This they share with the dominant culture of architecture that they claim to explicitly reject: if architectural formalism can be easily dismissed for its fetishization of intentionality through authorship, architectural activism often falls victim to the same temptation, even if the intentions are political rather than formal. Not surprisingly, the debate changes fundamentally in tone when the focus shifts away from judging the effects rather than the intentions of such projects. Some of them, despite their benevolent rhetoric and good intentions, are increasingly criticized for being vehicles of a new "humanitarian imperialism" or engendering urban gentrification. Meanwhile, neither the formalist nor the activist agenda has yet been able to address where exactly architecture can stand against the larger forces that shape the built environment today.

Mass housing, New Towns, and other large-scale urban developments are by no means conditions of the past. Only architecture seems to have shifted to the sidelines now. And while that sideline itself has become subject to increasing scrutiny, the sweeping urbanization of large parts of the world with sectors of mass housing continues to go underexplored. Recent architectural history—which has similarly privileged radical practices and unbuilt work over mainstream building—has done little to counter this dominant tendency to revel in the margins. Just as the social ambitions of modernism did not exist in a vacuum—but were intimately tied to national economic development, liberal capitalism, technocracy, social democracy, and the welfare state—we have to ask what the broader regime of production and consumption is that shapes architecture today.

During the midcentury decades of what contemporary observers—often pejoratively—call bureaucratic modernism, architecture not only belonged to architects: its social project was enmeshed with a range of institutions and collectives at different levels, from the local inhabitant associations of new housing estates to the centralized state and the international nongovernmental institutions of the Cold War. Now, in contrast, the architect appears to stand alone. That is the case for star architects, behind whom are hidden not just droves of hardworking interns but an entire network of media and other institutions that support their existence. But it is also true for the contemporary "critical practitioner," a figure in which dissent and entrepreneurship have become indistinguishable. If architecture's horizons shift with such paradigms, reimagining its social role and responsibility requires a critical understanding of architecture's production as much as its consumption, and thus its failures as much as its successes.

An analysis of the social project of architecture today therefore can no longer remain within the realms of intent, form, or representation—at least without tying these to consequence and effect. And that means taking the messiness of materiality more seriously. The call to judge architecture on what it does rather than how it represents is commonplace in architectural culture and yet it is rarely taken up. In some ways, this mirrors the recent calls within a wide range of humanities and social science for a renewed materialism. That trend should logically find fertile ground in architecture: it is hard to imagine a discipline traditionally better placed to think through issues of materiality and their social and human repercussions. And yet, architecture's materialism is often as idealistic as the type of reductive Marxism that Bruno Latour so cogently dismisses in his recent work.[23] The tendency within the academy to treat architecture discursively—as a means to argue—does not always prove useful for gauging its social importance. Architecture is too often understood as a realm of forms merely representing the social, rather than as a process of production that takes place in a larger social world and also helps shape that world. Shifting the lens thus means reconnecting architectural production—in the widest possible sense: design, policy, construction—with its consumption and use.

The direct equivalence of politics with form—perpetuated by an alliance between practitioners and theorists during the 1990s—has largely been discredited.[24] But its withering has only laid bare an older and more fundamental fallacy of architectural theory, whose basic assumption is that of *pars pro toto*: singular works of architecture illuminate the contemporary condition to such extent that the larger production of the built environment is but a footnote of similitude. Such a lens freezes the complex social materiality of building into ideology and representation. It comes as no surprise, then, that the history of mass housing has been relegated to the critique of a symbol—whether it be a vehicle of social progress or a symptom of state control. Yet the complex causes and effects that make up this kind of architecture trouble any such a priori categorizations. Sound insulation and maintenance budgets have been architectural determinants of social success or failure, perhaps more than the layout of rooms or the aesthetics of the facade. The architectural history you have just waded through employs such an empirically attuned lens to reveal the complexity of the built environment. Breaking with the current devotion to the discursively radical or the formally progressive, it has analyzed architecture not as an image of the political, but as part of a more complex process in which design matters as much as the various actors actually producing and consuming it.

A final implication of this study, then, lies in the nature of architectural knowledge. For much of the profession today, attributing a social role to architecture is nothing but a hollow gesture, which seems simply naive if not disingenuous. It is no longer commonly accepted that architects should have legitimate expertise in the realms of housing, dwelling, or everyday life in its most mundane forms. Such knowledge, which used to be squarely situated in the field of architecture, is now cause for disciplinary anxiety. Yet the persistent conviction that engaging other forms of knowledge threatens the discipline of architecture does not hold up against its history—nor contemporary practice, for that matter. Over the course of the twentieth century, architectural knowledge was not a closed realm internal to a single discipline; its vitality depended on the way architecture engaged with foreign domains of knowledge—in the case of this study, the social sciences. Experimentation could thus include not only form, process, and production, but also reception and use. The development of strategies for social engagement in architecture today cannot be imagined without such an expanded realm of architectural knowledge. Concomitantly, an expanded architectural history—of which this book is but an episode—could play a crucial role, once again, in our understanding of architecture's situated agency and thus its social project today.

NOTES

Archival Sources

Archives nationales, Centre des archives contemporaines, Fontainebleau (CAC)
Archives nationales, Paris, Fonds École nationale supérieure des Beaux-Arts (AN ENSBA)
Centre d'archives d'architecture du XXe siècle, Institut français d'architecture, Paris (CAA)
Caisse des dépôts, Fonds Société centrale immobilière de la Caisse, Paris (CDC/SCIC)
Archives départementales du Val d'Oise (AD Val d'Oise)
Archives départementales de l'Essonne (AD Essonne)
Archives municipales de Sarcelles (AM Sarcelles)
Maison du patrimoine de Sarcelles (MP Sarcelles)
Archives municipales de Grenoble (AM Grenoble)
Private archives of COFREMCA, now called Socio-vision (COFREMCA)

Library Collections

Bibliothèque nationale de France (BNF)
Centre de documentation de l'urbanisme (CDU)
Sciences-Po, Dossiers de presse: Villes nouvelles (SP)
Harvard Loeb Library: Vertical Files (Loeb)
Bibliothèque universitaire Paris V-Descartes, Sciences humaines et sociales (SHS)
Institut national de l'audiovisuel (INA)

Introduction

1. At the time of writing, a part of these archives in Fontainebleau were planned to be moved to a new archival complex designed by Massimiliano and Doriana Fuksas, located in Pierrefitte, another suburb of Paris.

2. Manuel Castells, *The City and the Grassroots: A Cross-Cultural Theory of Urban Social Movements* (Berkeley: University of California Press, 1983), 75.

3. Charles Jencks, *The Language of Postmodern Architecture* (New York: Rizzoli, 1977). For a historical analysis, see Katharine G. Bristol, "The Pruitt-Igoe Myth," *Journal of Architectural Education* 44, no. 3 (1991): 163–71.

4. Despite this exclusion, there are some groundbreaking histories of postwar mass housing and New Towns, such as Bruno-Henri Vayssière, *Reconstruction, déconstruction: Le hard French, ou l'architecture française des trente glorieuses* (Paris: Picard, 1988); Miles Glendinning and Stefan Muthesius, *Tower Block: Modern Public Housing in England, Scotland, Wales, and Northern Ireland* (New Haven: Paul Mellon Centre for Studies in British Art/Yale University Press, 1994); Kimberly Elman Zarecor, *Manufacturing a Socialist Modernity: Housing in Czechoslovakia, 1945–1960* (Pittsburgh: University of Pittsburgh Press, 2011).

5. The term *trente glorieuses* was first coined by Jean Fourastié, *Les trente glorieuses, ou la révolution invisible de 1946 à 1975* (Paris: Fayard, 1979). On French modernization and its relation to national identity, see Herrick Chapman, "Modernity and National Identity in Postwar France," *French Historical Studies* 22, no. 2 (1999); Gabrielle Hecht, *The Radiance of France: Nuclear Power and National Identity after World War II* (Cambridge: MIT Press, 1998); Richard F. Kuisel, *Seducing the French: The Dilemma of Americanization* (Berkeley: University of California Press, 1993).

6. Viviane Claude speaks about "l'État urbaniste" between the 1940s and the 1980s in *Faire la ville: Les métiers de l'urbanisme au XXᵉ siècle* (Marseille: Parenthèses, 2006). In this study, I treat the French state not as a monolithic or coherent entity, but as a complex site composed of diverse and often-competing actors and institutions. For a historical account of intrastate competition and the complexity of state policy with regard to architecture, see Éric Lengereau, *L'État et l'architecture, 1958–1981: Une politique publique?* (Paris: Picard/Comité d'histoire du Ministère de la Culture, 2001).

7. See Jean-Claude Thoenig, *L'ère des technocrates: Le cas des Ponts et chaussées* (Paris: L'Harmattan, 1987).

8. Existing accounts have tended to explain postwar mass housing as a direct result of earlier forces and ideologies, from the Athens Charter and the technocratic movements of the 1930s to colonial experimentation or aerial photography. In doing so, they have failed to address their design and transformation *during the time they were actually built*.

9. This study thus contributes to the emerging literature on the history of public housing across the Atlantic, by shifting the question away from failure or success. For the United States, see, for instance, Bradford D. Hunt, *Blueprint for Disaster: The Unraveling of Chicago Public Housing* (Chicago: University of Chicago Press, 2010); Nicholas Dagen Bloom, *Public Housing That Worked: New York in the Twentieth Century* (Philadelphia: University of Pennsylvania Press, 2008).

10. Key scholarship on postwar architectural modernism includes Team 10, Max Risselada, and Dirk van den Heuvel, *Team 10: 1953–81, in Search of a Utopia of the Present* (Rotterdam: NAi, 2005); Tom Avermaete, *Another Modern: The Post-War Architecture and Urbanism of Candilis-Josic-Woods*

(Rotterdam: NAi, 2005). On the links of these groups with the construction of mass housing, see Bruno Fayolle Lussac and Rémi Papillault, *Le Team X et le logement collectif à grande échelle en Europe: Un retour critique des pratiques vers la théorie. Actes du séminaire européen, Toulouse 27–28 mai 2004* (Pessac: Maison des sciences de l'homme d'Aquitaine, 2008). Key scholarship in the urban history of postwar France includes Danièle Voldman, *La reconstruction des villes françaises de 1940 à 1954: Histoire d'une politique* (Paris: L'Harmattan, 1997); Rosemary Wakeman, *Modernizing the Provincial City: Toulouse, 1945–1975* (Cambridge: Harvard University Press, 1997); Christine Mengin, "La solution des grands ensembles," *Vingtième siècle. Revue d'histoire* 64 (1999): 105–11; François Tomas, Jean-Noël Blanc, and Mario Bonilla, *Les grands ensembles: Une histoire qui continue* (Saint-Étienne: Publications de l'Université de Saint-Étienne, 2003); Annie Fourcaut, "Les premiers grands ensembles en région parisienne: Ne pas refaire la banlieue?" *French Historical Studies* 27, no. 1 (2004): 195–218; Nicole Rudolph, "At Home in Postwar France: The Design and Construction of Domestic Space 1945–1975," Ph.D. dissertation, New York University, 2005; Annie Fourcaut and Loïc Vadelorge, eds., *Villes nouvelles et grands ensembles, Histoire urbaine*, no. 17 (2006); Thibault Tellier, *Le temps des HLM 1945–1975: La saga urbaine des Trente Glorieuses* (Paris: Autrement, 2007); Brian William Newsome, *French Urban Planning, 1940–1968: The Construction and Deconstruction of an Authoritarian System* (New York: Peter Lang, 2009); Rosemary Wakeman, *The Heroic City: Paris 1945–1958* (Chicago: University of Chicago Press, 2009); Gwenaëlle Le Goullon, "Les grands ensembles en France: Genèse d'une politique publique (1945–1962)," Ph.D. dissertation, Université de Paris 1-Panthéon-Sorbonne, 2010. The history of the *grands ensembles* in France is the subject of a research team led by Annie Fourcaut at the Centre d'histoire sociale in Paris. The history of the *villes nouvelles* has been the subject of a large-scale state-sponsored collective research project, the Programme interministériel d'histoire et d'évaluation des villes nouvelles. On the architecture of French postwar reconstruction, see Vayssière, *Reconstruction, déconstruction*; Nicholas Bullock, "Developing prototypes for France's mass housing programme, 1949–53," *Planning Perspectives* 22, no. 1 (2007): 5–28. On the relationship of postwar French urbanism to a longer intellectual history of territory, see Marc Desportes and Antoine Picon, *De l'espace au territoire: L'aménagement en France XVIᵉ–XXᵉ siècles* (Paris: Presses de l'École nationale des Ponts et chaussées, 1997). Finally, the histories of social science on which this study builds include Michel Amiot, *Contre l'État, les sociologues: Éléments pour une histoire de la sociologie urbaine en France, 1900–1980* (Paris: Éditions de l'École des hautes études en sciences sociales, 1986); Alain Drouard, *Le Développement des sciences sociales en France au tournant des années soixante* (Paris: Éditions du Centre national de la recherche scientifique/Institut d'histoire du temps présent, 1983); Alain Drouard, "Réflexions sur une chronologie: Le développement des sciences sociales en France de 1945 à la fin des années soixante," *Revue française de sociologie* 23, no. 1 (1982); Pierre Lassave, *Les sociologues et la recherche urbaine dans la France contemporaine* (Toulouse: Presses Universitaires du Mirail, 1997).

11. This study builds on recent scholarship that has begun to connect the histories of architecture, planning, and social science in postwar France: Łukasz Stanek, *Henri Lefebvre on Space: Architecture, Urban Research, and the Production of Theory* (Minneapolis: University of Minnesota Press, 2011); Jeanne Haffner, *The View from Above: The Science of Social Space* (Cambridge: MIT Press, 2013); Jean-Louis Violeau, *Les architectes et mai 68* (Paris: Éditions Recherches, 2005).

12. See Larry Busbea, *Topologies: The Urban Utopia in France, 1960–1970* (Cambridge: MIT Press, 2007); Simon Sadler, *The Situationist City* (Cambridge: MIT Press, 1998).

13. For Sweden, see Helena Mattsson and Sven-Olov Wallenstein, eds., *Swedish Modernism: Architecture, Consumption, and the Welfare State* (London: Black Dog, 2010). For Britain, see Nicholas Bullock, *Building the Post-War World: Modern Architecture and Reconstruction in Britain* (London: Routledge, 2002). See also Tom Avermaete and Dirk Van den Heuvel, eds., *The European Welfare State Project: Ideals, Politics, Cities, and Buildings, Footprint* 5, no. 2 (2011).

14. The dictionary took up the word in 1933. See *Le Petit Robert: Dictionnaire de la langue française* (Paris: Dictionnaires Le Robert, 1967).

15. Jean-Pierre Daviet placed the first origins of the notion well into the nineteenth century and showed that it was not only a matter of administrative law but was also shaped by socialist ideas. See Jean-Pierre Daviet, "Le service public et l'usager, entre le droit administratif et la philosophie politique (1873–1945)," in *Consommateur, usager, citoyen: Quel modèle de socialisation?*, ed. Chantal Horellou-Lafarge (Paris: L'Harmattan, 1996), 23–48.

16. See Michel Foucault's later work on biopolitics and governmentality, including *Sécurité, territoire, population* (Paris: Seuil, 2004).

17. Historians have described the development of the welfare state since the end of the nineteenth century, but it was the experience of World War II that laid the basis for the development of the comprehensive interventionism of welfare in postwar Europe. See Tony Judt, *Postwar: A History of Europe since 1945* (New York: Penguin Books, 2005), 362; Richard F. Kuisel, *Capitalism and the State in Modern France: Renovation and Economic Management in the Twentieth Century* (Cambridge and New York: Cambridge University Press, 1981); Stephen Padgett and William Paterson, *A History of Social Democracy in Postwar Europe* (London and New York: Longman, 1991), 141. For France in particular, see François Ewald, *L'État providence* (Paris: B. Grasset, 1986).

18. Kristen Ross has shown how modernization and decolonization are intimately linked in French postwar culture. See Kristin Ross, *Fast Cars, Clean Bodies: Decolonization and the Reordering of French Culture* (Cambridge: MIT Press, 1995).

19. Yet there was constant resistance to American influence. See Victoria de Grazia, *Irresistible Empire: America's Advance through Twentieth-Century Europe* (Cambridge: Belknap Press of Harvard University Press, 2005).

20. Lizabeth Cohen, *A Consumers' Republic: The Politics of Mass Consumption in Postwar America* (New York: Knopf, distributed by Random House, 2003), 8.

21. Henri Lefebvre uses the term "la société bureaucratique de consommation dirigée" in *La vie quotidienne dans le monde moderne* (Paris: Gallimard, 1968).

22. See Mark Solovey and Hamilton Cravens, eds., *Cold War Social Science: Knowledge Production, Liberal Democracy, and Human Nature* (New York: Palgrave Macmillan, 2012).

23. Michel Foucault, "La fonction politique de l'intellectuel," in *Dits et Écrits* (Paris: Gallimard, 1994), 109–14.

24. See, for instance, Gwendolyn Wright, *The Politics of Design in French Colonial Urbanism* (Chicago: University of Chicago Press, 1991).

25. See, for instance, Hecht, *The Radiance of France*; Jennifer S. Light, *From Warfare to Welfare: Defense Intellectuals and Urban Problems in Cold War America* (Baltimore: Johns Hopkins University Press, 2003).

26. See Antoine Picon, *Les saint-simoniens: Raison, imaginaire et utopie* (Paris: Belin, 2002).

27. This contrasts with Gabrielle Hecht's argument of a clear opposition between technocrats and humanists during the 1950s and 1960s. See Gabrielle Hecht, "Planning a Technological Nation: Systems Thinking and the Politics of National Identity in Postwar France," in *Systems, Experts and Computers: The Systems Approach in Management and Engineering*, ed. Agatha C. Hughes and Thomas P. Hughes (Cambridge: MIT Press, 2000), 138.

28. On the nature of expertise in French urbanism during this period, see Gilles Verpraet, *Les professionnels de l'urbanisme: Socio-histoire des systèmes professionnels de l'urbanisme* (Paris: Economica/Anthropos, 2005); Claude, *Faire la ville*; Gilles Massardier, *Expertise et aménagement du territoire: L'État savant* (Paris: L'Harmattan, 1996); Thoenig, *L'ère des technocrates*.

29. On the intellectual notion of the everyday, see Michael Sheringham, *Everyday Life: Theories and Practices from Surrealism to the Present* (Oxford: Oxford University Press, 2006). On Lefebvre's influence on architecture, see Stanek, *Henri Lefebvre on Space*.

30. In France, many of these have themselves been inspired by sociological studies such as Henri Coing, *Rénovation urbaine et changement social l'ilôt nº 4 (Paris 13ᵉ)* (Paris: Éditions ouvrières, 1966); Manuel Castells et al., *Crise du logement et mouvements sociaux urbains: Enquête sur la région parisienne* (Paris: Éditions de l'École des hautes études en sciences sociales, 1978).

31. Paul Rabinow, *French Modern: Norms and Forms of the Social Environment* (Cambridge: MIT Press, 1989).

32. See Tyler Stovall, "French Communism and Suburban Development: The Rise of the Paris Red Belt," *Journal of Contemporary History* 24, no. 3 (1985): 437–60; Annie Fourcaut, *Banlieue rouge 1920–1960: Années Thorez, années Gabin: Archétype du populaire, banc d'essai des modernités* (Paris: Autrement, 1992).

33. See Newsome, *French Urban Planning, 1940–1968*.

34. The phrase "sous les pavés, la plage" was one of the famous slogans of May 1968.

35. See Philip Nord, *France's New Deal: From the Thirties to the Postwar Era* (Princeton, N.J.: Princeton University Press, 2012); Wakeman, *The Heroic City*.

36. This argument has already been made for management techniques by Luc Boltanski and Eve Chiapello, *Le nouvel esprit du capitalisme* (Paris: Gallimard, 1999). See also the critiques of Jean Baudrillard, Guy Debord, and Henri Lefebvre, as well as the more popular cultural expressions of it in the work of Georges Perec and the films of Jacques Tati.

37. Jean-Pierre Dormois, *The French Economy in the Twentieth Century* (Cambridge: Cambridge University Press, 2004).

38. For a social-geographic account of this shift, see Jacques Barou, *La place du pauvre: Histoire et géographie sociale de l'habitat HLM* (Paris: L'Harmattan, 1992).

39. See Sylvie Tissot, *L'État et les quartiers: Genèse d'une catégorie de l'action publique* (Paris: Seuil, 2007).

1. Streamlining Production

1. Alain Girard, *Une enquête par sondages: Désirs des Français en matière d'habitation urbaine* (Paris: Presses Universitaires de France/INED, 1947), 11.

2. François Clanché and Anne-Marie Fribourg, "Évolution des politiques du logement," in *Loge-ment et habitat: L'état des savoirs,* ed. Marion Segaud, Catherine Bonvalet, and Jacques Brun (Paris: La Découverte, 1998), 85.

3. See *Annuaire rétrospectif de la France, Séries longues, 1948–1988* (Paris: INSEE, 1990). See also "Le financement de la construction, Ministère de la construction, 1962–63" (CAC 19910319/011).

4. The term *grand ensemble* was first used by Maurice Rotival in a 1935 article. It became domi-nant in the 1950s, but never completely replaced other terms such as *nouvel ensemble urbain, unité de voisinage, ville neuve, ville nouvelle, cité neuve,* and so on. See Maurice Rotival, "Les grands ensembles: Problème général et implantation des cités," *L'Architecture d'aujourd'hui* 1, no. 6 (1935): 57–72; Adrien Spinetta, "Les grands ensembles pensés pour l'homme," *L'Architecture d'aujourd'hui,* no. 46 (1953). On the vague definition of the *grand ensemble,* see Christine Mengin, "La solution des grands ensembles," *Vingtième siècle. Revue d'histoire* 64 (1999): 105–11; Annie Fourcaut and Loïc Vadelorge, eds., *Cahiers de l'IHTP (Institut d'histoire du temps présent),* no. 17, Villes nouvelles et grands ensembles (2006).

5. See Michel Lescure, *Histoire d'une filière: Immobilier et bâtiment en France, 1820–1980* (Paris: Hatier, 1982).

6. See Gérard Dupont, "Évolution de la construction et de l'urbanisme depuis 1950," *Urbanisme* 80 (Theme: Bilan et objectifs) (1963): 33.

7. See Voldman, *La reconstruction des villes françaises de 1940 à 1954.* Also, state planners were sur-prisingly discrete about housing; see Frédérique Boucher, "Les planificateurs et le logement (1942–1952)," *Cahiers de l'IHTP (Institut d'histoire du temps présent)* 5 (1985): 83–102.

8. Tony Judt, *Postwar: A History of Europe since 1945* (New York: Penguin Books, 2005), 67.

9. Anthony Sutcliffe, *An Economic and Social History of Western Europe since 1945* (London and New York: Longman, 1996), 40–52.

10. See Nord, *France's New Deal.* This argument goes back to Richard F. Kuisel, "Technocrats and Public Economic Policy: From the Third to the Fourth Republic," *Journal of European Economic His-tory* 2 (1973): 55–99. For an intellectual history of technocratic thought in France, see Rabinow, *French Modern.*

11. See Mary McLeod, "'Architecture of Revolution': Taylorism, Technocracy and Social Change," *Art Journal* 43, no. 2 (1983): 132–47.

12. See Cecil O. Smith, "The Longest Run: Public Engineers and Planning in France," *American Historical Review* 95 (1990): 657–92.

13. See Rémi Baudouï, *Raoul Dautry, 1880–1951: Le technocrate de la République,* Biographies (Paris: Balland, 1992).

14. The ministry was established from Vichy institutions such as the Commissariat technique à la reconstruction immobilière (CRI) and the Délégation générale à l'équipement national (DGEN), both of which were charged with reconstruction. See Voldman, *La reconstruction des villes françaises de 1940 à 1954;* Baudouï, *Raoul Dautry, 1880–1951.*

15. See Hecht, *The Radiance of France;* Hecht, "Planning a Technological Nation."

16. See Richard F. Kuisel, *Capitalism and the State in Modern France: Renovation and Economic Management in the Twentieth Century* (Cambridge and New York: Cambridge University Press, 1981), 255.

17. See Thoenig, *L'ère des technocrates.*

18. See Kuisel, *Capitalism and the State in Modern France*.

19. See Saul Estrin and Peter Holmes, *French Planning in Theory and Practice* (London and Boston: G. Allen & Unwin, 1983), 92; Hecht, "Planning a Technological Nation."

20. See Irwin M. Wall, *The United States and the Making of Postwar France, 1945–1954* (Cambridge and New York: Cambridge University Press, 1991), 182–83. Frédérique Boucher has shown that while the 1946 Monnet Plan allotted significant sums to reconstruction and housing construction, its subsequent revisions of 1948 and 1949 remained silent about these issues. See Boucher, "Les planificateurs et le logement (1942–1952)."

21. See Sutcliffe, *An Economic and Social History of Western Europe since 1945*, 48.

22. See Haffner, *The View from Above*.

23. Desportes and Picon, *De l'espace au territoire*.

24. Gabriel Dessus, Pierre George, and Jacques Weulersse, *Matériaux pour une géographie volontaire de l'industrie française* (Paris: Armand Colin, 1949).

25. Benoît Pouvreau, "La politique d'aménagement du territoire d'Eugène Claudius-Petit," *Vingtième siècle. Revue d'histoire*, no. 79 (2003): 43–52.

26. Jean-François Gravier, *Paris et le désert français* (Paris: Portulan, 1947).

27. Jean Labasse, *L'organisation de l'espace, éléments de géographie volontaire* (Paris: Hermann, 1966).

28. See my forthcoming article in Stephen Cairns and Jane M. Jacobs, eds., *Architecture/Geography: Inter-disciplining Space, Re-imagining Territory* (London: Routledge, 2014).

29. See chapter 5 in Sheila Crane, *Mediterranean Crossroads: Marseille and Modern Architecture* (Minneapolis: University of Minnesota Press, 2011).

30. See Voldman, *La reconstruction des villes françaises de 1940 à 1954*; Anatole Kopp, Frédérique Boucher, and Danièle Pauly, *L'architecture de la reconstruction en France, 1945–1953* (Paris: Le Moniteur, 1982).

31. Nicole Rudolph, "Domestic Politics: The Cité expérimentale at Noisy-le-Sec in Greater Paris," *Modern and Contemporary France* 12, no. 4 (2004): 483–95; *Petites maisons construites depuis la guerre: La cité expérimentale de Noisy-le-Sec* (Paris: Ch. Massin & Cie/Librairie Centrale des Beaux-Arts, 1951).

32. See Segaud, Bonvalet, and Brun, *Logement et habitat*, 227.

33. On Belgian postwar suburbanization, see Bruno De Meulder et al., "Sleutelen aan het Belgische stadslandschap," *Oase* 52 (1999): 78–113.

34. Levitt France was established in 1963, and their first project was finished in 1965. See Isabelle Gournay, "Levitt France et la banlieue à l'américaine: Premier bilan," *Histoire urbaine* 5 (2002): 167–88.

35. Ross, *Fast Cars, Clean Bodies*.

36. Fourcaut, "Les premiers grands ensembles en région parisienne."

37. Susanna Magri, "Le pavillon stigmatisé: Grands ensembles et maisons individuelles dans la sociologie des années 1950 à 1970," *L'année sociologique* 58, no. 1 (2008): 171–202.

38. See "Courses by André Gutton and Robert Auzelle" (AN ENSBA AJ/52/978).

39. See Kopp, Boucher, and Pauly, *L'architecture de la reconstruction en France, 1945–1953*.

40. On Le Corbusier at Saint-Dié, see Baudouï, *Raoul Dautry, 1880–1951*, 313–16.

41. See Le Goullon, "Les grands ensembles en France." See also Nicholas Bullock, "Developing Prototypes for France's Mass Housing Programme, 1949–53," *Planning Perspectives* 22, no. 1 (2007): 5–28.

42. On the history of this relationship, see Antoine Picon, *Architectes et ingénieurs au siècle des Lumières* (Marseille: Parenthèses, 1988).

43. Ernst Neufert, *Bauordnungslehre* (Berlin: Volk und Reich Verlag, 1943).

44. Dominique Barjot, "Industrie du bâtiment et logements populaires après 1945," in *Ouvriers en banlieue, XIXe–XXe siècle,* ed. Jacques Girault (Paris: Éditions de l'Atelier/Éditions ouvrières, 1998), 225. See also Yvan Delemontey, "Le béton assemblé: Formes et figures de la préfabrication en France, 1947–52," *Histoire urbaine* 3, no. 20 (2008): 15–38.

45. See Lescure, *Histoire d'une filière;* Dominique Barjot, "Introduction," in *Histoire des métiers du bâtiment aux XIXe et XXe siècles: Séminaire des 28, 29 et 30 novembre 1989 à la Fondation Royaumont,* ed. Jean-François Crola and André Guillerme (Paris: Plan Construction et Architecture, 1991): 9–37.

46. See A. M. Sarcelles, "Sarcelles ville nouvelle, SCIC, 1969" (AD Val d'Oise BIB D618).

47. See Lescure, *Histoire d'une filière,* 56.

48. The first shantytowns emerged in Nanterre in 1951. They were later studied by Monique Hervo. See Monique Hervo and Marie-Ange Charras, *Bidonvilles* (Paris: Maspero, 1971).

49. See Bruno Duriez and Michel Chauvière, eds., *Cahiers du GRMF (Groupement de recherche sur les mouvements familiaux),* no. 7, *La bataille des squatters et l'invention du droit au logement 1945–1955* (1992). See also Wakeman, *The Heroic City,* 138–45.

50. "Loi du 15 avril 1953 facilitant la construction de logements économiques," *Journal officiel de la République française* (April 16, 1953). See Annie Fourcaut, "Introduction," in *Faire l'histoire des grands ensembles: Bibliographie 1950–1980,* ed. Annie Fourcaut and Frédéric Dufaux (Lyon: Éditions ENS, 2003).

51. See Christine Tréboulet, *Habitat social et capitalisme: Les comités interprofessionnels du logement dans les rapports État/Patronnat* (Paris: L'Harmattan, 2001).

52. Roughly 120,000 homes were built in 1953 and 320,000 in 1959. See *Annuaire rétrospectif de la France, Séries longues, 1948–1988.*

53. See Gwenaëlle Le Goullon, "La politique des cités d'urgence 1954–1958," Master's thesis, University of Paris, 2000.

54. For an economic history of this category of housing production, established in 1950, see Sabine Effosse, *L'invention du logement aidé en France: L'immobilier au temps des Trente Glorieuses* (Paris: Comité pour l'histoire économique et financière de la France, 2003).

55. See Jean-Paul Flamand, *Loger le peuple: Essai sur l'histoire du logement social en France* (Paris: La Découverte, 1989), 201.

56. See Effosse, *L'invention du logement aidé en France,* 419–22.

57. See Paul Landauer, "La Caisse des dépôts et consignations face à la crise du logement, 1953–1958," Ph.D. dissertation, Université de Paris I, 2004.

58. For instance, of the 270,000 dwelling units built in 1957 only 22,000 were privately financed. See "Le financement de la construction, Ministère de la construction, 1962–63" (CAC 19910319/011).

59. During the immediate postwar, the landscape of HLM organizations was fragmented, and their relationship with the state was neither stable nor always productive. During the 1950s, that relationship became much more univocal. See Flamand, *Loger le peuple.*

60. See Maurice Imbert, "Logement, autoconstruction, solidarité: L'exemple des Castors," in *Les formes de la solidarité* (Paris: DRAC Île-de-France/CNRS, 1999): 61–83.

61. See Anselme's introduction in Albert Meister, *Coopération d'habitation et sociologie du voisinage: Étude de quelques expériences pilotes en France* (Paris: Minuit, 1957).

62. In the words of inhabitants, "We have come here to be housed, not to live in a phalanstery" (ibid., 130).

63. See Brian William Newsome, "The Struggle for a Voice in the City: The Development of Participatory Architectural and Urban Planning in France, 1940–1968," Ph.D. dissertation, University of South Carolina, 2002, 166–68.

64. See Marie-Jeanne Dumont, *Le logement social à Paris 1850–1930: Les habitations à bon marché* (Liège: Mardaga, 1991); Janet Horne, *A Social Laboratory for Modern France: The Musée Social and the Rise of the Welfare State* (Durham, N.C., and London: Duke University Press, 2002).

65. Art. 17, "Loi no. 50-854 du 21 juillet 1950 relative au développement des dépenses d'investissement pour l'exercice 1950 (prêts et garanties)," *Journal officiel de la République française*, July 23, 1950.

66. Charles Carrodan, "Minimum vital ou social?" *Économie et humanisme*, no. 16 (1950): 211–13.

67. Patrice Noviant, Bruno Vayssière, and Rémi Baudouï, "Normation sociale et naissance du logement d'état," in *Dossiers et documents IFA: Les trois reconstructions 1919–1940–1945* (Paris: Institut français d'architecture, 1983), 30. On "mininum vital," see Dana Simmons, "Minimal Frenchmen: Science and Standards of Living, 1840–1960," Ph.D. dissertation, University of Chicago, 2004.

68. See "Évaluation des besoins en logement de la France pour les périodes 1957–1963 et 1963–1970. Rapport du Groupe spécialisé 'Besoins en logements' à la Commission de la Construction du Commissariat Général au Plan de Modernisation et d'Équipement," n.d., around 1957 (CAC 19770816/007).

69. See Jean Bosvieux, "Besoin et demande de logement," in Segaud, Bonvalet, and Brun, *Logement et habitat*, 91–99.

70. See, for instance, the Groupe d'études des problèmes du logement, which brought together Paul Vieille, Pierre Clément, and Louis Couvreur to study the "methodological problems of the evaluation of quantitative needs in terms of housing." See Conference, "Centre d'Études Économiques, 30.01.1959: Méthodologie besoin en logement" (CAC 19770775/007).

71. INSEE, "Une enquête par sondage sur le logement," *Études statistiques* (April–June 1957): 35–48.

72. *Catalogue des plans types: Logements économiques et familiaux*, juin 1953, Ministère de la reconstruction et de l'urbanisme (CAC 19771096/001).

73. CAC 19771096/001.

74. "Projets-types homologués, classified per department" (CAC 19771096/001–002).

75. See "Plan d'examen des projets sous l'aspect qualité de l'habitat et de l'architecture" (CAC 19771096/001).

76. Susan R. Henderson, "A Revolution in the Woman's Sphere: Grete Lihotzky and the Frankfurt Kitchen," in *Feminism and Architecture*, ed. Debra Coleman, Elizabeth Danze, and Carol Henderson (New York: Princeton Architectural Press, 1996): 221–53.

77. Marcel Lods, in Paul-Henry Chombart de Lauwe, *Famille et habitation*, vol. 1: *Sciences humaines et conceptions de l'habitation* (Paris: CNRS, 1960), 159.

78. Rudolph, "At Home in Postwar France."

79. On the breaking up of traditional class structures in postwar France, see Henri Mendras, *Social Change in Modern France: Towards a Cultural Anthropology of the Fifth Republic* (Cambridge and Paris: Cambridge University Press/Éditions de la Maison des Sciences de l'Homme, 1991).

80. Dumont, *Le logement social à Paris 1850–1930.*

81. See Rudolph, "At Home in Postwar France."

82. See "Décret no. 55-1394 du 22 octobre 1955 fixant les règles générales de construction des bâtiments d'habitation, visé à l'article 22 du code de l'urbanisme et de l'habitation," *Journal officiel de la République française,* October 25, 1955. Pierre Sudreau also published a complement to these laws on June 2, 1960: "Cahier des prescriptions techniques et fonctionnelles minimales unifiées," *Journal officiel de la République française,* July 3, 1960.

83. Jacques Riboud, *Les erreurs de Le Corbusier et leurs conséquences* (Paris: Mazarine, 1968).

84. Le Corbusier, "L'habitation moderne," *Population* 3, no. 3 (1948): 417–40.

85. Georges Gromort, *Essai sur la théorie de l'architecture: Cours professé à l'École nationale supérieure des beaux-arts de 1937 à 1940* (Paris: Vincent Fréal, 1946).

86. See Joseph Abram, *L'architecture moderne en France,* vol. 2: *Du chaos à la croissance, 1940–1966,* ed. Gérard Monnier (Paris: Picard, 1999), 120–25.

87. *L'Architecture d'aujourd'hui* 74, "Habitations collectives" (1957): 62–65, and *L'Architecture française* 205–6 (1957): 54–59. See also Bernard Marrey, "Les Grandes terres à Marly-le-Roi," in *Habiter la modernité,* ed. Xavier Guillot (Saint-Étienne: Publications de l'Université de Saint-Étienne, 2006), 75–83.

88. An observation by Gabi Dolff-Bonekämper, lecture at conference Network 45+: Post-War Architecture in Europe, TU Berlin, July 11, 2011.

89. *L'Architecture française* 205–6 (1957): 62–64; *Urbanisme* 68 (1960): 24–25. See also Abram, *L'architecture moderne en France,* 2:125–29.

90. Christiane Rochefort, *Les petits enfants du siècle* (Paris: Bernard Grasset, 1961), 62.

91. Robert Auzelle, *Technique de l'urbanisme: L'aménagement des agglomérations urbaines,* Que sais-je? (Paris: Presses Universitaires de France, 1953), 31.

92. See Bernard Granotier, *Les travailleurs immigrés en France* (Paris: Maspero, 1970), 94–111; Marie-Claude Blanc-Chaléard, "Les immigrés et le logement en France depuis le XIXe siècle," *Hommes et Migrations,* no. 1264 (2006): 20–35.

93. Choukri Hmed, "Loger les étrangers 'isolés' en France: Socio-histoire d'une institution d'État, la Sonacotra (1956–2006)" (Université de Paris I Panthéon-Sorbonne, 2006).

94. Alain Touraine, *Le HLM: Une société petite-bourgeoise* (Paris: Centre de recherche sur l'urbanisme, 1966).

95. Henri Lefebvre, "Les nouveaux ensembles urbains, un cas concret: Lacq-Mourenx et les problèmes urbains de la nouvelle classe ouvrière," *Revue française de sociologie* 1, no. 2 (1960): 186–201.

96. See, for instance, René Kaës, *Vivre dans les grands ensembles* (Paris: Éditions ouvrières, 1963), 85.

97. See various reports and conference proceedings in CAC 19770775/005.

98. The norms were promulgated not only by the UIOF itself, but also by the Fédération internationale de l'urbanisme de l'habitation et de l'aménagement des territoires. See specialized journals such as *HLM* and *L'habitation,* and the proceedings of the Congrès mondial de la famille, in CAC 19770775/006-007.

99. See CAC 19770775/005.

100. Sepp Stein, "Adaptation des plans de logements aux impératifs familiaux: Recherche de solutions non-traditionnelles, Contribution by Sepp Stein to the 1961 UIOF Conference in Coventry" (CAC 19770775/005).

2. A Bureaucratic Epistemology

1. See "L'appartement référendum," *Techniques et architecture* 19, no. 2 (1959): 114.

2. See Nicole Rudolph, "At Home in Postwar France: The Design and Construction of Domestic Space 1945–1975," Ph.D. dissertation, New York University, 2005; Newsome, *French Urban Planning, 1940–1968.* Newsome especially tends to emphasize the participatory aspect of this initiative.

3. See Rabinow, *French Modern.*

4. Le Corbusier, *Les constructions "murondins"* (Paris and Clermont Ferrand: Étienne Chiron, 1942), 3.

5. Ibid., 7.

6. See Jean-Louis Cohen, *André Lurçat, 1894–1970: Autocritique d'un moderne* (Liège: Mardaga, 1995), 243–61.

7. André Lurçat, "Synthèse d'une collaboration étroite entre techniciens et population," *Urbanisme* 37–38 (1954): 100.

8. Robert Venturi, Denise Scott Brown, and Steven Izenour, *Learning from Las Vegas* (Cambridge: MIT Press, 1972).

9. This chapter builds on a wealth of existing studies on Paul-Henry Chombart de Lauwe: Amiot, *Contre l'État, les sociologues;* Paul-Henry Chombart de Lauwe and Marc Augé, *Les hommes, leurs espaces, et leurs aspirations: Hommage à Paul-Henry Chombart de Lauwe* (Paris: L'Harmattan, 1994); Paul-Henry Chombart de Lauwe, *Un anthropologue dans le siècle: Entretiens avec Thierry Paquot* (Paris: Descartes & Cie, 1996); Jean Remy, ed., *Paul-Henry Chombart de Lauwe et l'histoire des études urbaines en France, Espaces et Sociétés,* no. 103 (Paris: L'Harmattan, 2001).

10. See Haffner, *The View from Above.*

11. See chapter 4 in Wakeman, *The Heroic City.*

12. Ibid.

13. Gerd-Rainer Horn and Emmanuel Gerard, eds., *Left Catholicism, 1943–1955: Catholics and Society in Western Europe at the Point of Liberation* (Leuven: Leuven University Press, 2001).

14. Paul-Henry Chombart de Lauwe, *Paris et l'agglomération parisienne* (Paris: Presses Universitaires de France, 1952).

15. This argument has been developed by Jeanne Haffner, "Historicizing the View from Below: Aerial Photography and the Emergence of a Social Conception of Space," in The Proceedings of Spaces of History/Histories of Space: Emerging Approaches to the Study of the Built Environment (Berkeley: College of Environmental Design, University of California, Berkeley, 2010).

16. Simon Sadler, *The Situationist City* (Cambridge: MIT Press, 1998).

17. On "habitat," see Oxford English Dictionary and Grand Robert dictionary of the French language.

18. See Eric Mumford, *The CIAM Discourse on Urbanism, 1928–1960* (Cambridge: MIT Press, 2000).

19. André Wogenscky, "Programme of CIAM 9," CIAM papers (Harvard University Graduate School of Design–Special Collections, 1953).

20. Tom Avermaete, *Another Modern: The Post-war Architecture and Urbanism of Candilis-Josic-Woods* (Rotterdam: NAi, 2005), 74. My analysis here is more generally indebted to Avermaete's scholarship on Team X.

21. Team 10, Max Risselada, and Dirk van den Heuvel, *Team 10: 1953–81, In Search of a Utopia of the Present* (Rotterdam: NAi, 2005), 30–33. See also Victoria Walsh and Nigel Henderson, *Parallel of Life and Art* (London: Thames and Hudson, 2001); Claude Lichtenstein and Thomas Schregenberger, eds., *As Found: The Discovery of the Ordinary* (Baden: Lars Müller Publishers, 2001).

22. Jean-Louis Cohen and Monique Eleb, *Casablanca: Colonial Myths and Architectural Ventures* (New York: Monacelli, 2002).

23. Zeynep Çelik, "Learning from the Bidonville: CIAM Looks at Algiers," *Harvard Design Magazine* 18 (2003): 476–79; Sheila Crane, "The Shantytown in Algiers and the Colonization of Everyday Life," in *Use Matters: An Alternative History of Architecture*, ed. Kenny Cupers (London: Routledge, 2013), 103–20.

24. As described in chapter 4, the latter three would become future members of the Atelier de Montrouge, which would play a key part in the changing architecture culture following the social critiques around 1968.

25. Catherine Blain and Dominique Delaunay, *L'Atelier de Montrouge: La modernité à l'œuvre, 1958–1981* (Paris: Actes sud/Cité de l'architecture et du patrimoine, 2008), 20, 84–88.

26. CIAM-Paris, "Introduction à l'étude d'une grille de présentation, juillet 1953" (CAA 395 IFA 1/1). See also Catherine Blain, "Du 'droit à l'habitat' au 'droit à la ville': L'héritage des CIAM chez les architectes de l'atelier de Montrouge," in *Autour du CIAM 9 d'Aix-en-Provence, 1953*, ed. Jean-Lucien Bonillo, Claude Massu, and Daniel Pinson (Marseille: Imbernon, 2006), 218–31.

27. On Thurnauer and Ecochard, see Catherine Blain, "Gérard Thurnauer et le groupe CIAM-Paris," in Bonillo, Massu, and Pinson, *Autour du CIAM 9 d'Aix-en-Provence, 1953*, 273–76.

28. Jean-Louis Violeau, "A Critique of Architecture: The Bitter Victory of the Situationist International," in *Anxious Modernisms: Experimentation in Postwar Architectural Culture*, ed. Sarah Williams Goldhagen and Réjean Legault (Montreal and Cambridge, Mass.: Canadian Centre for Architecture and MIT Press, 2000), 239–60.

29. Chombart de Lauwe, *Paris et l'agglomération parisienne*, 240.

30. Ibid., 228–40.

31. See Gaston Bardet, "Marcel Poëte," *News Sheet of the International Federation for Housing and Town Planning* 17 (1950); Marcel Poëte, *Introduction à l'urbanisme*, ed., foreword, and preface by Hubert Tonka; letter from Françoise Bardet; in memory of Gaston Bardet (Paris: Sens & Tonka, 2000). See also Donatella Calabi, *Marcel Poëte et le Paris des années vingt: Aux origines de "l'histoire des villes"* (Paris: L'Harmattan, 1998).

32. Gaston Bardet, *Le nouvel urbanisme* (Paris: Vincent, Fréal & Cie, 1948).

33. See Frédéric Bertrand, "La Cité de la Plaine à Clamart," in *Les bâtisseurs de la modernité*, ed. Bernard Marray (Paris: Le Moniteur, 2000), 181–87.

34. See "Visite au Groupe de l'Office d'HLM de Clamart, Quartier de la Plaine, 3 sep 1963" (CAC 19771142/019).

35. See Denis Pelletier, *Économie et humanisme: De l'utopie communautaire au combat pour le Tiers-monde, 1941–1966* (Paris: Éditions du Cerf, 1996).

36. Robert Auzelle, "Vers une généralisation des enquêtes sur l'habitat," *Urbanisme* 7–8 (1951); "Théorie générale de l'urbanisme, Cours Robert Auzelle, année 1959–1960, Institut d'Urbanisme de Paris Créteil" (CAC 19890277/002).

37. See Haffner, *The View from Above*.

38. Chombart de Lauwe, *Famille et habitation*, 1:11.

39. Ibid., 17–18.

40. Paul-Henry Chombart de Lauwe, "Sciences humaines, planification et urbanisme," *Annales (ESC)* 16, no. 4 (1961): 686–98.

41. Paul-Henry Chombart de Lauwe, Jacques Jenny, and Louis Couvreur, "Logement et comportement des ménages dans trois cités nouvelles de l'agglomération bordelaise," *Cahiers du CSTB (Centre scientifique et technique du bâtiment)* 30, no. 282 (1958): 55.

42. The Groupe d'ethnologie sociale became part of the large research group of the Centre d'études sociologiques after 1959. During the 1960s, it was moved to Montrouge and was renamed Centre d'ethnologie sociale et psychosociologie. The Centre d'étude des groups sociaux was renamed Centre de sociologie urbaine. See Christian Topalov, "Centre de recherche: Le Centre de sociologie urbaine," *Politix* 5, no. 20 (1992): 195–201.

43. Chombart de Lauwe, "Sciences humaines, planification et urbanisme," 686.

44. Ibid., 691.

45. They came together in political clubs such as the Club Jean Moulin, the Association d'étude pour l'expansion de la recherche scientifique, and the Centre d'études prospectives.

46. Larry Busbea, *Topologies: The Urban Utopia in France, 1960–1970* (Cambridge: MIT Press, 2007).

47. Jean Fourastié, *Les trente glorieuses, ou la révolution invisible de 1946 à 1975* (Paris: Fayard, 1979).

48. Busbea, *Topologies*.

49. See "Colloque national de démographie, Strasbourg 1960" (CAC 19770775/007).

50. A recent revision of Lefebvre's work in this vein is Łukasz Stanek, *Henri Lefebvre on Space: Architecture, Urban Research, and the Production of Theory* (Minneapolis: University of Minnesota Press, 2011).

51. Lefebvre, "Les nouveaux ensembles urbains, un cas concret," 191.

52. Coing, *Rénovation urbaine et changement social l'îlot n° 4 (Paris 13e)*, 12.

53. Chombart de Lauwe, "Sciences humaines, planification et urbanisme," 690.

54. Chombart de Lauwe, *Famille et habitation*, 1:19.

55. Chombart de Lauwe, "Sciences humaines, planification et urbanisme," 688.

56. Paul-Henry Chombart de Lauwe, "Sociologie de l'habitation," *Urbanisme* 65 (1959): 10.

57. Chombart de Lauwe, *Famille et habitation*, 1:17.

58. Ibid., 209.

59. See Chombart de Lauwe, Jenny, and Couvreur, "Logement et comportement des ménages dans trois cités nouvelles de l'agglomération bordelaise." The results of this study were deemed less than impressive by those who commissioned it and did not leave a substantial impact on urban policy in Bordeaux.

60. Ibid., 53.

61. Ibid., 53–54.

62. Statement by Émile Aillaud during a debate titled "L'Architecte peut-il et doit-il influer sur le mode de vie de ses contemporains?" See "Commission de la vie dans les grands ensembles, 1957–58" (CAC 19770816/005).

63. See Chombart's interviews with architects in Chombart de Lauwe, *Famille et habitation*, vol. 1.

64. See chapter 4.

65. Until 1954, André Trintignac worked in the office Besoins en logements et programmes at the Direction de l'aménagement du territoire of the ministry. Between 1954 and 1959, he worked in the office Service de l'aménagement national—Groupe des études: Territoire et population, aménagement régional, where he further developed his expertise in demographic and housing studies. Between 1959 and 1963, he led the office of Documentation et synthèse and then the Service de l'habitation, Bureau des études sociologiques de l'habitat. In 1967, he directed a working group on the resorption of shantytowns, resulting in the "rapport Trintignac," which argued for the necessity of social work and education as indispensable elements of urban renewal projects to demolish shantytowns. He was also associated with DATAR and the first generation of experimental programs that eventually led to the Habitat et vie sociale policies during the 1970s. See CAC 19770775 (introduction to the deposit in the catalog).

66. Chombart mentioned a list of such studies in "Le logement, le ménage et l'espace familial" (1955). See "Reports by Chombart de Lauwe" (CAC 19770775/004).

67. "Conference proceedings of the Congrès mondial de la famille, Paris 1958" (CAC 19770775/006-007).

68. "Conseil International du Bâtiment pour la recherche, l'étude et la documentation" (CAC 19770775/006).

69. CAC 19770775/004.

70. Amiot, *Contre l'État, les sociologues*, 35–46.

71. Drouard, *Le Développement des sciences sociales en France au tournant des années soixante*, 35.

72. De Grazia, *Irresistible Empire*.

73. Personal interview with Alain de Vulpian, October 2008.

74. The firm was renamed COFREMCA in 1959. It still exists today, under the name Sociovision (personal interview with Alain de Vulpian, October 2008).

75. CAC 19770775/004.

76. "June 1957 meeting minutes" (CAC 19770775/004).

77. Ibid.

78. Duriez and Chauvière, *Cahiers du GRMF*.

79. "Robert-Henri Hazemann, Les implication psychologiques de l'urbanisme, Entretiens de Bichat, 1960" (CAC 19770775/047).

80. Claude, *Faire la ville*, 168–78.

81. CAC 19770775/007.

82. For instance, after the 1958 Commission de la vie dans les grands ensembles, Sudreau established the Centre de recherche sur l'urbanisme and the Centre d'études des équipements résidentiels (CEDER). The goal of the latter was to make preliminary studies of urban areas to determine the necessary collective amenities and to plan these (see chapter 3).

83. See "CGP, Commission de l'Équipement urbain, groupe de travail no. 5, Études urbaines," September 1965 (CAC 19920405/009).

84. Rabinow, *French Modern*.

85. Drouard, *Le Développement des sciences sociales en France au tournant des années soixante*.

86. Solovey and Cravens, *Cold War Social Science*.

87. Vera Lutz, *Central Planning for the Market Economy: An Analysis of the French Theory and Experience* (London: Longmans, Green and Co., 1969), 4.

88. *Le 4ème Plan 1962–1965* (Paris: La Documentation française, 1962).

89. Drouard, *Le Développement des sciences sociales en France au tournant des années soixante*.

90. Drouard, "Réflexions sur une chronologie."

91. "Groupe de travail pour l'étude de l'industrialisation et l'accroissement de la productivité dans la construction, 1958" (CAC 19770816/007), 2.

92. At the same time, the report recognized the inevitability of individualized projects and thus argued for preliminary studies. These were nevertheless limited to the implantation of the project and the constraints of the site (ibid.).

3. *Animation* to the Rescue

1. Gérard Dupont, "Le grand ensemble, facteur de progrès social et de progrès humain," *Urbanisme* 62–63 (1959): 6.

2. See "Grille d'équipement d'un grand ensemble d'habitation," *Urbanisme* 62–63 (1959): 12–14.

3. On the urban policies of Pierre Sudreau, see Annie Fourcaut, "L'animation dans le béton: Autogérer les grands ensembles?" in *Autogestion, la dernière utopie?*, ed. Christian Chevandier and Frank Georgi (Paris: Presses de la Sorbonne, 2003); Fourcaut, "Les premiers grands ensembles en région parisienne"; Annie Fourcaut, "Trois discours, une politique?" *Urbanisme*, no. 322 (2002): 39–45; Lengereau, *L'État et l'architecture, 1958–1981*, 28–37. For a biographical account of Pierre Sudreau, see Christiane Rimbaud, *Pierre Sudreau: Un homme libre* (Paris: Cherche Midi, 2004).

4. CAC 19770816/006.

5. "Letter by Pierre Sudreau directed at the Prime Minister, 1958" (CAC 19770816/004).

6. "Constatations faites au cours de visites d'HLM, Groupe sociale et culturelle, Commission Grands ensembles" (CAC 19770816/004).

7. CAC 19770775/044.

8. Kaës, *Vivre dans les grands ensembles*, 144.

9. Pierre Sudreau, "Introduction," *Urbanisme* 62–63 (1959): 9.

10. This included national newspapers such as *Le Figaro* and *France Observateur*, popular science magazines such as *Science et Vie*, and specialized press such as *Revue Logement*, *Le Castor*, and *Habitation*.

11. Kaës, *Vivre dans les grands ensembles*, 70–71.

12. Henri Théry and M. Garrigou-Lagrange, *Équiper et animer la vie sociale* (Paris: Centurion, 1966), 34–35.

13. See "La vie des ménages de quatre nouveaux ensembles de la région parisienne (1962–63), Résumé général de l'étude, CINAM (Compagnie d'études industrielles et d'aménagement du territoire), Ministère de la construction (CAC 19771152/002).

14. Louis Caro, "Psychiatres et sociologues dénoncent la folie des Grands Ensembles," *Science et Vie* 504 (1959): 30.

15. "Study by Balladur and Prieur analyzing the first public critiques of the grands ensembles, Commission de la vie dans les grands ensembles, 1959" (CAC 19770816/005).

16. "Record of speech by Pierre Randet, 11ᵉᵐᵉ jour mondial de l'urbanisme, Mulhouse 08.11.1960" (CAC 19770775/047).

17. Lefebvre, "Les nouveaux ensembles urbains, un cas concret," 201; Henri Lefebvre, "Utopie expérimentale: pour un nouvel urbanisme," *Revue française de sociologie* 2, nos. 2–3 (1961): 191–98.

18. Jacques Loew, "Les grands ensembles, mal inévitable mais mal tout de même," *L'habitation* 72 (April 1959). On the Castor movement, see chapter 1.

19. Pierre Sudreau, cited in Fourcaut, "Trois discours, une politique?" 42.

20. "Speech by Pierre Sudreau at UNESCO Conference, 'Comment réussir la construction et l'équipement des ensembles immobiliers,' 21–23 January 1960" (CAC 19770816/004).

21. Chombart de Lauwe, Jenny, and Couvreur, "Logement et comportement des ménages dans trois cités nouvelles de l'agglomération bordelaise."

22. See, for instance, "Conference proceedings of the Congrès mondial de la famille, Paris 1958" (CAC 19770775/006-007).

23. "Les équipements résidentiels: Techniques d'étude des besoins dans les ensembles d'habitation, Bloch-Lemoine, INEP Malry-le-Roi, Octobre 1962" (CAC 19780633/001).

24. See Fourcaut, "Les premiers grands ensembles en région parisienne."

25. "Loi du 7 août 1957 tendant à favoriser la construction de logements et les équipements collectifs," *Journal officiel de la République française*, August 10, 1957.

26. See "Décrets relatifs aux plans d'urbanisme directeurs et de détail, aux lotissements, aux zones à urbaniser par priorité, à la rénovation urbaine, aux associations syndicales de propriétaires en vue de la réalisation d'opérations d'urbanisme," *Journal officiel de la République française*, December 31, 1958.

27. Jean Lemoine, cited in "Les équipements résidentiels: Techniques d'étude des besoins dans les ensembles d'habitation, Bloch-Lemoine, INEP Malry-le-Roi, octobre 1962" (CAC 19780633/001), 7.

28. See "Rapport du groupe équipement commercial" (CAC 19770775/044).

29. "Équipement commercial des grands ensembles," *Urbanisme* 62–63 (1959): 58–59.

30. Mumford, *The CIAM Discourse on Urbanism, 1928–1960*, 180–81, 203–8.

31. Jacqueline Tyrwhitt, Joseph Lluis Sert, and Ernesto Rogers, *CIAM 8: The Heart of the City* (New York: Pellegrini & Cudahy, 1952).

32. "Grille d'équipement d'un grand ensemble d'habitation," 12–14.

33. François Parfait, "Conception, organisation, réalisation des ensembles d'habitation," *Urbanisme* 65 (1959): 22.

34. See "Les équipements résidentiels: Techniques d'étude des besoins dans les ensembles d'habitation, Bloch-Lemoine, INEP Malry-le-Roi, octobre 1962." See also Yohei Nakayama, "La construction de logements et les investissement d'équipement annexes des années 1930 au milieu des années 1960," *Histoire urbaine* 3, no. 20 (2008): 55–69.

35. Christian Topalov, "Traditional Working-Class Neighborhoods: An Inquiry into the Emergence of a Sociological Model in the 1950s and 1960s," *Osiris* 18 (2003): 213–33.

36. Louis Chevalier, *Classes laborieuses et classes dangereuses à Paris pendant la première moitié du XIXe siècle* (Paris: Plon, 1958). On Économie et humanisme, see chapter 2 and Isabelle Astié and Jean-François Laé, "La notion de communauté dans les enquêtes sociales en France: Le groupe d'Économie et humanisme, 1940–1955," *Genèse* 5 (1991): 81–106; Denis Pelletier, *Économie et humanisme: De l'utopie communautaire au combat pour le Tiers-monde, 1941–1966* (Paris: Éditions du Cerf, 1996).

37. See chapter 2.

38. See Haffner, *The View from Above.*

39. Lucy Creagh, "From acceptera to Vällingby: The Discourse on Individuality and Community in Sweden (1931–54)," *Footprint* 5, no. 2 (2011): 5–23.

40. *Urbanisme* 62–63 (1959): 11.

41. See, for instance, Chombart de Lauwe, "Sociologie de l'habitation."

42. Maurice-François Rouge, "D'une doctrine des structures à l'esquisse d'une charte: Essai de synthèse," *Urbanisme* 66 (1960): 11.

43. Jacques Maziol, "Introduction," *Urbanisme* 75–76 (1962): 3.

44. Dupont, "Évolution de la construction et de l'urbanisme depuis 1950," 38.

45. See *Urbanisme* 90–91 (1965): 75. See also Joffre Dumazedier and Maurice Imbert, *Espace et loisir dans la société française d'hier et de demain,* vol. 2 (Paris: Centre de recherche sur l'urbanisme, 1967), 65–66.

46. Yves Aubert, "Espaces extérieurs et domaine socio-culturel," *Urbanisme* 90–91 (1965): 5.

47. Ibid., 9.

48. Ibid., 5.

49. Pierre Randet, "L'évolution de la doctrine," *Urbanisme* 77 (1962).

50. Roger Macé, "L'administration et les urbanistes," *Urbanisme* 82–83 (1964): 37. See also Kaës, *Vivre dans les grands ensembles,* 239.

51. See CAC 19770775/044.

52. Guy Houist, "Domaine socio-culturel," *Urbanisme* 90–91(1965): 67–68.

53. See "Contribution by J. P. Imhof, Journée d'études sur les problèmes posés par l'animation des nouveaux ensembles d'habitation, 1965" (CAC 19771142/020).

54. See Richard Klein, "Des maisons du peuple aux maisons de la culture," in *André Malraux et l'architecture,* ed. Dominique Hervier (Paris: Le Moniteur, 2008), 108–30.

55. "Le centre social, brochure, Fédération des centres sociaux de France (FCSF), 1965" (CAC 19771142/022).

56. See Robert Durand, *Histoire des centres sociaux: Du voisinage à la citoyenneté* (Paris: La Découverte, 2005); Jacques Eloy et al., *Les centres sociaux 1880–1980: Une résolution locale de la question sociale?* (Villeneuve d'Ascq: Presses Universitaires du Septentrium, 2004).

57. "IIème Congrès national des centres sociaux et socio-culturels, 2–4 mai 1969, Lyon" (CAC 19771142/022).

58. See "Équipement social, culturel, cultuel," *Urbanisme* 62–63 (1959): 45.

59. Ibid., 36.

60. Vincent Dubois and Philippe Poirrier, *La Politique culturelle: Genèse d'une catégorie d'intervention publique* (Paris: Belin, 1999); Philippe Urfalino, *L'invention de la politique culturelle* (Paris: La Documentation française/Comité d'histoire du ministère de la culture 1996).

61. Urfalino, *L'invention de la politique culturelle*, 15.

62. See Dubois and Poirrier, *La Politique culturelle*; "Équipement culturel et patrimoine artistique" (CAC 19771152/001). See also Alexis Korganow, "L'équipement socio-culturel, trajectoire architecturale d'un type contrarié d'édifice public à l'ère des loisirs, 1936–1975," Ph.D. dissertation, Université de Paris 8/Institut français d'urbanisme, 2003, 125–216.

63. Françoise Tétard, "Le phénomène blousons noirs en France fin années 50–début années 1960," *Révoltes et sociétés, Histoire au Présent* 2 (1989); Anne-Marie Sohn, *Âge tendre et tête de bois: Histoire des jeunes des années 1960* (Paris: Hachette, 2001), 266–72.

64. Michel de Saint-Pierre, *L'école de la violence* (Paris: Table Ronde, 1962).

65. Jacques Jenny, *Les équipements socio-culturels pour les jeunes dans les nouveaux groupes d'habitation, problèmes psycho-sociologiques* (Paris/Montrouge: Groupe d'ethnologie sociale/Centre d'études des groupes sociaux, 1961), 1. See also the chapter by Jacques Jenny in Paul-Henry Chombart de Lauwe, Jacques Jenny, and Louis Couvreur, *Famille et habitation II: Un essai d'observation expérimentale* (Paris: CNRS, 1960), 197–220.

66. Laurent Besse, *Les MJC de l'été des blousons noirs à l'été des Minguettes 1959–1981* (Rennes: Presses Universitaires de Rennes, 2008), 45, 361.

67. "Le centre social et le quartier: Le directeur de Centre social, ses méthodes de travail, analyse d'expériences," Union nationale des caisses d'allocations familiales, 1968 (CAC 19771142/024).

68. Some reports even went so far as to argue that the notion of the sociocultural itself came directly out of the *grille Dupont*. See "Bilan sommaire des études et des expériences concernant les problèmes posés par l'animation socio-culturelle dans les nouveaux ensembles d'habitation, Jean-Paul Imhof, 1967" (CAC 19771142/020).

69. Durand, *Histoire des centres sociaux*, 128–30.

70. See Houist, "Domaine socio-culturel"; "Bilan sommaire des études et des expériences concernant les problèmes posés par l'animation socio-culturelle dans les nouveaux ensembles d'habitation, Jean-Paul Imhof, 1967."

71. "Rapport de la commission nationale équipement animation, Haut Comité de la Jeunesse" (CAC 19771142/021).

72. "Étude des problèmes posés par la coordination des équipements socio-culturels, CINAM [Compagnie d'études industrielles et d'aménagement du territoire], 1965" (CAC 19771152/001), 11.

73. Henry Théry was *délégué général* of the Union nationale des Centres d'études et d'action sociale, and secrétaire général des Semaines sociales de France. See Théry and Garrigou-Lagrange, *Équiper et animer la vie sociale*.

74. Henri Théry, "L'animation des collectivités urbaines," *Recherche sociale* 1 (1965): 44.

75. Fourcaut, "L'animation dans le béton"; Tellier, *Le temps des HLM 1945–1975*, 132.

76. "Bilan sommaire des études et des expériences concernant les problèmes posés par l'animation socio-culturelle dans les nouveaux ensembles d'habitation, Jean-Paul Imhof, 1967."

77. For instance, the housing projects of Red Vienna. See Eve Blau, *The Architecture of Red Vienna, 1919–1934* (Cambridge: MIT Press, 1999).

78. Le Corbusier, *Manière de penser l'urbanisme* (Paris: Éditions de l'Architecture d'aujourd'hui, 1946), 60. The idea of is also developed in Le Corbusier, "L'habitation moderne," *Population* 3, no. 3 (1948): 417–40. For Chombart, see Chombart de Lauwe, Jenny, and Couvreur, "Logement et comportement des ménages dans trois cités nouvelles de l'agglomération bordelaise."

79. Circulaire no. 60-36 of 02.06.1960. See "Letter of the Director of Construction to the Minister, 8 June 1967" (CAC 19771142/020).

80. A working group derived from the Commission de la vie dans les grands ensembles was ordered to follow up on the development of these locaux collectifs résidentiels. The group reported that developers were not inclined to provide them, funding was absent, and there was a lack of experience of how to manage them (CAC 19771142/020).

81. Circulaire no. 65-29 of 09.06.1965. See ibid.

82. "Projet concernant les activités, Commission de la vie dans les grands ensembles" (CAC 19770816/006).

83. The first anthropological analyses of Lévi-Strauss had been published in the journal *Forum*, edited by Aldo van Eyck, between 1956 and 1962.

84. Tom Avermaete, *Another Modern: The Post-war Architecture and Urbanism of Candilis-Josic-Woods* (Rotterdam: NAi, 2005), 43.

85. Dominique Rouillard, "La théorie du cluster: Généalogie d'une métaphore," in *Le Team X et le logement collectif à grande échelle en Europe: Un retour critique des pratiques vers la théorie. Actes du séminaire européen, Toulouse 27–28 mai 2004*, ed. Bruno Fayolle Lussac and Rémi Papillault (Pessac: Maison des sciences de l'homme d'Aquitaine, 2008); Dominique Rouillard, "Dix-neuf-cent-soixante [1960]: Candilis, Josic, Woods," *Le moniteur architecture AMC* 103 (1999): 126–37.

86. Georges Candilis, "À la recherche d'une structure urbaine," *L'Architecture d'aujourd'hui* 101 (1962): 50–51.

87. In "Paysage urbain," *Urbanisme* 90–91 (1965): 19.

88. See Sandra Parvu, "Du territoire à la ville, histoire d'une limite," *Urbanisme* 358 (2008): 33–36; "Bures-Orsay ZUP des Ulis," *Techniques et architecture* 31, nos. 3–4 (1969): 51.

89. "ZUP de Bures-Orsay," *Urbanisme* 102–3 (1967): 64.

90. Ibid.

91. Xavier Arsène-Henry, "L'animation urbaine," *Urbanisme* 98 (1967): 32–37.

92. Ibid., 35.

93. See AM Sarcelles, Dossiers Permis de Construire.

94. Xavier Arsène-Henry, "L'art dans les villes nouvelles," *Techniques et architecture* 4 (1961): 82–83. For Aillaud, see Jean-François Dhuys, *L'architecture selon Émile Aillaud* (Paris: Dunod, 1983).

95. Guy Habasque, "Émile Aillaud, pour un urbanisme sans monotonie," *L'Œil*, no. 102 (June 1963): 36.

96. Alain Devy and Gérald Gassiot-Talabot, *La Grande Borne* (Paris: Hachette, 1972), 149–50.

97. Ibid., 69. The team of artists included Fabio Rieti, Gilles Aillaud, Cremonini, Lucio Fanti, François Lalanne, Eva Lukasiewicz, and Laurence Rieti.

4. The Expertise of Participation

1. "La presse et les Grands Ensembles," *L'A.S.*, no. 15 (June 1960).

2. Kaës, *Vivre dans les grands ensembles*, 13.

3. Ibid., 202, 46.

4. Gérard Marin, "Vivre dans les cités nouvelles," *Le Figaro*, February 12, 1963.

5. See "Un univers concentrationnaire," *Le Figaro*, January 14, 1965; "Un silo à hommes," *Le Figaro*, January 15, 1965; "Les raisons de la sarcellite," *L'Humanité*, November 5, 1963.

6. The term *sarcellite* was most likely used for the first time in the press in 1962 in an article in *L'Écho Régional* on March 22. See Alain Vulbeau, "De la sarcellite au malaise des banlieues: Trente ans de pathologie des grands ensembles," *Lumières de la ville*, no. 5 (June 1992): 31–37. On *brasilite*, see James Holston, *The Modernist City: An Anthropological Critique of Brasília* (Chicago: University of Chicago Press, 1989), 24–25.

7. Jean Duquesne, *Vivre à Sarcelles?* (Paris: Éditions Cujas, 1966), 31.

8. On the history of SCIC, see René Pares, *La SCIC au service du pays* (Paris: SCIC, 1992); François Bloch-Lainé and Françoise Carrière, *Profession fonctionnaire* (Paris: Seuil, 1976), 136–42.

9. See délibération municipal, 25.09.1954 (AM Sarcelles). For the Castor movement, see chapter 1. Findings on Sarcelles in this chapter are based largely on research at the Municipal Archives of Sarcelles.

10. Jacques-Henri Labourdette studied architecture at the École national supérieure des Beaux-Arts, first in the atelier of Roger Expert, then with Eugène Beaudouin and Charles Lemaresquier. In 1945, he created an office with Roger Boileau, the son of Louis-Hippolyte Boileau, the architect of hotel Lutétia and the Trocadéro in Paris. The office Boileau-Labourdette built more than sixty-five thousand housing units over their career, but received relatively few mentions in professional reviews.

11. See chapter 3.

12. See François Chaslin, "Hommage Jacques Henri-Labourdette (1915–2003)," *Urbanisme*, no. 331 (2003): 14–15.

13. Duquesne, *Vivre à Sarcelles?*, 67.

14. See "Bulletin d'information des entreprises participant au programme de construction à caractère social de la Caisse des Dépôts, 1956" (CDC/SCIC); Kaës, *Vivre dans les grands ensembles*, 76; Duquesne, *Vivre à Sarcelles?*, 28.

15. Many thanks to Catherine Roth for information about housing allocation policies in Sarcelles.

16. Jean Marty, "Une chance offerte à l'Église: Le cas de Sarcelles," in *Vers une nouvelle civilisation urbaine* (Paris: Librairie Arthème Fayard/Centre catholique des intellectuels français, 1962), 115.

17. Many thanks to Catherine Roth for pointing this out to me. See Didier Vaillant and Catherine Roth, eds., "*Migrations*," *Collections Patrimoine en Val de France* 10 (2012).

18. Claude Mezrahi, *Regards et témoignages sur Sarcelles* (Paris: Idéographic Éditions, 1991), 173. See also Duquesne, *Vivre à Sarcelles?*, 73.

19. Only 6 percent of new inhabitants came from rural municipalities. See Paul Clerc, *Grands ensembles, banlieues nouvelles: Enquête démographique et psycho-sociologique* (Paris: Presses Universitaires de France, 1967).

20. Kaës, *Vivre dans les grands ensembles*, 89.

21. This was a more general feature of the suburbs around Paris. See Annie Fourcaut, *Banlieue rouge 1920–1960: Années Thorez, années Gabin: Archétype du populaire, banc d'essai des modernités* (Paris: Autrement, 1992); Tyler Stovall, "French Communism and Suburban Development: The Rise of the Paris Red Belt," *Journal of Contemporary History* 24, no. 3 (1985): 437–60.

22. See local periodicals such as l'A.S. and *En famille* (AM Sarcelles, Bibliothèque nationale de France).

23. "La Sarcellite," *En famille* (January 1965).

24. See Catherine Roth and Gilbert Morin, eds., *Textes et images du grand ensemble de Sarcelles 1954–1976*, Collection Les Publications du Patrimoine en Val de France, no. 10 (Villiers-le-Bel: Éditions de la Mission Mémoires et Identités en Val de France, 2007).

25. Kaës, *Vivre dans les grands ensembles*, 287. For the late 1960s and 1970s, see Manuel Castells et al., *Crise du logement et mouvements sociaux urbains: Enquête sur la région parisienne* (Paris: Mouton, 1978).

26. Henri Lefebvre, "Les nouveaux ensembles urbains, un cas concret: Lacq-Mourenx et les problèmes urbains de la nouvelle classe ouvrière," *Revue française de sociologie* 1, no. 2 (1960): 186–201. In La Duchère, near Lyon, the local association was modeled explicitly after the Association Sarcelloise. See "Lyon La Duchère, documentation folder" (CAC 19771142/019).

27. "La SCIC: Une entreprise," *CDC*, no. 134 (1980).

28. "Extrait du Journal Officiel, Débats parlementaires—Assemblée nationale, no. 98 du 20.11.1965," *En famille* (February 1966). See also "Vivre ou végéter?" *En famille* (December 1965).

29. See Christian Topalov, *Le logement en France: Histoire d'une marchandise impossible* (Paris: Presses de la Fondation nationale des sciences politiques, 1987).

30. On the Confédération nationale du logement, see Sébastien Jolis, "Un syndicalisme de locataires? La Confédération nationale du logement (CNL) de la Libération aux années 1970," Université de Paris-1, 2009.

31. See Bernard Roux, "Le rôle des associations d'usagers dans le domaine du logement," *Recherche sociale*, no. 46 (April–June 1973): 5–24.

32. Kaës, *Vivre dans les grands ensembles*, 294–303; Claude Neuschwander, "Pour un syndicalisme de l'habitat," *Le Monde*, March 1, 1966. For a theoretical account of French self-management movements, see Pierre Rosanvallon, *L'âge de l'autogestion* (Paris: Seuil, 1976). See also Henri Lefebvre, *L'irruption de Nanterre au sommet* (Paris: Anthropos, 1968), 94–100.

33. See "Nouvelles de nos bâtiments," *L'A.S.*, no. 7 (February 1959).

34. "Indépendance ou affiliation," *L'A.S.*, no. 13 (March 1960).

35. "L'A.S. demande que l'on passe des project aux réalisations," *L'A.S.*, no. 27 (April 1962).

36. See Roth and Morin, *Textes et images du grand ensemble de Sarcelles 1954–1976*.

37. See chapter 3.

38. Mezrahi, *Regards et témoignages sur Sarcelles*, 166. About the design and construction of the urban center of Sarcelles, see chapter 6.

39. Kaës, *Vivre dans les grands ensembles*, 151–62.

40. "Sarcelles en noir ou en rose?" *En famille* (November 1964).

41. "Ni enfer ni paradis," *L'A.S.*, no. 4 (September 1958); "Sarcelles, une ville modèle? Oui, mais dans cinq ou dix ans!" *L'A.S.*, no. 5 (October 1958).

42. Duquesne, *Vivre à Sarcelles?*, 265.

43. "Augmenter le nombre des adhérents: Une nécessité vitale pour l'A.S.," *L'A.S.*, no. 9 (September 1962).

44. "La presse et les Grands Ensembles."

45. "Pour l'équipement collectif de la Cité, il reste encore beaucoup à faire . . . ," *L'A.S.*, no. 16 (July 1960).

46. "L'A.S. mène l'enquête," *L'A.S.*, no. 19 (December 1960).

47. See CINAM (Compagnie d'études industrielles et d'aménagement du territoire), "La vie des ménages de quatre nouveaux ensembles de la région parisienne (1962–63)," 2 vols. (Paris: Ministère de la construction, 1963).

48. See "Bron-Parilly, Documentation folder" (CAC 19771142/019).

49. The SCIC archives, managed by CDC, are inaccessible, which means it is not entirely clear at this point what motivated SCIC to organize resident councils. My interpretation is based on the periodicals published by SCIC and CDC, available for consultation at the CDC/SCIC in Paris.

50. Claude Jannoud, *La première ville nouvelle* (Paris: Mercure de France, 1974), 115.

51. Groupe de travail sur les relations entre promoteurs et résidents dans les grands ensembles, "Les relations entre propriétaires et locataires dans les grands ensembles" (Paris: Fondation nationale des sciences politiques/SCIC, June 1964), 5.

52. The participating organizations were the Union nationale des associations familiales, the CNL, the Confédération nationale des associations populaires familiales (CNAPF), la Confédération syndicale des familles, and the local Sarcelles ones, Association Sarcelloise and the Association familiale of Sarcelles.

53. J. M. Boucher and Elisabeth Théry, "L'expérience des conseils de résidents," *Habitat et vie sociale*, no. 2 (January–February 1974): 3–24.

54. See, for instance, the article by Jean Lagarde (chef du service "études de l'Habitat" at SCIC), "Les grands ensembles douze ans après," *Urbanisme*, no. 106 (1968): 30–34.

55. "Avec l'A.S. construisez Lochères," *Ville-nouvelles*, no. 1 (1968).

56. See municipal deliberations of June 8, 1962, October 30, 1963, and December 13, 1963 (AM Sarcelles).

57. On Sarcelles's municipal politics, see Manuel Castells, *The City and the Grassroots: A Cross-Cultural Theory of Urban Social Movements* (Berkeley: University of California Press, 1983), 83–84. See also the personal account by Henri Canacos, *Sarcelles ou le béton apprivoisé* (Paris: Éditions sociales, 1979).

58. See SCIC letter to the mayor on December 8, 1965 (AM Sarcelles).

59. See municipal deliberations of October 29, 1965, January 27, 1966, March 25, 1966, and November 18, 1966 (AM Sarcelles).

60. See municipal deliberations of January 12, 1967, March 3, 1967, May 17, 1967, December 6, 1968 (AM Sarcelles).

61. See "Urbanisme," *Ville-nouvelles*, no. 5 (1968); "Si la SCIC ne modifie pas son attitude, le Conseil de résidents est décidé à dénoncer la Convention," *Ville-nouvelles*, no. 6 (1968).

62. "À quoi sert ce journal?" *Ville-nouvelles*, no. 31 (July 1971).

63. Jannoud, *La première ville nouvelle*, 118.

64. Castells et al., *Crise du logement et mouvements sociaux urbains*, 359–61.

65. Boucher and Théry, "L'expérience des conseils de résidents," 19.

66. Ibid., 25.

67. See municipal periodicals, early 1980s (AM Sarcelles).

68. Many thanks to Catherine Roth for pointing this out to me. See Vaillant and Roth, *"Migrations," Collections Patrimoine en Val de France.*

69. Jannoud, *La première ville nouvelle.* For quantitative indication, see the municipal census of 1968 published in the *Bulletin Officiel Municipal* in January 1970.

70. In 1959, the population of Sarcelles was 47 percent working-class; in the early 1970s, it was only 33 percent, less than the average for the Paris suburbs. During the same period, the social group of "cadres moyens" increased from 17 to 31 percent, more than the national average (Jannoud, *La première ville nouvelle,* 26, 126). This contradicts the general opinion that equates *grands ensembles* and social housing, with the latter becoming, as Jacques Barou calls it, "the place of the poor" (Jacques Barou, *La place du pauvre: Histoire et géographie sociale de l'habitat HLM* [Paris: L'Harmattan, 1992]).

71. J. M. Offner, "Développement local et réseaux: Un entretien avec Claude Neuschwander," *Flux,* no. 20 (1995): 46–49. Through Publicis, he also had an important role in the promotion of the *villes nouvelles* (see chapter 5).

72. H. Toinet, "Animation, participation, information dans les villes nouvelles: Comparaison avec l'expérience britannique. Rapport de stage" (Paris: Ministère de l'équipement et du logement, November 1970).

73. Jean-François Parent, "Villeneuve de Grenoble Échirolles: Objectifs et réalisations (1961–1977)" (Société d'aménagement du département de l'Isère, 1977).

74. François Hollard, "Les unions de quartiers," *Urbanisme* 37, no. 107 (1968).

75. On private versus social housing development in Grenoble, see J. Lacoste, "Conception et production de l'habitat dans l'agglomération Grenobloise" (Grenoble: Unité d'enseignement et de recherche Urbanisation-aménagement, January 1977), 50.

76. Jean Verlhac, "AUAG [Agence d'urbanisme de l'agglomération Grenobloise]: Un instrument d'action municipale," *Urbanisme* 37, no. 107 (1968): 9.

77. Pascale Blin, *L'AUA: Mythe et réalités. L'Atelier d'urbanisme et d'architecture, 1960–1985* (Paris and Milan: Moniteur/Electa, 1988).

78. See "A.U.A. et architecture urbaine," *Architecture française,* no. 391 (1973): 76–100.

79. Rose Bergouignan and Simone Martin, "La Villeneuve de Grenoble" (Grenoble: Agence d'urbanisme de l'agglomération Grenobloise [AUAG], March 1973), Annex 1.

80. "Description de la rue intérieure du quartier 1" (AM Grenoble: 858W 40 October 1970).

81. Parent, "Villeneuve de Grenoble Échirolles," 52.

82. The school was modeled after the CES-MJC of Val d'Yerres, which had opened recently. See Agence d'urbanisme de l'agglomération Grenobloise (AUAG), "Quartier 1: Programme d'équipements collectifs–Dossier provisoire" (AM Grenoble: 858W 3610 April 1969). See also chapter 6.

83. "Correspondance avec les administrations et comptes rendus de réunions, 1969–1971" (AM Grenoble: 858W 33).

84. Parent, "Villeneuve de Grenoble Échirolles," 64.

85. For planners' intentions, see "Réflexions sur une politique du logement à propos du Quartier 1 Villeneuve" (AM Grenoble: 858W 40: Quartier 1: Études d'aménagement June 1971). For a list of what was eventually built, see Parent, "Villeneuve de Grenoble Échirolles," 54.

86. "Centre Commercial Arlequin: Études, 1970–1979" (AM Grenoble: 858W 238).

87. Jean-François Parent, "Évaluation de l'Arlequin 9.12.1976—Données démographiques" (AM Grenoble: 858W 43: Évaluations sur la vie du quartier I, 1974–77).

88. "Du gazon pas de béton" (AM Grenoble: 10Z.39: Le Manteau de l'Arlequin May 1973); "Les mots et les choses" (AM Grenoble: 10Z.39: Le Manteau de l'Arlequin May 1973).

89. "Arlequin, Premier Bilan" (AM Grenoble: 858W 43: Évaluations sur la vie du quartier I, 1974–1977 March 1977).

90. Eva Radwan, "Les mètres-carrés sociaux du Quartier de l'Arlequin" (AM Grenoble 858W 34: Études–projet quartier I, 1971–1972 14 May 1973).

91. Eva Radwan, "Observation de l'Arlequin" (AM Grenoble: 858W 43: Évaluations sur la vie du quartier I, 1974–1977 April 1974).

92. "Arlequin, Premier Bilan," 41.

93. In the mid-1970s, the total number of foreigners was 14 percent. In the housing units of l'Arlequin itself, this group was made up of 8 percent Italian, 7 percent Spanish, 4 percent Portuguese, 63 percent North African, 18 percent other. See Parent, "Évaluation de l'Arlequin 9.12.1976—Données démographiques."

94. Abouzaïd Mohammed, "Mémoire de sciences politiques sur Grenoble-Villeneuve" (AM Grenoble: 858W 43: Évaluations sur la vie du quartier I, 1974–1977–1976).

95. Agence d'urbanisme de l'agglomération Grenobloise (AUAG), "Observation du Quartier de l'Arlequin" (AM Grenoble 858W 34: Études–projet quartier I, 1971–1972).

96. Radwan, "Observation de l'Arlequin."

97. "Arlequin, Premier Bilan."

98. Judith Rueff, "À Grenoble, la Villeneuve au bout de ses utopies," *Urbanisme* 264–65 (1993): 32–35.

99. Jean Giard, "La ville-neuve ouvre ses portes" (AM Grenoble: Folder of Publicity Brochures 1975).

100. Manuel Castells and Francis Godard, *Monopolville: Analyse des rapports entre l'entreprise, l'État et l'urbain à partir d'une enquête sur la croissance industrielle et urbaine de la région de Dunkerque* (Paris: Mouton, 1974); Édmond Preteceille, *La production des grands ensembles: Essai d'analyse des déterminants de l'environnement urbain* (Paris: Mouton, 1973); Topalov, "Centre de recherche," 195–201.

101. See, for instance, the archive deposits of *GRECOH* [Groupe de recherches et d'études sur la construction et l'habitation] *Service de l'habitation,* under direction of André Trintignac (CAC 19771141, 19771142, 19771152).

102. See "Le Groupe permanent de coordination 'Habitat et vie sociale,'" *Habitat et vie sociale,* no. 1 (November–December 1973). See also chapter 2.

103. For Sarcelles, see Boucher and Théry, "L'expérience des conseils de résidents." For Grenoble, see J. M. Boucher and A. Gotman, "Animation globale et équipement intégrés: Le quartier de l'Arlequin à Grenoble," *Habitat et vie sociale,* no. 1 (November–December 1973); Albert Rousseau and Roger Beaunez, *L'expérience de Grenoble: L'action municipale, ses possibilités, ses limites* (Paris: Éditions ouvrières, 1971).

104. J. Sebastianelli, "Dans les Bouches-du-Rhône, un dispositif de concertation 'Habitat et vie sociale,'" *Habitat et vie sociale,* no. 2 (January–February 1974).

105. Françoise de Barros, "Genèse de la politique de Développement Social des Quartiers: Éléments de formalisation d'un 'problème des banlieues,'" DEA (Diplôme d'études approfondies) thesis, Université Paris 1, 1994.

106. Tissot, *L'État et les quartiers*; Jacques Donzelot, *Faire société: La politique de la ville aux États-Unis et en France* (Paris: Seuil, 2003).

107. Michael Miller, *The Representation of Place: Urban Planning and Protest in France and Great Britain, 1950–1980* (Aldershot and Burlington, Vt.: Ashgate, 2003).

108. See "Consultation revitalisation Les Flanades" (AM Sarcelles W25).

109. Ibid.; "Sarcelles ouvre son cœur, brochure" (AD Val d'Oise BIB D613).

5. Programming the *Villes Nouvelles*

1. Pierre Viot, "Les villes nouvelles en France: Avenir ou fiction?" *Revue Projet* (July–August 1969).

2. See *Schéma directeur d'aménagement et d'urbanisme de la région de Paris*, (Paris: District de Paris/Premier Ministre, 1965). See also François Fourquet and Lion Murard, *La naissance des villes nouvelles: Anatomie d'une décision (1961–1969)* (Paris: Presses de l'École nationale des Ponts et chaussées, 2004).

3. See Roselyne Chenu, *Paul Delouvrier ou la passion d'agir* (Paris: Seuil, 1994).

4. *Schéma directeur d'aménagement et d'urbanisme de la région de Paris*, 70–71. See also Frédérique Boucher, "Les modèles étrangers," *Cahiers de l'IHTP (Institut d'histoire du temps présent)*, no. 17 (1990): 23–34.

5. "La banlieue sous-équipée," in *Schéma directeur d'aménagement et d'urbanisme de la région de Paris*, 50.

6. "Comment se bâtissent les villes nouvelles—Les constructeurs ont une hantise: ne pas recommencer Sarcelles," *Paris-Presse*, June 5, 1966. See also "Note concernant la conception et la réalisation des centres urbains des villes nouvelles de la région parisienne, IAURP, June 1969" (CAC 199110585/011).

7. "Déclaration sur les orientations de la politique urbaine, par Olivier Guichard à l'Assemblée nationale," *Journal officiel de la République française*, May 17, 1973.

8. See Annie Fourcaut and Loïc Vadelorge, eds., *Histoire urbaine* (theme: "Villes nouvelles et grands ensembles"), no. 17 (2006).

9. "Sondage sur les villes nouvelles, SIGMA, 1969–1970" (CAC 19840342/391).

10. See AM Sarcelles. About the uses of the term *ville nouvelle*, see Laurent Coudroi de Lille, "'Ville nouvelle' ou 'grand ensemble': Les usages localisés d'une terminolgie bien particulière en région parisienne (1965–1980)," *Histoire urbaine*, no. 17 (2006): 47–66.

11. Annie Fourcaut, "Les grands ensembles ont-ils été conçus comme des villes nouvelles?" *Histoire urbaine*, no. 17 (2006): 7–25.

12. Pierre Sudreau, "Déclaration," *L'Architecture d'aujourd'hui*, no. 66 (July 1956).

13. "Problèmes posés par la vie dans les grands ensembles d'habitation, déclaration de Gérard Dupont, 1959" (CAC 19770816/005).

14. "Pour une expérience pilote d'action sur l'environnement urbain: La ville nouvelle d'Évry et la mise en œuvre d'une politique de l'environnement, 1970" (CAC 19780319/001).

15. Pierre Merlin, *Les villes nouvelles: Urbanisme régional et aménagement* (Paris: Presses Universitaires de France, 1969).

16. "Réunions du groupe de travail interministériel sur les villes nouvelles de la région parisienne, compte rendu 28 June 1966" (CAC 199110585/002).

17. "Cergy-Pontoise: Un cœur de ville dans une éprouvette de béton," *Le Monde*, November 3, 1970; "Il n'y a pas encore d'habitants et pourtant . . . Cergy-Pontoise vit déjà grâce à sa préfecture," *La Croix*, June 6, 1971.

18. Hashim Sarkis, "A Second Functionalism: Form, Flexibility, and the Architecture of Schools in the United States during the 1950s," lecture at Harvard Humanities Center, November 9, 2011.

19. Stanley Mathews, *From Agit-prop to Free Space: The Architecture of Cedric Price* (London: Black Dog, 2007).

20. After Bloch-Lainé's lecture "À la recherche d'une 'économie concertée'" (Paris, 1959). See Henry Ehrmann, "French Bureaucracy and Organized Interests," *Administrative Science Quarterly* 5, no. 4 (1961): 553.

21. Richard F. Kuisel, *Capitalism and the State in Modern France: Renovation and Economic Management in the Twentieth Century* (Cambridge and New York: Cambridge University Press, 1981), 256.

22. De Grazia, *Irresistible Empire*.

23. Saul Estrin and Peter Holmes, *French Planning in Theory and Practice* (London and Boston: George Allen & Unwin, 1983).

24. On the *grille Dupont*, see chapter 3.

25. On French shopping-mall development, see chapter 6.

26. "Rapports généraux de la Commission du bâtiment et des travaux publics, et de la Commission de l'habitation, IV Plan, n.d. /1964?" (CAC 19771152/001). See also Bruno Lefebvre, Michel Mouillart, and Sylvie Occhipinti, *Politique du logement, cinquante ans pour un échec* (Paris: L'Harmattan, 1992).

27. See "Financement de la Construction (1966–68): Avis et rapport du Conseil économique et social, 26.03.1968" (CAC 19771142/045).

28. On single-family home development, see chapter 7.

29. See chapter 1.

30. Chenu, *Paul Delouvrier ou la passion d'agir*.

31. See Jean-Charles Fredenucci, "L'entregent colonial des ingénieurs des Ponts et chaussées dans l'urbanisme des années 1950–1970," *Vingtième siècle, Revue d'histoire* 3, no. 79 (2003): 79–91.

32. Labasse, *L'organisation de l'espace, éléments de géographie volontaire*.

33. Extrait des avis recueillis sur le Schéma directeur d'aménagement et d'urbanisme de la région de Paris, published by La Documentation française in 1966, quoted in Jean-Paul Alduy, "L'aménagement de la région de Paris entre 1930 et 1975: De la planification à la politique urbaine," *Sociologie du Travail*, no. 2 (April–June 1979): 179.

34. Pierre Merlin, *Les villes nouvelles en France* (Paris: Presses Universitaires de France, 1991), 38.

35. "Pontoise-Cergy ville nouvelle, brochure de promotion, 1968" (CAC 199110585/009).

36. Jean-Claude Richez and Léon Strauss, "Un temps nouveau pour les ouvriers: Les congés payés," in *L'avènement des loisirs, 1850–1960*, ed. Alain Corbin (Paris: Champs/Flammarion, 1995).

37. Joffre Dumazedier and Maurice Imbert, *Espace et loisir dans la société française d'hier et de demain*, 2 vols. (Paris: Centre de recherche sur l'urbanisme, 1967).

38. Ibid., 1:10.

39. "Compte rendu, 28 avril 1969, présentation Albin Chalandon, Ministère de l'équipement" (CAC 19840342/023).

40. "Notes d'Alain Lagier sur les villes nouvelles, 11 avril 1969, Ministère de l'équipement" (CAC 19840342/023).

41. "L'action de l'État en matière foncière dans les villes nouvelles, note de Jean-Eudes Roullier, 22 mars 1969" (CAC 19840342/023).

42. In 1954, the region counted 67,000 inhabitants, and in 1967 150,000 inhabitants. See "La ville nouvelle d'Évry, par Jean-Louis Faure, Institut d'études politiques de Paris" (CAC 199110585/009).

43. Jacques Guyard, *Évry Ville Nouvelle 1960–2003: La troisième banlieue* (Évry: Espaces Sud, 2003), 45.

44. "Groupe I: Structures urbaines, Commission de l'Équipement urbain, CGP: Rapport définitif, 1966" (CAC 19920405/007).

45. "L'expérience française des villes nouvelles, Fondation nationale des sciences politiques (n.d.), Jean-Eudes Roullier" (CAC 19840342/171).

46. Melvin Webber, "The Urban Place and the Non-Place Urban Realm," in *Explorations into Urban Structure* (Philadelphia: University of Pennsylvania Press, 1964), 79.

47. Derek Walker, *The Architecture and Planning of Milton Keynes* (London: Architectural Press, 1982).

48. André Darmagnac, François Desbruyères, and Michel Mottez, *Créer un centre ville: Évry* (Paris: Éditions du Moniteur, 1980), 32; "Évry, centre urbain nouveau et ville nouvelle," *Cahiers de l'IAURP* 15 (1969).

49. Thoenig, *L'ère des technocrates*.

50. Hecht, "Planning a Technological Nation."

51. Thoenig, *L'ère des technocrates*, 99–112, 16.

52. Pierre George, "Enseignement et recherche en urbanisme," *Annales de géographie* 74, no. 406 (1965): 733–36.

53. "Le Centre de recherche sur l'urbanisme," *Urbanisme* 75–76 (1962).

54. Dumazedier and Imbert, *Espace et loisir dans la société française d'hier et de demain*, 1:1.

55. "Editorial," *Urbanisme* 93 (1966): 1.

56. Claude, *Faire la ville*, 103–55; Viviane Claude, "Les équipes d'aménagement des villes nouvelles," *Annales de la recherche urbaine*, no. 98 (2005): 14–24.

57. "La ville nouvelle d'Évry, par Jean-Louis Faure, Institut d'études politiques de Paris," 12.

58. J. M. Boyer, "La programmation urbaine et architecturale: L'expérience des villes nouvelles," Ph.D. dissertation, École des hautes études en sciences sociales, 1983.

59. CERFI, "Généalogie des équipements collectifs: Première synthèse" (Paris: Copedith, 1973), 9.

60. Ibid., 72–73.

61. CERFI, "La programmation des équipements collectifs dans les villes nouvelles: Les équipements d'hygiène mentale" (January 1972).

62. CERFI, "Programme général provisoire des équipements d'hygiène mentale de la ville nouvelle d'Évry" (February 1973).

63. Gilles Deleuze and Félix Guattari, *L'Anti-Œedipe: Capitalisme et schizophrénie* (Paris: Minuit, 1972).

64. CERFI, "Programme général provisoire des équipements d'hygiène mentale de la ville nouvelle d'Évry." The group also established programs for Melun-Senart and Marne-la-Vallée.

65. See, for instance, the interview with Foucault, Deleuze, and Guattari conducted by François Fourquet in Michel Foucault, "Equipments of Power: Towns, Territories and Collective Equipments," in *Foucault Live (Interviews, 1961–1984),* ed. Sylvère Lotringer (New York: Semiotext[e], 1989), 105–12. This interview first appeared in *Recherches* 13 (December 1973).

66. Bernard Hirsch, *Oublier Cergy . . . L'invention d'une ville nouvelle, Cergy-Pontoise 1965–1975. Récit d'un témoignage* (Paris: Presses de l'École nationale des Ponts et chaussées, 1990), 58.

67. Ibid., 73.

68. Ibid., 146.

69. Ibid., 149.

70. See Jean-Paul Trystram et al., "Sociologie et développement urbain" (Paris: Ministère de la construction, 1966).

71. Jean-Paul Trystram, ed., *Sociologie et urbanisme* (Paris: Fondation Royaumont–Éditions de l'Epi, 1970).

72. See Pierre Lassave, *Les sociologues et la recherche urbaine dans la France contemporaine* (Toulouse: Presses Universitaires du Mirail, 1997).

73. Hubert Tonka, "Pratique urbaine de l'urbanisme," *Urbanisme* 106 (1968): 7.

74. For a compilation of the journal in English, see Craig Buckley and Jean-Louis Violeau, *Utopie: Texts and Projects, 1967–1978* (Los Angeles: Semiotext[e], 2011).

75. See Claude Parent, *Claude Parent: L'œuvre construite, l'œuvre graphique* (Orléans: HYX, 2010).

76. Michel Mottez, *Carnets de campagne: Évry 1965–2007* (Paris: L'Harmattan, 2003), 39.

77. See "Programmes d'actions concertées, 1966–1970" (CAC 19771142/041).

78. See Jeannine Verdes-Leroux, "Les Candidats-aménageurs dans une organisation en quête de finalité: Le Service technique central d'aménagement et d'urbanisme" (Paris: Copedith, 1972).

79. Michel Conan was inspired by U.S. urban research and was very critical of quantitative models (interview by the author with Anne Querrien, February 25, 2008).

80. "Programmes d'actions concertées, 1966–1970." See also DGRST research programs of 1972–1974 (CAC 19910319/045&047).

81. "Rapport du Groupe V: Études urbaines, septembre 1965" (CAC 19920405/009). See also Claude, *Faire la ville*, 168–78.

82. See, for instance, Topalov, "Centre de recherche."

83. Amiot, *Contre l'État, les sociologues*, 41.

84. Violeau, *Les architectes et mai 68.*

85. See Michel Denès, *Le fantôme des Beaux-Arts: L'enseignement de l'architecture depuis 1968* (Paris: La Villette, 1999). See also Lengereau, *L'État et l'architecture, 1958–1981*, 85–106; Jacques Lucan, *Architecture en France, 1940–2000: Histoire et théories* (Paris: Moniteur, 2001), 187–200.

86. "Courses by André Gutton and Robert Auzelle" (AN ENSBA AJ/52/978). See also André Gutton, "SATG 1961–1973 Séminaire et Atelier Tony Garnier," *Urbanisme* 142 (1974).

87. André Gutton, "Séminaire et Atelier Tony Garnier: L'enseignement de l'urbanisme à l'ENSBA," *Urbanisme* 82–83 (1964): 100. See also his published courses: André Gutton, *Conversations sur l'architecture*, vol. 6: *L'architecte et l'urbaniste* (Paris: Vincent Fréal & Cie, 1962).

88. "Introduction à la sociologie urbaine, Cours de Margot-Duclot, année 1961–1962, Institut d'Urbanisme de Paris Créteil" (CAC 19890277/002).

89. "Théorie générale de l'urbanisme, Cours Robert Auzelle, année 1959–1960, Institut d'Urbanisme de Paris Créteil" (CAC 19890277/002).

90. *Atelier populaire, présenté par lui-même: 87 affiches de mai–juin 1968* (Paris: Bibliothèque de Mai, U.U.U. [Usines, Universités, Union], 1968).

91. See "L'institut d'urbanisme en autogestion: Commission d'étude de l'enseignement," *Urbanisme* 106 (1968).

92. Monique Eleb and Christian Gaillard, "Le savoir et la provocation," in *Espaces des sciences humaines: Questions d'enseignement en architecture*, ed. Centre de recherche en sciences humaines (Paris: Institut de l'environnement, 1974), 13–26.

93. See Jean-Louis Violeau, "Why and How 'To Do Science'? On the Often Ambiguous Relationship between Architecture and the Social Sciences in France in the Wake of May '68," *Footprint*, no. 1 (2007): 9; Denès, *Le fantôme des Beaux-Arts*, 111–15.

94. See, for instance, *Besoin(s): Analyse et critique de la notion. Cahiers pédagogiques*, no. 5 (Paris: Institut de l'environnement/Centre de recherche en sciences humaines, 1975).

95. Jean Baudrillard, "Genèse idéologique des besoins," *Cahiers internationaux de sociologie* 16, no. 47 (June–December 1969): 61.

96. See, for instance, Françoise Bedos et al., eds., *Les besoins fonctionnels de l'homme en vue de leur projection ultérieure sur le plan de la conception architecturale, compte rendu de fin de contrat* (Paris: CRAUC [Centre de recherche d'architecture, d'urbanisme et de construction], 1970).

97. Michèle Teboul, "Ailleurs, Colloque 1972," in Centre de recherche en sciences humaines, *Espaces des sciences humaines*, 36.

98. Bernard Huet edited the important issue "Recherche + Habitat" of *L'Architecture d'aujourd'hui* in 1974.

99. "Presentation of the office AUA, sent in by the architects, n.d." (CAC 19840342/324).

100. Blin, *L'AUA*.

101. See Claire Brossaud, *Le Vaudreuil Ville Nouvelle (Val-de-Reuil) et son imaginaire bâtisseur: Identification d'un champ autour d'une ville* (Paris: L'Harmattan, 2003). For a first-person historical account, see Jean Maze, *L'aventure du Vaudreuil: Histoire d'une ville nouvelle* (Paris: Dominique Vincent, 1977). See also Frédéric Saunier, "L'urbanisation en Basse-Seine: Regards sur la conception et l'évolution des grands ensembles et de la ville nouvelle du Vaudreuil," *Histoire urbaine*, no. 17 (2006): 129–46.

102. See the publications of Catherine Blain based on Catherine Blain, "L'Atelier de Montrouge (1958–1981): Prolégomènes à une autre modernité," Ph.D. dissertation, Université Paris 8, 2001.

103. For a brief history of the office, see Catherine Blain and Dominique Delaunay, *L'Atelier de Montrouge: La modernité à l'œuvre, 1958–1981* (Paris: Actes sud/Cité de l'architecture et du patrimoine, 2008), 15–23.

104. See Busbea, *Topologies*.

105. Catherine Blain, "L'Atelier de Montrouge et Le Vaudreuil," *Ethnologie française*, no. 1 (January–March 2003): 45.

106. André Grandsard, "Le recours aux sciences humaines dans la conception de la ville nouvelle de Vaudreuil, 1967–1973," Ph.D. dissertation, École des hautes études en sciences sociales, 1989, 30.

107. Interview with Gérard Héliot in ibid., 56.

108. Ibid., 84.

109. Blain, "L'Atelier de Montrouge et Le Vaudreuil," 44.

110. "Le Vaudreuil, ville nouvelle: Premières recherches, MEBS/Atelier de Montrouge, avril 1968" (CAA ATM 162 IFA 712).

111. Jean Renaudie, "Pour une connaissance de la ville," *L'Architecture d'aujourd'hui*, no. 146 (October–November 1969): 12.

112. Ibid., 13. For Jean Renaudie's critique of CIAM functionalism, see Paul Bossard, Claude Parent, and Jean Renaudie, "Trois architectes répondent," *L'Architecture d'aujourd'hui*, no. 138 (June–July 1968): 30–33.

113. Jean-François Sirinelli, "Les années 1960, première manière," in *Histoire culturelle de la France: Le temps des masses, le vingtième siècle*, vol. 4, ed. Jean-Pierre Rioux and Jean-François Sirinelli (Paris: Seuil, 1998), 260; Jean-Pierre Delas and Bruno Milly, *Histoire des pensées sociologiques* (Paris: Dalloz/Sirey, 1997), 233–59.

114. "Patterns for Le Vaudreuil, SAR Eindhoven, mai 1971, étude pour MEVNV" (CAA ATM 162 IFA 1551/1).

115. "Notes sur la création des villes par leurs habitants ou le droit à l'architecture, Pierre Riboulet, octobre 1968, in Recherches pour la ville nouvelle du Vaudreuil, 1972" (CAA ATM 162 IFA 713).

116. Henri Lefebvre, *Le droit à la ville* (Paris: Anthropos, 1968), 155.

117. Henri Raymond et al., *L'habitat pavillonnaire* (Paris: Centre de recherche d'urbanisme, 1964).

118. Philippe Boudon, *Pessac de Le Corbusier, 1927–1967: Étude socio-architecturale* (Paris: Dunod, 1969); translated as *Lived-in Architecture: Le Corbusier's Pessac revisited* (London: Humphries, 1972).

119. Łukasz Stanek, "Henri Lefebvre and the Concrete Research of Space: Urban Theory, Empirical Studies, Architecture Practice," Ph.D. dissertation, Delft University of Technology, 2008, 118.

120. Bedos et al., *Les besoins fonctionnels de l'homme en vue de leur projection ultérieure sur le plan de la conception architecturale, compte rendu de fin de contrat*, 2.

121. "La mobilité dans l'architecture en tant que moyen d'appropriation, Pierre Riboulet, décembre 1968, in Recherches pour la ville nouvelle du Vaudreuil, 1972" (CAA ATM 162 IFA 713), 4.

122. "Groupe de réflexion sur les équipements socio-éducatifs, séance du 18 septembre 1969, notes de Pierre Riboulet" (CAA ATM 162 IFA 1540/3).

123. "La mobilité dans l'architecture en tant que moyen d'appropriation, Pierre Riboulet, décembre 1968, in Recherches pour la ville nouvelle du Vaudreuil, 1972," 1.

124. "Objectifs et méthode, Thurnauer & Héliot, MEVNV juin 1969" (CAA ATM 162 IFA 1540/3).

125. Stanek, "Henri Lefebvre and the Concrete Research of Space," 118–49.

126. Irénée Scalbert, *A Right to Difference: The Architecture of Jean Renaudie* (London: Architectural Association, 2004), cover citation.

127. "Notes sur la création des villes par leurs habitants ou le droit à l'architecture, Pierre Riboulet, octobre 1968, in *Recherches pour la ville nouvelle du Vaudreuil, 1972*"; Renaudie, "Pour une connaissance de la ville."

128. See chapter 6.

129. "Le Vaudreuil: Une méthode d'étude et de réalisation," *Cahiers de l'IAURP* 30 (February 1973): 1.

130. This was the slogan of the poster for the 1972 exhibition (Blain, "L'Atelier de Montrouge et Le Vaudreuil," 47).

6. Megastructures in Denial

1. "Évry: L'intendance a précédé," *Le point*, March 24, 1975.

2. "Une oasis au milieu du désert," *Le Figaro*, February 27, 1975.

3. "Des commerces mais aussi des lieux de rencontre: Une place à l'anciennce pour la ville nouvelle d'Évry," *Le Monde*, March 18, 1975.

4. "Fermera-t'on l'agora d'Évry? Le financement des investissements publics," *Le Monde*, March 20, 1975.

5. "Rapport sur les villes nouvelles, Commission des villes–Groupe ad hoc 'villes nouvelles,' 1969" (CAC 199110585/002).

6. Jean-François Gravier, *Paris et le désert français* (Paris: Portulan, 1947).

7. Bernard Lepetit, *Les villes dans la France moderne, 1740–1840* (Paris: Albin Michel, 1988).

8. Nicholas Dagen Bloom, *Suburban Alchemy: 1960s New Towns and the Transformation of the American Dream* (Columbus: Ohio State University Press, 2001).

9. "Évry An II: Le cœur d'une ville se crée sous nos yeux," *La vie française*, October 22, 1971.

10. Tyrwhitt, Sert, and Rogers, *CIAM 8*.

11. Gilles Ragot and Mathilde Dion, *Le Corbusier en France: Projets et réalisations* (Paris: Moniteur, 1997), 284–89.

12. On Gruen's mall designs, see Alex Wall, *Victor Gruen: From Urban Shop to New City* (Barcelona: Actar, 2005), 65–92.

13. See Dossiers permis de construire (AM Sarcelles).

14. On the history of the *dalle*, see Virginie Lefebvre, "Les origines de l'architecture sur dalle," in *Les années ZUP: Architectures de la croissance 1960–1973*, ed. Gérard Monnier and Richard Klein (Paris: Picard, 2002), 251–80; Virginie Lefebvre, *Paris, ville moderne: Maine-Montparnasse et La Défense, 1950–1970* (Paris: Éditions Norma, 2003). See also Rosemary Wakeman, "Les Dalles: French Modernism and the Architecture of Public Space," presentation at conference "Sanctioning Modernism: A Symposium on Post–World War II architecture," University of Texas at Austin School of Architecture, March 2, 2007.

15. See Busbea, *Topologies*.

16. See Mark Wigley, "Network Fever," *Grey Room* 4 (2001): 82–122.

17. Busbea, *Topologies*.

18. Hadas A. Steiner, *Beyond Archigram: The Structure of Circulation* (London: Routledge, 2009).

19. Maurice Doublet quoted in Jean-Eudes Roullier, "Les villes nouvelles et l'innovation," *Revue 2000* (January 1973): 10.

20. See Jean Labasse, "Signification et avenir des centres," *Urbanisme* 120–21 (1970); Paul Rendu, "Rôle fonctionnel du centre," *Urbanisme* 120–21 (1970).

21. Guyard, *Évry Ville Nouvelle 1960–2003*, 43; Darmagnac, Desbruyères, and Mottez, *Créer un centre ville*. See also chapter 5.

22. "Ville nouvelle d'Évry, Brochure, Mission d'étude et d'aménagement de la ville nouvelle d'Évry, 1969" (CAC 199110585/009).

23. Maurice-François Rouge, "La logique du non quantifiable," *Urbanisme* 9 (1967): lix.

24. On Paris urban renewal, see Jacques Lucan, "Cinq cent mille hectares à reconquérir," in *Eau et gaz à tous les étages. Paris, 100 ans de logements*, ed. Jacques Lucan (Paris: Picard, 1992): 136–51.

25. Interview with André Lalande in "Une ville latine moyenne phare d'une région: Voilà ce que veulent réaliser les bâtisseurs d'Évry, mais cela ne va pas sans poser de sérieux problèmes . . . ," *Le journal du dimanche*, March 18, 1973.

26. "Colloque Centres Urbains: Texte des conférences et débats, 2–3–4 juillet, 1969" (Paris: Bureau des villes nouvelles, Direction de l'aménagement foncier et de l'urbanisme, Ministère de l'équipement et du logement).

27. Maze, *L'aventure du Vaudreuil*, 98.

28. "Journée d'études du 17 octobre 1973 sur les centres urbains" (CAC 19840342/334), 32–33.

29. Aymeric Zublena, Patrice Noviant, and Xavier Triplet, "Les centres urbaines des villes nouvelles françaises" (Paris: Ministère de l'équipement/Secrétariat général du Groupe central des villes nouvelles, 1972), 17 (CAC 19840342/335).

30. See chapter 3.

31. On *équipement intégré* in French New Towns, see Korganow, "L'équipement socio-culturel, trajectoire architecturale d'un type contrarié d'édifice public à l'ère des loisirs, 1936–1975," 217–310; Alexis Korganow, Tricia Meehan, and Clément Orillard, *L'interaction ville-équipement en ville nouvelle: Réception et adaptation de la formule d'équipement socio-culturel intégré* (Paris: Atelier IV: Architecture, formes urbaines et cadre de vie, Programme interministériel d'histoire et d'évaluation des villes nouvelles françaises, 2005).

32. Quote from "Les équipements intégrés, La Documentation française, 1974. Foreword by Augustin Girard" (CAC 19840342/191).

33. "Circulaire sur les orientations et procédures à suivre en matière d'intégration des équipements," *Journal officiel de la République française*, November 19, 1973.

34. Agence d'urbanisme de l'agglomération grenobloise, "Les équipements intégrés, Rapport final. Agence d'urbanisme de l'agglomération grenobloise (8 fascicules)" (Paris: Ministère de l'éducation nationale/Ministère de l'aménagement du territoire, de l'équipement et du tourisme, February 1973), fasc. 1, 7.

35. Nicole Chartier, "Les équipements intégrés" (Paris: Institut d'études politiques, n.d., around 1972), 44.

36. "Circulaire sur les orientations et procédures à suivre en matière d'intégration des équipements."

37. "Révolution administrative et financière nécessaire pour créer de véritables centres urbains dans les villes nouvelles: Le cloisonnement entre les ministères empêche la polyvalence et le regroupement des équipements," *Le Figaro*, October 27, 1970.

38. See, for example, Jean Chauchoy, "L'intégration des équipements collectifs urbains," *Urbanisme* 125 (1971): 13–15.

39. Joseph Belmont, *L'architecture, création collective* (Paris: Éditions ouvrières, 1970).

40. Francis Strauven, *Aldo van Eyck: The Shape of Relativity* (Amsterdam: Architecture & Natura, 1998).

41. See, for instance, French school architecture in *L'Architecture d'aujourd'hui* 72 (1957).

42. See chapter 4.

43. Henry Théry quoted in Jean Chabanne and Philippe Cougnot, "Réflexions sur l'intégration des équipements," *Urbanisme* 125 (1971): 22.

44. Ionel Schein, *Espace global polyvalent* (Paris: Vincent, Fréal & Cie, 1970), 1.

45. Ibid., 9.

46. See, for instance, "Pays-Bas, espace polyvalent: Centres socio-culturels à Dronten et à Lelystad," *Techniques et architecture* 32, no. 1 (1970): 36–41. See also CAC 19840342/191.

47. "Équipements publics et privés: Montage d'une cohabitation, bilan sur l'exemple d'Évry, André Darmagnac, n.d." (CAC 19840342/191).

48. On the Agora and other works of van Klingeren, see Marina van den Bergen and Piet Vollaard, *Hinder en Ontklontering: Architectuur en Maatschappij in het Werk van Frank van Klingeren* (Rotterdam: Uitgeverij 010, 2003).

49. Schein, *Espace global polyvalent*, 14.

50. Ibid.

51. Ivan Illich was a standard reference for the French post-1968 generation. See, for instance, "Dans le laboratoire des villes nouvelles: Faire coïncider la vie quotidienne avec les structures," *Le Monde*, June 3, 1976.

52. "Les lieux du spectacle," *L'Architecture d'aujourd'hui* 152 (October–November 1970): entire issue.

53. Chartier, "Les équipements intégrés," 70.

54. A first conference titled "Équipements intégrés et villes nouvelles" took place on October 24, 1970, under direction of Paul Delouvrier. See conference proceedings in "Équipements intégrés et villes nouvelles," *Pour*, nos. 23–24 (October 1971): entire issue.

55. "Colloque Centres Urbains."

56. Zublena, Noviant, and Triplet, "Les centres urbaines des villes nouvelles françaises," 17.

57. The first urban self-service supermarkets opened in the late 1940s; see de Grazia, *Irresistible Empire*, 382. The first *suburban* self-service supermarket opened around 1955. See "Les centres commerciaux péri-urbains: Difficultés d'une adaption," *CDC*, no. 62 (1973).

58. See chapter 2.

59. Jean-Marc Villermet, *Naissance de l'hypermarché* (Paris: Armand Colin, 1991); Christian Lhermie, *Carrefour ou l'invention de l'hypermarché* (Paris: Vuibert, 2003); Jacques Marseille, ed., *La révolution commerciale en France: Du "bon marché" à l'hypermarché* (Paris: Le Monde-Éditions, 1997); René Péron, *La fin des vitrines: Des temples de la consommation aux usines à vendre* (Paris: Cachan/Éditions de l'École nationale supérieure, 1993); Solange Jungers, "L'invention de l'hypermarché," in *Les Années ZUP: Architectures de la croissance 1960–1973*, ed. Gérard Monnier and Richard Klein (Paris: Picard, 2002).

60. Villermet, *Naissance de l'hypermarché,* 125–29.

61. See "L'équipement commercial doit être un facteur d'urbanisme," *CDC* (March 1969).

62. See "Centre commercial de Parly 2, brochure, n.d." (CAC 199110585/011). The information in the brochure was based on a research report by CECOD titled "Les commerçants des nouveaux centres" for the Ministry of Finance.

63. See "L'équipement commercial des ensembles résidentiels: Réalisation des centres commerciaux, M. Le Besnerais, INEP Marly-le-Roi, 1961" (CAC 19780633/001).

64. See Commissariat général du plan d'équipement et de la productivité, "Rapport général de la Commission du Commerce, IVᵉ Plan, 1962–1965" (Paris: Imprimerie nationale, 1962), 118.

65. See Hervé Martin, "Dix ans d'urbanisme commercial ou les leçons d'un échec," *Libre-Service Actualités,* no. 286 (1968). See also the official directive of 1969: "Place de l'équipement commercial dans le développement urbain," *Journal officiel de la République française,* August 27, 1969.

66. Jean-Louis Solal, "Le centre commercial région de Parly 2," *Urbanisme* 108–9 (May–June 1968); "Centre commercial régional de Parly 2," *Urbanisme* 114 (June 1969).

67. Michel Sauquet and Pierre Di Meglio, "L'expérience d'implantation des centres urbains nouveaux de la région parisienne" (Paris: Cerau-Beture/Université Paris IX, Dauphine/UER Sciences et organisations, July 1971).

68. Victor Gruen and Larry Smith, *Shopping Towns U.S.A.* (New York: Reinhold, 1960).

69. See Korganow, Meehan, and Orillard, *L'interaction ville-équipement en ville nouvelle,* 91.

70. "Centres urbains AREAUR, Études de P. Dimeglio: Memento de la journée d'études du 23.10.1973, organisé par un groupe étude et recherche, DAFU" (CAC 19840342/335), 3–4.

71. See "Centre commercial régional Rosny 2, brochure, n.d." (CAC 19840342/335).

72. Anne Fournié, "Planification et production des centres commerciaux régionaux en France de 1965 à 1981," Ph.D. dissertation, Université Paris 12, 1982.

73. Serge Goldberg and Guy Édouard, *Programmation des centres commerciaux régionaux et intercommunaux en région parisienne* (Paris: IAURP, 1965).

74. See "Les centres commerciaux péri-urbains: Difficultés d'une adaption."

75. Ibid., 19.

76. Jean Baudrillard, *La société de consommation: Ses mythes, ses structures* (Paris: S.G.P.P., 1970), 21–24.

77. Ibid., 27.

78. Schein, *Espace global polyvalent,* 5–6.

79. Jacques Chaban-Delmas quoted in Baudrillard, *La société de consommation,* 298.

80. Jeffrey M. Hardwick, *Mall Maker: Victor Gruen, Architect of an American Dream* (Philadelphia: University of Pennsylvania Press, 2003).

81. Gruen and Smith, *Shopping Towns U.S.A.,* 23–24.

82. Wall, *Victor Gruen;* Victor Gruen, "The Sad Story of Shopping Centers," *Town and Country Planning* 46 (1978): 350–53.

83. "Report by Victor Gruen for IAURP, August 1968" (CAC 19840342/337). On the cellular metropolis idea, see Victor Gruen, *The Heart of Our Cities: The Urban Crisis, Diagnosis and Cure* (New York: Simon & Schuster, 1964), 266–96.

84. Korganow, Meehan, and Orillard, *L'interaction ville-équipement en ville nouvelle,* 94–98.

85. Ibid., 86.

86. Sauquet and Di Meglio, "L'expérience d'implantation des centres urbains nouveaux de la région parisienne," 8–9.

87. See Sandra Parvu, *Grands ensembles en situation: Journal de bord de quatre chantiers* (Geneva: Mētis Presses, 2010).

88. The initiative for the new development came from the municipality and the department. There was already a *grand ensemble* at Mont-Mesly by SCIC, separated from the existing village. The New Town was to mend both. See "Pose de la première pierre de la ville nouvelle de Créteil," *Le Figaro*, April 2, 1969.

89. Jungers, "L'invention de l'hypermarché," 166.

90. "Colloque Centres Urbains," 10.

91. "Journée d'études du 17 octobre 1973 sur les centres urbains."

92. "Nordweststadt," *L'Architecture d'aujourd'hui*, no. 146 (1969). On Valencia city center, see Wall, *Victor Gruen*, 216.

93. AD Essonne 1523W/638.

94. "Journée d'études du 17 octobre 1973 sur les centres urbains."

95. "Pour une expérience pilote d'action sur l'environnement urbain: La ville nouvelle d'Évry et la mis en œuvre d'une politique de l'environnement, 1970" (CAC 19780319/001), III.1.

96. Le Couteur was chosen by André Lalande and the minister of culture, according to Mottez, *Carnets de campagne*, 64.

97. "Journée d'études du 17 octobre 1973 sur les centres urbains," 39.

98. Michel Mottez, for instance, called them "vulgaires" (Mottez, *Carnets de campagne*, 63).

99. Korganow, Meehan, and Orillard, *L'interaction ville-équipement en ville nouvelle*, 102.

100. "Centre Commercial Régional: Rapport au Conseil d'Administration, EPEVRY, 20 juin 1972" (AD Essonne 1523/W358).

101. "Journée d'études du 17 octobre 1973 sur les centres urbains."

102. "Avec la préfecture 'l'Agora' constituera le cœur de la ville nouvelle d'Évry," *Le Croix*, May 9, 1971.

103. Korganow, Meehan, and Orillard, *L'interaction ville-équipement en ville nouvelle*, 101.

104. "Les équipements intégrés, La Documentation française, 1974. Foreword by Augustin Girard," 22.

105. Guyard, *Évry Ville Nouvelle 1960–2003*, 76.

106. "Évry ou l'espoir de ne plus être une banlieue," *Le Monde*, February 3, 1976.

107. Guyard, *Évry Ville Nouvelle 1960–2003*, 77–80.

108. Similar accounts exist for Cumbernauld—one of Britain's most truthful realizations of the urban center megastructure. See Reyner Banham, *Megastructure: Urban Futures of the Recent Past* (New York: Icon Editions, 1976).

109. At Sarcelles, and also at Évry, for instance, one of the two magnets was a discount store and the other a department store.

110. See Péron, *La fin des vitrines*.

111. "Centres urbains AREAUR, Études de P. Dimeglio: Memento de la journée d'études du 23.10.1973, organisé par une groupe étude et recherche, DAFU [Direction de l'aménagement foncier

et de l'urbanisme]," 24. This was confirmed again in the subsequent report: "Les équipements intégrés, La Documentation française, 1974. Foreword by Augustin Girard," 44.

112. Korganow, Meehan, and Orillard, *L'interaction ville-équipement en ville nouvelle*, 5.

113. Ibid., 62.

114. See, for instance, Diane Ghirardo, *Architecture after Modernism* (London: Thames & Hudson, 1996).

115. "Banham: La Megastrutture é Morta," *Casabella* 375 (1972): 2.

116. Banham, *Megastructure*, 9–10.

117. Manfredo Tafuri, *Theories and History of Architecture* (London: Granada, 1980), 236; originally published in Italian in 1969.

118. Utopie, *Utopia e/o Rivoluzione* (Turin: Editrici Magma, 1969), 34.

119. Banham, *Megastructure*, 10.

7. The Ultimate Projects

1. Quoted in "Modèles innovation 1973–1974–1975" (CAC 19840342/324).

2. Monique Dagnaud, *Le mythe de la qualité de la vie et la politique urbaine en France: Enquête sur l'idéologie urbaine de l'élite technocratique et politique, 1945-1975* (Paris and The Hague: Mouton, 1978).

3. Jacques Riboud, "La maison individuelle et son jardin dans la ville nouvelle: Un récit sur la création de La Haie Bergerie à Villepreux (Yvelines)" (Paris: Éditions Mazarine, n.d.).

4. ADROS (Association pour le développement de la recherche sur l'organisation spatiale), "Les nouveaux villages" (Paris: CRAUC [Centre de recherche d'architecture et d'urbanisme et de construction], 1976), 2.

5. "France: A Lesson from Levitt," *Time*, December 10, 1965.

6. Isabelle Gournay, "Levitt France et la banlieue à l'américaine: Premier bilan," *Histoire urbaine* 5 (2002): 167–88.

7. Paul Delouvrier and Roland Nungesser, in "Villages urbains: Concours 'Habitat individuel' organisé par le District de la région de Paris," *Urbanisme* 82–83 (1964).

8. See Anne Meistersheim, *Villagexpo* (Paris: Dunod, 1970).

9. "Inauguration de Villagexpo, discours de Roland Nungesser, Secrétariat d'État au logement, septembre 1966" (CAC 19771142/019).

10. "Une nouvelle politique de l'urbanisme: Place et rôle de la maison individuelle. Conférence de Monsieur Albin Chalandon à Paris, Chambre de commerce et d'industrie, 7 mai 1969" (CAC 19840342/171).

11. "Concours international de la maison individuelle, brochure, n.d." (CAC 19840342/229), 4.

12. See "Une nouvelle politique de l'urbanisme," 2.

13. In 1972, another such initiative was organized under the name "jeu de construction." In 1975, regional competitions for individual homes were organized in order to diversify typologies for individual home developments. See CAC 19840342/330; C. Damery, P. Vetter, and G. Weil, "Une maison 'jeu de construction,'" *Techniques et architecture*, no. 296 (December 1973): 48–53.

14. See "L'habitat individuel dans le Bassin parisien: Situation et évolution du marché en 1976, IRCOM [Institut de recherche sur les civilisations de l'occident moderne], décembre 1976" (CAC 19840342/330).

15. Very little scholarship exists on the history of these mobility patterns, in part because of the relative absence of data on race and ethnicity, and in part because of social historians' neglect of the topic thus far. See Jacques Barou, *La place du pauvre: Histoire et géographie sociale de l'habitat HLM* (Paris: L'Harmattan, 1992), 114–23.

16. "Note sur la ségrégation, GRECOH [Groupe de recherches et d'études sur la construction et l'habitation], septembre 1970" (CAC 19771142/036).

17. Jean-Claude Chamboredon and Madeleine Lemaire, "Proximité spatiale et distance sociale: Les grands ensembles et leur peuplement," *Revue française de sociologie* 11, no. 1 (January–March 1970): 3–33.

18. See Amiot, *Contre l'État, les sociologues*, 209–16.

19. Jean-Marie Reinert, "La présence des étrangers dans les zones d'habitation," *CDC*, no. 62 (1973).

20. "Rapport final, groupe du long terme, Commission de l'habitation, CGP, 1970" (CAC 19771142/036).

21. "Note sur la ségrégation, GRECOH [Groupe de recherches et d'études sur la construction et l'habitation], septembre 1970."

22. Ibid., 14.

23. "Rapport général, Commission de l'habitation, CGP, mars 1971" (CAC 19771142/035).

24. "Note sur la ségrégation, GRECOH [Groupe de recherches et d'études sur la construction et l'habitation], septembre 1970," 27.

25. "Rapport final, groupe du long terme, Commission de l'habitation, CGP, 1970," 24.

26. "Consommation et mode de vie, Étude par Agnès Pitrou, Compte rendu du Groupe IV Long terme, CGP" (CAC 19771142/036).

27. "Olivier Guichard décide d'interdire les grands ensembles, Note 21 mars 1973, distribué 26 mars 1973" (CAC 19840342/023). See also "Déclaration sur les orientations de la politique urbaine, par Olivier Guichard à l'Assemblée nationale," *Journal officiel de la République française*, May 17, 1973.

28. "Press release of Guichard's speech at the National Assembly on 17 May 1973" (CAC 19840342/023).

29. Ibid.

30. Lefebvre scholars have shown how his theories became appropriated in state planning and urban policy during the 1970s. See Laurent Devisme, *Actualité de la pensée d'Henri Lefebvre: La question de la centralité* (Tours: Maison des sciences de la ville/CNRS-UMS/Université de Tours, 1998); Jean-Pierre Garnier and Denis Goldschmidt, *La comédie urbaine* (Paris: Maspéro, 1970); Jean-Pierre Garnier, "La vision urbaine de Henri Lefebvre," *Espaces et sociétés*, no. 76 (1994): 123–45.

31. See Pierre Chemillier, *Les techniques du bâtiment et leur avenir* (Paris: Le Moniteur, 1977).

32. Christian Moley, "L'innovation architecturale dans la production du logement social: Bilan des opérations du Plan-construction, 1972–1978" (Paris: Plan Construction, May 1979).

33. "Cinq ans de Plan Construction: Entretien avec M. Paul Delouvrier, Président du Plan Construction, n.d." (CAC 19840342/327), 23.

34. "Rapport présenté par le groupe de travail 'Architecture' en vue de l'élaboration du Vème Plan, 22 juin 1965" (CAC 19920405/009).

35. On Val d'Yerres, see Castells et al., *Crise du logement et mouvements sociaux urbains*, 283–372; Bernard Marrey, "Le Val d'Yerres," in *Les bâtisseurs de la modernité*, ed. Bernard Marrey (Paris: Le Moniteur, 2000), 192–96.

36. Joseph Abram and Daniel Gross, "Bilan des réalisations expérimentales en matière de technologie nouvelle: Plan Construction 1971–1975" (Paris: Plan Construction, 1980), 15.

37. Anne Bouret, "Plan Construction: Trois ans d'activité, mai 1971–décembre 1974" (Paris: Ministère de l'équipement et du logement, 1974), 3.

38. "Plan Construction," *TEL—Tourisme, équipement, logement*, no. 180 (December 1972).

39. See the internal notes of the *Plan Construction* in CAC 19840342/326.

40. "Plan Construction," *TEL—Tourisme, équipement, logement*, no. 155 (February 1972).

41. See "Le Plan Construction et la qualité de l'habitat: Colloques d'information sur les problèmes généraux de l'urbanisme et de l'aménagement" (Marly-le-Roi: Institut national d'éducation populaire, October 1972), 26–33.

42. "Rapport du groupe de travail 'Méthodes de programmation des actions du Plan-Construction,' 10 février 1972" (CAC 19840342/326).

43. "Plan Construction," *TEL—Tourisme, équipement, logement*, no. 155 (February 1972).

44. "Réunion du comité directeur du Plan Construction, 21 juin 1972" (CAC 19840342/326).

45. Christian Arnaud, "Modèles innovation: Interview avec Robert Lion," *Urbanisme* 153–54 (1976): 22. See also "Circulaire No. 72-93 relative à la politique des modèles," *Journal officiel de la République française*, June 23, 1972.

46. Bouret, "Plan Construction," 20.

47. "Plan Construction," *TEL—Tourisme, équipement, logement*, no. 180 (December 1972): 31.

48. See chapter 5.

49. Bernard Hamburger, Gérard Bauer, and Philippe Boudon, "Série industrielle et diversité architecturale" (Paris: DGRST, 1971), 3.

50. Philippe Boudon, *Pessac de Le Corbusier, 1927–1967: Étude socio-architecturale* (Paris: Dunod, 1969).

51. Hamburger, Bauer, and Boudon, "Série industrielle et diversité architecturale," 3.

52. Paul Chemetov, "Création architecturale et industrialisation: Pour une architecture de composants industriels" (Paris: Fondation pour le développement culturel, 1971).

53. Henri-Pierre Maillard, Paul Ducamp, and Michel Bancon, "Les outils de la création collective," *Techniques et architecture* 34, no. 6 (April 1972): 65–71.

54. Henri-Pierre Maillard, "Du prototype à la série," *Techniques et architecture*, no. 341 (1982): 104–7.

55. Robert Durand, "Réflexion sur les quartiers nouveaux et leur équipement," *Recherche sociale* 46 (1973): 88.

56. SERES (Société d'études et de recherches en sciences sociales), "Le logement évolutif: Approche historique" (Paris: DGRST, 1972), 1.

57. "L'Exposition 'Habitat et innovation,'" *Habitat et vie sociale*, no. 3 (1974). For a more conceptual approach to architectural flexibility, see "Architecture évolutive," *Techniques et architecture*, no. 298 (May 1974).

58. See, for instance, Giancarlo De Carlo, "Une architecture de participation," *Le Carré bleu*, no. 3 (1972): 8–10.

59. See Manfredo Tafuri's analysis, "The Crisis of Utopia: Le Corbusier at Algiers," in Manfredo Tafuri, *Architecture and Utopia: Design and Capitalist Development* (Cambridge: MIT Press, 1976), 125–49.

60. See, for instance, Eva-Marie Neumann, "Architectural Proportion in Britain 1945–57," *Architectural History* 39 (1996): 197–221. See also Ezra D. Ehrenkrantz, *The Modular Number Pattern: Flexibility through Standardization* (London: A. Tiranti, 1956).

61. For an analysis of Swedish examples, see Manuel Periáñez, "L'habitat évolutif: Du mythe aux réalités" (Paris: Plan Construction et Architecture, 1993).

62. Claude Parent and Ionel Schein, "Essai pour un habitat individuel évolutif," *L'Architecture d'aujourd'hui*, no. 49 (1953): 4–5.

63. "L'habitation évolutive," *Techniques et architecture* 20, no. 3 (May 1960).

64. Georges Candilis, Alexis Josic, and Shadrach Woods, "Proposition pour un habitat évolutif," *Techniques et architecture* 19, no. 2 (1959).

65. See Rémi Papillault, "Le Team X, les bâtiments et les théories qui les font naître: Toulouse-Le Mirail et la cellule de l'habitat," in *Le Team X et le logement collectif à grande échelle en Europe: Un retour critique des pratiques vers la théorie. Actes du séminaire européen, Toulouse 27–28 mai 2004*, ed. Bruno Fayolle Lussac and Rémi Papillault (Pessac: Maison des sciences de l'homme d'Aquitaine, 2008), 199.

66. Interview with Luc and Xavier Arsène-Henry in "Architecture évolutive: Les Architectes prennent position," *Techniques et architecture*, no. 292 (April 1973): 93.

67. See Luc Arsène-Henry, "L'expérience de Montereau," *Les Cahiers du CSTB [Centre scientifique et technique du bâtiment]*, no. 167 (March 1976): 59–66; A. Martel, "An experiment with adaptable housing at Montereau," *Industrialization Forum* 5, no. 5 (1974): 59–64.

68. Manuel Periáñez and M. Routon, *Les logements à plans adaptables de Montereau-Surville* (Paris: Association Anthropologie Appliquée, 1972), 2.

69. See Manuel Periáñez and Isabelle Marghieri, "Le développement de l'habitat évolutif" (Paris: CSTB/Plan Construction et Architecture, 1985), 75.

70. Periáñez and Routon, *Les logements à plans adaptables de Montereau-Surville*. See also "Nouveau projet de recherche sur le quartier de Bordeaux-le-Lac, Association Antropologie Appliquée, 19 juillet 1971" (CAC 19780319/013).

71. Periáñez and Routon, *Les logements à plans adaptables de Montereau-Surville*, 21.

72. Arsène-Henry, "L'expérience de Montereau," 61.

73. CAPEM (Centre d'analyse et de prévisions immobilières), "Enquêtes auprès des utilisateurs: Rapport de synthèse" (Paris: Plan Construction, 1974), 42.

74. See "GEAI [Groupement pour l'étude d'une architecture industrialisée]—L.D.B.," *Techniques et architecture*, no. 292 (April 1973): 76–77.

75. See Marcel Lods, "Une expérience de 500 logements HLM à Rouen dans la ZUP de la Grand-Mare en système industrialisé GEAI [Groupement pour l'étude d'une architecture industrialisée]," *Techniques et architecture* 29, no. 5 (September 1968): 62; "La Grand Mare, à Rouen," *Bâtir*, no. 174 (April 1969): 42–51.

76. Lods, "Une expérience de 500 logements HLM à Rouen dans la ZUP de la Grand-Mare en système industrialisé GEAI [Groupement pour l'étude d'une architecture industrialisée]," 62.

77. See Abram and Gross, "Bilan des réalisations expérimentales en matière de technologie nouvelle," 61.

78. Monique Fichelet and Raymond Fichelet, "Le logement évolutif" (Paris: SERES [Société d'études et de recherches en sciences sociales], 1973), 35.

79. André Nicolas Bouleau, "Concours et villes nouvelles: Témoignage des recherches contemporaines," *Urbanisme* 146 (1975).

80. "Ville nouvelle du Vaudreuil: Consultation pour un programme expérimental de 4000 logements," *Techniques et architecture* 34, no. 6 (April 1972): 45.

81. The system was nominated as "Modèle innovation" under the name "Solfège" in 1974. See "La première tranche du germe de ville; Le protoytype," *Techniques et architecture*, no. 302 (December 1974–January 1975).

82. Evelyne Pierre, "Expérimentation dans un atelier à parois mobiles au Vaudreuil," *Les Cahiers du CSTB [Centre scientifique et technique du bâtiment]*, no. 167 (March 1976).

83. See Éric Rohmer, *Logement à la demande*, INA (Institut national de l'audiovisuel), 1975.

84. See Periáñez and Marghieri, "Le développement de l'habitat évolutif," 303–5.

85. Abram and Gross, "Bilan des réalisations expérimentales en matière de technologie nouvelle," 112–19.

86. See "Espace construit adaptable," *Techniques et architecture*, no. 292 (April 1973); "Architecture évolutive: Habitation," *Techniques et architecture*, no. 292 (April 1973); Georges Maurios and Michel Herrou, "Les Marelles, une structure servante irriguée de fluides," *Les Cahiers du CSTB [Centre scientifique et technique du bâtiment]*, no. 167 (March 1976).

87. See John M. Habraken, *De dragers en de mensen: het einde van de massawoningbouw* (Amsterdam: Scheltema & Holkema, 1961); See: Koos Bosma, Dorine van Hoogstraten, and Martijn Vos, *John Habraken and the SAR, 1960–2000* (Rotterdam: NAi, 2000).

88. Jean-Pierre Maurios and Michel Herrou, "Les Marelles: 1. Expérimentation" (Paris: Environnement et comportement, 1975), 1.

89. Ibid., 17.

90. Jean-Pierre Maurios and Michel Herrou, "Les Marelles, habitat adaptable: Les premiers acquéreurs" (Paris: Environnement et comportement, 1974).

91. For the complete analysis of the process, see ibid.; Maurios and Herrou, "Les Marelles: 1. Expérimentation"; Jean-Pierre Maurios and Michel Herrou, "Les Marelles: 2. Monographies" (Paris: Environnement et comportement, 1975).

92. Already pointed out by Christian Moley in "L'innovation architecturale dans la production du logement social," 69.

93. See the 1976 issue of *Techniques et architecture* (no. 311) with the theme "La question du logement: 1. du rêve participationniste à la flexibilité."

94. Ibid.

95. See Hilde Heynen, "New Babylon: The Antinomies of Utopia," *Assemblage*, no. 29 (April 1996): 24–39; Mark Wigley, *Constant's New Babylon: The Hyper-Architecture of Desire* (Rotterdam: 010 Publishers, 1999).

96. Quote from the back cover of Thierry Vilmin and Jean-Jacques de Alzua, *Évry-Courcouronnes: Le logement intermédiaire et l'urbanisme* (Bagneux: Architecture et construction, 1978).

97. The competition was launched in May 1971 by Maurice Doublet, the prefect of the Paris region, and Michel Boscher, mayor of Évry and president of the Établissement public d'Évry. The competition jury was composed of state representatives including Boscher himself, André Lalande, and Michel Arrou-Vignod, and architects including Jacob Bakema, Joseph Belmont, and Gérard Thurnauer.

98. "Évry I: Concours Conception-Réalisation—note de présentation, 1971" (CAC19780319/001), V.1.

99. Ibid., V.2.

100. "Concours Évry I: Rapport de la commission administrative et financière & Rapport de la commission Habitat" (CAC 19780319/001).

101. Korganow, Meehan, and Orillard, *L'interaction ville-équipement en ville nouvelle*, 78–80.

102. Jean-Louis Cohen and Monique Eleb, *Casablanca: Colonial Myths and Architectural Ventures* (New York: Monacelli, 2002), 341.

103. For a first overview, see "Habitat intermédiaire: Individualisation du collectif ou collectivisation de l'individuel?" *Architecture française*, no. 391 (June 1975).

104. See chapter 3.

105. Luc Thomas and Gérard Pele, "Évry I: Concours d'aménagement urbain," *Cahiers de l'IAURP* 31 (April 1973): 77–78.

106. "Un concours international pour la construction du premier quartier de la ville nouvelle d'Évry," *Le Monde*, May 20, 1971.

107. "La vie à Évry I, brochure UCY, n.d." (CAC 19780319/001).

108. Henri Raymond et al., *L'habitat pavillonnaire* (Paris: Centre de recherche d'urbanisme, 1964). See also Nicole Haumont, "Les pavillonnaires et la pratique de l'habitat," *Urbanisme* 151 (1976). See also chapter 5.

109. Marc Gaillard, *Andrault-Parat Architectes* (Paris: Dunod, 1979), 220.

110. See Pascale Buffard, *Jean Renaudie* (Paris: Sodedat 93/Institut français d'architecture/Carte Segrete, 1993). See also Irénée Scalbert, *A Right to Difference: The Architecture of Jean Renaudie* (London: Architectural Association, 2004).

111. Moley, "L'innovation architecturale dans la production du logement social," 26.

112. See Françoise Lugassy, *Les réactions à l'immeuble Danièle Casanova à Ivry*, vol. 1: *Réactions avant l'aménagement*; vol. 2: *Les processus d'appropriation* (Paris: Compagnie française d'économistes et de psychosociologues, 1974); Anne Denner, *Étude des réactions à l'habitat angulaire à partir des modèles at home, trirème et D. Casanova* (vol. 1); *Rapport deuxième phase de la recherche* (vol. 2) (Paris: Ministère de l'équipement et du logement, July 1977).

113. Lugassy, *Les processus d'appropriation*, 2:143.

114. See "EPA de la ville nouvelle de Lille-Est, Pont de Bois, Concours d'architecture et de composition urbaine," *Techniques et architecture*, no. 293 (1973). The project was also featured in "Habitat intermédiaire," 58–59.

115. The project was featured in Pierre Quercy, "Programme Architecture Nouvelle," *Urbanisme* 152 (1976): 80–81.

116. See Mark Swenarton, "Reforming the Welfare State: Camden 1965–73," *Footprint* 5, no. 2 (2011): 41–48, and Mariana Mogilevich, "Designing the Urban: Space and Politics in Lindsay's New York," Ph.D. dissertation, Harvard University, 2012.

117. Moley, "L'innovation architecturale dans la production du logement social," 22. See also Jean-François Paoli, Claude Ricordeau, and François Faraut, "L'habitat intermédiaire: Étude sur les usages d'un logement à terrasse" (Paris: Institut pour le développement de la recherche appliquée en sciences sociales [IDRASS], 1978).

118. Jacques Bardet cited in "Habitat intermédiaire," 42. His project at Val d'Yerres was La Nérac, begun after he won the 1964 competition by the District of Paris.

119. A director of a local social housing organization quoted in Moley, "L'innovation architecturale dans la production du logement social," 25.

120. Ibid., 53.

121. Gérard Monnier, ed., *L'architecture moderne en France*, vol. 3: *De la croissance à la compétition, 1967–1999* (Paris: Picard, 2000), 25.

122. Lescure, *Histoire d'une filière*, 59.

123. See Barjot, "Introduction."

124. Violeau, "Why and How 'To Do Science'?"; Violeau, *Les architectes et mai 68*, 382–92.

125. See for, instance, Lucan, *Architecture en France, 1940–2000*. See also Roland Castro et al., "1975: On repense à la ville," *Techniques et architecture*, no. 306 (1975): 101.

126. The project by Christian Portzamparc, "Architecturer la ville," at the PAN (Plan architecture nouvelle) competition of 1975 was exemplary of this new interest in the qualities of traditional urbanity.

127. Édith Girard, "Enfin libres et soumis," *L'Architecture d'aujourd'hui*, no. 174 (July–August 1974): 11–12.

Conclusion

1. See Lengereau, *L'État et l'architecture, 1958–1981*, 257–446.

2. Michel Ragon, *L'architecte, le Prince et la Démocratie: Vers une démocratisation de l'architecture?* (Paris: Albin Michel, 1977).

3. See "Atelier Lucien Kroll," *Architecture française*, no. 401 (April 1977); "Portrait de Lucien Kroll," *L'Architecture d'aujourd'hui*, no. 183 (January–February 1976). On Alma-Gare, see Michael Miller, *The Representation of Place: Urban Planning and Protest in France and Great Britain, 1950–1980* (Aldershot and Burlington, Vt.: Ashgate, 2003).

4. "Loi portant réforme de l'urbanisme," *Journal officiel de la République française*, December 31, 1976.

5. On legislation designed by Raymond Barre, see "Loi portant réforme de l'aide au logement," *Journal officiel de la République française*, January 3, 1977.

6. Michel Foucault, *Sécurité, territoire, population* (Paris: Seuil, 2004).

7. Segaud, Bonvalet, and Brun, *Logement et habitat*, 227.

8. De Barros, "Genèse de la politique de développement social des quartiers"; Sylvie Tissot, *L'État et les quartiers: Genèse d'une catégorie de l'action publique* (Paris: Seuil, 2007).

9. Céline Loudier-Malgouyres, "L'espace défendable aux États-Unis et en France," *Urbanisme* 337 (2004): 51–56.

10. See, for instance, the French architecture and urbanism debates of the 1980s in Monique Yaari, *Rethinking the French City: Architecture, Dwelling, and Display after 1968* (Amsterdam: Rodopi, 2008).

11. See Lengereau, *L'État et l'architecture, 1958–1981*; Éric Lengereau, "Du coup d'arrêt de la circulaire Guichard au 'cadre de vie' giscardien," *Urbanisme*, no. 322 (2002).

12. "Allocution prononcée par M. Valéry Giscard d'Estaing à l'occasion du symposium organisé par l'Académie d'Architecture 'Pour une politique de l'architecture,' Maison de l'UNESCO, 20 octobre 1977" (CAC 19840342/323).

13. Philippe Panerai, Jean Castex, and Jean-Charles Depaule, *Formes urbaines: De l'îlot à la barre* (Paris: Dunod, 1977).

14. "Allocution prononcée par M. Valéry Giscard d'Estaing à l'occasion du symposium organisé par l'Académie d'Architecture 'Pour une politique de l'architecture,' Maison de l'UNESCO, 20 octobre 1977," 8.

15. See Kenny Cupers, ed., *Use Matters: An Alternative History of Architecture* (London: Routledge, 2013).

16. The critique that follows is adopted in my opinion piece "Where Is the Social Project?" *Journal of Architectural Eduction* 68, no. 1 (2014): 6–8.

17. For a recent overview of the debate, see Lee Stickells, "The Right to the City: Rethinking Architecture's Social Significance," *Architectural Theory Review* 16, no. 3 (2011): 213–27. See also Bryan Bell and Katie Wakeford, eds., *Expanding Architecture: Design as Activism* (New York: Metropolis Books, 2008).

18. See, for instance, Andres Lepik, *Small Scale, Big Change: New Architectures of Social Engagement* (Basel: Birkhäuser, 2010).

19. See, for instance, John Chase, Margaret Crawford, and John Kaliski, *Everyday Urbanism* (New York: Monacelli Press, 1999).

20. See Michel de Certeau, *L'invention du quotidien: 1. Arts de faire* (Paris: Union générale d'éditions, 1980). Its English translation in 1984 was titled *The Practice of Everyday Life*.

21. See Michael Sheringham, *Everyday Life: Theories and Practices from Surrealism to the Present* (Oxford: Oxford University Press, 2006).

22. See Luc Boltanski and Eve Chiapello, *Le nouvel esprit du capitalisme* (Paris: Gallimard, 1999). This problem also guides Łukasz Stanek's study of Lefebvre, *Henri Lefebvre on Space*.

23. Bruno Latour, "Can We Get Our Materialism Back, Please?" *Isis*, no. 98 (2007): 138–42.

24. For a brief overview of this debate, see Thomas A. Dutton and Lian Hurst Mann, "Problems in Theorizing 'the Political' In Architectural Discourse," *Rethinking Marxism: A Journal of Economics, Culture, and Society* 12, no. 4 (2000): 117–29. The observation itself is Frederic Jameson's, in "Architecture and the Critique of Ideology," in *Architecture Criticism Ideology*, ed. Joan Ockman (New York: Princeton Architectural Press, 1985), 71.

INDEX

All locations are in France unless otherwise indicated.

KENNY CUPERS is assistant professor of architectural history at the University of Illinois at Urbana–Champaign.